THE PSYCHOLOGY OF
TEACHING METHODS

THE PSYCHOLOGY OF
TEACHING METHODS

The Seventy-fifth Yearbook of the National Society for the Study of Education

PART I

By

THE YEARBOOK COMMITTEE

and

ASSOCIATED CONTRIBUTORS

Edited by

N. L. GAGE

Editor for the Society

KENNETH J. REHAGE

19 NSSE 76

Distributed by THE UNIVERSITY OF CHICAGO PRESS • CHICAGO, ILLINOIS

The National Society for the Study of Education

The purposes of the Society are to carry on investigations of educational problems and to publish the results of these investigations as a means of promoting informed discussion of important educational issues.

The two volumes of the seventy-fifth yearbook (Part I: *The Psychology of Teaching Methods* and Part II: *Issues in Secondary Education*) continue the well-established tradition, now in its seventy-sixth year, of serious effort to provide scholarly and readable materials for those interested in the thoughtful study of educational matters. The yearbook series is planned to include at least one volume each year of general interest to all educators, while the second volume tends to be somewhat more specialized.

A complete list of the Society's past publications, including the yearbooks and the recently inaugurated series of paperbacks on Contemporary Educational Issues, will be found in the back pages of this volume.

It is the responsibility of the Board of Directors of the Society to select the subjects to be treated in the yearbooks, to appoint committees whose personnel are expected to insure consideration of all significant points of view, to provide for necessary expenses in connection with the preparation of the yearbooks, to publish and distribute the committees' reports, and to arrange for their discussion at the annual meeting. The editor for the Society is responsible for preparing the submitted manuscripts for publication in accordance with the principles and regulations approved by the Board of Directors.

Neither the Board of Directors, nor the Society's editor, nor the Society is responsible for the conclusions reached or the opinions expressed by the Society's yearbook committees.

All persons sharing an interest in the Society's purposes are invited to join. Regular members receive both volumes of the current yearbook. Those taking out the "comprehensive" membership receive the yearbook volumes and the volumes in the current series of paperbacks. Inquiries regarding membership may be addressed to the Secretary, NSSE, 5835 Kimbark Avenue, Chicago, Illinois 60637.

Library of Congress Catalog Number: 6-16938

Published 1976 by
THE NATIONAL SOCIETY FOR THE STUDY OF EDUCATION

5835 Kimbark Avenue, Chicago, Illinois 60637

Copyright, 1976, by KENNETH J. REHAGE, Secretary

First Printing, 9,000 Copies

Printed in the United States of America

iv

Officers of the Society
1975-76
(Term of office expires March 1 of the year indicated.)

JEANNE CHALL
(1977)
Harvard University, Cambridge, Massachusetts

LUVERN L. CUNNINGHAM
(1976)
The Ohio State University, Columbus, Ohio

JACOB W. GETZELS
(1978)
University of Chicago, Chicago, Illinois

JOHN I. GOODLAD
(1976)
University of California, Los Angeles, California

A. HARRY PASSOW
(1978)
Teachers College, Columbia University, New York, New York

KENNETH J. REHAGE
(Ex-officio)
University of Chicago, Chicago, Illinois

RALPH W. TYLER
(1977)
Director Emeritus, Center for Advanced Study in the Behavioral Sciences
Stanford, California

Secretary-Treasurer

KENNETH J. REHAGE
5835 Kimbark Avenue, Chicago, Illinois 60637

v

The Society's Committee on
The Psychology of Teaching Methods

N. L. GAGE

(Chairman)
Professor of Education and Psychology
School of Education
Stanford University
Stanford, California

DAVID C. BERLINER

Associate Laboratory Director for Research
Far West Laboratory for Educational Research and Development
San Francisco, California

JOHN B. CARROLL

Kenan Professor of Psychology
Director, L. L. Thurstone Psychometric Laboratory
University of North Carolina
Chapel Hill, North Carolina

ROBERT M. GAGNÉ

Professor of Education
College of Education
Florida State University
Tallahassee, Florida

BARAK ROSENSHINE

Professor of Educational Psychology
Bureau of Educational Research
University of Illinois
Urbana, Illinois

Associated Contributors

C. VICTOR BUNDERSON

Professor of Computer Science and Instructional Science
Director, Institute for Computer Uses in Education
Brigham Young University
Provo, Utah

DOUGLAS G. ELLSON

Professor of Psychology
Indiana University
Bloomington, Indiana

GERALD W. FAUST

President, Courseware, Inc.
Orem, Utah
Adjunct Professor of Instructional Science
Brigham Young University
Provo, Utah

JOYCE P. GALL

Associate Research Scientist
American Institutes for Research
Palo Alto, California

MEREDITH D. GALL

Associate Professor of Education
College of Education
University of Oregon
Eugene, Oregon

AIMÉE DORR LEIFER

Assistant Professor of Education
Graduate School of Education
Harvard University
Cambridge, Massachusetts

JOHN MC LEISH

Professor of Educational Psychology
University of Alberta
Edmonton, Canada

ERNST Z. ROTHKOPF

Head, Learning and Instruction Department
Bell Laboratories
Murray Hill, New Jersey

CONSTANCE J. SEIDNER

Assistant Professor of Education
Boston University
Boston, Massachusetts

RICHARD J. SHAVELSON

Associate Professor of Education
University of California
Los Angeles, California

Editor's Preface

At the invitation of the Society's Board of Directors, I presented the idea of this Yearbook on February 23, 1972. The Board had made earlier inquiries in various quarters as to the desirability and feasibility of a yearbook in "educational psychology." Those inquiries had revealed serious doubts as to whether the broad field of educational psychology—in all its present ramifications—could be encompassed in any single yearbook. As a result, my proposal focused on just one important area within educational psychology—the psychology of teaching methods. A yearbook in that area would represent a continuation of part of what several previous yearbooks —*The Psychology of Learning* in 1942, *Learning and Instruction* in 1950, and *Theories of Learning and Instruction* in 1964—had dealt with. Such a continuation was characterized in the proposal as

warranted by recent developments in the field of educational psychology. These developments have turned the field more directly toward the needs of the teacher for theory and practical help on *what to do* and *how to do it*. With the advent of educational technology, the role of the human teacher needs to be reexamined, redefined, and improved. The proposed yearbook on the Psychology of Teaching Methods would be devoted to these purposes. One possible approach to the organization of the yearbook would be to categorize existing methods according to the size of the student group for which they are appropriate.

Upon approval of the proposal by the Board, the Committee on the Psychology of Teaching Methods was appointed. In meetings at Stanford University in February 1973, and in Montreal, during the American Psychological Association meetings, in September 1973, it decided upon the list of chapter titles, brief characterizations of each chapter's contents, and possible authors. I then issued invitations to the authors. In due course, manuscripts for the chapters were received, edited by me, and then further edited and prepared for the printer by the Society's editor.

As with all NSSE yearbooks, the main thanks must go to the authors, whose devotion and scholarship are manifested in their chapters. My fellow members of the Committee also deserve much gratitude for adding this yearbook to their responsibilities. Professor Herman G. Richey, formerly Secretary-Treasurer of the Society, graciously consented to prepare the index for the volume. Finally, I wish to thank the Society's Board of Directors for much valuable advice at all stages of the work. Everyone concerned with this volume can only hope that it does justice to the opportunities for improving education that an NSSE yearbook provides.

N. L. GAGE
Stanford, California
December 1975

Table of Contents

PAGE

THE NATIONAL SOCIETY FOR THE STUDY OF EDUCATION iv

OFFICERS OF THE SOCIETY v

THE SOCIETY'S COMMITTEE ON THE PSYCHOLOGY OF TEACHING
    METHODS vi

ASSOCIATED CONTRIBUTORS vi

EDITOR'S PREFACE, *N. L. Gage*. ix

CHAPTER

   I. THE PSYCHOLOGY OF TEACHING METHODS, *David C. Berliner*
     and *N. L. Gage* 1
       Historical Introduction. Recent Trends. The Definition
       of Teaching Methods. Group Size and Teaching Meth-
       ods. Teaching Methods and Psychologizing. Descriptive
       Concepts for Particular Teaching Methods. Descriptive
       Concepts Yet to be Developed. Teaching Methods and
       Student Achievement. Teaching Methods and Teachers'
       Choices.

  II. THE LEARNING BASIS OF TEACHING METHODS, *Robert M. Gagné*   21
       Introduction. Learning Models. Phases of Learning and
       Phases of Instruction. Outcomes of Learning. Other
       Learning Theories. Summary: Implications for Instruc-
       tion.

 III. PROGRAMMED AND COMPUTER-ASSISTED INSTRUCTION, *C. Victor
     Bunderson* and *Gerald W. Faust* 44
       A Characterization of PI and CAI. PI: The State of the
       Art. CAI: The State of the Art. Concluding Remarks.

 IV. WRITING TO TEACH AND READING TO LEARN: A PERSPECTIVE ON
     THE PSYCHOLOGY OF WRITTEN INSTRUCTION, *Ernst Z. Roth-
     kopf* 91
       Written Material as Nominal Stimulus. Processing.

  V. TUTORING, *Douglas G. Ellson* 130
       The Current Status of Tutoring. The Effectiveness of
       Tutoring. Psychological Aspects of Tutoring. Pro-
       grammed Tutoring. Estimates of the Cost-effectiveness
       of Tutoring. Summary.

CHAPTER   PAGE

VI. THE DISCUSSION METHOD, *Meredith D. Gall* and *Joyce P. Gall*   166
    Attributes of the Discussion Method. Discussion Group Dynamics. Effectiveness of the Discussion Method. Individual Differences. Concluding Remarks.

VII. TEACHING WITH SIMULATIONS AND GAMES, *Constance J. Seidner*   217
    Socialization Function of Play. Types of Simulations and Games. Relationships of Simulation/Games to Other Teaching Techniques. Learning from Simulation/Games. Goals for Which Simulation/Games May be Appropriate. Effectiveness of Simulation/Games. Correlates of the Effectiveness of Simulation/Games. Research Issues. Role of the Teacher in Using Simulation/Games.

VIII. THE LECTURE METHOD, *John McLeish*   252
    Introduction. Systematic Experiments on the Lecture Method. Improving the Lecture.

IX. TEACHING WITH TELEVISION AND FILM, *Aimée Dorr Leifer* .   302
    Introduction. Content That Television and Film May Convey. Processes of Learning from Television and Film. Designing or Evaluating Programming. Utility of Television and Film Teaching. Integrating Television and Film Teaching with Classroom Teaching. Conclusion.

X. CLASSROOM INSTRUCTION, *Barak Rosenshine*   335
    Summary Publications since 1970. Reviews of Selected Instructional Variables. The Direct Instruction Model. Summary.

XI. TEACHERS' DECISION MAKING, *Richard J. Shavelson* . . .   372
    Teaching as Decision Making. Abilities in Decision Making. Decisions Intended to Optimize Student Outcomes. The Decision Perspective and Teacher Training. Summary and Implications for Research.

INDEX   415

INFORMATION CONCERNING THE SOCIETY   427

LIST OF PUBLICATIONS OF THE SOCIETY   429

CHAPTER I

The Psychology of Teaching Methods

DAVID C. BERLINER AND N. L. GAGE

Historical Introduction

Psychology and education have had a long though sometimes disappointing marriage. In America, the marriage began with great enthusiasm just before the turn of the century, when science had won the grudging admiration of influential educators. Empirical research, primarily psychological, seemed to be only a few short years away from solving the problems of education by providing the scientific underpinnings for instructional practice.[1] In the early years of this century, psychological insights of value to educators came from the child centered movement, for which Dewey was a spokesman, and from the connectionism of Thorndike. The latter's emphasis on measurement and statistical analysis in education gave special status to psychology, which appeared to be the only discipline that cared to apply a fundamental empiricism and thorough-going scientific methodology to educational problems.[2]

In the first third of this century, yearbooks of the National Society for the Study of Education provided testimony to the psychologist's contribution to the educator's understanding of the new testing movement and the improvement of the teaching of reading, social studies, arithmetic, and other subjects. The psychology of teaching different subject matters was an especially

1. Lee J. Cronbach and Patrick Suppes, eds., *Research for Tomorrow's Schools* (New York: Macmillan, 1969); Geraldine J. Clifford, "A History of the Impact of Research on Teaching," in *Second Handbook of Research on Teaching*, ed. Robert M. W. Travers (Chicago: Rand McNally, 1973), pp. 1-46.

2. Frederick J. McDonald, "The Influence of Learning Theories on Education (1900-1950)," in *Theories of Learning and Instruction*, ed. Ernest R. Hilgard, Sixty-third Yearbook of the National Society for the Study of Education, Part I (Chicago: University of Chicago Press, 1964), pp. 1-26.

profitable area of investigation because the young science of psychology had much to say about the sequencing of instruction, organization of practice, effectiveness of drill, transfer of learning, and testing of comprehension.[3] But the intensity of this application of psychology to instruction declined after the 1930s, as general psychology and educational psychology moved apart.[4] The Forty-first Yearbook of the Society, *The Psychology of Learning*, reflected this schism.[5] That yearbook focused on the continuing debate in general psychology between advocates of competing theories of learning. Singled out for presentation at that time were the theories associated with conditioning, connectionism, and Gestalt psychology. Notably missing were Tolman's work on purposiveness and Skinner's first statement of a more radical behaviorism,[6] theories that had just begun to generate some interest among educators. It became increasingly evident that these theories were concerned with rats and pigeons or with internal states of consciousness and perceptual organization. Implications for the instruction of students in classrooms—students attempting to learn meaningful verbal material—were not easily discerned.

The era of grand theory building ended in the early 1940s, partly because of World War II. As Allport noted, theories went into the ash can for the duration of the war.[7] Under wartime pressures, atheoretical but sound psychological thinking and measurement led to considerable success in the promotion of social engineering. By 1947 the nadir of laboratory experimental psychology had been reached.[8] Problems of the real world became more im-

3. Edward L. Thorndike, *The Psychology of Arithmetic* (New York: Macmillan, 1922).

4. Paul Woodring, "Reform Movements from the Point of View of Psychological Theory," in *Theories of Learning and Instruction*, pp. 286-305.

5. *The Psychology of Learning*, ed. Nelson B. Henry, Forty-first Yearbook of the National Society for the Study of Education, Part II (Chicago: University of Chicago Press, 1942).

6. Ernest R. Hilgard, "Postscript: Twenty Years of Learning Theory in Relation to Education," in *Theories of Learning and Instruction*, pp. 416-18.

7. Gordon W. Allport, "Scientific Models and Human Morals," *Psychological Review* 54 (July 1947): 182-92.

8. B. F. Skinner, "The Flight from the Laboratory," in *Current Trends in Psychological Theory* (Pittsburgh: University of Pittsburgh Press, 1961), pp. 50-69.

portant in the minds of many, and a slow return of psychologists to the problems of education began. In 1950, the Society's yearbook on *Learning and Instruction* initiated a transition toward putting concern with instruction and teaching on a level nearly equal to concern with learning. After two sections on learning, that yearbook presented a five-chapter section on "Applying Principles of Learning to the Improvement of Instruction at Different Levels of School Work." By 1964, when the Society's yearbook on *Theories of Learning and Instruction* again tried to focus attention on theories of learning, it was apparent first that learning theories had become more molecular and were accompanied by mathematical models whose applicability to classroom instruction was still unknown;[9] second, that the need for theories of instruction or theories of teaching was almost as important to educational psychologists as was the need for theories of learning;[10] and third, that the military experience of many psychologists, unencumbered by rigid theoretical allegiances, had had a salutary effect on the application of psychological concepts and principles to problems of instruction and learning, although it became increasingly obvious that laboratory-derived principles were strikingly inadequate for the design of effective instructional situations.[11] But at least psychologists appeared once again to be giving serious attention to education.

Recent Trends

The 1960s saw the continuing rise of Skinner's behaviorism, less for its elegance as a theoretical position than for its increasing usefulness in understanding and controlling human behavior. In part, that behavioral orientation gave rise to programmed instruction, and an instructional technology began to flourish. But cognitive psychology also continued to influence educational thought and practice: Bruner's essays were widely read;[12] Piaget's ideas became

9. William K. Estes, "Toward a Statistical Theory of Learning," *Psychological Review* 57 (March 1950): 94-107.

10. Jerome S. Bruner, "Some Theorems on Instruction Illustrated with Reference to Mathematics," in *Theories of Learning and Instruction*, pp. 306-35; N. L. Gage, "Theories of Teaching," ibid., pp. 268-85.

11. Robert M. Gagné, "Military Training and Principles of Learning," *American Psychologist* 17 (February 1962): 83-91.

12. Jerome S. Bruner, *Toward a Theory of Instruction* (Cambridge, Mass.: Harvard University Press, 1966).

better known in the United States; and "understanding" and "discovery" became important notions in the curriculum reform movements of the decade.[13] The first handbook of research on teaching was compiled at this time,[14] and the structural approach to learning gained in importance as an analytic tool for examining instruction.[15]

As the committee for the present yearbook considered another volume chronicling the marriage of psychology and education, the influences of one field on the other seemed increasingly diffuse and thoroughly reciprocal. And the marriage seemed stronger than ever. True, it is acknowledged that laboratory laws of learning are untrustworthy guides to classroom practice.[16] We also know that "the sequence from basic research, to applied research, to development, to practice and application on which most of us were weaned is no longer applicable if, in fact, it ever was." [17] But psychology still brings to education its concepts, its principles (however fragile), its methods, and perhaps most important, its sense of what variables are or are not important in particular settings. In recent years information-processing models have been used in this kind of application of psychology to an understanding of school learning (see chapter 2). Implications for instruction come not from general theories but from tentative models of learning built up from empirical data. These restricted models give meaning to a set of concepts that are presumed to be useful in influencing the process of learning and improving achievement of the intended outcomes of instruction.

Through psychologizing of this model-based type, the discipline is bringing its concepts and empiricism, tempered by the sociological and political realities of the schools, to the study of subject matter areas, media of instruction, and the evaluation of educational

13. L. S. Shulman and E. R. Keislar, eds., *Learning by Discovery* (Chicago: Rand McNally, 1966).

14. N. L. Gage, ed., *Handbook of Research on Teaching* (Chicago: Rand McNally, 1963).

15. Robert M. Gagné, *Conditions of Learning*, 2nd ed. (New York: Holt, Rinehart and Winston, 1970).

16. Wilbert J. McKeachie, "The Decline and Fall of the Laws of Learning," *Educational Researcher* 3 (March 1974): 7-11.

17. Robert Glaser, "Educational Psychology and Education," *American Psychologist* 28 (July 1973): 557.

programs. Among such important applications, the psychology of
teaching methods has received the least recent attention from the
National Society for the Study of Education and from the rest of
the profession. In these new ideas we find the origins of this yearbook of the Society, which has carefully documented the marriage
of psychology and education from their original infatuation, their
years of occasional estrangement, and their newly rekindled mutual
interest.

The Definition of Teaching Methods

Teaching methods are recurrent instructional processes, applicable to various subject matters, and usable by more than one teacher.
They are *recurrent* in that the activities are repeated over intervals
measured in minutes or weeks. They are *instructional processes*, such
as patterned teacher behavior (for example, lecturing, discussion,
and recitation); delivery systems for curriculum (for example,
printed matter, film, programmed instruction, and computer-assisted
instruction); and organizational structures for promoting learning
(for example, tutoring and independent study).

These instructional processes promote student learning of different kinds in various subject matters. The term "teaching method"
should not be applied to instructional processes that are useful in
teaching only, say, arithmetic (for example, using Cuisenaire rods),
or reading (for example, conducting phonics drill). The ways in
which the teaching of specific subject matter goes on we call "teaching techniques," which are studied in courses on curriculum and
instruction in reading, science, social studies, mathematics, English,
and the like. The requirement that a teaching method be *usable by
more than one teacher* means that it should not depend upon the
talents, traits, or resources unique to an individual teacher. Rather,
the use of a teaching method should, in principle, be accessible to
any trained teacher.

Admittedly, this rough definition of the term *teaching method*
provides only a general concept with much surplus meaning. Some
methods have been found in classrooms for centuries, like lecturing,
discussion, and the use of printed matter, and other methods, such
as computer-assisted instruction and simulation games, are hardly
more than ten years old.

Group Size and Teaching Methods

The organization of this book is based upon the proposition that one powerful determiner of teaching method is the size of the group to be taught. The average public school classroom contains about thirty students. But there are times in every school when teachers work with considerably more or fewer students. Certain organizational structures, such as team teaching, flexible scheduling, and differentiated staffing, facilitate such modifications of group size. Federally, state, and locally financed programs bring in technology and paraprofessional teaching aides that give teachers more flexibility as to the size of the groups they interact with. And certain teaching methods are more appropriate for groups of some of these different sizes than for others.

In chapters 3 through 5 we deal with that end of the continuum in which the "group" size is one. Individual students work by themselves. The teacher may not be highly involved in the delivery of instruction, as when programmed instruction or computer-assisted instruction is used to bring about learning (see chapter 3). Or the instruction may be delivered through printed texts, widespread since Gutenberg (see chapter 4). Or teachers may work with individuals within elaborately organized systems of instruction, such as PLAN (Program for Learning in Accordance with Needs), IPI (Individually Prescribed Instruction), or IGE (Individually Guided Education).[18] Finally, with one student as the focus, the teacher or her surrogate may spend time in tutorial work, providing either enrichment or remedial experiences for particular students (see chapter 5).

In chapters 6 and 7 we deal with teaching methods appropriate for small groups of perhaps two to twenty students. The most traditional of small-group teaching methods, the discussion method, is as popular as ever in certain curriculum areas. And from the social psychological literature come insights and understandings about how the discussion method operates and induces learning (see chapter 6). Another method of growing importance for instruction in small groups uses simulations and games, in which instructional ends are served through gamelike activities (see chapter 7).

18. Because these systems have recently been the subject of another publication of the Society they are not treated in the present volume. See Harriet Talmage, ed., *Systems of Individualized Education* (Berkeley, Calif.: McCutchan Publishing Corporation, 1975).

In chapters 8 and 9 we consider first the teaching method with the longest historical record, the lecture. Much maligned, the lecture is still often the method of choice when older students are to be taught in large groups of forty or more. The reasons for the survival of this method of instruction are examined in chapter 8, along with approaches to the improvement of the method. Another way to instruct large groups of students is by means of film and television. Mediated instruction of this type is playing an increasing role, although the full implications of using these more recent techniques have seldom been fully articulated (see chapter 9).

In chapters 10 and 11 we deal with the most frequently occurring size of instructional groups—that which ranges between twenty and forty students. In such classroom configurations, the "recitation method" is often found,[19] and recent reviews have brought together the research on teaching that has been done with classroom-size groups.[20] Several hitherto unreviewed, recent, and relatively large-scale studies of classroom teaching are brought together and analyzed in chapter 10.

Because, in addition to the recitation method, all the other methods for groups of various sizes are in principle available to the classroom teacher, the volume ends with a consideration of decision making in the classroom (see chapter 11). Such decision making is needed to choose among these methods in ways appropriate to educational objectives and student characteristics. The choices will result in a kind of "orchestration" that is only now beginning to be seen as a part of the classroom teacher's role.

Teaching Methods and Psychologizing

Psychologists cannot resist trying to explain, or at least describe, how learning takes place in various settings. All of the various teaching methods described in this book are capable of helping students achieve educational objectives, and yet, on the surface, the methods

19. John I. Goodlad, M. Frances Klein, and Associates, *Looking behind the Classroom Door* (Worthington, Ohio: Charles A. Jones Publishing Co., 1970).

20. Barak Rosenshine, *Teaching Behaviors and Student Achievement* (Slough, Eng.: National Foundation for Educational Research in England and Wales, 1971); Michael J. Dunkin and Bruce J. Biddle, *The Study of Teaching* (New York: Holt, Rinehart and Winston, 1974).

appear to differ radically. How is it that learning takes place in these different methods?

OPERANT CONDITIONING THEORY

One set of concepts to describe learning is available from the systematic studies of operant conditioning theorists. As Skinner elaborated it, such theory begins with the simple proposition that an organism will show an increase in the strength of any *response* that is *reinforced*.[21] The first emission of the response is unexplained, but later responses come to be controlled by *discriminative stimuli*. In the case of the individual student working alone, say with programmed instructional material, the student is exposed to a discriminative stimulus in the form of some sentences of instructional material—a statement of some facts, relationships, definitions, examples, and so forth. This instructional material, or "frame," usually ends with a question or an incomplete statement. As a result of the student's previous learning, the incomplete statement or question—a discriminative stimulus—elicits an *overt or covert response* of a certain kind. After the student emits his response, he receives immediate *feedback* about the correctness of that response to that stimulus. The information that a response is correct is assumed to be a *positive reinforcer*, and learning is presumed to have occurred. Information that a response is incorrect operates as a form of mild *punishment* and serves also as a discriminative stimulus indicating that the student should try again, but make a different response. After making a correct response, the student goes on to the next frame and the process is repeated. Programmed materials are designed to have low error rates. Thus as the student goes through the program, his responses are usually reinforced. In this manner, for example, the student may be put into contact with frames from a program about igneous rocks, and the student learns their distinguishing characteristics. Later, on a field trip, he may find a piece of obsidian and correctly identify it as igneous rather than sedimentary or metamorphic in origin. Thus we find that instructional goals are served because, through the processes of stimulus *general-*

21. B. F. Skinner, *Science and Human Behavior* (New York: Macmillan, 1953).

ization and *discrimination,* the appropriate *transfer of learning* has taken place.

In other kinds of individualized instruction, the process differs in superficial ways, but the same concepts of operant conditioning apply. In tutoring, the "frame" may be provided vocally by the teacher. The teacher makes a comment, points out an error, suggests, criticizes, clarifies, or asks a question. The teacher's words serve as a discriminative stimulus, and the student speaks or writes his response. The teacher's next comment provides feedback informing the student about the correctness or incorrectness of his response. Reinforcement or punishment is provided in this way, and the teacher-student interaction progresses much as it does in programmed instruction.

In the discussion method, where group size is from two to twenty, the same concepts can be used to describe how learning takes place. Discriminative stimuli are supplied by the teacher and other students. These serve as signals for the emission of responses from other group members. One group member's response may be overt and audible, while another group member may merely listen and make covert, or silent, responses. The person providing the discriminative stimulus, say a description and question on the forces producing igneous rock, gets responses from one or more other group members, who in turn are given feedback about the correctness or appropriateness of their responses. The non-participants, through *vicarious learning* (observing and sympathetically participating in the experience of another) receive reinforcement and punishment in a form similar to that of the persons actually participating in the discussion. In this way, all members of the discussion group acquire the knowledge, understanding, values, and the like, that are transmitted by the participating members of the group.

In cases where the group size is greater than twenty when, say, lectures are used, we see an extension of the operant conditioning concepts into areas where their appropriateness for describing learning strains our credulity. The concepts have to be applied to conditions where learning occurs in spite of the fact that students may make no overt responses, that is, produce no written notes, and emit no audible or visible responses. Yet many of those who hear lectures on earth science also learn to classify obsidian as igneous in origin. Operant conditioning concepts applied to the lecture situation require us to believe that students are regularly responding, but covertly, as the lecture goes on. The student may respond by anticipating in some way the lecturer's subsequent statement or word or phrase. He may predict the exact word or phrase of the lecturer or merely its grammatical form or structure, and within some limits, its meaning. In a way almost unrecognized by himself, he may predict whether the next word or phrase will be a verb, a noun, an adverbial phrase, and so on. He may predict that the next word or phrase will have a certain meaning related to what has gone before. As the lecturer proceeds, the student may, in a sense, "run along side," broadly predicting the lecturer's next intellectual move. Confirmations of his predictions mean that the student is understanding, and they reinforce the student, thereby inducing learning. Unconfirmed predictions mean that the student goes unreinforced and therefore does not learn. When the student gets too few reinforcers, his predictive responses become extinguished, and he stops paying attention to what the lecturer is saying. Thus a second grader listening to a high school lecture on earth science is unable to make the appropriate predictive responses to the lecturer's statements, which serve as discriminative cues. So the second grader goes unreinforced, stops predicting, and learns nothing from the lecture. The same process would occur during those parts of small-group discussion that are filled with long discourse by group members. The same process of operant conditioning could be considered to account for learning from written discourse which, like the lecture, takes the form of a lengthy string of verbal knowledge-to-be-learned. As Skinner put it, "The student who is paying attention to a lecture or text is reinforced when the words he hears or sees correspond to responses he has anticipated—an important ingredient in listening or reading with 'understanding.'" [22]

CONTIGUITY THEORY

Other theoretical descriptions of the learning process provide other concepts to help us understand how teaching methods result in student learning. Thus the concept of *contiguity learning*, central

22. B. F. Skinner, *The Technology of Teaching* (New York: Appleton-Century-Crofts, 1968), p. 157.

to the theories of Edwin R. Guthrie and William K. Estes, describes how verbal associations and chains may be learned in any of the teaching methods simply as a result of the closeness of two stimuli in time or space (for example, igneous rocks → volcanic origins; metamorphic rocks → pressure and heat origins; sedimentary rocks → deposits of wind, water, or ice). Contiguity theory parsimoniously describes how drill activities, such as those in individualized computer-assisted instruction, result in learning (for example, "9 × 9 = _____"; "Pick the word that means something you ride in: LAR, BAR, CAR").

RESPONDENT LEARNING THEORY

The kind of conditioning described by Ivan Pavlov and John B. Watson was labeled "respondent conditioning" by Skinner.[23] In such learning, a previously ineffective stimulus, when it regularly and closely precedes an effective (unconditioned) one, becomes able to elicit a response very similar to that elicited by the unconditioned stimulus and becomes a conditioned stimulus. Such learning provides useful concepts for understanding how attitudinal learning takes place. In the small-group discussion, a teacher's voice and facial expression may show tension and discomfort when discussing "oil cartels." The teacher's discomfort may be considered an *unconditioned stimulus*, eliciting, in turn, feelings of aversion in the student. The student's aversion is an *unconditioned response*, occurring as the student watches the teacher and listens to the discussion of "oil cartels." The new and until then neutrally valued term, "oil cartel," is considered a *conditioned stimulus*. Because it is regularly paired with the teacher's discomfort, in time it becomes capable of eliciting a response similar to that elicited by the unconditioned stimulus. This response, the *conditioned response*, is an aversion to the term "oil cartel." Following this basic Pavlovian paradigm, we see how attitudes toward such concepts as "democracy," "Jews," "abortion," and "justice" may be conditioned in the various teaching methods.

OBSERVATIONAL LEARNING

The concept of *observational learning* comes from studies of modeling and imitation. From observing a model, a student can learn

23. Skinner, *Science and Human Behavior*.

new behavior, have already learned behavior facilitated, or have already learned behavior inhibited or disinhibited.[24] A student learns to carry 10 from the "ones" column and add it to the numeral in the "tens" column in the way he saw his teacher do it in their tutoring session. Another student learns how to use a microscope from the way a filmed laboratory worker, serving as a model, prepared his slide, adjusted his microscope, and focused his lenses. Other students may learn how to chair a meeting from games in which one student uses Robert's *Rules of Order* and thus teaches the others through behavior modeling.

COGNITIVE LEARNING

Conceptions of *cognitive learning* have been used to account for the acquisition of verbal knowledge, viewed as one important outcome of instruction in all these methods. Cognitive learning theorists have concerned themselves with the organization of information and its *meaningfulness*. The description of learning from the information-processing model in chapter 2 seems more appropriate for describing learning from written discourse and lecturing than does the operant conception of learning. Here, emphasis is not placed on the responses of students. Concepts such as reinforcement and contiguity are seen as factors that affect *performance* but not necessarily the basic *acquisition*, or learning, of responses and information. Instead, emphasis is placed on the learner's receiving, perceiving, and organizing the ideas of the lecturer, tutor, writer, or film. These ideas are the definitions, concepts, principles, evidence, logic, illustrations, instances, and the like, that make up the verbal message to be *coded*, *stored* and *retrieved*. The model presented by Gagné in chapter 2 schematizes this information-processing conception of cognitive psychology, one that has wide application to all the teaching methods when they are employed to transmit verbal information and intellectual skills.

Descriptive Concepts for Particular Teaching Methods

Thus far the concepts used to describe learning have been derived from theory. More modest sets of concepts are also used by

24. Albert Bandura, *Principles of Behavior Modification* (New York: Holt, Rinehart and Winston, 1969).

psychologists to describe unique aspects of each of the various teaching methods. Thus in psychologizing about how people learn from programmed instruction and computer-assisted instruction, terms such as *terminal performance, branching,* and *response latency* find their way into our discourse and help us to understand better learning occurring in these settings. In describing learning from written discourse, concepts like *mathemagenic behavior* and *opportunity to learn* become important. In tutorial methods the concepts of *diagnostic questions, practice* and, of course, *motivation,* take on special meaning. Understanding simulation and games requires familiarity with such concepts as *strategies, reward structure,* and *control beliefs.* In making sense of the small-group discussion, we use *all-channel communication network, low-consensus fields,* and *yielding* as descriptive categories.

Psychology's concepts are applied to particular phenomena in order to make those phenomena more readily comprehensible. A powerful concept language, which psychology tries to supply, lets us more easily understand, predict, and control the behavior of teachers engaged in some teaching method and the learning of the students involved. This yearbook is an attempt to bring concepts with this kind of utility to the foreground. But not all the concepts needed to understand school learning by these methods are at hand. New conceptualizations of the learning process in the various methods are required. A starting point for examining the different teaching methods with such a new perspective is described next.

Descriptive Concepts Yet to be Developed

The fact that socially significant amounts of student learning occur regardless of the teaching method used has important implications. It means that, at some level yet to be understood, the information value of the material presented by the various methods is often equivalent.[25] Perhaps the information conveyed by the various teaching methods is coded, stored, and retrieved from memory in similar ways by different people, no matter how the information was first obtained. Such a supposition seems necessary to explain why several students, each exposed to only one of several different

25. David R. Olson, "On a Theory of Instruction: Why Different Forms of Instruction Result in Similar Knowledge," *Interchange* 3, no. 1 (1972): 9-24.

teaching methods, learn the same concept, principle, or behavior. Thus, they may all learn to classify a piece of obsidian as igneous in origin. Three general stages, or types, of learning predominate between childhood and adolescence.[26] In the most mature stage, *symbolic* learning may occur. One student may have learned his earth science through programmed instruction; another student, from a lecture; and another, from a textbook. At a less mature stage, *iconic* learning, from visual representations, or pictures, predominates. Thus students may acquire knowledge of earth science by looking at pictures or diagrams, or by observing how a discussion leader classifies rocks, or by watching a film of a geologist exhibiting classificatory behavior, with relevant cues highlighted in the film. At the least mature stage, students may learn primarily from *enactive*, or physical, manipulations of the requisite knowledge. Thus a tutor may bring in specimens of particular rocks for handling. Or, in the course of a classroom discussion or recitation, the teacher may pass out mineral samples to be examined.

To use a metaphor from Chomsky,[27] although the surface structure of the information being presented appears to be different, the deep structure of the information presented to students is the same. All of the methods allowed students to derive sufficient understanding of the origins of rocks to display the appropriate transfer of learning. That deep-structure equivalence may be effected inside the learner's head as the information is being processed. In numerous forms and with different degrees of efficiency, information is presented, attended to, rehearsed, coded, stored, generalized, and retrieved. Many of the previously noted descriptions of how learning takes place in different teaching methods may be inadequate. They may be concerned only with the surface structure of the method. In the cognitions of the learner, where only the deeper structure of the information is processed, new kinds of concepts to describe learning may be more appropriate. Thus, Attneave proposed that we posit the existence of language-like representational structures, whose elements have word-like status and provide meaning to all

26. Bruner, *Toward a Theory of Instruction.*

27. Noam Chomsky, *Language and Mind* (New York: Harcourt, Brace, Jovanovich, 1968).

forms of our experience.[28] Again, to use an analogy, there must be an elemental internal language that extracts meaning from symbolic, iconic, and enactive experiences, in much the same way as that in which a computer processes information from FORTRAN, ALGOL, and COBOL entry languages.

As the concepts that describe the basic cognitive information-processing mechanisms of learners become better understood, the equivalence among teaching methods, as far as the learning of verbal information and intellectual skills is concerned, will probably become more evident. This hypothesized equivalence of methods implies that we should only expect different teaching methods to be more or less appropriate for different kinds of objectives, more or less efficient in time and other costs, and more or less appropriate for students with different levels of various traits or aptitudes. If this analysis is correct, different teaching methods should *not* have different effects on student outcomes when the content to be learned is similar. We turn now to that issue.

Teaching Methods and Student Achievement

We should expect any teaching method to be about as "good" as any other when the criterion is student achievement or knowledge or understanding, and the content coverage of the methods is similar. The data support this conclusion. For example, Dubin and Taveggia reviewed the data for several scores of comparisons of the lecture and discussion methods at the college level.[29] Of eighty-eight comparisons between traditional lecture and traditional discussion methods, as reported in thirty-six experimental studies, 51 percent favored the lecture method and 49 percent favored the discussion method. When they standardized the criterion test scores from these studies, making them comparable from study to study, the average difference between average test performances following exposure to lecture or discussion methods, across studies, was very close to zero. Similar results were found in comparisons of (a)

28. Fred Attneave, "How Do You Know?" *American Psychologist* 29 (July 1974): 493-99.

29. Robert Dubin and Thomas C. Taveggia, *The Teaching-learning Paradox: A Comparative Analysis of College Teaching Methods* (Eugene, Ore.: Center for the Advanced Study of Educational Administration, University of Oregon, 1968).

lecture and lecture-discussion methods in seven studies, (b) discussion and lecture-discussion methods in three studies, (c) lecture methods and supervised independent-study methods in fourteen studies, and (d) lecture-discussion methods and supervised independent-study methods in nine studies. The authors concluded that college teaching methods do not differ in their effectiveness in determining achievement on final examinations.

Nevertheless, as Hilgard and McLeish have pointed out, in most school learning studies, there is an "equalizer" effect.[30] In such studies, students usually learn from printed material (for example, the textbook) as well as from lectures, discussion, computer-assisted instruction, and the like. Students who know they will take a final examination compensate for any inadequacies in the teaching method by which they are taught by relying heavily upon the textbook. Thus it is hard to uncover differences in the effects of teaching methods when achievement tends to be equalized by use of a textbook common to the different methods and by a final examination based in large part on the textbook.

In another review of the effectiveness of different teaching methods, Jamison, Suppes, and Wells (1974) examined instructional radio as a teaching method.[31] They concluded that instructional radio, supplemented with appropriate printed material, can be used to teach almost any subject as effectively as any of the other typical classroom teaching methods. It is not better or worse than the other methods. Similarly, programmed instruction is generally as effective as traditional instructional methods. Further, they concluded that "as in other methods of instruction surveyed in this report, no simple uniform conclusions can be drawn about the effectiveness of computer-assisted instruction."[32]

From 421 comparisons of instructional television with traditional instructional methods, Chu and Schramm concluded that 308 yielded no significant difference, 63 comparisons showed instructional

30. Ibid., quoting a communication from Hilgard; John McLeish, *The Lecture Method* (Cambridge, Eng.: Cambridge Institute of Education, 1968).

31. Dean Jamison, Patrick Suppes, and Stuart Wells, "The Effectiveness of Alternative Instructional Media: A Survey," *Review of Educational Research* 44 (Winter 1974): 1-67.

32. Ibid., p. 55.

television to be more effective, and 50 comparisons showed traditional teaching methods to be more effective.[33] Again the equivalence of methods in effectiveness overwhelms any alternative conclusion.

From a different perspective come similar data. Walker and Schaffarzick examined the results of over twenty studies comparing "new" and traditional curricula.[34] "We began as people always begin, naively, to look for signs of superiority of innovative curricula over traditional curricula. What we found was not superiority, but parity: each curriculum did better on the distinctive parts of its own program, and each did about equally well on the parts they held in common."[35] They concluded that where content coverage and content emphasis were roughly equal, achievement in the different curricula was also roughly equal.

In general, the evidence is sufficient to support the conclusion that different teaching methods yield similar average results when achievement of knowledge is used as the criterion. But this conclusion in no way means that different teaching methods are equivalent in other ways. For example, it seems reasonable to conclude that programmed instruction may decrease the amount of time required for a student to achieve specific educational goals. At the elementary school level, computer-assisted instruction has been shown to be an important supplement to traditional instruction. But this teaching method usually requires increased monetary expenditures for computer equipment and programs. In small-group discussion, knowledge may not be enhanced but the attitudes of students are often affected. And the motivation of students playing instructional games is obvious to any observer. Thus many considerations enter into the choice of a teaching method.

It is also important to remember that different teaching methods are likely to have different effects on students with different aptitudes. Such "aptitude-treatment interactions" are being revealed

33. Godwin C. Chu and Wilbur Schramm, *Learning from Television: What the Research Says* (Stanford, Calif.: Institute for Communication Research, Stanford University, 1967).

34. Decker F. Walker and Jon Schaffarzick, "Comparing Curricula," *Review of Educational Research* 44 (Winter 1974): 83-111.

35. Ibid., p. 108.

more frequently as the search for them intensifies.[36] Dowaliby and Schumer found, for example, that high-anxiety students performed better than low-anxiety students in a teacher-centered situation of the lecture type. Students low in anxiety performed better than students high in anxiety in a student-centered situation of the discussion type.[37] Doty found that social needs of students were positively correlated with achievement when the lecture and discussion methods were used ($r = .40$ and $.65$, respectively).[38] But the social needs of students were negatively correlated with achievement when audio-taped lectures were used ($r = -.53$). Also, the correlations between creativity and achievement in conventional lecture and audio-taped lecture courses was negative ($r = -.21$ and $-.16$, respectively). But when the teaching method used was small-group instruction, the correlation between creativity and achievement was .37. Thus, although one teaching method may not be superior to another teaching method when class averages are looked at, students with different aptitudes may very well perform differently, depending on which teaching method is used.

The costs for staff and materials, time required to reach criterion, attitudes of the students, and their aptitudes must enter into our decisions when choosing between teaching methods. And each teaching method must be examined in the light of its unique contribution to the attainment of objectives other than the acquisition of knowledge.

In short, it appears that, when properly used, the different teaching methods are roughly equivalent, when compared on their effectiveness in fostering the acquisition of knowledge. But we have had relatively few studies of effectiveness *within* teaching methods. We have all had experiences with "good" and "poor" lecturers. The lecturer's behavior—his enthusiasm, fluency, organization, humor,

36. Lee J. Cronbach and Richard E. Snow, *Aptitudes and Instructional Methods* (New York: Irvington Publishers/Naiburg Publishing Corp., in press).

37. Fred J. Dowaliby and Harry Schumer, "Teacher-centered versus Student-centered Mode of College Classroom Instruction as Related to Manifest Anxiety," *Journal of Educational Psychology* 65 (April 1973): 125-32.

38. B. A. Doty, "Teaching Method Effectiveness in Relation to Certain Student Characteristics," *Journal of Educational Research* 60 (April 1967): 363-65.

and other behavioral dimensions—make him or her more or less effective. Similarly, anecdotal reports on the use of educational television reveal that the teacher's introduction to televised lessons affects the students' learning from such lessons. Small-group discussions are sometimes aimless, filling up the school day but not serving educational goals. But sometimes such discussions give students important opportunities to explore controversial topics, clarify their values, and practice public speaking. It is probably time to de-emphasize comparisons of different teaching methods on the same objectives and to focus more sharply on the ways in which each method can be optimally used. There is a place in the design of education for all the teaching methods.

Teaching Methods and Teachers' Choices

There is a narrow range of average class size in this country. Most teachers have approximately thirty students per class. While teachers continue to argue for a reduction in class size, it seems unlikely that great changes will occur in the near future. Estimates from an analysis of this problem in one large state revealed that a decrease in class size of one student throughout the state would cost almost 100 million dollars annually, a decrease of two students per class would cost over 200 million dollars, and a decrease of three students per class would cost approximately 450 million dollars.[39] With school finances being what they are, no radical changes in class size can be expected. Thus the teacher's job is to find ways, within the framework of classroom teaching, in which the different teaching methods, each with its own advantages for different purposes and different students, can be used.

At times the lecture is an appropriate method; it can transmit information to the entire class. At times small discussion groups will be appropriate, and the teacher can organize the class to make them possible. At other times, printed material can be used to further instructional purposes, and it can be supplemented with computer-assisted instruction, programmed instruction, games, or films. Tutor-

39. Personal communication from Dr. Alexander I. Law, Chief, Program Evaluation and Research, California State Department of Education. The estimates were obtained by taking 1/29th of costs for instruction in 1973-74 for the reduction of class size by one pupil; 1/28th, for the reduction of class size by two pupils; and so on.

ing can be done by older students, paraprofessionals, or the regular classroom teacher, if that teacher makes the necessary organizational changes to make the tutorial method feasible. The methods discussed in this yearbook differ in efficiency and in their appropriateness for different objectives and different types of learners. But they do not differ in some kind of undifferentiated "general effectiveness."

So teachers should learn to make decisions about teaching methods (see chapter 11) as carefully as they choose content and objectives. And by learning to use many different methods, teachers will provide students with the kind of variation in teaching methods that will best serve the variety—of objectives and students—that characterizes American education today.

CHAPTER II

The Learning Basis of Teaching Methods

ROBERT M. GAGNÉ

Introduction

The practice of teaching incorporates both the planning and delivery of instruction. As suggested by the chapters of this volume, teaching in both these aspects may be done with individuals or groups; by the use of a number of different methods and their combinations—lecturing, discussion, tutoring, or the use of games; and by using various media including printed texts, pictures, television, and films. And, of course, teaching is done in connection with a great variety of subjects—from reading in an elementary classroom to the traditional categories of the high school curriculum and to the vocational and avocational pursuits of adult education.

With all of this variety of means and modes, it nevertheless remains true that the central purpose of teaching is the promotion of *learning* in individuals called students. As a consequence, it seems reasonable to expect that, whatever particular method or style the teacher may choose on any given occasion, or whatever variation in teaching approach he may consider desirable, he will continue to maintain the support of learning as his primary goal. In pursuit of this goal, it is evident that the teacher must make a host of individual decisions concerning what kinds of stimulation to present to the learner, what communications to make, what questions to ask, what sorts of confirmation of the learner's productions to provide, and many other decisions of this general sort. These decisions are based upon the teacher's understanding of what is happening to the student as a learner; that is, they are influenced by the teacher's conceptualization of the *processes* of learning and the *expected outcomes* to which these processes lead.

Descriptions of the procedures and methods of teaching, such as are contained in this volume, must likewise take into account the goal of promotion of learning, including remembering and the transfer of learning. The events that are planned by the teacher, and responded to by the teacher as parts of the instructional situation, are conceptually related to processes that are operating within the student to produce outcomes that are newly learned, retained, and applied. Accordingly, a *model* of these processes provides an essential framework for describing the activities of teaching that are designed to support or otherwise influence them. In the following sections of this chapter three questions are considered for the purpose of providing a reference framework of learner processes to which the actions of the teacher may be related. These questions are:

1. What are the processes involved in learning, retention, and transfer of learning? (Processes of learning)

2. What is the sequence of transformations brought about by these processes? (Phases of learning)

3. What kinds of outcomes of learning processes can be inferred from human performance? (Capabilities and dispositions produced by learning)

Learning Models

A model of learning has the function of identifying the structures and processes that need to be taken into account in giving an adequate rational explanation for the learning event. These structures and their associated processes are derived as hypothetical constructs from empirical research findings, by means of rational inference. Their existence as constructs also depends upon continued verification from empirical data. As customarily used, a model serves to identify the structures and processes involved in learning, but does not necessarily predict the quantitative values of the operation of these processes. Thus, a model is merely the beginning of a learning theory; in fact, alternative theories of individual processes or combinations of processes may be equally compatible with a given model.

A PROTOTYPICAL MODEL

While it seems reasonable that theories of learning that make possible quantitative prediction of learning outcomes may have important implications for instruction, such theories have not yet achieved this state of development. Models that identify learning structures and processes, however, are currently available and appear to have substantial applicability to the understanding of instructional events. There are several such models, employed as frameworks for a variety of theories of human learning and memory.[1] Recent trends in such theories have been reviewed by Greeno and Bjork,[2] who also developed a basic model emphasizing common features of other models. A similar prototype is shown in figure 1.

In brief, the model depicts the following flow of information from one hypothesized structure to another: a stimulus input from the receptors enters the sensory register (a very short-lived memory store), and then the short-term memory, where it persists for about thirty seconds or less. Rehearsal by the learner can maintain information here for longer periods. It is then coded for storage and transferred to the long-term memory, assumed to be a permanent repository. Later the information is retrieved, following a search, and when recovered is transferred again to the short-term memory (in a sense, to the "forefront" of memory). At this point its appropriateness is considered, resulting in a decision for further search, or for the generation of responses that result in performance, by activation of the response generator. Important components of the model are the executive control processes, by means of which the various kinds of information transfer are activated and modified. A similar function may be proposed for expectancies established in preparation for an act of learning.[3] Specific flow

1. Prominent examples are described in: R. C. Atkinson and R. M. Shiffrin, "Human Memory: A Proposed System and Its Control Processes," in *The Psychology of Learning and Motivation*, vol. 2, ed. Kenneth W. Spence and Janet T. Spence (New York: Academic Press, 1968), pp. 89-195; Donald A. Norman, ed., *Models of Human Memory* (New York: Academic Press, 1970); Endel Tulving and Wayne Donaldson, eds., *Organization of Memory* (New York: Academic Press, 1972); Arthur W. Melton and Edwin Martin, eds., *Coding Processes in Human Memory* (Washington, D.C.: Winston, 1972).

2. James G. Greeno and Robert A. Bjork, "Mathematical Learning Theory and the New 'Mental Forestry,'" *Annual Review of Psychology* 24 (1973): 81-116.

3. Cf. William K. Estes, "Reinforcement in Human Behavior," *American Scientist* 60 (November-December 1972): 723-29.

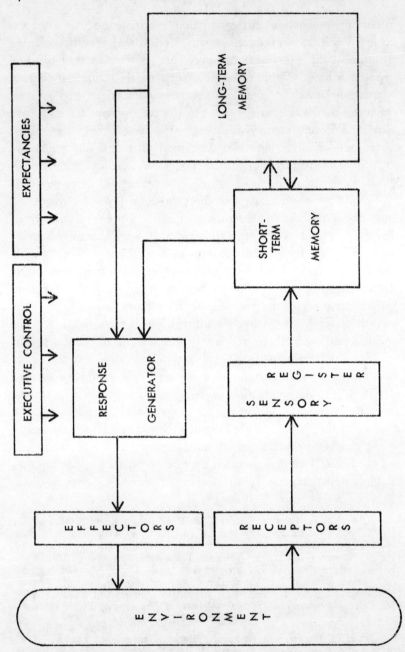

FIG. 1. A prototype of models employed by contemporary information-processing theories of learning and memory

Source: Robert M. Gagné, *Essentials of Learning for Instruction* (Hinsdale, Ill.: Dryden Press, 1974). Reproduced by permission of the Dryden Press.

connections of these processes are not indicated in the figure, since most theories do not identify them in detail.[4]

When described in this brief manner, it is evident that the model provides little more than a framework to which can be added descriptions of the processes required to make the necessary transformations of information from one structure to another. It is these processes that are the targets of explanation, in part or in whole, for contemporary theories of learning and memory. Accordingly, the model in figure 1 can well serve the purpose of a referent learning model relevant to teaching. A detailed review of research findings relevant to the model has been presented by Kumar.[5]

LEARNING PROCESSES

The model for learning and memory may be examined to reveal the processes it identifies that occur during an act of learning. Some of these processes are entirely familiar, in the sense that they have been investigated over a period of many years (for example, attention, selective perception). Others, like coding and retrieval, have more recently come into prominence as parts of contemporary theory.

Motivation. As given in figure 1, the model includes the process whereby the motivation of the learner is brought to bear upon learning and memory. It seems reasonable to assume that this process exerts its effects by means of a *set* or *expectancy* established prior to the act of learning itself. Such an interpretation is suggested by Estes.[6] An expectancy set, persisting during the learning act, may be seen as one kind of "executive control process." Such a set may act to guide a number of other processes involved in learning. In particular it may be expected to influence the type of performance that eventuates from learning, thus setting the

4. However, see R. C. Atkinson, D. J. Herrmann, and K. T. Wescourt, *Search Processes in Recognition Memory*, Technical Report No. 204 (Stanford, California: Institute for Mathematical Studies in the Social Sciences, Stanford University, 1973).

5. V. K. Kumar, "The Structure of Human Memory and Some Educational Implications," *Review of Educational Research* 41 (December 1971): 379-417.

6. Estes, "Reinforcement in Human Behavior."

stage for the feedback that serves to confirm the expectancy. The notion of expectancy is associated with the concept of reinforcement, the implications of which for an information-processing model have been examined by Atkinson and Wickens.[7] As will be pointed out later, the process of expectancy is of singular importance in its implications for teaching.

Attention; selective perception. These processes (or this process) serve the important function of modifying the information flow from the sensory register to the short-term memory (figure 1). The array of stimulation that reaches the learner through his sensory register is acted upon selectively by means of this process, in such a way that certain salient features of it are "attended to" and "perceived." Thus they are "perceptually coded" for storage or further processing in the short-term memory.

Rehearsal. Without further processing, the contents of short-term memory decay fairly rapidly. They may, however, be maintained for longer periods by means of a control process called rehearsal. Since short-term memory is often considered to function as a "working memory,"[8] rehearsal processes are conceived as playing an active role in the relating of new information to that previously acquired.

Coding. The information in the short-term memory is transformed in several different ways for entry into long-term memory. The individual learners may have available alternative control processes that can be utilized for the purpose of coding. Relating the newly learned item to larger organized bodies of information is one example of a coding process; transforming it into an image is another. Most importantly, coding transforms the material into conceptual form for storage as propositions, as conceived by Kintsch[9] or by Anderson and Bower.[10]

---

7. Richard C. Atkinson and Thomas D. Wickens, "Human Memory and the Concept of Reinforcement," in *The Nature of Reinforcement*, ed. Robert Glaser (New York: Academic Press, 1971), pp. 66-120.

8. Atkinson and Shiffrin, "Human Memory."

9. Walter Kintsch, "Notes on the Structure of Semantic Memory," in Tulving and Donaldson, *Organization of Memory*, pp. 247-308.

10. John R. Anderson and Gordon H. Bower, *Human Associative Memory* (Washington, D.C.: Winston, 1973).

Search and retrieval. Retrieval is generally conceived as a process of search, aided by cues from the learner's environment or from other parts of his memory. Material which is stored in memory becomes "accessible"[11] when revived by such cues. Frequently, selected portions of what has been learned are retrieved and recovered to the short-term memory (the "working memory") where they may be used in further learning or as inputs in response generation.

Generalization; transfer of learning. Presumably, the transfer of acquired knowledge to new situations depends in part upon how this knowledge is stored, and also upon what cues are available for recovering it in the new situation. This conception implies that there can be "coding for transfer" as one form of "coding for retrieval." It seems likely that the transfer of learning may require processes beyond those of storage and retrieval. Transferability of knowledge and skill is of course a matter of great importance to the design and conduct of instruction.

Response generation. The contents of long-term memory, or of information recovered to the working (short-term) memory, are transformed into the performances of the learner. It is these performances, of course, that enable the external observer to verify that learning has in fact taken place.

Feedback. An act of learning is completed when the learner receives information to the effect that his performance has met certain expectations. There is, in other words, a confirmation of the expectancy that was activated at the initiation of the learning act. Some theorists interpret feedback in ways that do not involve expectancy confirmation. Virtually all, however, agree in identifying as *reinforcement* those events that provide positive feedback.

Phases of Learning and Phases of Instruction

The processes required to account for the phenomena of learning are *internal* processes, rational constructs of the model builder. Many of them, however, and perhaps all of them, are affected by events that are *external* to the learner, that is, external sources of

11. Endel Tulving and Zena Pearlstone, "Availability Versus Accessibility of Information in Memory for Words," *Journal of Verbal Learning and Verbal Behavior* 5 (August 1966): 381-91.

stimulation from his environment. It is these external events that may be planned and executed in ways that serve to activate, maintain, facilitate, or enhance the internal processes of learning. When planned and conducted to promote learning by any of these means, these external events are called *instruction*. They are, accordingly, the particular province of the teacher.

THE PHASES OF INSTRUCTION

The sequence of transformational events effected by learning processes follows the sequence in which these processes are listed in the previous section. As these events unfold in the course of an act of learning, they may be influenced to a greater or lesser degree, and in a number of different ways, by the external events of instruction. Some processes (for example, the establishment of expectancy) are obviously affected by instruction, whereas others (for example, the internal processes of memory storage) may be only indirectly influenced. It seems reasonable, therefore, to distinguish as successive *phases of instruction* those interactions of external stimulation and learning processes that can most clearly alter the course of learning. Designating instructional phases in this way helps to emphasize the function of instruction as supportive of learning, and thus to suggest the variety of tasks involved in teaching.

Parenthetically it may be noted that as the learner develops in sophistication, many of the events of instruction, initially observed as planned external events, come to be accomplished by the learner himself. In other words, to a greater or lesser degree, he becomes a "self-learner." He may supply his own motivation, develop his own system of coding, initiate strategies of search and retrieval, and supply his own feedback. Naturally, the teacher wishes to encourage this growing tendency toward independent learning. This is done in a number of ways, including the progressive reduction in external "cueing" for coding and retrieval processes as the learner develops.

The phases of instruction, as related to the processes of learning previously described, may be identified as follows:

Motivation phase. The preparation for learning is accomplished by instruction, which activates motivation by appealing to student interests. Communications of the teacher during this phase have the additional purpose of relating these interests to an expectancy of "what the student will be able to do" once he has learned.

Apprehending phase. During this phase, teaching is concerned with arousing attention in a general sense, and also with providing stimulation (often verbal), which "directs" attention so that particular features of the stimulus situation are selectively perceived.

Acquisition phase. This phase of instruction supports the process of entry into long-term store. Coding processes may be provided or suggested. Alternatively, a set to employ a strategy of coding may be activated by communications from the teacher.

Retention phase. This phase pertaining to "storage" is included for the sake of completeness. The manner in which internal processes of storage (such as interference, simplification, and the like) can be directly influenced by instruction, if indeed they can be, is not entirely clear. It seems evident, however, that indirect influence can be brought to bear by suitable arrangement of learning conditions, as, for example, in presenting dissimilar stimuli together rather than highly similar ones, thus reducing the possibility of interference.

Recall phase. External instructional events during this phase may take the form of providing cues to retrieval, or of monitoring the process of retrieval to insure that suitable strategies of search are employed. Teaching also includes the conduct of "spaced reviews," providing opportunities for retrieval to occur.

Generalization phase. During the generalization phase, the teacher provides situations (which may be verbally described) calling for the transfer of learned knowledge and skills in novel ways, and providing cues for application to previously unencountered situations.

Performance phase. Instruction oriented to this phase of learning is largely a matter of setting occasions for the student to "show" that he has learned. Obviously, these occasions set the stage for the feedback that comes next.

Feedback phase. The feedback phase is one in which information is supplied to the student concerning the extent to which his performance has reached or approached a criterion standard reflected in his expectancy. What is accomplished in this phase is the confirmation of the expectancy, affecting the process of reinforcement.

Outcomes of Learning

The processes of learning, supported by events of instruction, result in the establishment of more or less permanent states within the individual learner. These states are, of course, inferred from observations of his performances, as these are exhibited in specifiable situations on two or more occasions. To emphasize the learned and also the persisting nature of these states, they may be called *capabilities* and *dispositions*.

It is customary in describing the varieties of outcomes of school learning to deal with them in terms of subject matter. Thus, one may speak of a student's having learned American history, or algebra, or typing, or biology, or auto repair. Such categories, however, although they may be necessary for the conduct of logistical operations of school instruction, are grossly inadequate for purposes of differentiating the kinds of outcomes resulting from learning. The reasons are as follows:

1. Learning is not unique to subject matter. There is no sound rational basis for such entities as "mathematics learning," "science learning," "language learning," or "history learning," except as divisions of time devoted to these subjects during a school day or term.

2. The same varieties of learning outcome occur in different subjects. For example, the student may learn the fact that Newton invented the calculus in the subject called "mathematics," whereas he may learn the fact that Bell invented the telephone in a subject called "history."

3. Different varieties of learning outcomes occur within the same subject. In "biology," a student may learn a capability, for example, the skill of deriving the expected genetic constitution of the offspring of cross-mated animals. In the same course he may also acquire a disposition, for example, an attitude of avoidance of harmful drugs. The classes of performance that these learning outcomes make possible are distinctly different.

Varieties of outcomes of the learning process are important to teaching because they create different requirements for instruction.[12] While the phases of instruction described in the previous section imply certain general characteristics for the events controlled by the teacher, these events also require more specific design related to the type of learning outcome expected. For example, the acquisition phase of learning is concerned with the coding of stimulation, and may be influenced by a means of coding suggested by a teacher or a textbook. Obviously, though, the coding of a motor skill like shooting baskets cannot be greatly influenced by externally suggested codes; the ineffectiveness of "verbal guidance" in facilitating the learning of motor skills is well known. In contrast, the learning of information, such as the steps in passage of a law by Congress, can be highly influenced by the suggestion of appropriate coding procedures and retrieval cues. Thus the learning of these two kinds of capabilities (motor skill, verbal information) requires two quite different procedures of instruction, even though they both may be undertaken during the acquisition phase.

VARIETIES OF LEARNED CAPABILITIES AND DISPOSITIONS

There are five classes of learned capabilities and dispositions, which differ from each other in the essential nature of the performances they mediate, their characteristics in retention and transfer, and the conditions of instruction that may be employed to support or enhance them. These five varieties of learning outcome have been identified as (a) verbal information, (b) intellectual skills, (c) cognitive strategies, (d) attitudes, and (e) motor skills.[13] For present purposes, the most important differentiating feature of these classes of capabilities resides in the fact that they require different approaches to the support of processes involved in learning them. In other words, for each of these classes of learning something different has to be done about instruction by the teacher, the textbook, the ITV tape, or any other medium.

Verbal information. The student learns a great deal of information in school—names, facts, generalizations about what things are,

12. Robert M. Gagné and Leslie J. Briggs, *Principles of Instructional Design* (New York: Holt, Rinehart and Winston, 1974).

13. Robert M. Gagné, "Domains of Learning," *Interchange* 3, no. 1 (1972): 1-8.

what has happened, where things are located, and so on. Information is identified as "verbal," not because it is necessarily stored that way, but because verbal information is the outcome. One knows that the student has learned verbal information because he can *state* it. In a fundamental sense, it has a sentence (or propositional) form.

Presumably, verbal information is often (or perhaps usually) stored in the form of internally organized bodies of knowledge. Various forms of organization have been proposed for such storage, including hierarchical networks and mental imagery.[14] The retrieval of verbal information is greatly facilitated by externally supplied cues, and cues may also be supplied by the learner himself.

Modern research suggests that the most critical feature of instruction for the learning of any item of verbal information is the *provision of a larger meaningful context* with which the item can be associated, or into which it can be incorporated.[15] Ausubel proposes that new items of information are "subsumed" into more comprehensive cognitive structures.[16] Another possibility is that verbal information is transformed into visual images.[17] Presumably, whatever the nature of the larger context, it is this that makes it possible for the item of information to be most readily searched for and retrieved. The implication for instruction is clear, at least in a general sense: the teacher and the medium must either separately or together provide a meaningful context at the time a new item or set of items is presented for learning.

Intellectual skills. The learning of intellectual skills begins with the acquisition of simple discriminations and chains.[18] School learn-

14. See, for example, Gordon Wood, "Organizational Processes and Free Recall," in Tulving and Donaldson, *Organization of Memory*, pp. 49-91; Gordon H. Bower, "Mental Imagery and Associative Learning," in *Cognition in Learning and Memory*, ed. Lee W. Gregg (New York: Wiley, 1973), pp. 51-88.

15. Anderson and Bower, *Human Associative Memory*.

16. David P. Ausubel, *Educational Psychology: A Cognitive View* (New York: Holt, Rinehart and Winston, 1968).

17. Allan Paivio, *Imagery and Verbal Processes* (New York: Holt, Rinehart and Winston, 1971).

18. Robert M. Gagné, *The Conditions of Learning*, 2d ed. (New York: Holt, Rinehart and Winston, 1970).

ing, although it may sometimes include these simpler forms, is mainly concerned with the learning of *concepts* and *rules*. These are the kinds of capabilities that make it possible for the student to *do* something with the symbols representing his environment. While verbal information has to do with knowing "what," intellectual skills have to do with knowing "how."

Many varieties of intellectual skills are learned in formal education, beginning with the basic skills of manipulating language and number symbols. The concepts and rules that are acquired in the subjects of the curriculum offered in later grades may be viewed as increasingly elaborate and complex forms that incorporate the simpler forms within them. As opposed to information learning, the learning of intellectual skills appears to be cumulative in nature. The learning of a new rule, for example, requires the availability of the simpler rules or concepts that compose it.

Intellectual skill learning requires the "combining" of simpler intellectual skills (rules, concepts), which have been previously learned and can be retrieved. (In terms of the learning model, they must be "recovered" in short-term memory.) The implications for instruction, therefore, are clear. First, the teacher must insure that the prerequisite skills have been learned. This prior learning may have taken place in an immediately preceding lesson, or in a lesson that occurred a long time ago. If the necessary prerequisite skills have not been learned, then instruction must be given to establish them. Second, cues must be given to enable the student to retrieve the previously learned skills. And third, some kinds of externally provided cues must usually be provided to suggest the nature of the "combination" to be learned. This function of instruction is most typically performed by verbal means; the new rule or concept is stated verbally. Minimal cues for such learning characterize the method of "discovery learning," an alternative sometimes employed to good effect.

It should be pointed out that although the learning of intellectual skills under ideal conditions appears to be a simple and straightforward matter, their storage and retrieval may involve other complications. For example, the student who has acquired the rule for transforming Fahrenheit temperature into Celsius may know "how," but may find that he has forgotten the formula (information) that enables him to recover the skill. It appears, then, that informational cues often need to be learned, besides the skill itself. The full implications of this state of affairs cannot currently be described. However, the importance of *spaced reviews* for retrieval of intellectual skills has more than once been verified.[19]

Cognitive strategies. Cognitive strategies are internally organized skills that govern the individual's behavior in attending, learning, remembering, and thinking. In terms of the learning model previously described, they are *control processes*. Presumably, some of these processes may be inborn, but most of them are learned. Processes of attention and selective perception may be acquired in perceptual learning, as the work of E. J. Gibson indicates.[20] The operation of strategies for storage and retrieval of word pairs has been investigated by Rohwer and his associates.[21] Strategies of problem solving and thinking are prominently emphasized in the writings of Bruner.[22]

On the whole, knowledge of how cognitive strategies are learned is meager. Accordingly, the arrangement of instruction to promote the learning of these strategies appears correspondingly primitive. The usual recommendation is to provide frequent opportunities for the student to practice the use of cognitive strategies, and presumably to refine them by so doing. Thus, provision is often made for the student to solve challenging novel problems, to write original essays or stories, or to undertake projects requiring the application and transfer of knowledge and skills. It is widely believed that such procedures are effective in promoting the learning and improve-

19. For example, James H. Reynolds and Robert Glaser, "Effects of Repetition and Spaced Review Upon Retention of a Complex Learning Task," *Journal of Educational Psychology* 55 (October 1964): 297-308; Lorraine R. Gay, "Temporal Position of Reviews and Its Effect on the Retention of Mathematical Rules," *Journal of Educational Psychology* 64 (April 1973): 171-82.

20. Eleanor J. Gibson, *Principles of Perceptual Learning and Development* (New York: Appleton-Century-Crofts, 1969).

21. William D. Rohwer, Jr. et al., "Pictorial and Verbal Factors in the Efficient Learning of Paired Associates," *Journal of Educational Psychology* 58 (October 1967): 278-84.

22. Jerome S. Bruner, *The Relevance of Education* (New York: Norton, 1971).

ment of cognitive strategies, although the evidence for this belief is sadly lacking. The importance of this kind of learning objective is universally acknowledged, and the description of increasingly effective instructional methods may be hoped for in the near future.

Attitudes. The school is usually considered responsible for establishing a number of kinds of attitudes in students, and for modifying preexisting attitudes. Among other attitudes, self-concept and self-esteem are often considered important by educational scholars. In addition, it is expected that such attitudes as tolerance, consideration for the feelings of others, honesty, kindness, and helpfulness will be acquired and reinforced by school learning experiences. Then there are attitudes toward school subjects, such as a liking for mathematics, literature, music, or sports. Included also are such negative attitudes as aversion to drug abuse and avoidance of accidents and disease. Obviously, this is a very large category of school learning, sometimes referred to as the affective domain.[23] This particular title, however, should not lead us to neglect the behavioral aspects of attitudes.

Attitudes are learned dispositions that influence the choice of personal action toward classes of things, events, or persons. In the terms of a learning model, they bear a resemblance to cognitive strategies in being internally organized control processes. However, since they do not actually determine behavior, but only influence it, they may perhaps better be described as "moderator processes." They are often identified as "tendencies," which may be either positive or negative in their influence on actions.

So far as instruction is concerned, a number of techniques for establishing and maintaining attitudes can be employed. Perhaps the first point to be noted is the striking ineffectiveness of verbal communications (in and of themselves) as means of establishing or modifying attitudes. Telling students to "avoid harmful drugs" or "be kind to animals," whether these communications are couched in terms of rational arguments, exhortations, or emotional appeals, is not a technique that changes attitudes. In other words, attitudes cannot be established or changed simply by having the student

23. David R. Krathwohl, Benjamin S. Bloom, and B. B. Masia, *Taxonomy of Educational Objectives, Handbook II: Affective Domain* (New York: McKay, 1964).

learn verbal information. This fact has been verified many times.[24]

Attitudes are often learned under conditions in which the student experiences success, or receives reinforcement following a choice of action that he deliberately makes. Perhaps equally important for instruction, if not more so, are methods providing vicarious reinforcement by way of a human model, as described by Bandura.[25] The human model may in some circumstances be the teacher. Other possibilities are respected public personalities, sports figures, famous men and women, and (by extension) heroes of literature. Effective conditions for attitudinal change require that the student observe the human model making the desired choice of action (avoiding harmful drugs, being a cautious driver, placing personal trash in a container) and subsequently being rewarded (reinforced) for this action.

Motor skills. The learning of motor skills, while not a large component of school learning, is nevertheless a part that can readily be identified. Motor skills are prominent in physical education and sports, and in a number of specialties of the performing arts and vocational education. They also occur as learning outcomes in such activities as printing letters and words, and in the pronunciation of language sounds.

The learning of smoothness and timing of responses is a critical feature of motor skills, and these aspects are influenced by kinesthetic feedback from the muscles and other elements of the response system. Accordingly, instruction mainly takes the form of providing reinforced *practice* of the motor responses. Sometimes, the learning can be facilitated by arranging conditions so that feedback is made more nearly immediate, or more precise, or both.

In addition to the learning of increased smoothness and accuracy of responding, motor skills often require that the student acquire a procedure that determines the sequence of his actions. This aspect of motor skill learning is called an *executive subroutine* by Fitts and Posner.[26] Besides learning to pitch a baseball accurately and

24. Harry C. Triandis, *Attitudes and Attitude Change* (New York: Wiley, 1971).

25. Albert Bandura, *Principles of Behavior Modification* (New York: Holt, Rinehart and Winston, 1969).

26. Paul M. Fitts and Michael I. Posner, *Human Performance* (Belmont, Calif.: Brooks/Cole, 1967).

smoothly, the pitcher must learn to wind up, check first base, place his foot properly, and so on. A procedure of this sort has the nature of a sequence rule, and is presumably acquired as are other intellectual skills. Intellectual skills of this kind can accordingly be influenced by verbal cues as a part of instruction; in contrast, the essential motor skill cannot be so influenced, and must be practiced. Of course, both of these components need to be present in instruction of a practically useful skill.

Other Learning Theories

It is not possible within the confines of the present chapter to make comparisons of the details of theories that use the information-processing model, nor to compare them with other types of learning theories. However, some points of similarity and difference can perhaps be pointed out concerning issues specifically related to teaching. Particularly can this be done in terms of the previously described dimensions of instruction, namely, the phases of instruction and the outcomes of instruction.

The facts seem to be that in their sometimes incidental attempts to suggest the critical variables in instruction, different learning theorists have emphasized different instructional phases. Likewise, they have directed their theoretical ideas toward particular learning outcomes, and ignored others. Some examples of theoretical views that are addressed to linkages between learning and instruction may serve to illustrate these points.

BEHAVIORIST VIEWS

One variety of learning theory of the behaviorist type is that of Hull,[27] who accounted for learning in terms of postulated intervening variables affecting the strength of associations (S-Rs). Advocating a "liberalized" version of this basic viewpoint is N. E. Miller,[28] who also described the implications for instruction of

27. Clark L. Hull, *Principles of Behavior* (New York: Appleton-Century-Crofts, 1943).

28. Neal E. Miller, "Liberalization of Basic S-R Concepts: Extensions to Conflict Behavior, Motivation and Social Learning," in *Psychology: A Study of a Science*, vol. 2, ed. Sigmund Koch (New York: McGraw-Hill, 1959), pp. 196-292.

learning theory of this general sort.[29] Miller proposes that an effective sequence of instruction, in any medium, includes provision for *motivation, cue, response,* and *reward.* As a first step, instruction must invoke and channel existing motivation of the student. Second, it must aid the student in distinguishing the relevant cues. Third, the student must be given the opportunity to do something, that is, to exhibit his learned response. And finally, knowledge of his achievement must be fed back to the student, that is, reinforcement must occur.

There is obviously a strong resemblance between the implications for instruction described by Miller and those derived from contemporary information-processing theories. Assuming that both accept the necessity of motivation, made explicit by Miller, the two sets of implications begin the same way (with attention) and end the same way (with performance and feedback). The difference lies in the middle—with "cue" and what follows. For Miller, the externally provided cue serves the primary purpose of supporting attention and perception processes. Information-processing theory, however, expands the notion of cue to encompass the provision of additional context for coding and also for the support of retrieval and transfer. Although they supplement Miller's views in this manner, the proposals of contemporary theory are obviously highly compatible with his.

The brand of behaviorism espoused by Skinner presents a rather different picture.[30] In the first place, Skinner maintains that the internal processes postulated by contemporary information-processing theories are irrelevant for analysis and unnecessary for the prediction of behavior. In brief, he advocates accounting for learning on the basis of external events that act upon the learner, including the arrangement of contingencies for reinforcement.[31]

The implications of these views for instruction, however, do not

29. Neal E. Miller, *Graphic Communication and the Crisis in Education* (Washington, D.C.: Department of Audio-Visual Instruction, National Education Association, 1957).

30. B. F. Skinner, *Science and Human Behavior* (New York: Macmillan, 1953).

31. B. F. Skinner, *The Technology of Teaching* (New York: Appleton-Century-Crofts, 1968).

differ greatly from those of information-processing theory; the differences appear to be largely matters of emphasis. Thus, Skinner provides for the motivation of the learner through initial selection of a preferred activity, which becomes a "reinforcer" for the act to be acquired when set in a contingency sequence. Skinner's next point of emphasis is on the response and feedback phases of instruction, providing the occasion for positive reinforcement to have its effect. Between these two sets of events are "prompting," "fading," and "gradual stimulus change." It is conceivable that these forms of learning guidance, when put into practical usage, sometimes take on the characteristics of coding and of cueing for retrieval. Whereas the coding and cueing functions are incorporated in information-processing theory, they are not explicitly formulated in Skinner's theory, nor are they implied as instructional events.

COGNITIVE THEORIES

Some cognitive theorists postulate a fairly complex set of internal mechanisms to account for learning and retention. In this respect their theories resemble information-processing theories, even though a different nomenclature is employed. Prominent among such theorists is Ausubel.[32] In brief, Ausubel proposes that the information to be learned must be (a) selectively perceived, (b) meaningfully structured, (c) encoded by being subsumed within a previously learned cognitive structure, (d) differentiated within that structure for later retrieval, and (e) subjected to further consolidation and "reconciliation" to promote transfer.

If one allows for differences in terminology, resemblances between Ausubel's theory and contemporary information-processing models are substantial. Ausubel emphasizes the operational processes of meaningful coding, and the storage of information in propositional form. His ideas about the differentiation and dissociability of material stored in memory imply the need for instruction that concerns itself with cueing for retrieval and transfer. In contrast to behaviorist theories previously described, Ausubel's theory focuses on the middle set of events for instruction, that is, on the presentation of stimulus material, its coding and cueing. Not much is said

32. Ausubel, *Educational Psychology*.

in his theory about the beginning and end of the instructional process, that is, on the establishment of motivation, on the one hand, and the provision of feedback, on the other.

As a cognitive theorist, Bruner presents wide-ranging views, including ideas about the social and biological foundations of education[33] and the cognitive development of children[34] as well as the design of effective instruction.[35] Perhaps the most important point of emphasis, so far as instruction itself is concerned, is the use of discovery methods of teaching,[36] with the aim of developing cognitive strategies.[37] Cognitive strategies are processes by which the learner controls his own attending, learning, and thinking behavior. As a general class, they may be considered equivalent to the executive control processes that form a part of the information-processing model. Although Bruner acknowledges that intellectual skills constitute a substantial part of most school subjects to be learned,[38] it is the strategies of learning and productive thinking that he considers worthy of greatest attention in instruction.

The theoretical ideas advanced by Bruner would apparently not conflict with notions derived from information-processing theories, insofar as the latter concern matters of coding, storage, and retrieval. The contrast is again one of emphasis. Although the information-processing model depends heavily upon the operation of executive control processes, it does not have much to say about how such processes are acquired, developed, stored, or activated by the learner. It is these matters that are of greatest concern to Bruner. His theory implies that the learner must have considerable freedom of exploration to develop these processes, and at the same time frequent intellectual challenges to stimulate his thinking and allow discovery to take place.

33. Bruner, *The Relevance of Education*.

34. Jerome S. Bruner, "The Growth of Mind," *American Psychologist* 20 (December 1965): 1007-17.

35. Jerome S. Bruner, *Toward a Theory of Instruction* (Cambridge, Mass.: Harvard University Press, 1966).

36. Jerome S. Bruner, "The Act of Discovery," *Harvard Educational Review* 31 (Winter 1961): 21-32.

37. Bruner, *The Relevance of Education*.

38. Ibid., pp. 109-10.

A SOCIAL LEARNING THEORY

Another variety of theory that has significance for instruction is social learning theory, of which Bandura is a leading proponent.[39] As indicated previously, this theory emphasizes the role of imitation of human models as a mode of learning. Instruction takes the form of demonstration of desired behavior by the model. The student learns by observing the behavior, and noting also the evidences of satisfaction and reward to the model. Feedback is provided in this situation as "vicarious reinforcement," which may lead, under suitable conditions, to "self-reinforcement."[40]

Learning by human modeling provides still another example of a theory having instructional implications that do not appear inherently incompatible with those of information-processing theory. Modeling represents a somewhat different way of dealing with motivation, with coding, and with feedback. The major point of difference lies in the area of what is being learned. Most prominently, social learning theory deals with the learning of attitudes and motor skills, kinds of learning outcomes that information-processing theories have not attempted to encompass.

LEARNING THEORIES AND LEARNING OUTCOMES

The place occupied by Bandura's theory of human modeling, largely outside the purview of contemporary theories of learning and memory, serves to illustrate a more general point about the latter theories. All of them are, in a sense, partial theories. They do not cover the range of learning phenomena that occur in the school, and are therefore the concern of the teacher. It is for this reason that, in thinking about instruction in an analytical sense, one needs to bear in mind the total range and variety of learning outcomes described in the previous section of this chapter. In educational environments, students are learning more than information; they are also learning intellectual skills, motor skills, cognitive strategies, and attitudes.

Contemporary information-processing theory concerns itself almost exclusively with the learning and retention of verbal informa-

39. Bandura, *Principles of Behavior Modification.*

40. Albert Bandura, "Vicarious and Self-reinforcement Processes," in Glaser, *The Nature of Reinforcement,* pp. 228-78.

tion of the sort that is exhibited as propositional knowledge. Other theorists have given attention to other kinds of learning outcomes they see as relevant to school instruction: Bruner to cognitive strategies, Bandura to attitudes, Gagné to intellectual skills. Evidently, a truly comprehensive theory of human learning will ultimately account for learning processes that are differentially applicable to all of the kinds of capabilities and dispositions that human beings can and do learn.

Summary: Implications for Instruction

As viewed from the standpoint of learning models of the information-processing variety, each act of learning involves the operation of a number of internal processes. The inputs to these processes come partly from the learner himself, that is, they are recovered from his memory and thus depend to a considerable extent upon previous learning. These inputs can also be altered, modified, and enhanced in various ways by stimulation from the learner's external environment. It is these actions that constitute *instruction*.

The essential task of the teacher is to arrange the conditions of the learner's environment so that the processes of learning will be activated, supported, enhanced, and maintained. Thus the teacher needs to be aware of what the processes of learning are and of the specific influences he can exert on them in order to provide successful instruction. It will be convenient for him to look upon an act of learning as having a number of phases, beginning with the arousal of a motivational state of expectancy and proceeding to the point at which feedback is provided to confirm this expectancy. In this view, there are eight phases to learning, each of which may be influenced by events of instruction to a greater or lesser degree, and each in a different way.

An orthogonal dimension of instruction to be taken into account in teaching concerns the matter of *what* is to be learned, or the nature of the *learning outcome* to be expected. The effects of learning consist in the establishment of human capabilities, of which there are five major varieties: verbal information, intellectual skills, cognitive strategies, attitudes, and motor skills. While the phases of learning that reflect underlying processes are presumably common for all of these learning outcomes, their learning differs with respect

6999

to which phases are most subject to external influence by instruction. The coding of verbal information for retrieval, for example, appears to be greatly influenced by externally suggested schemes, whereas coding of the smoothness and timing of motor skills can be influenced little, if at all, by such schemes. Accordingly, it is desirable for the teacher to be aware of, and to make adequate provision for, certain critical conditions of instruction relating to each type of learning outcome.

Models of learning thus make possible a conceptual frame of reference within which learning can be viewed as a set of sequentially ordered processes leading to the establishment and retention of more or less permanent human capabilities. At the same time, these models provide a conceptualization of what instruction can and cannot accomplish, when considered as a set of planned external events designed to influence the ongoing processes of learning.

CHAPTER III

Programmed and Computer-Assisted Instruction

C. VICTOR BUNDERSON AND GERALD W. FAUST

In this chapter programmed instruction (PI) and computer-assisted instruction (CAI), viewed in their primary roles as methods of teaching one person at a time, are defined and reviewed. Neither PI nor CAI is seen to be a subset of the other, for the first is defined as a systematic development process rather than a product form, and the second is still too complex to be characterized as a kind of instructional medium. A synthesis is possible, however, around the idea of a "design science of instruction."

A Characterization of PI and CAI

PROGRAMMED INSTRUCTION: A PROCESS DEFINITION

In the early 1960s, definitions of programmed instruction focused on easily recognized features of format (small frames, requirements for responses, and the like). Susan Markle wisely pointed out that such definitions unnecessarily restrict the class of instructional materials that can be called "programs."[1] Instead, she proposed a definition that focused on the characteristics of the process of development rather than the characteristics of the product of that development. She defined an instructional program as a "reproducible sequence of instructional events designed to produce a measurable and consistent effect on the behavior of each and every acceptable student." This definition and very similar statements have received widespread acceptance, and the term "programmed in-

1. Susan M. Markle, "Empirical Testing of Programs," in *Programed Instruction*, ed. Phil C. Lange, Sixty-sixth Yearbook of the National Society for the Study of Education, Part II (Chicago: University of Chicago Press, 1967), p. 104.

struction" has in many circles become synonomous with the term
"validated instruction." [2]

It has been shown, however, that even validated instruction can
be worthless.[3] A program may teach irrelevant objectives extremely
well, thus meeting external criteria of validation as set forth in
Markle's definition, while being of little value in terms of accomplishing worthwhile educational goals. Geis has suggested that the
term "validated instruction" should be reserved for instruction that
(a) is the result of an empirical development process that guarantees
that it meets its stated objectives, (b) is directed at objectives that
reflect meaningful real-world performances, and (c) includes tech-
nically accurate instructional content.[4]

Whatever definition one chooses, obvious problems arise when
one attempts to define instruction that encompasses a variety of
media, from striped pages and interactive lectures to tape-slide and
television productions, and employs a myriad of techniques derived
from different psychological theories and a number of clever rules
of thumb. Yet there seems to be some agreement. It is the process
of developing instructional programs that determines whether experts
in the field will accept a given piece of instruction as being "programmed." And this process must include an empirical validation
step in which student performance after instruction is compared to
stated program objectives. This definition can be extended if we
make some inferences based on the term "validated instruction."
The definitions of Markle and Geis both include references to the
comparison of postprogram student performance with program
objectives.[5] This kind of definition allows us to infer two phases

2. A. A. Lumsdaine, "Educational Technology, Programed Learning, and
Instructional Science," in *Theories of Learning and Instruction*, ed. Ernest R.
Hilgard, Sixty-third Yearbook of the National Society for the Study of Edu-
cation, Part I (Chicago: University of Chicago Press, 1964), p. 385; Francis
Mechner, "Science Education and Behavioral Technology," in *Teaching
Machines and Programed Learning, II: Data and Directions*, ed. Robert Glaser
(Washington, D.C.: Department of Audiovisual Instruction, National Educa-
tion Association, 1965), p. 444.

3. David G. Markle, "In Which It Is Demonstrated That a Program That
Works May Well Be Worthless," *Improving Human Performance* 3 (Fall
1973): 175-80.

4. George L. Geis, "A Comment on Validated Instruction," *Improving
Human Performance* 3 (Fall 1973): 161-64.

5. Ibid.; Susan Markle, "Empirical Testing of Programs."

of the process of program development—one in which evaluation of student performance on objectives takes place and one in which the program objectives are developed. Certainly this kind of definition indicates that there must be a phase during which instructional objectives are used to direct the development of the instructional program.

This reasoning leads to an even fuller description of a three-step process required to produce validated instruction. The process involves (a) some form of problem analysis that focuses on desirable real-world performances and results in specific statements of instructional objectives the achievement of which is measurable; (b) a design and development process that insures instructional materials (displays, frames) directed at fostering achievement of the stated objectives, using the most efficient and effective instructional strategies or techniques; and (c) an evaluation-validation phase. During this third step, students representative of the intended target population use the program and then are evaluated as to their achievement of the stated objectives, changes are made in the program wherever the students do not achieve the objectives, and the evaluation-revision process is continued until the program demonstrates that it does indeed have a measurable and consistent effect on the behavior of students who meet entry-level requirements.

Thus, programmed instruction is instruction that results from a systematic development process in which the developer assumes the responsibility for student learning.

COMPUTER-ASSISTED INSTRUCTION: A DELIVERY SYSTEM DEFINITION

The early literature on computer-assisted, computer-aided, computer-based, and computer-managed instruction is filled with a variety of not too enlightening attempts to define and distinguish the three-letter acronyms beginning with "C" and ending with "I." Computers and specialized terminal devices can be engineered and programmed to perform work needed in any of the processes of instructional management, delivery to an individual or to a group, design and development, and evaluation, research, and administration. The more generic term, "computer uses in education" (CUE), does not limit the use of computers prematurely to models and applications that have gained early prominence.

In this chapter, "CAI" is used as a primitive term, not an acronym, to refer to that class of situations wherein a student may, for educational purposes, interact with an electromechanical device that (a) can display information in one or more forms, such as printed graphic, audio, and tactual displays or mechanical movements, and (b) can receive responses from the student in one or more forms, such as keyboard responses, pointing responses, movements of mechanical objects, vocal responses, or recorded changes in physiological measures. The educational purposes at which this interaction is aimed may encompass cognitive, affective, or psychomotor objectives and also exploration, creative problem solving, design, testing, diagnosis, and prescription within an individualized multimedia instructional environment. In short, CAI is defined as an interaction between a student, a computer controlled display, and a response-entry device for the purpose of achieving educational outcomes.

This definition excludes batch jobs (slow turn-around programs submitted by students) submitted without benefit of an interactive terminal, but not a computer-managed instructional interaction wherein the student gets a test scored and receives a diagnosis and prescription within five minutes or less. It excludes data collection for management or research purposes, which may also be accomplished through recording data from the above-defined cybernetic interaction between student and artifact. It excludes the interactions between teacher, proctor, and operator that may occur at the same student terminal or at a special terminal used to assist in the monitoring and management of groups and of single students. It excludes the interactions that may occur at a terminal among instructional designers, authors and media packagers to promote the development and revision of instructional materials. All these are important aspects of the more general term "computer uses in education."

This definition focuses on the operational constraints on display and response, and on the control and measurement, that can be applied to the contingent relationships between subsequent displays and responses. CAI limits display types and formats to what can be shown on a particular device. Some examples are teletypes (upper-case alphanumeric characters), a television or plasma display (alphanumeric characters and graphics), movies, audio, a Braille typewriter, or a "Turtle."[6] For the purposes of interpreting alternatives and controlling contingent actions, CAI limits responses to a sequence of key depressions on a keyboard, a pointing response with a finger or light-pen, or other more esoteric methods of entering data into a computer.[7] It should be noted that instructional designers do not always limit themselves to responses that can be received by the device and used to direct contingent actions.[8]

There is no conceivable limit to the variety of algorithms that can be implemented. These algorithms control the content and sequence of displays and feedback messages. The algorithms can be made contingent upon student responses, historical data about students, temporal variables, and models of the student and of the learning process. The hardware of display and response serves to limit and bring under control the events of display and response. Similarly, the algorithms programmed into the computer make explicit, limit, and control the sequential and contingent processes occurring in an episode of instructional interaction.

CAI thus offers itself as instrumentation and, through its explicit algorithms, as notation for a new science and technology of instruction. Its potential has barely been tapped. It is the epitome of instructional technology. Performance objectives introduced the limit-

6. One kind of "Turtle" is a mechanical device, connected to a computer, that can roll in four directions and raise and lower a pen. It is controlled by a simple computer program that a child can write. See Seymour Papert, "Teaching Children Thinking," in *World Conference on Computer Education, 1970*, Part I (New York: International Federation of Information Processing Societies, Science Associates/International, 1970), pp. 73-78.

7. The University of Illinois PLATO terminal may be equipped with a touch panel. The student touches a portion of the screen and his computer replies with an audible sound to indicate receipt of response, then takes action contingent on the response. A light-pen is sometimes used for a pointing response, as in the IBM 1500 system. See *IBM 1500 Operating System, Computer-Assisted Instruction, Coursewriter II*, CAI-4036-1 (San Jose, Cal.: IBM, Product Publication Department, n.d.).

8. Children watching "Sesame Street" are encouraged to repeat, answer, sing, clap, and move about. Victorine Abboud and C. Victor Bunderson had students write Arabic characters on a television screen, project the correct characters under the writing for visual comparison, wipe it off, and repeat. See *A Computer-Assisted Instruction Program in the Arabic Writing System*, Technical Report No. 4 (Austin, Texas.: University of Texas CAI Laboratory, 1971). ERIC 052603.

ing of instruction to a display specification, a response specification, and a performance standard. In so doing, they evoked the often valid complaints of humanists that the tacit components of person-to-person instruction were being lost.[9] CAI limits display and response no more than does programmed instruction, for a computer can control—or reference—any kind of media. CAI brings the *process* under greater control, however, and thus invades the domain of human teachers in a more threatening and potent way.

CAI will bring a new science and technology of instruction and can further strip away certain valued tacit components of learning. Or, if it is used wisely in concert with organized patterns of human interaction (student-to-student and student-to-teacher), it can effect a resurgence of the human aspects of learning and teaching. It can help both by highlighting what is *not* essentially human and by freeing teachers from those tasks.

The Three Technologies of CAI

The three technologies of hardware, software, and courseware elaborate CAI's essential features of explicit and limited display, response, and contingent processing. The designers of CAI systems must span, in one person or as a team, many specialties. Expertise in hardware must include a knowledge of (a) a variety of display and response devices, (b) techniques and tradeoffs in data communication, (c) varieties of information storage devices, (d) the capabilities of various new microcircuits, and (e) kinds of memory storage devices and ways to organize them hierarchiacally to achieve design objectives. Special hardware technologies for audio and video storage and reproduction, as well as for computer graphics, are evolving rapidly.[10] Creation of the architecture of the various hardware elements that make up a CAI system may be as deceptively simple as adapting an existing intelligent terminal with a built-in

9. An articulate and persuasive case for the tacit component in all knowledge is made by the philosopher of science, Michael Polanyi, in *Personal Knowledge* (Chicago: University of Chicago Press, 1962). See especially his chapter on skills, pp. 49-63.

10. A good review of computer hardware, with emphasis on instructional uses of computers, is found in Roger Levien, *The Emerging Technology: Instructional Uses of the Computer in Higher Education* (New York: McGraw-Hill Book Co., 1972), pp. 251-326.

microcomputer,[11] or as complex and responsive to different purposes and philosophies as the architecture of PLATO and TICCIT, which are discussed later in this chapter.[12]

Software is distinguished from courseware in CAI parlance because the "software" of systems analysis and programming is distinctly different from the "software" of instructional materials development, although their relationship is full of provocative analogies. Systems programming gives authors, teachers, and students access, by means of command language statements and a hierarchy of levels of control, to the hardware features of the terminal and the central computing and storage devices. Operating systems, structured file-access systems, and languages for entering, editing, and revising any course materials must be provided. Artificial intelligence promises to make this software more sophisticated and general.

The courseware itself is seen as consisting of special purpose programs and data files, which require for their implementation the general purpose software provided by the systems programmers. Courseware also includes instructional materials coordinated with the computer programs, but not provided through the computer, such as workbooks, videotapes, slides, and audiotapes. The nature of the emerging science and technology underlying courseware design and development has been elaborated in previous yearbooks of the National Society for the Study of Education[13] and is discussed further in the next major section of this chapter.

An Intellectual Bifurcation in CAI

A bifurcation exists between the computer science perspective

11. Martin Kamp and John A. Starkweather, "A Return to the Dedicated Machine for Computer-Assisted Instruction," *Computers in Biology and Medicine* 3 (October 1973): 293-98.

12. Donald Bitzer and Dominic Skaperdas, "The Economics of a Large-Scale Computer-Based Education System: PLATO IV," in *Computer-Assisted Instruction, Testing, and Guidance,* ed. Wayne H. Holtzman (New York: Harper and Row, 1970), pp. 17-29. The architecture of TICCIT, a minicomputer-based system with color television terminals, is described in *An Overview of the TICCIT Program,* Technical Report M74-1 (McLean, Va.: The MITRE Corporation, 1974).

13. See especially *Theories of Learning and Instruction* and *Programed Instruction.*

and the instructional science perspective. Persons proficient in the hardware and software technologies underlying CAI (primarily electrical engineering and computer science) have a different perspective than those proficient in the courseware technologies (instructional psychology and media).

The former group sees the intellectual history of CAI in terms of (a) the development of time-sharing capability, which has afforded mass access to computer terminals and computer power, (b) issues in man-machine interaction, programming, computer simulation, and artificial intelligence, and (c) fundamental computer science concepts, such as data structures, alternative representational schemes, and alternative algorithms. To them the computer is of profound intellectual interest in and of itself, not just as a possible new method of mediating old subject matter in old ways. It is itself a message and a metaphor.[14] Learning to use formal languages, create models, and implement them in a computer is seen as worthwhile in its own right. More than that, it is seen as an indispensable part of the creative professionals' future problem-solving and design activities. For the teacher in any field, the notions of data structure and formal model may generate new ways of conceiving the very structure and organization of a portion of one's subject matter. The use of computer graphics, computational power, and information retrieval power suggests alternate ways of presenting the subject matter to students. Computer applications in research and instruction in one field serve as metaphors to prompt restructuring and invention in other fields. The *Proceedings* of six national conferences on Computers in the Undergraduate Curriculum have documented a diverse array of computer applications to instruction in a wide variety of undergraduate disciplines.[15] These efforts by creative faculty members are for the most part notably untouched

---

14. Arthur W. Luehrmann, "Should the Computer Teach the Student or Vice Versa?" in *Proceedings of the Spring Joint Computer Conference* (Mondale, N.J.: AFIPS Press, 1972).

15. The *Proceedings* of these conferences, which have been held at the University of Iowa (1970), Dartmouth College (1971), Atlanta, Georgia (1972), Claremont, California (1973), Washington State University (1974), and Texas Christian University (1975), are available through the University of Iowa, 1245 Lindquist Center, Iowa City, Iowa 52242. The conferences have been supported by the National Science Foundation.

by much knowledge of programmed instruction as defined above. Yet the great majority of instructional activities on computers that fit our definition of CAI fall into this category.[16]

The courseware technologists see a different intellectual history behind the use of CAI.[17] Fitting CAI into a framework of systematic design and evaluation makes it a medium of instruction. Its capabilities for dynamic branching, storing large files of data, score keeping, dynamic graphic display, and the like, might be implied by a set of performance objectives and a list of implementation constraints.[18] Like any good medium, it will then be designed into a total individualized instructional environment where it can meet certain requirements uniquely well, or better than any other medium, and still keep costs within bounds. This "mainline" use of the computer as a part of a total instructional system stands in contrast to the adjunctive approach that emanates from the "computer qua computer" perspective.[19]

It may be possible in the near future for a synthesis to occur, based perhaps on the analytic PI approach described below. The result, a more mature science and technology of instruction, could encompass the unique aspects of both PI and CAI within a coherent intellectual framework. In the meantime, faculty members at all

16. As Levien shows (*The Emerging Technology*, pp. 123-421), the number of uses of the computer to teach *about* computers far exceeds the uses of CAI to teach other subjects. Contrast this with chapter 3 of the excellent new book by Beverly Hunter, Carol Kastner, Martin Rubin, and Robert J. Seidel, *Learning Alternatives in U.S. Education: Where Student and Computer Meet* (Englewood Cliffs, N.J.: Educational Technology Publications, 1975). Relatively few of the 5,560 programs summarized by Hunter et al. (p. 47) have been developed systematically or validated; hence most do not fit the definition of PI used in this chapter.

17. The previously cited volumes of the National Society for the Study of Education carry much of the history, written by psychologists and educators.

18. Glaser was one of the first to consider hardware design as a function of educational objectives. See Robert Glaser and William W. Ramage, "The Student-Machine Interface in Instruction," in *1967 IEEE International Convention Record, Part 10* (New York: Institute of Electrical and Electronic Engineers, 1967), pp. 52-59.

19. C. Victor Bunderson, "Justifying CAI in Mainline Instruction," in *Proceedings of the Conference on Computers in the Undergraduate Curricula*, Gerard P. Weeg, chairman (Iowa City, Iowa: University of Iowa Center for Conferences and Institutes, 1970), pp. 12.5-12.16.

levels of education and in almost all disciplines are trying their hands at CAI without benefit of PI's hard-won knowledge of how to specify, design, and validate good instruction.

CAI's Economic and Intellectual Potential

CAI could well be likened to the invention of printing, which brought another technology, the book, into wide use. CAI represents a potential breakthrough of similar social and intellectual significance. Economically it is a breakthrough in the capability of performing the work involved in teaching one person at a time and managing the learning environment required.[20] Individualized instruction often founders on the problem of work, which expands enormously in the initial production of materials, the updating and revision of materials, the management of individual paths to learning, and the provision of detailed practice with feedback.

CAI as defined here does not itself reduce the work involved in the authoring and updating of materials. Even as the algorithms for student instruction are made explicit and operational, however, the processes involved in authoring are being made explicit. Generative CAI is one result. At the Ontario Institute for Studies in Education, an extensive system of remedial mathematics modules has been developed. Only one prototype problem for each exercise format and test item format is provided, and random numbers are generated according to parameters to create an infinitely large problem file.[21] Using state-of-the-art PI techniques outlined in this chapter, the TICCIT project introduced an authoring approach, described below, that has simplified the process of developing large volumes of courseware.[22] The rapid editing and updating capabili-

20. The authors are indebted to Dr. Dustin Heustin, Headmaster of Spence School in Manhattan, N.Y., and a CAI pioneer in elementary and secondary applications, for his as yet unpublished and thoughtful analysis of the work breakthrough afforded by CAI.

21. W. P. Olivier, R. S. McLean, J. W. Brahan, and C. Payne, "A Canadian Cooperative Computer-aided Learning Project," in *Computers in Education: IFIP Second World Conference*, ed. L. Lecarme and R. Lewis (Amsterdam, Holland: North Holland Publishing Co., 1975), pp. 491-96.

22. C. Victor Bunderson, "Team Production of Learner-Controlled Courseware: A Progress Report," *International Journal of Man-Machine Studies* 6 (July 1974): 479-91.

ties of computers, coupled with data collection routines that can summarize student data to pinpoint revision needs, provides powerful assistance in the work involved in updating and revision.

The problem of managing individual paths to learning is easily handled by CAI systems, which can maintain a representation of the complete set of individualized instructional modules, along with a record of which ones any student has completed, still needs, or is working on. Using this information, the system can provide reports to teachers or instructional managers on the status of students, alone or in groups, summarizing exceptions for action.

It is difficult to find a teacher willing and patient enough to work with individual students to provide detailed practice on problems or exercises in such areas as basic mathematical and language skills. Tutoring bureaus at colleges attest to the need for such services. CAI provides this high volume of detailed, tedious (to a human) work for many students at once. The established success of drill-and-practice CAI in elementary schools is a notable example of the work breakthrough at the level of repetitive practice.

While there is increasing understanding of how to use computers to perform instructional work, the prices of computer equipment are still dropping rapidly, even during these inflationary times.[23] CAI was oversold during the middle sixties, and overoptimistic claims have deserved much of the criticism they received.[24] Past errors of overselling CAI should not be repeated. But so long as intensive individualization is a valid educational goal, the work potential of CAI, its increasing availability, and its decreasing costs make its expanded use likely.

PI: The State of the Art

The programmed instruction movement hit the fields of educa-

23. See Levien, *The Emerging Technology*, pp. 1-10, for a review of computer cost trends. Since Levien's work was written, the downward trends have continued. A number of new and established computer companies offer a microcomputer and a television terminal in kit form (to be assembled by the purchaser) for from $500 to $900. These companies can be identified in the trade journals.

24. Anthony G. Oettinger and Sema Marks, *Run, Computer, Run: The Mythology of Educational Innovation* (Cambridge, Mass.: Harvard University Press, 1969). See also R. W. Simonsen and K. S. Renshaw, "CAI—Boon or Boondoggle?" *Datamation* 20 (March 1974): 90-102.

tion and training like a whirlwind in the early 1960s. Educators were told that here at last was a guaranteed method of teaching, and trainers seized on PI as a cost-effective method for increasing the performance capabilities of their charges. Striped textbooks and small steps became the order of the day and literally thousands of "programs" began to flood the market. Small companies of programmers sprang up and almost anyone who had "taken" a program began to write one. Guidance for the novice programmer was limited with only a few texts providing much help (for example, Markle's *Good Frames and Bad*).[25]

The claims of programmers generally far outreached their skill, and the shelves began to fill with unused programs that provided mute testimony to the fallacy that small steps and overt responding ensure effective instruction. The product definition of programmed instruction contributed to a rapid demise of the field. The easily recognized and reproduced features of format that were used as defining characteristics of programmed instruction deluded many into thinking they could be programmers. These same features deluded publishers into thinking that a book with "frames" is a program. The calls for validation were often looked upon as little more than signs of weakness or lack of confidence on the part of overly systematic psychologists.

By the late 1960s and early 1970s, the realization that effective programmed instruction had to be the result of a systematic and empirical development process had been added to the earlier experiences to instill a new maturity into the field. Publishers had seriously retrenched, with most of them leaving the programmed text business. The output of programmed materials had slowed to a trickle.

The military and industrial training communities had come through the 1960s with a relatively healthy respect for programmed instruction. This was due mainly to their contact with several professional groups (for example, the American Society for Training and Development, the National Society for Performance and Instruction, and the Association for Educational Communications and Technology), to their commitment to internal training departments,

25. Susan Markle, *Good Frames and Bad* (New York: John Wiley & Sons, 1969).

and to regulations or policies that outlined procedures and made "systems approaches" to training mandatory. Today the military and industrial communities continue to support a modern brand of programmed (validated) instruction. Many millions of dollars were expended in 1975 on programmed materials for the Training Extension Courses (TEC) of the U.S. Army alone. The TEC program continues to flourish with an even greater expenditure expected in 1976.

THREE APPROACHES TO ONE PROCESS

The process of developing instructional programs described earlier in this chapter is diagrammed in figure 1. Phase I of this process yields a complete list or hierarchy of objectives. Phase II results in the completed instructional materials, and Phase III yields a specification for revision that may result in a refinement of the objectives or a revision of the materials or both. There is considerable agreement concerning the need for an instructional development process which involves these phases. An analysis of current trends, however, reveals a plethora of specific methodologies, techniques, and models for implementing such an approach.

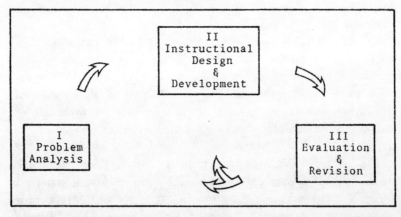

FIG. 1. Three basic phases in a systematic approach to instructional development

Although some procedures for Phases I and III of the instructional development process differ, an analysis of most systematic models reveals considerable agreement. The major differences in technique and in attitudes toward instructional development are found in the activities of the design and development efforts of Phase II.

Three basic approaches or philosophies can be used to bring some order to the variation in the design and development phase of the systematic models that have been proposed. Models seem to focus on either empirical, artistic, or analytical approaches to the development of instructional materials.

The Empirical Approach

The empirical approach is probably the longest-lived and most written about. It is a product of the basic psychology laboratories that spawned programmed instruction in the late 1950s and 1960s. The Skinnerian (operant conditioning) model of observing student behavior and of reinforcing successively closer approximations of desired performances has its analogue among program developers. The developer produces frames, presents them to students, and observes reactions. Frames that do not produce desired behavior are changed, and gradually the program is "shaped" by the close interaction of developer and trial student. Gilbert describes the programming procedure as one in which you "take your first crude effort to the student." He describes a trial and error procedure in which "the important thing to remember is to keep varying your behavior until you are successful." This procedure is repeated with several students until the program is reaching desired levels of effectiveness. Gilbert predicts that "after fewer than ten tries you will have a program which will teach 98 percent of the students."[26]

This much reliance on an empirical approach can have several problems, not the least of which are the inefficiencies in development and learning times that can result. The empirical approach provides little guidance as to the design (sequence, strategy, and the like) of the initial sequence of frames. Therefore, the initial sequence could be extremely ineffective and provide little that can eventually be used to teach students. Inefficiencies can also be a problem on the learner's side of the table. The initial program may

26. Thomas F. Gilbert, "On the Relevance of Laboratory Investigation of Learning to Self-Instructional Programming," in *Teaching Machines and Programmed Learning: A Source Book*, ed. A. A. Lumsdaine and Robert Glaser (Washington, D.C.: Department of Audio-Visual Instruction, National Education Association, 1960), pp. 479-80.

not contain all that is needed for learning; or it may contain considerably more explanation, practice, or other verbiage than the student will need. The problem is that the empirical approach provides limited data concerning such inefficiencies. Lean programming and related techniques have been developed in order to produce programs that present just enough material to teach, and no more.[27] The advice to programmers is to start with only a few frames and add frames only where they are needed.

In general, the small-group tryout and reliance on individual and small-group data advocated by those using empirical approaches are not only reasonable but are also extremely important components of other approaches. Nonetheless, reliance on these techniques during the design and development phases places considerable strain on the talents of the programmer. He must be extremely observant, must establish excellent rapport with trial students, and must be able to make both content and strategy decisions based on individual data. History indicates that few good programmers can use this model effectively.

The Artistic Approach

The artistic approach arises from a totally different intellectual base. It involves heavy reliance on communications concepts and technology. This approach assumes that subject matter experts or teachers know what to teach and how to teach, but that they need assistance in delivering their instruction to the learner. The emphasis, therefore, is on the design and development of effective delivery systems or instructional media. The techniques and procedures used either are intuitive or stem from the literature concerning the medium being used (for example, television, film, graphics). The products of this approach are generally judged on the basis of their aesthetic appeal.

The artistic approach is by far the most widely used approach to instructional development. Publishers, film makers, and educational television studios are generally staffed by persons who come from the editing, layout, film production, or educational and broad-

27. Geary A. Rummler, "The Economics of Lean Programming," *Improving Human Performance* 3 (Fall 1973): 211-16.

cast television communities. These persons tend to assume an artistic model when confronted with instructional development projects. Materials developed through an artistic approach are usually not systematic in the sense of being directed at specific objectives and evaluated with measures of student performance. Certainly much instruction is developed in an unsystematic manner. The users of artistic approaches, however, are the most likely to abandon the three-step process outlined above in favor of less systematic procedures.

For the true artist, the medium is the message and evaluation and validation based upon student performance are of little importance. In most cases, validation can be extremely expensive for those who use the artistic approach. Since the bulk of the dollar investment in instructional development goes into the production of "hard copy" media, even small changes can double or triple the cost.

Whenever major emphasis is placed on hardware technology or its design and development, the artistic approach is easily adopted. This has been true in the field of CAI. Institutions or organizations that have focused on the development of interactive graphics, simulations, and gaming have tended to ignore principles of systematic instructional development and to focus on the affective and aesthetic qualities of their product.

The Analytic Approach

The analytic approach is based on the belief that instructional science has developed to the point where prescriptive rules can be derived and used to develop effective instructional materials that have a high probability of first-trial success. This approach assumes that the subject matter expert may know what there is to teach but needs help in determining exactly what, how much, and how to teach. The approach emphasizes systematic analysis of instructional outcomes and content, and the design of effective instructional strategies. The procedures used are based on prescriptive propositions developed through basic and applied research on human learning and the instructional process. Products of this approach are judged on the degree to which they work to help students achieve prescribed objectives. But the goal is to predict probable effectiveness of particular instructional programs in advance of extensive tryout and revision.

The analytic approach can be likened to the approach taken by the architect. The architect knows that carpenters and bricklayers may subtly modify his plans, but he still uses a host of conventions and prescriptive rules (eighteen-inch centers, stress models, and the like) to develop a blueprint that, when followed exactly, has a very high probability of resulting in a house of the desired quality, durability, and aesthetic appeal. Similarly, the instructional developer using an analytic approach applies the output of instructional science to develop an instructional blueprint that, if followed, has a high probability of meeting his goals in terms of affect and instructional effectiveness.

Generally speaking, we see the analytic approach offering the greatest hope of providing specific guidance to the instructional developer on the specific rules to apply in order to go from instructional objectives to effective instructional materials. This approach is the newest and least developed, yet its rate of progress and ultimate promise justify considerable excitement.

Proponents of the analytic approach have directed their efforts at solving problems in three major areas of concern: the selection and sequencing of content, the development of instructional strategies, and the selection or design of instructional delivery systems. To provide a basis for the attack on these problem areas, taxonomies of terms and concepts that could be used to describe instructional phenomena had to be developed. The taxonomies provide a basis for the analysis of instructional phenomena, the identification of instructional variables, and the precise communication of research results. Once developed, the taxonomies can be evaluated through research on relationships between instructional phenomena and instructional outcomes. These relationships, when stated in the form of propositions, become the prescriptive rules that can be used for developing instructional materials.

Attempts at developing systems (taxonomies) to describe instructional phenomena first concentrated on descriptions of classes or levels of learning outcomes. The pioneering effort by Bloom resulted in a taxonomy of educational objectives that, while historically important, was difficult to apply in the area of prescriptive rules for instructional design.[28] Later taxonomies of instructional outcomes have been simpler and easier to use and have provided a basis for research and development on prescriptive rules.[29] It is from these prescriptive rules that analytic instructional development models have been developed.

The propositions used in analytic approaches fall into two basic categories: those allowing diagnosis or prescriptions concerning content structures or sequences and those useful in diagnosing and prescribing instructional strategies and tactics.

Content analysis procedures. A variety of procedures have been developed for analyzing instructional outcomes or contents.[30] These procedures are variously designed to aid the instructional developer in (a) selecting those objectives that should be taught from the myriad that could be taught, (b) determining the most effective instructional sequence, and (c) presenting instruction in such a way that it will be easily remembered and used by students.

Gagné's hierarchical task analysis focuses on the coordinate and subordinate relationships between tasks, or between terminal and enabling objectives. It provides the developer with a task structure that indicates what students should be able to do after instruction (terminal tasks or objectives) and what must be learned (enabling tasks or objectives) in order for the student to be able to perform satisfactorily. It also provides a hierarchy of tasks or objectives—a hierarchy that indicates prerequisite learning relationships usable in instructional sequencing. The entailment structure method of Pask, as well as the content analysis method proposed by Merrill, con-

28. Benjamin S. Bloom et al., *Taxonomy of Educational Objectives, Handbook I: Cognitive Domain* (New York: David McKay, 1956).

29. Robert M. Gagné, *The Conditions of Learning*, 2nd ed. (New York: Holt, Rinehart and Winston, 1970); M. David Merrill and N. D. Wood, *Instructional Strategies: A Preliminary Taxonomy*, Mathematics Education Report, ERIC/SMEAC (Columbus, Ohio: The Ohio State University, 1974). See also idem, rev. ed., Technical Report 1R (Orem, Utah: Courseware, Inc., 1975).

30. Two contrasting approaches are those of Gagné and Pask. See Robert M. Gagné, "Learning Hierarchies," *Educational Psychologist* 6 (November 1968): 1-6, reprinted in *Instructional Design: Readings*, ed. M. David Merrill (Englewood Cliffs, N.J.: Prentice-Hall, 1971). See also Gordon Pask, D. Kallikourdis, and B. C. E. Scott, "The Representation of Knowables," (Unpublished manuscript, System Research Ltd., Richmond, Surrey, England, 1972).

siders the structure of content and the desired behavior of students separately in arriving at aids for the instructional developer.[31]

Strategy analysis procedures. Methods for analyzing and prescribing instructional strategies fall into two basic categories—those derived from operant models of learning and those derived from cognitive or information processing models of the learning process. Proponents of an operant approach have developed methods that require analysis of the behavioral chains and the stimuli that signal the beginning and end points of those chains.[32]

Merrill and his associates, Markle and Tiemann, Gagné and Briggs, and Gerlach and Ely have attempted to develop a set of principles that can be applied in the design and development of instructional materials.[33] Each position begins with some classification scheme by which objectives can be classified and appropriate instructional strategies selected.

One of the most complete systems to date is that represented by the Instructional Strategy Diagnostic Profile (ISDP) developed by Merrill and Wood.[34] The ISDP is based on a detailed system for classifying objectives and an extensive taxonomy of instructional variables. The ISDP is both diagnostic and prescriptive. It consists of five separate sets of evaluative statements that can be used to

31. M. David Merrill, "Content and Instructional Analysis for Cognitive Transfer Tasks," *AV Communication Review* 21 (Spring 1973): 109-25.

32. William A. Deterline, *Principles and Practices of Instructional Technology: A Mediated Training Course* (Palo Alto, Cal.: General Programmed Teaching Corporation, 1967); Francis Mechner, "Behavioral Analysis and Instructional Sequencing," in *Programed Instruction,* ed. Phil C. Lange, Sixty-sixth Yearbook of the National Society for the Study of Education, Part II (Chicago: University of Chicago Press, 1967), pp. 81-103.

33. M. David Merrill, Gerald W. Faust, and Edward E. Green, *Concepts* (Orem, Utah: Courseware, Inc., 1974). See also Merrill and Wood, *Instructional Strategies;* Susan M. Markle and P. W. Tiemann, *Really Understanding Concepts: Or in Frumious Pursuit of the Jabberwock* (Chicago: Tiemann Associates, 1969); Robert M. Gagné and Leslie J. Briggs, *Principles of Instructional Design* (New York: Holt, Rinehart and Winston, 1974); V. S. Gerlach and D. P. Ely, *Teaching and Media: A Systematic Approach* (Englewood Cliffs, N.J.: Prentice-Hall, 1971).

34. The propositional basis for the ISDP is presented in M. David Merrill and N. D. Wood, *Rules for Effective Instructional Strategies* (Orem, Utah: Courseware, Inc., 1975). See also M. David Merrill and Norman D. Wood, *The Instructional Strategy Diagnostic Profile,* Technical Report No. 5 (Orem, Utah: Courseware, Inc., 1975).

rate instructional strategies. The five sets of statements were generated from five analogous sets of prescriptive rules for the effective
teaching of concepts and rules (principles). Each set of statements
and rules is related to a hypothesis concerning instruction. The hypotheses deal with the role of consistency, learner control of strategy, the selection of instances for use in instructional sequences, the
representation form (for example, object, symbol, picture) of instructional components, and the presentation of mathemagenic
(comprehension-facilitating) information (for example, algorithms,
heuristics, prompts, and the like). The profile has been used to predict the effectiveness of several sets of instructional materials, as
measured by student performance on criterion tests. Early results,
although limited because of restriction in the sample materials evaluated (that is, all had been developed systematically and were rated
relatively effective) have shown high correlations ($r = .80$ to $.90$)
between strategy ratings and program effectiveness.[35] The descriptive rules from which the profile was developed have also been
used in a prescriptive manner to develop design and authoring guides
for instructional developers, and these guides have been shown to
be effective in streamlining the design and development process.[36]

SYSTEMATIC DELIVERY SYSTEM SELECTION

The design and selection of instructional methods and media
have long been influenced by technological innovations, salesman-
ship, and political and economic constraints. Many attempts at classifying methods and media by capabilities have been made to provide some systematization of the process. But the categorization
schemes have been all too general, have usually been of value only
to the novice developer, and have been proven wrong time and
again by the creative developer who can mix methods and media
to increase overall capability. For example, the statement that television cannot be interactive, allow for student practice, or provide

35. Norman D. Wood, "Prediction of Student Performance on Rule Using
Tasks from the Diagnosis of Instructional Strategies" (Doctoral diss., Brigham
Young University, 1975).

36. Jonah P. Hymes and Gerald W. Faust, *Macro- and Micro-models in
Large-scale Instructional Development*, Technical Report No. 4 (Orem,
Utah: Courseware, Inc., 1975).

feedback is generally true until the energetic developer uses video-tape players to present a variety of situations, stops the tape, has students respond, and then presents feedback to their responses.

As the analytic models have been developed and their associated taxonomies and rules have been refined, a broad base has been established from which more sophisticated media-selection algorithms can be developed. The most promising of such algorithms consider basic learning requirements, rules for selecting an effective strategy, and the level of learning to be achieved, as well as the more common considerations of display capabilities (for example, dynamics, graphics, audio). One such model was developed by a team of psychologists for the Navy's S-3A Air Crew Training Program.[37]

The model was developed after careful consideration of resource constraints, basic learning requirements, and the capabilities of specified instructional methods and media. The first step in the process was to analyze budget, facilities, and other constraints to determine a variety of delivery systems (for example, film, CAI, workbook, and the like) that could possibly be used on the project. Then an analysis of the basic instructional requirements for learning different types of objectives was completed, following the procedures of Merrill and Wood. This analysis was used in prescribing the components of instruction for various instructional strategies (again keyed to objective types) that could be built into the methods and media available for the project. Detailed specifications for methods and media were then developed. For example, a lecture method was designed that incorporates important components for concept and principle learning objectives (for example, sets of examples, opportunities for student practice, instructor feedback on practice, and the like). The methods and media, specified in this way, provide an instructional capability considerably greater than "traditional" uses of these same delivery systems. In all, ten "high capability" methods were specified for this project. These were then analyzed as to their display capability appropriateness for use with different objective types and a method/media decision model was developed.

The model is presented as a flow chart by Hymes et al. to guide

37. Jonah P. Hymes, John A. Hughes, and Gerald W. Faust, *Method and Media Selection*, Technical Report No. 3 (Orem, Utah: Courseware, Inc., 1975).

the decisions of the designer.[38] It can be used to select from among the specified methods and media those that are most appropriate for teaching a particular kind of objective. The developer, therefore, must have his objectives specified and classified before using the model.

This model, although it has some generality, is valid only as long as the specifications for the methods and media are followed. It does not apply to the usual "artistic" conventions for using these same media. Further, the model does not concern itself with costs except before the fact (for example, in selecting media that will be used as possible end points for the selection algorithms). The design of complete media selection models continues, and there is much work to be done. Models like the one discussed above, however, are a definite step in the right direction in that they focus on learning and teaching requirements of specific learning situations as major factors in method and media selection.

CAI: The State of the Art

HISTORICAL NOTES

The literature on CAI is voluminous. It emanates from a variety of disciplines and from many perspectives within and across these disciplines.[39] During the 1960s, much of it was found primarily in technical reports, informal newsletters, and the like, rather than in referenced journals or books. This situation is slowly changing as studies involving CAI become more professional and editorial policies become more accepting.

Four Pioneers

This chapter is not the place for a history of CAI. Other sources

38. Ibid.

39. A good summary of the professional and commercial organizations that provide publications on CAI and other computer uses in education is found in Appendix 3 of Hunter et al., *Learning Alternatives in U.S. Education*, pp. 359-67. Since much information is found in technical reports, brochures, papers, and the like from service networks and university laboratories and centers, Appendix 4 of this same volume (pp. 369-73) may be consulted for a recent listing of such sources.

may be consulted to piece together this short history.[40] For the purposes of this chapter, only four centers where early work (prior to 1965) established trends will be mentioned: Dartmouth College, the University of Illinois, Stanford University, and the IBM Corporation.

Dartmouth College. The BASIC language and time-sharing system, developed at Dartmouth College, made computing easy to learn and more readily available to students and teachers. Software and applications that have led to sales of minicomputers and microcomputers to schools today trace their history to this development. The adjunctive use of CAI in many disciplines from elementary school through graduate school represents by far the heaviest use of CAI as defined here. All of the better established computer companies have a version of BASIC available. Some of them, notably Digital Equipment Corporation and Hewlett-Packard, also have catalogs describing libraries of adjunctive curriculum packages consisting of printed manuals and interactive computer programs, primarily written in BASIC.

University of Illinois. In 1959, Donald Bitzer conceived PLATO I and undertook to implement it on a 1954 vintage Illiac I computer. PLATO is an acronym for Programmed Logic for Automated Teaching Operations. Since 1959, PLATO has gone through four versions. The present version, PLATO IV, is a computer-assisted instruction network utilizing a large-scale computer (CDC 6500) with 900 graphics terminals attached. Most of the terminals are in Illinois, but some are as far away as San Diego and Boston. They are located in universities, junior colleges, elementary schools, military training bases, and employee training centers.

Much has been written about PLATO and need not be repeated

---

40. See Lawrence M. Stolurow, *Teaching by Machine*, OE-34010, Cooperative Research Monograph No. 6 (Washington, D.C.: U.S. Government Printing Office, 1961). This monograph is a good review and synthesis of both PI and what little had been done with CAI. *Programmed Learning and Computer-based Instruction*, ed. John F. Coulson (New York: John Wiley & Sons, 1962) gives more emphasis to CAI, less to a synthesizing view. The early history was reviewed extensively in a dissertation by John G. Tuttle, "The Historical Development of Computer Capabilities Which Permitted the Use of the Computer as an Educational Medium in the United States from 1958 to 1968, with Implications of Trends" (Doctoral diss., Columbia University, 1970).

here.[41] Early publications and models from the PLATO project influenced the field indirectly, and the network of 900 terminals now connected to the Illinois computer brings a rich interactive graphics capability to many users who, because PLATO is a network, can share ideas and materials, conduct research, and train the next generation of CAI developers and users.

Also at the University of Illinois, Lawrence Stolurow developed an early CAI system called SOCRATES.[42] Because of his familiarity with training research and programmed instruction, his early research and writing influenced the development of the instructional science view of CAI.[43] SOCRATES did not survive as a viable hardware alternative. But PLATO did, and is discussed in more detail below.

Stanford University. The Institute for Mathematical Studies in the Social Sciences, headed by Patrick Suppes and Richard Atkinson, provided early leadership that continues today.[44] Two early contributions were the design, in cooperation with IBM, of the IBM 1500 CAI system, and the development, demonstration, and propagation of drill-and-practice systems in elementary mathematics and reading. This early work is well documented.[45] The drill-and-practice concept has been validated by others. Vinsonhaler and

41. Elizabeth R. Lyman, *PLATO Highlights*, CERL Technical Report (Urbana, Ill.: University of Illinois, 1974). Lyman lists 184 publications about PLATO from 1961 through April, 1974.

42. Lawrence M. Stolurow, *Computer-Based Instruction*, Technical Report No. 9 (Urbana, Ill.: Training Research Laboratories, University of Illinois, 1965).

43. Lawrence M. Stolurow, "Some Factors in the Design of Systems for Computer-Assisted Instruction," in *Computer-Assisted Instruction: A Book of Readings*, ed. Richard C. Atkinson and Harlaiee Wilson (New York: Academic Press, 1969), pp. 65-94.

44. Stanford's contributions to the field of CAI continue, including work in foreign language instruction, logic, computer language instruction, learning and instruction theory, artificial intelligence, and automatic speech synthesis and recognition. The Technical Report series of the Institute for Mathematical Studies in the Social Sciences contains over 260 entries, a healthy percentage of them related to CAI.

45. Patrick Suppes, Max Jerman, and Dow Brian, *Computer-Assisted Instruction: Stanford's 1965-66 Arithmetic Program* (New York: Academic Press, 1968); Patrick Suppes and Mona Morningstar, *Computer-Assisted Instruction at Stanford: 1966-68, Data Models and Evaluation of Arithmetic Programs* (New York: Academic Press, 1972).

Bass report the results of ten studies using Stanford's drill-and-practice programs.[46] These data show that ten to twenty minutes of drill per day at a teletype or at a simple cathode ray tube terminal will produce significant gains in the mathematical skills of elementary school children. Such programs are also successful with deaf and disadvantaged students. While drill-and-practice programs have been implemented widely, the largest CAI network for school children is in Chicago, where 1,000 terminals serve over sixty elementary schools. The justification is effectiveness. Disadvantaged children who are slipping behind each month (averaging .74 months gain on standardized tests for each month of work) start to catch up (averaging 1.1 months gain per month) when given a few minutes a day on the terminal.[47]

International Business Machines (IBM). There is no wish here to imply that the products of one computer company are superior to the products of others because of the influence of early contributions. Even a brief review of early influences on the field, however, must include IBM's development of the Coursewriter language and the 1500 system.

Seeing a potential market of vast size and social significance, IBM committed a substantial investment of capital and human talent to the task of realizing CAI. This investment has not yet yielded the expected return, but unlike smaller companies that made similar premature investments, IBM was large enough to absorb the losses and consolidate gains. In the mid 1960s, IBM entered into joint relationships with several universities—Pennsylvania State University, Florida State University, and the University of Texas. These agreements involved research on early typewriter-terminal systems using IBM's Coursewriter language. With Stanford University, IBM had meanwhile developed the 1500 system, with sophisticated displays providing cathode ray tubes with both limited graphics and textual display, computer-controlled random access image projection, and audio. Light-pen and keyboard response entry were available. About twenty-five of the IBM 1500 systems were placed in schools, colleges, military training centers, and industrial training centers. Good

46. John F. Vinsonhaler and R. K. Bass, "A Summary of Ten Major Studies on CAI Drill and Practice," *Educational Technology* 12 (July 1972): 29-32.

47. Harry Strassberg, Chicago Public Schools, personal communication.

maintenance and training support was given to the users.

By 1970, IBM management had withdrawn the research and development, marketing, and production support from the 1500 system and has since allowed the systems in the field to dwindle almost to extinction. Nevertheless, a great deal of knowledge was generated by the intense research and development activity around these systems, and many people were trained in CAI as a result. The Association for Development of Computer-based Instructional Systems, a professional society that now publishes its own journal,[48] was originally an IBM 1500 users group. The designers of the TICCIT instructional model described below were influenced by five years of research and development using the IBM 1500 in a learning resource center environment.

IBM users of System 360 and 370 Coursewriter still constitute the largest single group of users of tutorial CAI. The Coursewriter author language has influenced a host of newer CAI author languages. Yet, because of the narrow conception of instruction and learning strategies inherent in the primitive commands and intrinsic branching in Coursewriter, this influence has probably passed the peak of its usefulness.

Boom and Decline

The year 1965 marked the beginning of a boom in CAI. Great expectations for profits filled the minds of industrial leaders.[49] Computer companies were merging with publishing companies, in anticipation of a new educational market. Under the regime of President Johnson, federal aid for research and development in instruction flowed freely, and many projects were started in schools, colleges, universities, and industrial laboratories. Seven years later, however, the federal funding had begun to dry up, the hope for a new educational market had not materialized, and the computer companies had either retrenched or gone out of business.[50] By 1975,

48. The journal is the *Journal of Computer-Based Instruction*, 215 South Main St., Clarion, Iowa 50525.

49. Charles E. Silberman, "Technology Is Knocking on the Schoolhouse Door," *Fortune* 74 (August 1966): 120-25.

50. General Electric and RCA, active bidders during this period for educational dollars through CAI and other forms of technology, both gave up their computer businesses at a loss. CAI, of course, was not the only factor.

all of the publishing companies that had invested heavily in CAI had either withdrawn from the field or had sharply curtailed their activities.

CAI had been oversold, and the complexity of mastering its three technologies greatly underestimated. The problems inherent in the sociology of change in educational institutions had not been anticipated and were not well understood.

The PLATO and TICCIT Projects

In 1971 the National Science Foundation (NSF) funded two major demonstration projects.[51] The PLATO project was funded to stimulate the completion of the PLATO IV hardware and software, and to develop courseware for community colleges, elementary schools, and universities in order to demonstrate and test PLATO. The TICCIT (Time-shared Interactive Computer-Controlled Information Television) project was funded at the same time to develop, test, and demonstrate a minicomputer-based CAI system supporting 128 color television display terminals and delivering courses in freshman and remedial mathematics and English composition in two community colleges. The Educational Testing Service was given an independent contract to evaluate the effectiveness, technology, and costs of the two systems. Having observed the limited progress on many of the federally funded CAI projects undertaken during the middle and late 1960s,[52] NSF provided more substantial funding for a longer period of time. Both projects were given five years to deliver and demonstrate their alternative hardware, software, and courseware systems, and to be evaluated by the Educational Testing Service.

PLATO. The main emphasis of the PLATO project has not been to develop a computer-based curriculum but rather to develop a comprehensive set of hardware devices and the requisite software to operate them. Perhaps the most significant hardware development

---

51. Allen L. Hammond, "Computer-Assisted Instruction: Two Major Demonstrations," *Science* 176 (June 9, 1972): 1110-12.

52. The typical life cycle of these projects, usually two-year affairs, was to struggle to master the hardware and software for one year, clarify goals and do some courseware for the next six months, and look for new jobs the last six months.

has been the invention of the PLATO IV terminal. Unlike the familiar television tube, which must be refreshed sixty times per second to maintain a visible image, the PLATO IV plasma display panel remembers information displayed on it and requires no refreshing. The terminal contains a 22-centimeter square plasma panel consisting of 512×512 display positions, each of which may be turned bright orange by passing a current through neon gas trapped beneath each point. The display has high resolution, and the hardware and software developed to drive the display allows for flexible graphics capabilities, including selective erase, creation of special characters, animations, and alternative symbolic alphabets (for example, Russian or Chinese).

The TUTOR language, developed at the University of Illinois to assist the authoring of courseware, has graphics commands that allow for large-sized writing, figure rotation, and an extensive set of graph-generating commands. TUTOR also has extensive calculational, branching, and response-handling capabilities, and is considered by CAI experts to be a versatile programming language for generating interesting interactions on a graphics terminal.

In addition to the graphics capabilities of the plasma panel, each PLATO terminal may be equipped with a pneumatically driven random access microfiche projector. This retrieves one of 256 color images within a quarter of a second and projects it on the back of the translucent plasma panel. The terminals may also be equipped with a touch panel, which has been used to teach reading to elementary school children. A magnetic disc that provides random access to twenty-two minutes of audio messages has also been developed, but has not seen wide use. Because of the availability of PLATO terminals over telephone lines, the PLATO network now has a large number of users. These users have developed CAI programs in a variety of disciplines, at all educational levels, and in military and industrial training. Because of the flexibility and reliability of the PLATO hardware and software, and because it is a network that can reach many users throughout this and other countries, PLATO's influence will probably increase during the late 1970s. Bitzer has plans for adding another large computer for managing 1,000 more users after the first 950 terminals are installed on the present system. In the 1980s, a communications network servicing one million or more users and communicating by satellite is envisioned.[53]

TICCIT. The TICCIT system was conceived by the MITRE Corporation in 1969 as a stand-alone minicomputer-based configuration of primarily off-the-shelf hardware elements. Plans at that time were to utilize 128 television terminals with digital graphics capability for computer-managed elementary school instruction. In the late 1970s emphasis shifted to providing support for mathematics and English instruction at community colleges. The user interface specified required an "authoring system" with both hardware and software elements and a "learner control command language" to facilitate student interactions and promote self-directed, enjoyable learning. MITRE selected hardware that was low in cost in 1971. The costs have continued to decrease. The terminal is a twelve-inch Sony color television set modified to be refreshed by a solid state device located centrally. Characters can be modified "on the fly" to produce any character set or to compose any graphic, whether describable easily by an elementary function or as a digitized version of free-form artwork. A modified television camera and graphics entry system scans and digitizes the artwork, which is then stored centrally. The graphics editor permits authors to plot any elementary or parametric function and to edit these and the digitized artwork at will. Displays are composed on a grey background in seven brilliant colors. The crisp digital color displays are a hallmark of TICCIT.

Authoring systems have taken a variety of forms. The graphics camera and editor is only one part of the user interface designed to make the TICCIT computers easy for authors to use. The authoring system is more than an "authoring language" such as TUTOR or Coursewriter. Such languages are written to control the basic hardware and logical capabilities of a given CAI system. They do not include in their semantics the fundamental concepts of systematic instructional development, such as those described above as the analytic approach. An authoring system is an integrated set of computer programs, formatted manuscripts, and man-

53. Joyce Statz, "Interview with Don Bitzer, PLATO," *SIGCUE Bulletin* 9 (April 1975): 2-13.

agement procedures designed to facilitate the various steps in the instructional development process.

MITRE developed the operating systems, compilers, and related software for use by authors and students. Brigham Young University developed software to permit data entry and editing, graphics entry and editing, report generation for teachers and authors, and other user utility programs. Manuscript formats were developed for use by authors in producing "maps," tests, objectives, rules, examples, practice problems, and helps and the same formats were embodied in the authoring software. Similar manuscript formats and on line embodiments for coders were developed to provide for display specifications, file creation, and answer analysis coding.

This authoring system resulted in the production of a large body of courseware at Brigham Young University.[54] Starting with a review of arithmetic, the mathematics materials extended from a review of fractions through elementary and intermediate algebra and elementary functions (except trigonometry). The English materials provide two catalog courses, a remedial grammar and mechanics course, and a freshman composition course, in which the teacher's role is vital in generating ideas and grading writing assignments, but not in teaching structure or editing skills. Regardless of the success of the TICCIT community college courseware, the authoring system approach first implemented on TICCIT appears to be proliferating. A commercial company (Courseware, Inc., of Orem, Utah) has taught this approach to a number of customers in the military services, industry, and colleges.[55] The training has resulted in the production of tens of thousands of segments (objectives) of instruction, some on CAI and some in workbook or mediated forms.

It is useful to consider TICCIT's learner-control language in the context of historical developments in the field of computer-assisted instruction. Most early work in CAI can be divided into four pro-

54. C. Victor Bunderson, "Team Production of Learner-Controlled Courseware"; idem, "The TICCIT Project: Design Strategy for Educational Innovation," in *Improving Instructional Productivity in Higher Education*, ed. Shelley A. Harrison and Lawrence M. Stolurow (Englewood Cliffs, N.J.: Educational Technology Publications, 1975), pp. 91-111.

55. Gerald W. Faust, M. David Merrill, and C. Victor Bunderson, principals in the design of the TICCIT authoring system, were among the founders of Courseware, Inc.

gram categories: drill-and-practice, tutorial programs, simulations and games, and use of computer terminals in problem solving. Three of these categories—drill-and-practice, simulation, and problem solving—are adjunctive applications in which the computer is a supplement to the main instruction, provided by teachers. Tutorial programs could also be used in an adjunctive mode; they were designed, however, to handle a heavier burden of instruction, usually involving concepts and rules. Concepts and rules characterize most instruction above the junior high school level. By contrast, the objectives of drill-and-practice instruction focus on memorization skills. Simulations and games focus on the application of concepts, rules, and information rather than the initial acquisition of them. The early research revealed that considerable motivation accompanied work with simulation, games, and problem solving. By contrast, students caught in the network of preprogrammed branches that comprised a tutorial program expressed less motivation and enjoyment.

At the University of Texas considerable work was done on learner control in an effort to capture some of the motivation inherent in the use of problem-solving languages and simulations. Simultaneously, work was being done at Brigham Young University by Merrill and his coworkers on synthesizing the literature on concept and rule learning to provide a taxonomy of theorems for teaching concepts and rules.[56] The cybernetics models developed at Texas and the instructional psychology theorems developed at Brigham Young University ultimately came together in the TICCIT learner-control language.

The British cyberneticist, Gordon Pask, provided basic concepts for the design of the TICCIT learner-control language.[57] Pask's work, reviewed in more detail below, led to the concept of three levels of discourse—a concept liberally adapted by the designers of TICCIT, so that the resemblance between TICCIT and Pask's conception is now slight. However conceived, the concept of three levels of discourse affords a powerful model for designing man-

56. M. David Merrill and Richard Boutwell, "Instructional Development: Methodology and Research," in *Review of Research in Education*, ed. J. H. Kerlinger (Itasca, Ill.: Peacock, 1973), vol. 1, pp. 95-131.

57. Gordon Pask, "The Control of Learning in Small Subsystems of a Programmed Educational System," *IEEE Transactions on Human Factors in Electronics* 8 (June 1967): 88-93.

machine dialogues, and others have used the concept as well.[58] For
the purposes of TICCIT, it was useful to think of three levels of
discourse between student and machine: Level 0, Level 1, and Level
2. At each level is a language: L0, L1, or L2. L1 and L2 are meta-
languages for discourse about the next lower level language. At
Level 0 in any computer-assisted instruction system there exist commands that students can use for responding to questions and to the
solicited decision requests intrinsic to any preprogrammed network,
such as a tutorial program. Student control is limited by the author's
sequence strategy.

   L1 is a metalanguage for talking about the strategies that the
author may have used at Level 0. In learner control, L1 gives the
student control over sequence strategy. A strategy consists of at
least four phases: a survey phase, a learning tactics phase, an evaluation tactics phase, and a review phase. TICCIT provides general
commands to control all aspects of strategy. Most of these are implemented as special keys on a learner control panel.

   At Level 2 we can conceive of a metalanguage for talking about
L1 strategies in general. A Level 2 language would allow student-
machine dialogue concerning general aspects of strategy and tactics that are independent of content. How well is a student strategy
working? What other strategies are available to the student? In the
TICCIT system, an advisor program collects data on student performance. It uses color coding on structural representations (called
MAPS) of the course, unit, and lesson hierarchies to indicate which
segments, lessons, and units the student has passed (green), which
ones he has failed (red), and which ones are in progress (yellow).
The student may solicit status information at any time by pressing
the MAP key and observing the colors, and by pressing the ADVICE
key for more specific status information. General suggestions concerning the sequence the student might take through lesson and
unit MAPS and concerning evaluation and learning tactics are also
available from the advisor. The advisor also interjects unsolicited
advice on strategy and tactics.

   It is important to recognize that all the major CAI systems developed over the past twelve years, with the exception of TICCIT,

58. David Harrah, *Communication: A Logical Model* (Cambridge, Mass.:
MIT Press, 1963), pp. 11-12.

have worked primarily at Level 0. The drill and tutorial programs written in existing CAI languages have only occasional instances of Level 1 and Level 2 functions. This description applies to all the major CAI languages, including Coursewriter and TUTOR (the PLATO language). The description does not apply to the use of APL (IBM's array-oriented language based on a powerful rotation for applied mathematics), BASIC (the most widely used language for student programming) and other languages used for solving student problems. Here the student has complete control over the programs that he himself writes. These problem-solving applications, however, are not appropriate for mainline instruction in concepts and rules, nor do they provide Level 2 support to help students develop better strategies.

Development of a set of student commands, especially in the areas of survey tactics and learning tactics, required the application of research and theorems from instructional psychology related to the acquisition of concepts and rules. The taxonomy developed by Merrill served as the basis for the design of student commands. It was desired that student commands should manipulate important instructional variables. A further constraint was that the student would not be given a control command in an area where he had no information to guide his choice. The commands were implemented as buttons on a special learner-control keyboard, and as choice points on MAP displays on the Sony television terminal.

PLATO and TICCIT differ substantially in terms of all three technologies (hardware, software, and courseware), in total concept, and in philosophy. The major hardware difference comes in the mode of solving the data communications problem. PLATO is a network and distributes terminals to users at any location by means of telephone lines. TICCIT, like the old IBM 1500, is designed to centralize terminals in a learning resource center. Since centralized terminals can share hardware (for example, graphics, character, generation, audio) instead of duplicating it at each terminal, TICCIT terminals are considerably less expensive than PLATO terminals, but lack the dynamic graphics (except on videotape), large computer power, and network advantages of PLATO.

The authoring models of PLATO and TICCIT provided a sharp contrast initially, although each project has begun to adopt the strengths of the others in the authoring area. The TICCIT project evolved an analytic PI process and used differentiated teams of authors. These concepts, and learner control, were designed into the very hardware and software of TICCIT. The TUTOR language ignores the semantics of any particular instructional model, and of the PI process, and leaves the authors free to generate any strategy using a powerful and versatile computer language. This freedom typically results in the artistic approach, exploiting the dynamic graphics and calculation power of PLATO as message rather than medium.

ALTERNATIVE THEORETICAL POSITIONS

Design Science and Technology of Instruction

Hilgard has provided a synthesizing framework for alternate theories of learning and instruction.[59] He showed a continuum ranging from basic laboratory learning studies, having no immediate relevance to instruction, through field applications in the classroom having immediate relevance.[60] He placed the programmed instruction approach centrally, under technological research and development instead of under pure research, referring to the empirical and artistic approaches to programmed instruction that predominated at that time. The programmed instruction process using an analytical approach, as outlined earlier in this chapter, encompasses four of the six stages of Hilgard's continuum, from the use of data from human verbal learning and concept formation through tryout in a normal classroom.

Because of its scope of application, its use of research data, its "falsifiability," and the possibility of its being framed in a coherent alternative philosophy of instructional science that breaks down the dichotomy between basic research and educational practice, the programmed instruction process using an analytic approach represents a distinct theoretical alternative. This alternate philosophy would view learning and instruction as a design science instead of

59. Ernest R. Hilgard, "A Perspective on the Relationship between Learning Theory and Educational Practice," in *Theories of Learning and Instruction*, pp. 402-15.

60. Ibid., p. 406.

a natural science. Simon has dwelt on the possibilities of artificial sciences and has urged that the concepts of this artificial science of design should be a part of the liberal education of all professionals.[61]

Simon's distinction between a natural science and an artificial science is provocative.[62] The term "design science" will be used in this chapter despite the precedence of Simon's terms. A natural science deals with natural objects and phenomena while a design science deals with artificial or man-made objects and phenomena. The principal distinction, however, is that a natural science deals with efficient causes and material causes while a design science deals with goals and values (final causes) and the plans (formal causes) that motivate the shape of a design. The distinction is clarified by Aristotle's four-fold classification of cause.[63] A natural science deals with the material cause (that is, the composition of the materials in a natural object) and the efficient cause (that is, the sequence of mechanistically describable actions and the causal relationships among these actions). Adapting Aristotle's concept of formal cause to instructional design, we identify the pattern or blueprint (course, unit, and lesson specifications). His final cause corresponds to the training goals and the related and overarching set of values that motivate and shape the design.

A further distinction is that natural sciences are descriptive, whereas design sciences are prescriptive. That is, given the needs, goals, and operational design objectives, what prescriptive statements will allow us to achieve these design objectives under constraints of cost and time? Prescription can occur through the use of the analytic model described above, through the use of simulators to preassess alternatives, and through the use of optimization methods and other quantitative analytic techniques, such as Atkinson's, discussed below. Instead of repeating the term "design science

61. Herbert Simon, *The Sciences of the Artificial* (Cambridge, Mass.: MIT Press, 1969).

62. Ibid., pp. 1-20.

63. Aristotle's famous theory of four causes appears in many places throughout his works. A clear exposition for our purposes is found in "Physics," Book II, Chapter 3, in *Great Books of the Western World*, ed. Robert M. Hutchins (Chicago: Encyclopaedia Britannica Inc., 1952), vol. 8.

and technology of instruction" to characterize this approach, we shall use the term "designtech."

A Decision-Theoretic Analysis of Instruction

Atkinson has articulated an approach to the derivation of optimal instructional strategies that utilizes decision-theoretic analysis.[64] The approach is applicable to a variety of instructional decision situations, but in particular to the derivation of sequencing strategies in CAI. There are four criteria that must be satisfied in Atkinson's approach to a theory of instruction: (a) a model of the learning process must exist; (b) admissible instructional actions must be specified; (c) instructional objectives must be specified; and (d) a measurement scale must exist that permits costs to be assigned to each of the instructional actions, and values or payoffs to the achievement of each overall objective.

When a precise definition can be given for each of these four elements, then it is generally possible to derive an optimal instructional strategy, using powerful analytic tools recently developed. A model or theory of instruction defined in this manner proves to be a special case of what has come to be known as *optimal control theory* in the mathematical and engineering literature. The solution of instructional decision problems defined within this framework leads to the selection of the instructional policy or strategy (from several specified alternatives) that will yield positive gains and reduce possible costs in an optimal or near-optimal manner.

The TICCIT learner control model, a reflection of the "designtech" approach, is a distinct alternative to the optimization model of Atkinson, and to other approaches that are primarily program controlled rather than student controlled. The TICCIT approach posits that important gains can be achieved in learning strategies and in attitudes of approach and responsibility. These objectives are at least as important as the objectives of efficiency, effectiveness, and the minimization of costs sought by the optimization approach. Giving the student the choices inherent in a learner-control command language may be a necessary prerequisite to the achievement of these other educational goals, and need not sacrifice mastery and effi-

64. Richard C. Atkinson, "Ingredients for a Theory of Instruction," *American Psychologist* 27 (October 1972): 921-31.

ciency. The contrast is this: Program control may be shown ultimately to be applicable to complex cognitive learning, such as that involved in the mathematics and English courseware on the TICCIT system. Even so, those who espouse the learner-control and the "designtech" alternative would be loath to adopt program control insofar as it precludes the opportunity for student growth in areas of personality separate from the acquisition of specific content objectives.

For teaching vocabulary lists and other paired associate skills, however, it may be inadvisable to give students a choice over the detailed and precise sequences of individual items. In this application there would appear to be no conflict between learner-control approaches and optimization approaches. Learner control could be used for survey tactics, evaluation tactics, and for learning tactics related to the learning of concepts and rules, and program control for the sequencing of individual items in long lists. Optimization procedures could also be used at the general levels of the system for the scheduling of students to alternate media, as Atkinson has demonstrated elsewhere.[65]

Artificial Intelligence

The general goal of artificial intelligence (AI) research has been to emulate with computerized systems the intelligence exhibited by humans and to create machine extensions of human processes deemed to be intelligent. AI research and theory has affected CAI in at least two ways. One way is by metaphor to the kind of thought processes exemplified by AI; the other is by mechanism—the production of intelligent computerized teaching systems.

The metaphorical application of AI. The TURTLE project at MIT, directed by Papert, is beginning to affect many CAI projects because of its philosophy.[66] This philosophy is consonant with some of the basic propositions that have emerged from artificial intelligence research. Some of these basic propositions are: (a) to exhibit intelligence, a computer program must have a formal representation

65. Ibid., pp. 923-25. Atkinson solves an optimization problem in allocating the amount of time different students in a first-grade class should spend on CAI. Presumably, this procedure could be extended to optimize performance based on time spent on a variety of alternative media.

66. Papert, "Teaching Children Thinking."

of the problem domain; (b) the computer program must have a set of heuristics that can guide trial and error; (c) it must have a way of detecting errors in its tentative attempts to solve a problem, and it must have a way of correcting those errors; and (d) it must also have a way of incorporating the knowledge gained through experience with the class of problems and of using this knowledge to shorten the solution process in new problems. Why should students not have the same opportunities and characteristics shown to enhance the performance of supposedly intelligent computer programs? Papert thinks they should. He feels that students should be given the opportunity to build models, both in a formal language and in their heads, of various kinds of information processing sequences. Students should be given formal languages to enable them to represent these models, as well as tools to help them "debug" their own models and procedures. They should learn good debugging techniques, such as how to formulate simple but critical test cases. A student should be able to feel that, even though he may not have an adequate model at one point, he can make a better model through intelligent effort and the application of trial and error debugging procedures. This approach provides a strong contrast to the helplessness engendered by the prevalent notions in our culture about aptitudes and gifts related to mathematics and other forms of learning. Instead of this helplessness, the student should, through being given creative experiences with formal systems he can manipulate, develop confidence in his own ability to model processes of interest.

Papert has attempted to achieve some of these general goals by teaching children a version of computational geometry called "Turtle geometry." Students are taught to use a programmable robot called a Turtle, which maneuvers about on paper with its pen up or down, to draw geometric figures. By controlling the movements of the Turtle and the figures that it draws, students gain a feeling of control over the processes of constructing geometric patterns and figures. They come to understand the computation underlying the processes, for they must program each algorithm for producing the Turtle's movements, using the simple language called LOGO. When the Turtle does not do as the student intends, the student is able to debug the program and improve the model.

Minsky has commented on the absence of such techniques as mental modeling and debugging in the curriculum of schools: "This is not because educators have ignored the possibility of mental models, but because they simply had no effective way before the beginning of work on simulation of thought processes to describe, construct, and test such ideas."[67]

Artificially intelligent tutors. Early attempts to build intelligence into CAI tutors were more interesting for their promise than for their achievement. Even the influential paper by Carbonell illustrated the promise of this technique with an instructional paradigm of little efficacy (asking questions and getting answers about specific geographical facts related to South American geography).[68] What Carbonell did demonstrate was a question-answering system that permitted mixed initiative dialogues; that is, the dialogue exchanges can be initiated either by the student or by the computer. What information is presented by the computer depends on the model of the subject matter and on the depth of information already covered by the student. Carbonell's original system to teach geography is now being extended to embody various tutorial strategies.[69]

The most impressive artificial intelligence-based CAI system now developed is the system called SOPHIE (Sophisticated Instructional Environment).[70] This system was designed to provide a simulated electronic trouble shooting training laboratory interaction. The SOPHIE program makes possible a mixed initiative CAI interchange but, unlike earlier versions, SOPHIE uses several representations of subject matter and has inferencing procedures designed for each of these representations. The system contains an English language processor, a semantic interpreter, an electronic circuit simu-

67. Marvin Minsky, "Form and Content in Computer Science," *Journal of the Association for Computing Machinery* 17 (April 1970): 197-215.

68. Jaime R. Carbonell, "AI in CAI: An Artificial Intelligence Approach to Computer-Assisted Instruction," *IEEE Transactions in Man-Machine Systems* 11 (December 1970): 190-202.

69. A. Collins, E. H. Warnoch, and J. J. Passafiume, *Analysis and Synthesis of Tutorial Dialogues*, Technical Report No. 2789 (Cambridge, Mass.: Bolt, Baranek, and Newman, Inc., 1974).

70. John S. Brown, Richard R. Burton, Alan G. Bell, and Robert J. Bobrow, *SOPHIE: A Sophisticated Instructional Environment*, TR74-93 (Lowry Air Force Base, Texas: Air Force Human Resources Laboratory, 1974).

lator, and a semantic network. SOPHIE can randomly generate an easy or hard fault in a simulated circuit. The student then can ask in English for measurements at any test point in the circuit. The student may ask his questions in rather informal English, of the sort that can occur in a casual conversation between people working on devices in an electronics repair shop. The language interpreter uses previous information from the student to "disambiguate" his casual comments. The computer can provide the student with the simulated measurements he asks for in this informal version of English. It can also query him about his hypotheses and check whether they are consistent with the information previously given. All in all, the reading of a protocol of dialogue between a student and the SOPHIE program gives one the eerie feeling that a rather sophisticated and knowledgeable tutor is at work with the student.

SOPHIE is promising but requires much more extensive testing with students. The modeling procedures and natural language procedures used in SOPHIE also have implications for simplifying and upgrading the authoring of mixed initiative instructional dialogues in CAI.

Cybernetic Theory and Methodology

The last alternative theoretical position to be discussed bears some resemblance to AI modeling procedures. Unlike these procedures, that worked out by Gordon Pask in England is based on a comprehensive cybernetic theory, whereas the applications of AI to CAI in the United States have primarily had the purpose of engineering AI into specific applications to training. Pask's work is not well understood in this country, perhaps because of the extreme novelty of his concepts. In addition, it has been difficult to obtain a sufficiently complete set of his papers. This latter problem should be alleviated with the recent publication of two books summarizing Pask's experimental and theoretical work over the past decade.[71] Additional volumes are promised.

Pask attacks the natural science model that is at the foundation

---

71. Gordon Pask, *Conversation, Cognition, and Learning: A Cybernetic Theory and Methodology* (New York: Elsevier, 1975). Another new book, not reviewed for this chapter, is Gordon Pask, *The Cybernetics of Human Learning and Performance* (London: Hutchinson, 1975).

of psychological experimentation. In the standard psychological experiment, there is a clear distinction between observer and organism (or subject). The observer pretends to be objective and not influence the outcomes. The variables are usually changed singly, and the effects are noted. This paradigm runs into trouble when the variables are strongly related and when the organism changes or adapts while the experiment is in progress. Obviously this is what happens in an episode in which the student learns anything substantial.

Pask redefines a psychological experiment as a conversation between two or more participants on a series of topics that form a conversational domain. One participant is the subject; the other may be a machine or a person acting as the experimenter's agent. An experiment seen as a conversation fits what Pask calls a "normative" paradigm. In this paradigm, the experimenter negotiates an experimental contract in a metalanguage. This is an observational language for talking about experiments, describing the system in which the experiment will be conducted, prescribing actions to be taken to pose and test hypotheses, and negotiating the contract for the experiment.

The participant must agree to speak an object language throughout the course of the experiment. This object language is to be used inside a cybernetic learning environment. Because of the complexity of this environment, it usually involves some kind of complex electronic equipment. The object language has certain of the qualities of natural language. For example, it allows commands and questions of a certain form. Unlike natural language, it is formally stratified into an upper level and a lower level. The upper level is used for commands to the student to learn and requests for explanation by the student, and the lower level is used for commands and questions about the building of models within the cybernetic system. The construction of models amounts to a practical explanation of what the student has learned. (Compare the model-building activities of the TURTLE project discussed earlier). Given the contract between subject and experimenter to speak in precise languages, the knowledge and understanding of the experimenter and the student can be brought into the public arena. This conversational procedure for exhibiting learning and problem-solving strategies as observable behaviors is called Cooperative Externalization Technique. For Pask, then, an experiment is seen as a conversation between two or more participants within a well-defined conversational domain, with cooperative agreements to make aspects of the conversation explicit and measurable.

The conversational domain in which an experiment or learning episode takes place is specified by a large grid showing subject matter topics and their relationships. It is similar in some ways to Gagné's learning hierarchies and the maps of the TICCIT system. Pask calls this grid an entailment structure. The procedure for developing the entailment structure, however, is much more formal and systematic than procedures for developing learning hierarchies. It involves six steps, starting with a discussion with the subject matter expert, going through a series of manipulations based on graph theory, and ending in the entailment structure, the final product with which the student interacts. Using a large representation of an entailment structure developed for teaching elementary probability (called CASTE), Pask and his colleagues have conducted research to test his theory. Using this large grid, the student can specify goals—that is, the topics and the related performance capabilities he wishes to achieve. The nodes on the entailment structure convey status information as the student works. Signal lights indicate whether the node is a member of the set of topics the student is currently engaged in learning and whether the node is understood.

Understanding is demonstrated by both verbal and nonverbal procedures. The verbal procedure involves a verbal conversation between the student and the experimenter in which the student "teaches back" by explaining the subject to the experimenter. This externalizes concept reproduction and allows the experimenter and student to compare their explanations. The student also demonstrates his knowledge by creating a model. In the system built to teach probability a "Stat lab" is provided as a formal modeling facility for a strict conversation about probability. The student demonstrates topic relations by model-building activities that simulate real world statistical experiments.

Because of the breadth and novelty of the theory, Pask's approach is not strictly comparable to the other three theoretical positions (that is, designtech, optimization, and artificial intelligence) discussed above. Some comparative comments can be made, however. There are many superficial similarities between Pask's CASTE system and the TICCIT system, which is an embodiment of the designtech position. The map structures and their corresponding externalization of survey tactics and review tactics bear a definite resemblance to Pask's entailment structures. The maps, however, are developed by a rather pragmatic analysis of component behaviors, not by Pask's rigorous use of logic and graph theory. Pragmatically, it remains to be seen whether students may not learn about as well using maps developed by this less formal procedure. Theoretically, however, it makes a great difference, since an entailment structure is related to a model of the student himself. In Pask's system the entailment structure involves a set of relations between topics that can be expressed by some ordered combination of relational operators. The entailment structure, then, is a model of the same transformations as the cognitive operations that a student (or more generally, the "psychological individual") is assumed to have in his mental repertoire, but the transformations are not assumed to be identical with these cognitive operations. The TICCIT maps do not have this depth of theory underlying them. They are seen as pragmatic representations of what the student must accomplish —representations which enable him through survey tactics to plan an attack, and through the advisor to see what he has accomplished and where he is weak. The maps have a pragmatic utility for the author in that they structure the authoring process and allow this process to be monitored and managed.

TICCIT's evaluation procedures (tests available from the maps and items in the practice files) are also much more pragmatic and less theory-oriented than Pask's evaluation procedures. The combination of Pask's teach-back and modeling facility appears to be more powerful (but much more costly) than the sequential testing procedures used in TICCIT tests, or the simple mastery tests used in most CAI courseware in this country, except in the AI community.

Pask's system does not lay heavy stress on the careful design of instructional sequences or interactions to teach a particular topic represented in an entailment structure. The printed materials that the student may read in connection with mastering a given node are witness to this. In this area, the "designtech" approach seems to have some advantages. The analytic approach described in Section II has been cross-validated in the production of a large number of instructional materials in CAI, workbooks, slides, tapes, and lectures. The Instructional Strategies Diagnostic Profile is provocative of additional research and more elaborate theory building in the second phase of the PI process.

There are not as many points of contact between Pask's approach and the optimization procedure developed by Atkinson. The philosophies of science underlying Pask's approach and much of Atkinson's research appear radically different. Nevertheless, optimization is theoretically neutral and appears powerful as a technique for developing instructional sequences at the microscopic level—that is, within a node on Pask's entailment structure, or as a technique for optimizing the use of instructional resources in the institutional environment which houses a CAI system.

It would appear that the Pask theory of strict conversations might provide an overall theoretical framework for the mixed initiative dialogues now being implemented by the AI community. The AI community could also be of great service in providing a wide variety of modeling facilities analogous to Pask's statistical laboratory in which nonverbal understanding could be demonstrated.

The Pask theory may have considerable influence on future theories of learning and instruction and on the design of products based on these theories. But its implications could be even broader, with relevance to the epistemology of subject matter organization, and to the philosophy of science.

Concluding Remarks

Space does not permit a detailed prognosis of the future of PI and CAI. This future, however, promises to be exciting. The computer represents a breakthrough in man's ability to get done the work associated with instructional research, development, and delivery. Until the advent of the computer, we were unable to manage the work associated with tracking the diversity of student paths through individualized systems, providing detailed practice with feedback, and collecting precise data for the revision and improvement of courseware. If the work potential of the computer can be harnessed through the application of instructional science, a quantum leap in our capability to deliver effective instruction to individuals will result. This advance will occur especially in areas that require self-pacing and extensive practice, and in areas where materials must be developed, evaluated, and improved. In the past ten years the cost of computer components has dropped dramatically each year, and projections are that it will continue to drop for another ten years. As solid state technology has made calculators feasible for every teacher and most school children, so the microcomputer revolution (associated with such developments as the videodisc) should in the next five to ten years make CAI terminals widely available. Such low-cost terminals will have many of the capabilities of PLATO and TICCIT and be available in offices, proprietary education centers, homes, and schools.

The task of hammering this raw computer power into educational plowshares will fall to instructional science, which in the next five or ten years is likely to provide a rich base from which increasingly sophisticated analytic approaches to instructional design, development, and delivery will evolve. Manufacturers tend to design products for mass markets such as entertainment or business. The failure of the earlier boom in CAI has made them cautious. Yet if instructional technology is to have high impact, CAI systems must incorporate sophisticated instructional models to mediate the interactions (or conversations) between the student and the machine. As was noted in the previous section, some promising beginnings have been made toward the development of such models.

Another problem impeding the promised impact of computers is that of producing cost-effective and instructionally effective courseware. This problem is presently sharpened by the lack of generally available, tested, and prescriptive analytic models for development of such courseware. In addition, there is a lack of sophisticated programs for training authors to use these prescriptive models, and it is difficult to make this courseware technology usable with available hardware and software systems. The problems of training authors can be solved once the analytic models are developed, and progress is being made in this direction. To build design and development models for courseware into the hardware and software of computers will require the development of authoring systems, but not, however, merely the authoring languages that have been the stock in trade of computer-oriented CAI developers during the past fifteen years. Authoring systems will reflect and facilitate a systematic approach to instructional development. They will provide guides and editing tools for the author in the thinking stages of content and strategy analysis, in the design of intermediate products, and in the management of day-to-day production of intermediate and final design products. The computer can be engineered and programmed to facilitate the data-gathering, decision-making, and prompting stages that an author needs in order to go through each of the intermediate steps of the systematic design process. A computer for use by authors should not require them to learn computer programming, which, as now practiced, takes authors into a complex and demanding area essentially unrelated to the analysis of content, behavior, and strategy.

In addition to the need for authoring systems for tomorrow's low-priced and widely available computers, the problems of human factors have not been met. Teachers as a group are uneasy about the introduction of computers into the instructional process. Both because of the mystique of the computer as something difficult to understand, and because of the threat that automation will restructure or even replace jobs, teachers are often slow to seek out CAI. The teacher's role in relation to new instructional and computer technology is too broad a subject to be treated here. Suffice it to say that the teacher's role is radically changed—though not necessarily for the worse—when computers are introduced in a substantial manner into the instructional process. They become managers, helpers, provokers to creativity, instructional developers, and serve less as a kind of delivery system.

It is not only the knowledge of how to use computers, but the new knowledge brought by instructional science that challenges the existing education profession. The field of education has changed slowly in the past. It is probable that CAI and PI will be adopted more rapidly in military and industrial training, in proprietary educational institutions, and even in homes than in the schools.

Both PI and CAI have passed their infancy. Both have been oversold and have settled down to the sober and difficult task of building firm theoretical and empirical foundations, and of establishing traditions and technologies that will serve educational needs. The symptoms of this increased maturity are apparent in the field of PI and promising beginnings have been made in CAI. The synthesis of the two in the form of authoring systems, teacher-oriented management systems, and student-oriented learning environments could have profound implications for education.

CHAPTER IV

Writing to Teach and Reading to Learn: A Perspective on the Psychology of Written Instruction

ERNST Z. ROTHKOPF

Writing is one of the most important instructional means available to us. The scientists investigating the chemical basis of memory might look inside of inkwells instead of homogenized cerebral protein, for much of the memory of our culture is in the inky swirls of print. Writing has a useful role in practically all organs of our culture: to communicate, to debate, to guide, to link the past to the future and today to tomorrow. Writing plays an awesomely important role in the instruction of all people, whether young or old.

Written instructional material is mass produced in the United States by an industry with annual sales in the neighborhood of one billion dollars. This impressive output is supplemented by a thriving home industry equipped with numerous tools that range in technological sophistication from print-producing computers and electric typewriters to ball-point pens and dittoing devices. The amount of written material produced each year for instructional consumption is almost beyond estimate. Whole forests die so that knowledge (and also kitsch) may pass from one generation to the next, and skill from one hand to another. From the libraries of the world and from bookshelves everywhere, the voices and the hearts of both the living and dead, some wise and some foolish, speak to those who read.

The invention of writing and of printing presses and other reproduction machines has had a long and dramatic impact on human life. It was not until this century, however, that men began to think about writing as psychological or instructional technology. As literacy became widespread, educators, psychologists, and others became concerned with the nature of reading processes, and the characteristics that made writing an effective transmitter of instructional messages. Written instructional materials began to interest the educator as objects of scientific study and as important practical means that required decisions at a technical level.

KINDS OF INSTRUCTIONAL WRITING

The present discussion will concentrate primarily on discourse, that is, connected, cohesive presentations of some matter which, in style, more or less resembles connected speech. Discourse ranges in complexity and size from brief encyclopedia entries to instructional text and from programmed instructional material to essays, belles lettres, poetry, and novels. Other written materials that lack the connecting threads of discourse are also of substantial educational importance. The nondiscourse materials include tables, procedural directions, lists, and other similar displays. These may range in complexity and size from knitting directions to a concordance of the Bible. The distinction between discourse and nondiscourse is not always well marked. It is made here mainly for convenience because very little will be said about nondiscourse materials despite their importance.

It is useful to think of three kinds of discourse. First, there are materials intended primarily for general instructional purposes, such as texts and didactic expository articles. The second class consists of materials that have been prepared for a relatively circumscribed and well-specified purpose, such as programmed self-instructional materials. Finally, there is the great bulk of written material, scientific, technical, nonfiction, and literary, which is the collective experience treasury of any culture. This material was not deliberately written for instructional use (at least not for formal instruction). Nevertheless it is of overwhelming educational importance and is frequently not only the vehicle but also the object of instruction.

PROPERTIES OF WRITTEN INSTRUCTIONAL MATERIAL

The most important single characteristic of writing from a scientific or technical point of view is that it is a stable instructional system. An instructional system can be said to be stable when we can assume that the same instructional message will be reliably delivered to all students (although not necessarily received) each time the system is used. Stable instructional systems tend to have a tangible, documentary form, such as written material, film, audio-tape, and videotape recording.

Instructional systems differ very widely in degree of stability. Among the more stable forms are the documentary media referred to above. Among the least stable are the extemporaneous exchanges of classroom debate. Between these two extremes, every level of stability may be found. The teacher as lecturer, or the teacher in the free give and take of the classroom, is a relatively unstable instructional system.

Stable instructional systems readily lend themselves to scientific study and to systematic improvement by technological methods. There are two reasons why stable instructional means and particularly written material are suitable for systematic improvement by technological methods. First, most scientific or technical methods involve attempts to utilize experience to modify and improve instructional means. The very identity of an instructional system depends on its stability. It is difficult to evaluate an instructional chameleon. A stable documentary system is a complete definition of what has been delivered to the student and tends to leave little uncertainty as to what is to be evaluated.

Second, stable systems such as writing are suited for systematic technological applications because such systems can be modified by an iterative process, namely, editing or rewriting, to incorporate scientific principles of construction or to reflect the experience that has been gained during tryouts. Since the instructional means are documentary, the changes become a stable and reliable portion of the instructional program. Principles and experience can be used to modify the actual physical structure of the instructional program. Written instructional materials are permanently modified in editing. In fact, it is simpler to modify written material, by editing and re-writing, than other stable documentary forms such as films or tapes. It is not critically important whether written materials have been programmed for self-instruction or are in conventional forms, such as pamphlets or books. It should be noted, however, that ordinary written instructional materials tend to be somewhat less stable than highly structured forms of programmed instruction because the condition of use of ordinary text materials is not completely known.

The highly desirable attribute of stability stands in contrast against the singular dependency of written material on actions by the readers. Stability offers the possibilities of applying scientific knowledge to the development of instructional material. It offers the possibilities of careful product engineering. Yet the most carefully written and edited text will not produce the desired instructional results unless the student acts in a suitable way. The student has complete veto power over the success of written instruction. The student also has the opportunity to extend its scope substantially. To paraphrase an old Cappadocian saying: You can lead a horse to water, but the only water that reaches his stomach is what he drinks. Failure to read assignments and failure to prepare adequately by reading undoubtedly are large factors in academic failure and underachievement. The contrast between the opportunities for careful product design that are offered by the stability of written instructional materials and the vulnerability of these materials to the student's disposition is one of the main themes of the present chapter.

MEASURING OUTCOMES

Pragmatic discussion of an educational medium must consider how the results produced by the medium are to be measured. This measurement has often been approached in a deceptively simple manner with written material. The problem arises in no small measure from the fact that the term *understanding* is too readily accepted as a criterion of the degree to which results produced by reading are satisfactory.

The verb *to understand* without an object or with a reference to a language unit as an object carries with it the implication that any language unit such as a sentence or a paragraph has "true content." Understanding in that context means that this true content has been received. The acceptance of the word *understand* as a primitive term is common among linguists and certain students of cognition. This view may result in certain logical difficulties.

There are several reasons for these logical problems. *True content* implies that the interpretation of a linguistic unit is simple and unique and that the measurable consequences of the exposure to a written stimulus are completely enumerable. The specifications of these consequences are frequently sought either in the observed or inferred intention of the author or in a logical précis of the linguistic unit.[1] This approach is exemplified by measures of understanding based on "correct" responses using the completion method,[2] paraphrases or gist,[3] or completion techniques with linguistic transformations of the original stimulus.[4] Careful analysis suggests that these approaches have serious logical and practical limitations. The universe of acceptable consequences may be exceedingly large, and it may not be possible to enumerate them exhaustively. The number of conceivable consequences grows rapidly larger as the written unit increases in size from phrases or simple sentences to concatenations of sentences and paragraphs.[5]

The term *acceptable consequences* is equivalent to the number and nature of test items that can be generated by logical judgment or by certain logical rules from the instructive stimulus. The number of such acceptable items is large even with relatively small units, and performances on these test items are by no means perfectly correlated. Acceptable items range from paraphrases to the substantial class of items identified with "connotative meaning," and from collative responses to remembering locations of certain other information on pages.[6]

1. Edward J. Crothers, "Memory Structure and the Recall of Discourse," in *Language Comprehension and the Acquisition of Knowledge*, ed. Roy O. Freedle and John B. Carroll (Washington, D.C.: V. H. Winston and Sons, 1972), pp. 247-84; Carl H. Frederiksen, "Effect of Task-Induced Cognitive Operations on Comprehension and Memory Processes," ibid., pp. 211-46.

2. This is the cloze procedure; see, for example, Earl F. Rankin, Jr., "An Evaluation of Cloze Procedure as a Technique for Measuring Reading Comprehension" (Ph.D. diss., University of Michigan, 1958).

3. See, for example, Richard C. Anderson, "How to Construct Achievement Tests to Assess Comprehension," *Review of Educational Research* 42 (Spring 1972): 145-70.

4. John R. Bormuth, *On the Theory of Achievement Test Items* (Chicago: University of Chicago Press, 1970).

5. It should be noted here that the number of acceptable transformations and paraphrases increases markedly as the size of the relevant linguistic unit becomes larger.

6. For an example of collative responses, see Lawrence T. Frase, "A Structural Analysis of the Knowledge That Results from Thinking about Text,"

The issue thus raised about ways to evaluate the outcome of written instruction does not refer to the nature of the response required from the student—whether paraphrase, cloze, or multiple-choice recognition. The issue is whether a document itself should be used as a source of criterion test items or whether some external referent should be used. Such an external referent might be found in the pragmatics of instruction, for example, instructional goals. The argument here proposed is that, if the purpose of measurement is to describe or evaluate the skill of an individual, the read document *may* be an acceptable source of test items. But if the purpose of measurement is to evaluate a document, test items must be derived from an external referent.

The point is simple but easy to miss. If one is trying to decide which of two documents is more effective, one looks to some purpose that both documents are supposed to accomplish, rather than to the documents themselves, for a source of measurement.

DISTINCTION BETWEEN NOMINAL AND EFFECTIVE STIMULUS

In the analysis of learning from written material, it is useful to distinguish between attributes of the text and the internal representations that result when the reader processes the text. This is the distinction between the nominal and the effective stimulus that has been made by Rothkopf and others.[7] The nominal stimulus is characterized by analysis of the text. The effective stimulus is inferred indirectly. It is the consequence of the reader's operations on the nominal stimulus and is the main determinant of what is understood and remembered after reading. Learner performance thus is the result of both the nature of the nominal stimulus, that is, attributes of the text, and of processing operations by the reader. Written

---

Journal of Educational Psychology 60 (1969), Monograph Supplement 6. This monograph indicates the large number of test items that can be generated from four simple statements. See also Ernst Z. Rothkopf, "Incidental Memory for Location of Information in Text," *Journal of Verbal Learning and Verbal Behavior* 10 (December 1971): 608-13.

7. Ernst Z. Rothkopf, "A Measure of Stimulus Similarity and Errors in Some Paired-Associate Learning Tasks," *Journal of Experimental Psychology* 53 (February 1957): 94-101; Clark L. Hull, *Principles of Behavior* (New York: Appleton-Century, 1943); Benton J. Underwood, "Stimulus Selection in Verbal Learning," in *Verbal Behavior and Learning*, ed. C. N. Cofer and B. S. Musgrave (New York: McGraw-Hill, 1963), pp. 33-47.

material as nominal stimulus and processing will therefore serve as major organizational headings for the discussion that follows.

Written Material as Nominal Stimulus

The effectiveness of a written document in accomplishing selected instructional goals is influenced by certain characteristics of the document. These characteristics are summarized in table 1. They fall into three major divisions that would not have been novel to Aristotle: content, representation, and form. Not all of the rubrics in table 1 have received the same experimental or theoretical attention, nor are they all on the same conceptual level. Also shown in table 1 is whether each factor must be considered with reference to a specific set of goals or a specific student population in order to be evaluated. The classification scheme is useful as a summary of the nominal stimulus properties of written discourse.

TABLE 1

TEXT AS NOMINAL STIMULUS: ATTRIBUTES RELATED
TO INSTRUCTIONAL EFFECTIVENESS

Text Attributes	Goal-specific	Population-specific
Content		
Completeness..............	Yes	Yes
Accuracy...................	Yes	No
Goal guidance.............	Yes	No
Unrelated material	Yes	Yes
Representation		
Lexicon...................	No	Yes
Exposition................	No	Probably
Organization..............	No	Probably
Form		
Grammatical structure........	No	Yes
Grammatical complexity......	No	Yes

Content factors are related to the meaning or purpose of a written message. They include *givens* in the sense that some aspects of content are constrained by what the message is supposed to accomplish.

Representational factors include optional elements, such as the lexicon, that are used to represent the intended meaning. Many variables that have been studied in simple verbal learning experiments, such as familiarity, vividness, concreteness, and similarity, are presumably relevant to the choice of an instructionally desirable lexicon. Sequential organization and various modes of exposition are also included among representational factors.

Form factors include grammatical structure, complexity, and sentence length. It is assumed that grammaticality and sentence length can be varied without changing content, meaning, or representational form. It is, however, generally recognized that subtle changes in meaning are sometimes unavoidable in form changes.

We ask about content when we ask whether a document is accurate and complete enough to accomplish the intended purpose *if it were* understood. We ask about representation or form when we ask whether the choice of phrasing, lexicon, and other representation such as metaphor or simile produce efficient understanding, consistent with the purpose of the communication.

CONTENT

It has been argued that content has extremely important effects on instruction and may be the single most powerful characteristic of the nominal stimulus.[8] The position taken here is that for most purposes the content of a written document can only be evaluated pragmatically, that is, with reference to descriptions of specific instructional goals.

Content is characterized in four ways: (a) Is it complete? (b) Is it accurate? (c) Is goal guidance provided? (d) How much unrelated material is there? Techniques for characterizing text content are at present relatively imperfect, and no standard techniques for describing these attributes have evolved. The status of these attributes could be determined by a hypothetical, omniscient, and extremely patient observer. In practice this task is handled by a subject matter expert aided by a detailed checklist, or by a panel of expert judges.

Content factors are related to the purpose or meaning of a given message. Their status depends on *givens* in the sense that the

8. Ernst Z. Rothkopf, "Structural Text Features and the Control of Processes in Learning from Written Materials," in *Language Comprehension and the Acquisition of Knowledge*, ed. R. O. Freedle and John B. Carroll (Washington, D.C.: V. H. Winston and Sons, 1972), pp. 315-35.

evaluation of content is constrained by what a message is supposed to accomplish.

Completeness. This property of a written document refers to the completeness with which it covers the knowledge needed to attain a particular instructional goal. There may be many ways in which the competencies that correspond to the instructional goal may be produced. The judgment is simply made that the content of the document is sufficient for at least some nontrivial portion of a hypothetical student population. The student population must be taken into account because assumptions about previously acquired student knowledge enter to some extent in making the judgment of completeness. One technique for making a useful completeness judgment has been described by Koether, Rothkopf, and Smith.[9] It involved developing elaborate checklists of major points derived from an analysis of the proposed instructional content (see figure 1 for an example). The instructional document was inspected repeatedly to check for each point on the checklist.

Accuracy. This aspect hardly needs explanation. Written material must not contain misinformation. Accuracy poses special problems with written materials that deal with subjects outside of the traditional academic curriculum, such as practical guidance for assembling and making things where the writer is often also the primary collector of information.

Goal-guidance. The question asked here is whether the document specifically states for the student the nature of the preselected instructional aims. Material prepared for general instructional use may provide no guidance about emphasis or purpose. The judgment about the availability of goal-setting material in the instructional document is useful in deciding whether additional environmental supports are needed.

Unrelated material. When instructional goals have been chosen, it is possible to judge how much material that is *not* related to the goals is included in the instructional document. What the best quantitative units for such an estimate might be is not clear. The

9. Mary E. Koether, Ernst Z. Rothkopf, and Martin E. Smith, "The Evaluation of Instructional Text: I. Effectiveness as a Function of Method of Measuring Achievement" (Paper presented at the meeting of the American Educational Research Association, Minneapolis, March 1970).

SCORING SHEET - Page 3

FREQUENCY OF DUSTING - con't.

FOLLOW THE DIRECTIONS THAT APPEAR IN THE BOX YOU CHECK

	YES	NO	NOTE

32. Is powdered tannin or any of the synonyms given below mentioned in the definition? Synonyms for powdered tannin: chestnut, mimosa, myrobalans, tannic dust, tanning material, tanning powder, tanning substance, valonia. Terms not acceptable as synonyms: dust, chemicals, granular leather fibres, liquors, liquids, powder, special materials, used tannin.

33. Is the idea of the tannin being sprinkled, spread, or scattered on the hides mentioned? The following terms are acceptable synonyms if powdered tannin "is used in the first part of the definition: added to, applied, covered with, put on. Terms not acceptable as synonyms: brushed on, dusted, splattered, sprayed.

34. Is the idea of the tannin being sprinkled "on the hides" made explicit? Synonyms for on the "hides": butts, leather, sides and back, skins.

35. Does the essay state that the tannin is sprinkled "directly" on the hides? Other ways of emphasizing that the tannin powder goes on the hide rather than into the liquor that touch the hide are: as the hides are being put into the pit, beforedipping, before immersion, individually. Not acceptable: between the hides.

THE FORMATION OF BLOOM

36. Bloom is caused by dusting, or depends on the type of tannin used in dusting. Does the essay suggest this?

37. Bloom is a fawn-colored deposit that forms in and on the hide. Does the essay attempt to define bloom in this way? *SKIP TO 42*

38. Is "fawn-colored" part of the definition? Acceptable synonyms: tan, cream-colored.

39. Is the idea of deposit or residue included in the definition?

40. Is the formation of the deposit "in" the hide made clear?

41. Does the definition also present the idea that the deposit forms "on" the hide?

42. Bloom affects the leather by giving it weight and firmness and by waterproofing it. Does the essay mention any of these effects of bloom? *SKIP TO 46*

43. Is there a statement that bloom gives the leather weight or makes it heavy?

44. Is there a statement that bloom makes the leather firm or gives it strength?

45. Does the essay mention that bloom makes the leather waterproof (or water-repellent, or water resistant)?

FIG. 1. Sample scoring sheet for minimum content for articles and student essays on leather tanning

NOTE: This checklist, developed by M. E. Koether, included ninety instructional objectives and consisted of five scoring sheets.

number of sentences not directly related to any instructional goal
has been used to derive a suitable index. In a slightly different
context, Rothkopf and Kaplan employed a ratio of sentences of a
particular class to the total number of sentences in the text.[10] Relatively few good data are available on the effect of unrelated material on the achievement of instructional goals. Smith, Rothkopf,
and Koether have reported that the amount of unrelated material
in passages predicted goal achievement better than any other formal
characteristics of the nominal stimulus measured.[11] In that study
such unrelated material comprised materials which were related
to the main topic (leather tanning) but were not directly relevant
to the tanning procedures on which the student was tested.

REPRESENTATION

Documents judged to contain the same minimum content may
represent this content in different ways. It is useful to distinguish
three kinds of representation: lexicon, exposition, and organization
(see table 1). The distinctions among these three classes of representation are sometimes blurred, but the blurring does not detract
from the usefulness of the distinctions. The important point is
that representation may be changed without changes in content
and the representation involves primarily optional elements of a
message.

Lexicon. The lexicon of a document refers to the words that
have been selected to represent meaning. The substantial verbal
learning literature contains a good deal of information relevant to
the effects of various kinds of lexical representation on learning
from written text. Only summary reference to this research will
be made here.[12] The results of verbal learning research indicate that

10. Ernst Z. Rothkopf and Robert Kaplan, "An Exploration of the Effect of
Density and Specificity of Instructional Objectives on Learning from Text,"
Journal of Educational Psychology 63 (August 1972): 295-302.

11. Martin E. Smith, Ernst Z. Rothkopf, and Mary E. Koether, "The Evaluation of Instructional Text: II. Relating Measures of Recall to Text Properties"
(Paper presented at the meeting of the American Educational Research Association, Minneapolis, March 1970).

12. More extensive treatments can be found in Ernst Z. Rothkopf and Paul
E. Johnson, eds., *Verbal Learning Research and the Technology of Written
Instruction* (New York: Columbia University Teachers College Press, 1971).

associations (that is, arbitrarily determined pairings) between words are learned faster and remembered longer if the words evoke concrete images that are meaningful and familiar than if such images are not evoked.[13]

Scales based on judgments of vividness (imagery) and concreteness are available for small sets of words.[14] Since agreement among judges about vividness and concreteness has been found to be fairly high, the individual writer is probably capable of making reasonable estimates about these attributes for any word not found in the available lists. Similar scalings of words have been provided for meaningfulness and familiarity by Noble.[15] The most commonly used basis for estimating the familiarity of words, however, is obtained by counting the frequency of use of any word in printed material.[16]

The importance of such aspects of the lexicon as vividness, concreteness, meaningfulness, and familiarity derives partially from the previous experience of the reader. The available numerical indices are estimates of the likelihood that the words have been encountered, as well as the nature and variety of contexts in which they have been seen.[17] An implicit assertion is also made about the character of the associations established for each word and of the complexity of the memorial nets in which they are presumably stored.[18]

Experience and the consequent enriched memorial representa-

13. Allan Paivio, "Mental Imagery in Associative Learning and Memory," *Psychological Review* 76 (May 1969): 241-63; Clyde E. Noble, "Meaningfulness and Familiarity," in Cofer and Musgrave, *Verbal Behavior and Learning*, pp. 76-119.

14. See, for example, Allan Paivio, John C. Yuille, and Stephen A. Madigan, "Concreteness, Imagery, and Meaningfulness Values for 925 Nouns," *Journal of Experimental Psychology Monograph Supplement* 76 (January 1968): entire issue.

15. Noble, "Meaningfulness and Familiarity."

16. See, for example, Edward L. Thorndike and Irving Lorge, *The Teacher's Word Book of 30,000 Words* (New York: Bureau of Publications, Teachers College, Columbia University, 1944); Henry Kučera and W. Nelson Francis, *Computational Analysis of Present-Day American English* (Providence, R.I.: Brown University Press, 1967); John B. Carroll, P. Davies, and Bruce Richman, *The American Heritage Word Frequency Book* (New York: American Heritage Publishing Co., 1971).

17. See Ernst Z. Rothkopf and Ronald D. Thurner, "Effects of Written Instructional Material on the Statistical Structure of Test Essays," *Journal of Educational Psychology* 61 (April 1970): 83-89.

18. See John R. Anderson and Gordon H. Bower, *Human Associative Memory* (Washington, D.C.: V. H. Winston and Sons, 1973); Allan M. Col-

tions are considered to be critical to learned performance because it has been well established that new learning involving these words and concepts is greatly facilitated by the availability of previously acquired associations and other nonverbal representations evoked by the lexicon. It has also been reported that retrieval and recognition occur more quickly with familiar and meaningful words.[19] Such greater speed is important in an activity such as reading, where the ability to process words rapidly is presumed to be needed for effective performance.

Exposition. The concept of exposition refers to certain aspects of the presentation of concepts and relationships that are not captured by characterizations of the single-word lexicon. Among the expository expressions of particular interest here are instructional metaphors, similes, and various defining or referential phrases. It seems plausible that these expository devices parallel the lexicon to some degree in that familiarity and meaningfulness differ among expressions. For this reason, expository terms probably have a role in determining instructional effectiveness. Unfortunately the experimental literature contains little that is relevant to exposition. This situation probably prevails in part because expository devices are complex and the number of possibilities is large. No simple way of characterizing the potential psychological properties of exposition has been found. Another factor, which may be related to our neglect of the scientific study of expository expressions, is that semantically interesting expository phrases depend strongly on verbs. The experimental psychology of verbal learning has traditionally been a psychology of nouns. Relatively little experimental work has been done on verbs, although the recent analysis of verb characteristics

lins and M. Ross Quillian, "Retrieval Time from Semantic Memory," *Journal of Verbal Learning and Verbal Behavior* 8 (April 1969): 240-47; Barbara Hayes-Roth and Frederic Hayes-Roth, "Plasticity in Memorial Networks," *Journal of Verbal Learning and Verbal Behavior* 14 (October 1975): 506-522; David E. Meyer, "On the Representation and Retrieval of Stored Semantic Information," *Cognitive Psychology* 1 (August 1970): 242-300.

19. Kenneth I. Forster and Susan M. Chambers, "Lexical Access and Naming Time," *Journal of Verbal Learning and Verbal Behavior* 12 (December 1973): 627-35; Herbert Rubenstein, Lonnie Garfield, and Jane A. Millikan, "Homographic Entries in the Internal Lexicon," *Journal of Verbal Learning and Verbal Behavior* 9 (October 1970): 487-94; Robert F. Stanners, James E. Jastrzembski, and Allen Westbrook, "Frequency and Visual Quality in a Word-Nonword Classification Task," *Journal of Verbal Learning and Verbal Behavior* 14 (June 1975): 259-64.

by Schank may stimulate more work on this neglected area.[20]

Organization and sequence. The content of a passage using a given lexicon and a given ensemble of expository constructions may be organized in different sequences. The effect of organization or sequence on learning has been investigated in a number of studies. This research has demonstrated that the same sentences rearranged in different orders can produce different instructional results.[21] The experimental sequences compared in these studies were all equally acceptable (or unacceptable) as English text patterns. Nevertheless, different blocking of similar semantic features, such as attributes or names in the text sequences, favored high performance on different items on recall tests.

Our understanding of the effect of text organization on learning has not been aided so far by the emergence of unifying theoretical ideas. The experimental variables that have received attention in research include the organization by semantic attributes referred to above, comparison of deductive-to-inductive expository development with inductive-to-deductive sequences,[22] amount of text intervening between two redundant passage elements,[23] and within-paragraph order.[24]

20. Roger C. Schank, "Conceptual Dependency: A Theory of Natural Language Understanding," *Cognitive Psychology* 3 (October 1972): 552-631.

21. Lawrence T. Frase, "Influence of Sentence Order and Amount of Higher Level Text Processing upon Reproductive and Productive Memory," *American Educational Research Journal* 7 (May 1970): 307-19; Morton P. Friedman and Frank L. Greitzer, "Organization and Study Time in Learning from Reading," *Journal of Educational Psychology* 63 (December 1972): 609-16; Jerome L. Myers, Kathy Pezdek, and Douglas Coulson, "Effects of Prose Organization upon Recall," *Journal of Educational Psychology* 65 (December 1973): 313-20; Charles B. Schultz and Francis J. DiVesta, "Effects of Passage Organization and Note Taking on the Selection of Clustering Strategies and on Recall of Textual Materials," *Journal of Educational Psychology* 63 (June 1972): 244-52.

22. James L. Evans, Lloyd E. Homme, and Robert Glaser, "The Ruleg System for the Construction of Programmed Verbal Learning Sequences," *Journal of Educational Research* 55 (June-July 1962): 513-18.

23. Ernst Z. Rothkopf and Esther U. Coke, "Repetition Interval and Rehearsal Method in Learning Equivalences from Written Sentences," *Journal of Verbal Learning and Verbal Behavior* 2 (December 1963): 406-16; idem, "Variations in Phrasing, Repetition Intervals, and the Recall of Sentence Material," ibid. 5 (February 1966): 86-91.

24. See, for example, James Deese and Roger A. Kaufman, "Serial Effects in Recall of Unorganized and Sequentially Organized Verbal Material," *Journal*

FORM: GRAMMAR, STRUCTURE, AND SENTENCE LENGTH

It will not be possible to review the work on grammatical form in detail here. A fairly substantial experimental literature indicates that simple active sentences are reacted to more quickly than more complex transformations of the same sentence.[25] Some experimental evidence also indicates that trying to understand or remember a simple active sentence interferes less with the accomplishment of other simultaneous tasks than trying to understand more complex transformations.[26] Longer sentences have also been reported to be more difficult to understand.[27] It has been experimentally shown, however, that lengthening by use of conjunctions does not increase difficulty seriously.[28] Schlesinger has pointed out that sentence length is confounded with other important sentence variables such as grammatical structure and redundancy.[29] Schlesinger also provided a useful review of the literature on structure. An additional extensive literature survey has been compiled by Carroll.[30]

READABILITY

Readability indices are quantitative characterizations of text as

of *Experimental Psychology* 54 (September 1957): 180-87; Ernst Z. Rothkopf, "Learning from Written Sentences: Effects of Order of Presentation on Retention," *Psychological Reports* 10 (June 1962): 667-74.

25. See, for example, Philip B. Gough, "Grammatical Transformations and Speed of Understanding," *Journal of Verbal Learning and Verbal Behavior* 4 (April 1965): 107-11; Lee E. McMahon, "Grammatical Analysis as Part of Understanding a Sentence" (Doctoral diss., Harvard University, 1963).

26. See, for example, Harris B. Savin and Ellen Perchonock, "Grammatical Structure and the Immediate Recall of English Sentences," *Journal of Verbal Learning and Verbal Behavior* 4 (October 1965): 348-53.

27. Edmund B. Coleman, "Improving Comprehensibility by Shortening Sentences," *Journal of Applied Psychology* 46 (April 1962): 131-34.

28. Edmund B. Coleman, "Developing a Technology of Written Instruction: Some Determiners of the Complexity of Prose," in *Verbal Learning Research and the Technology of Written Instruction*, ed. Ernst Z. Rothkopf and P. E. Johnson (New York: Columbia University Teachers College Press, 1971), pp. 155-204.

29. I. M. Schlesinger, *Sentence Structure and the Reading Process* (The Hague: Mouton, 1966).

30. John B. Carroll, "Learning from Verbal Discourse in Educational Media," Research Bulletin 71-61 (Princeton, N.J.: Educational Testing Service, 1971).

nominal stimulus.[31] These indices will not be discussed in detail here because they are well known and because excellent reviews and discussions are available.[32]

The present discussion of readability measures will focus on their relationship to the document characteristics enumerated in table 1 and on certain general implications of the use of such indices. In 1963, Klare estimated that thirty-one different readability formulas had been proposed. Since then a number of others have been invented. The majority of them use two factors to predict reading difficulty. These two factors are word difficulty and sentence difficulty, and these, in many cases, are estimated by measures of length. Perhaps the best known of these readability formulas is the Flesch Reading Ease Formula. It will be used here to illustrate the relationship between readability indices and the stimulus characteristics of text discussed previously. The reading ease index is calculated in the following way: (a) unsystematically select 100-word samples from the materials to be measured; (b) determine the number of syllables per 100-word sample; this is the index of word length, wl; (c) determine the average number of words per sentence, sl; (d) calculate reading ease, RE, by the following formula:

$$RE = 206.835 - .846\,wl - 1.015\,sl$$

The two predictive variables in this formula are related to the lexicon and to grammatical form factors. Word length (wl) is related (although indirectly) to familiarity and to meaningfulness by the following argument.[33] The basic principle is Zipf's law, which states that word length is negatively related to the frequency of occurrence of that word in the language.[34] The plausible assumption

31. Examples of readability indices include Edgar Dale and Jeanne S. Chall, "A Formula for Predicting Readability," *Educational Research Bulletin* 27 (January 1948): 11-20; Rudolph Flesch, "A New Readability Yardstick," *Journal of Applied Psychology* 32 (June 1948): 221-33; and Robert Gunning, *The Technique of Clear Writing* (New York: McGraw-Hill, 1952).

32. George R. Klare, *The Measurement of Readability* (Ames: Iowa State University Press, 1963).

33. The rationales presented here were *not* those proposed by Flesch.

34. G. K. Zipf, *The Psycho-biology of Language* (Boston: Houghton-Mifflin, 1935).

is then made that the more frequent words in the language are more likely to be familiar and meaningful than rarer words. This assumption is supported by the findings of positive correlations between the counted frequencies of words and the meaningfulness measure (m) developed by Noble[35] as well as with rated familiarity. Average word length, however, is not a simple indicator of the meaningfulness and familiarity of the lexicon because it is strongly influenced by the number of short function words and personal pronouns in the text. Because of this, the word length measure reflects the form of the text sentences as well as characteristics of individual words.

The inclusion of sentence length in the readability formulas might be justified on the following basis. First, the assumption is plausible that longer sentences tend to be syntactically more complex. This assumption, coupled with the finding, referred to previously, that syntactically more complex sentences take longer to evaluate and demand more processing capacity, would suggest weighting readability formulas with sentence length. There are, of course, also the direct experimental results, described earlier, that longer sentences are more difficult to "understand." The finding that lengthening sentences by use of conjunctions does not have any substantial effects on comprehension measures, would tend to weaken expectations about the predictive usefulness of sentence-length measures.[36]

Several points are worth noting about the Flesch reading ease index, as well as most other readability formulas:

1. They are poor guides for writing because favorable values can be attained by trivial maneuvers. They are, however, reasonable first-order checks on the acceptability of text for certain user populations. Information about readability may now be obtained at very low cost. Modern printing technology brings text into computer-readable form very early in the production process. Many texts are now entered into the computer at the manuscript typing stage. This technological possibility coupled with the use of computer-based

35. Noble, "Meaningfulness and Familiarity."

36. Coleman, "Improving Comprehensibility."

readability formulas, such as that of Coke and Rothkopf,[37] makes the required word and sentence counts simple, accurate, and easy to obtain.

2. Current readability measures are relatively weak predictors of reading difficulties, particularly when the user is well motivated and is free of severe time constraints. Some of the probable reasons for this are discussed in detail by Rothkopf.[38]

3. Current readability indices use only a small number of the factors listed in table 1. The lexical characteristic chiefly tapped is familiarity. Vividness and concreteness are neglected. Exposition and organization are disregarded completely. Content factors are ignored.[39] The disregard for content factors diminishes the power of any predictor of learning in goal-oriented instructional situations. For many important general reading activities such as browsing, however, the absence of content weighting may actually be advantageous.

4. Readability indices may be viewed as statistical estimates of certain characteristics of text. These characteristics can be shown to be related to variables that have been exactly manipulated in simple experiments and that have been demonstrated to have powerful effects on learning. The lack of precision of the techniques for estimating the values of underlying variables from text characteristics is to some extent counteracted by the very large number of words to which the technique *could* be applied with computer techniques. This model for future applications of laboratory findings merits careful attention. It may not be possible to ascertain exactly the state of a given variable for a text, but useful although inexact statistical approximations may be found that can be applied to large aggregates such as text.

37. Esther U. Coke and Ernst Z. Rothkopf, "Note on a Simple Algorithm for a Computer-Produced Reading Ease Score," *Journal of Applied Psychology* 54 (June 1970): 208-10.

38. Ernst Z. Rothkopf, "Structural Text Features and the Control of Processes in Learning from Written Material."

39. A recently developed readability measure developed by Langer et al. for German texts has met some of these criticisms. See I. Langer et al., "Merkmale der Verständlichkeit schriftlicher Informations—und Lehr texte," *Zeitschrift für experimentelle und angewandte Psychologie* 20, no. 2 (1973): 269-86. The German technique, however, requires relatively laborious procedures.

Processing

The importance of the learner's processing activities and of the control of these activities by environmental circumstances outside the stimulus object, has only recently become widely recognized in experimental studies of human learning. Human learning theories during the last three decades treated learning as if it were the passive consequence of bombardment by environmental particles.[40] A noteworthy exception was the work of Postman, who clearly saw the importance of stimulus processing in determining learning outcomes.[41]

Research on the nature of prose learning has been somewhat ahead of conventional learning research in its concern with the role of the subject's activities in determining what was learned. In 1963, Rothkopf described the concept of inspection behaviors, or mathemagenic activities, in order to draw attention to the processing activities that are necessary for various learning outcomes.[42] This

---

40. See, for example, William K. Estes, "Toward a Statistical Theory of Learning," *Psychological Review* 57 (March 1950): 94-107; E. R. Guthrie, "Conditioning: A Theory of Learning in Terms of Stimulus, Response, and Association," in *The Psychology of Learning*, Forty-first Yearbook of the National Society for the Study of Education, Part II, ed. Nelson B. Henry (Chicago: University of Chicago Press, 1942), pp. 17-60.

41. Leo Postman, "Short-term Memory and Incidental Learning," in *Categories of Human Learning*, ed. A. W. Melton (New York: Academic Press, 1964), pp. 146-201.

42. The term "mathemagenic" is derived from Greek roots that mean giving birth to learning. The main purpose in coining the term was to emphasize the important role of the student in determining what is learned. The concept also draws attention to possibilities of manipulating the instructional environment as a form of educational intervention in contrast to manipulating instructional means or materials. See Ernst Z. Rothkopf, "Some Conjectures about Inspection Behavior in Learning from Written Sentences and the Response Mode Problem in Programmed Self-instruction," *Journal of Programmed Instruction* 2 (Winter 1963): 31-45. See also idem, "Some Theoretical and Experimental Approaches to Problems in Written Instruction," in *Learning and the Educational Process*, ed. J. D. Krumboltz (Chicago: Rand McNally, 1965), pp. 193-221; idem, "Two Scientific Approaches to the Management of Instruction," in *Learning Research and School Subjects*, ed. Robert M. Gagné and W. J. Gephart (Itasca, Ill.: F. E. Peacock, 1968), pp. 107-33; idem, "The Concept of Mathemagenic Activities," *Review of Educational Research* 40 (June 1970): 325-36; idem, "Experiments on Mathemagenic Behavior and the Technology of Written Instruction," in *Verbal Learning Research and the Technology of Written Instruction*, pp. 284-303.

formulation grew logically out of analysis of the role of response demands and knowledge of results in programmed instruction and out of recognition of the distinction between nominal and effective stimuli.[43] Processing activities were seen to determine the transformation of nominal into effective stimuli. Effective stimuli determined what was learned.

It is easy to understand why researchers on learning from written material should have become interested in processing conceptions. Learning from text, regardless of how carefully the text has been written, cannot succeed without important activities on the part of the student. The translation of written language into a useful internal representation obviously requires the exercise of highly skilled processing activities, which are not usually directly observable. This processing activity, for many different reasons, may be selectively exercised, that is, not all portions of the text may be translated, or elaborated through linkages with previous associations or other textual information, to the same degree. This kind of conception of reading activities is a reasonable although partial account of why some texts or some portions of them are not very well remembered while other aspects or other text segments are remembered well.

Recently, the importance of processing in determining learning outcomes has also gained some recognition in research on verbal learning. Articles that recognize the critical role of learner activities are beginning to appear with greater frequency in the learning literature.[44]

The work of Craik and Tulving illustrates how the concept of depth of processing has been applied in systematic experiments on human learning. They asked subjects to make one of four judg-

43. Rothkopf, "A Measure of Stimulus Similarity."

44. Samuel A. Bobrow and Gordon H. Bower, "Comprehension and Recall of Sentences," *Journal of Experimental Psychology* 80 (June 1969): 455-61; Fergus I. M. Craik and Robert S. Lockhart, "Levels of Processing: A Framework for Memory Research," *Journal of Verbal Learning and Verbal Behavior* 11 (December 1972): 671-84; Fergus I. M. Craik and Endel Tulving, "Depth of Processing and the Retention of Words in Episodic Memory," *Journal of Experimental Psychology: General* 104 (1975): 268-94; Thomas S. Hyde and James J. Jenkins, "Recall for Words as a Function of Semantic, Graphic, and Syntactic Orienting Tasks," *Journal of Verbal Learning and Verbal Behavior* 12 (October 1973): 471-80.

ments about a word. The judgments were (a) Was the word in capital letters? (b) Did it rhyme with a given word? (c) Did it belong to a given conceptual category? or (d) Did it fit into a given sentence? These judgments, according to Craik and Tulving, involved progressive increases in semantic involvement and hence "deeper processing." In an elegant series of experiments, it was shown that subsequent recall increased with depth of processing and that this effect could not be accounted for purely on the basis of increased processing time.[45]

A MODEL FOR LEARNING FROM TEXT

A conceptual model is useful in thinking about any practical problem and in keeping track of diverse empirical facts. For this reason, an effort will be made to describe a processing model for learning and understanding written material. This model is essentially a model of reading. It will be crude, inexact, and incomplete. It is unrealistic to expect more. Reading involves almost every aspect of human psychology—sensory capacity, perception, learning, motivation, and thinking. Reasonably complete and satisfactory models of reading activities can come into existence only when our understanding of human psychology has advanced considerably beyond its present state.

Figure 2 shows a general schema of the processes that may be involved in reading narrative text for some special purpose. The purpose assumed for figure 2 was to remember enough of the passage in order subsequently to paraphrase it. The eyes fixate on some text element for periods of approximately 200 milliseconds at each fixation. The pattern of fixations is usually a fairly systematic progression from left to right and down the page, but there are sometimes exceptions such as regressions, that is, movements from right to left. The fixations result in some initial internal representation, and these in turn become the object of some quasi-acoustic translation. There is currently considerable controversy about whether this quasi-acoustic translation is necessary for understanding but there seems to be no doubt that at times the musculature involved in speech, such as the lips and the tongue, is weakly but measurably activated during reading. The initial translation

45. Craik and Tulving, "Depth of Processing."

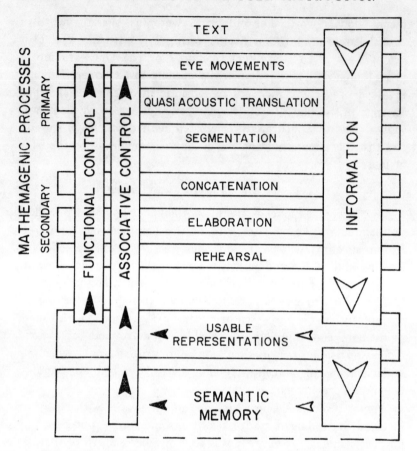

FIG. 2. Flow model for translating text into internal representation

Note: Functional control of mathemagenic processing comes from the usable representations including set; associative control arises both from usable representation and semantic memory. Usable representations are partially determined by information from mathemagenic activities, including recent experience, and partially through associative control from semantic memory.

process must also involve the segmentation of the quasi-acoustic representation in a manner functionally equivalent to a syntactic analysis. The initial translation activities involving eye fixations, quasi-acoustic translation, and segmentation are referred to in figure 2 as *primary mathemagenic processing*.

Two assumptions have been made about primary mathemagenic processing. The first is that its elements are partially under the control of certain environmental factors such as task demands made upon the reader, or more accurately the psychological dispositions that result from these demands.[46] This control is referred to as functional control in figure 2. The translation processes are also partially under associative control, that is, they are regulated to some extent by what the reader knows and by the resulting emerging interpretation of the text. The second assumption is that the primary analytic processes and the sources of their control result in an immediate representation of the text (called "usable representation" in figure 2), which is a reconstruction in the sense that it is created by a synthesis between partial interpretation of the text and what the reader knows. The immediate representation can be used to answer questions, solve problems, or interpret subsequent text segments. The psychological availability of the immediate representation decreases in time but portions of it produce a more or less permanent memorial representation.

Further analytic processes operate on usable representations. These are also partially under functional and partially under associative control. These processes (referred to in figure 2 as "*secondary mathemagenic processes*") collate and integrate information from usable representations, as well as from episodic and semantic memory. The functional results can be the concatenation and elaboration of text information and regulation of the nature of the transfer of usable representation into retrievable memorial representations.

This is a speculative but plausible model. It is not stated in a way that would make an empirical test possible. It is not intended as a theory of narrative reading but rather as a guide to intuition in thinking about reading.

Some features of this conception of a reading process are particularly important. First, successful use of written material depends on the execution of a series of skilled acts by readers. Readers may fail because they do not have the basic skills or because they do not exercise them. They may fail in interpretation because they

46. There are indications that some of the primary processes such as eye movements can fall under what looks like automatic control. Finding one's eye looking at the lower right corner after traversing the page "without having read anything" is a commonly reported experience that suggests the possibility of such automatic processes.

lack needed substantive knowledge or because they do not exercise the required analytic processes.

Second, the sources of failure may have different loci in the interpretative process. Failures may occur in the movements of the eyes or in quasi-acoustic translation. If these stages are effectively handled, the instructional purpose may not be achieved because of failures in later stages of the analytic process.

Decoding, segmentation, and higher level interpretation may fail because of task variables, unfamiliar words, difficult syntactic constructions, or the complexity of the goals that the reader seeks to satisfy. On the other hand, they may fail because the instructional environment has not shaped and maintained the needed dispositions in the reader.

MATHEMAGENIC ACTIVITIES

The various processing activities described in the above model are subsumed under what Rothkopf has called "mathemagenic activities." The concept of mathemagenic activities is discussed in detail elsewhere.[47] Not all mathemagenic activities are useful to the student, and some actually interfere with the attainment of instructional objectives. Most mathemagenic activities are inferred indirectly. These inferences are usually made through antecedent manipulation of the experimental environment such as directions to students, questions, or certain arranged contingencies between student activities and outcomes. On the consequent side, the hypothetical mathemagenic activities are anchored on the level of observation in expected performance on certain tests. Time observations have been used as both independent and dependent measures.

The chain of reasoning is illustrated in figure 3. The distinctive feature of most research on hypothetical internal processes, such as certain mathemagenic activities, is that the learning material is held constant across all experimental conditions. What is varied are environmental factors to affect the subject's processing mode and his disposition to process the experimental text. By contrast, most

47. Rothkopf, "Some Theoretical and Experimental Approaches"; idem, "Two Scientific Approaches to the Management of Instruction"; idem, "The Concept of Mathemagenic Activities"; idem, "Experiments on Mathemagenic Behavior."

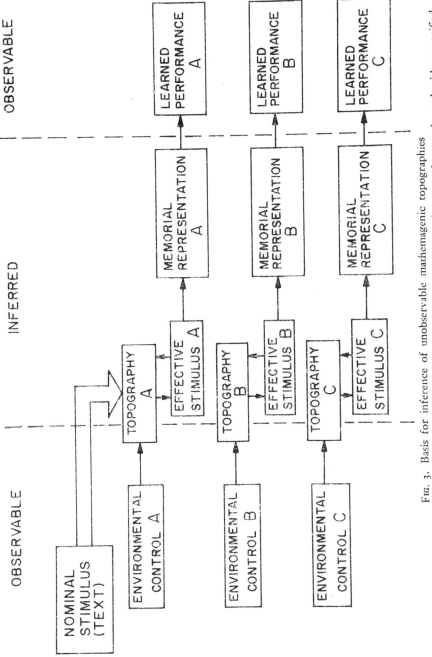

FIG. 3. Basis for inference of unobservable mathemagenic topographies

Note: Conjectures about mathemagenic topographies that result from certain environmental controls used with a specified text are tested by predicting certain learned test performances.

other learning research manipulates the text stimulus or the way it is presented.

It has been proposed that mathemagenic activities have topography.[48] This peculiarly neutral term was used to indicate that a stimulus object such as a passage can be processed in a variety of ways, and that different topographies result in different effective stimuli and hence different learning outcomes. This conception differs from the simple notion of *depth of processing* proposed by Craik and Lockhart.[49] According to those authors, variations in depth of processing are expected to affect *how much* is remembered. The topography idea, on the other hand, implies that topography affects *what* is processed, *how* it is processed, and therefore *what* is remembered. Topography is an especially interesting characteristic of processing in learning from text because of the unique demands for selection that are often made in text learning contexts. Selective reading and mental elaboration of various kinds for portions of the text are reflections of the topography of mathemagenic activity. Selection, mental elaborations, and other conceptions of topography such as mnemonics or integration with previously learned information, are largely inaccessible to direct observation. Their memorial consequences, however, become measurable through performances on various kinds of tests. These possibilities for inference of hypothetical topographical characteristics of mathemagenic activities on the consequent side are illustrated through the three types of test performances in figure 3.

CONTROL OF MATHEMAGENIC ACTIVITIES

The concept of mathemagenic activities has been employed with various degrees of success in a variety of situations. The two major classes of manipulation that have been used are *inductive* and *deductive* (or directive) controls. Changes in the effectiveness of mathemagenic activities as a function of length and recency of stimulus contacts have also been explored.

The deductive or directive control research has generally involved directions to learn, usually in the form of descriptions of

48. Rothkopf, "Some Theoretical and Experimental Approaches."
49. Craik and Lockhart, "Levels of Processing."

learning goals that are given to the student. Inductive controls have mainly involved the use of adjunct questions with text.

Directions describing learning goals. Studies of the deductive control of mathemagenic behavior follow a simple paradigm: all subjects receive the same text materials and the experimental treatments differ in what subjects are told to learn. Providing subjects with very explicit descriptions of learning goals results in marked increase on the recall of the goal-relevant material.[50] This effect must be attributed at least partially to changes in mathemagenic activities produced by directions. Alternative, although not necessarily conflicting, hypotheses have been considered. One plausible alternative explanation was that specific descriptions of goals are in themselves informative and therefore would contribute to learned performance in a way similar to the effects of repetition or review of material. A study by Kaplan and Simmons examined this possibility by experimenting with learning goals that were presented to subjects *after* reading the passage.[51] Subjects operating under this condition performed at the same level as a no-goal control group. Similar findings with directions to remember have been reported by Ausubel, Schpoont, and Cukier.[52]

Another plausible conjecture is that explicit descriptions of learning goals identify for students those sentences of the text that they should learn. When students encounter and recognize a target sentence, students initiate unspecified maneuvers that allow them to learn the appropriate information. Two kinds of experimental evidence discredit this conjecture or at least suggest that marking a sentence and having the intention to learn is not sufficient to account for the entire direction effect. The first line of argument

50. Robert Kaplan and Ernst Z. Rothkopf, "Instructional Objectives as Directions to Learners: Effect of Passage Length and Amount of Objective-Relevant Content," *Journal of Educational Psychology* 66 (June 1974): 448-56; Rothkopf and Kaplan, "An Exploration of the Effect of Density and Specificity."

51. Robert Kaplan and Francine G. Simmons, "Effects of Instructional Objectives Used as Orienting Stimuli or as Summary/Review upon Prose Learning," *Journal of Educational Psychology* 66 (August 1974): 614-22.

52. David P. Ausubel, Seymour H. Schpoont, and Lillian Cukier, "The Influence of Intention on the Retention of School Materials," *Journal of Educational Psychology* 48 (February 1957): 87-92.

against this conjecture rests on studies by Postman and his associates.[53] They have provided strong demonstrations that intention
is neither a necessary nor a peculiarly advantageous condition for
learning. Second, in an ingenious experiment Frase and Kreitzberg
have shown that identifying target sentences does not help much in
learning.[54] They specifically identified for subjects the eleven sentences in a twenty-two-sentence passage that they were *not* to learn
about. This condition, which might be called identification by ex-
clusion, provided as much information about what the subject was
to learn as a condition that specified the target sentences (that is,
by including them in the directions). Frase and Kreitzberg found
that *inclusive* specification facilitates goal-relevant learning while
exclusive specification did not help at all. Their findings are consistent with the generally poor results that have been obtained with
underlining as a learning aid.[55] These results tend to discredit the
marker cum intention hypothesis.

Deductive (that is, directive) control of mathemagenic activities
is subject to certain limitations that are not completely understood.
One limitation can be observed if the number of specific learning
goals is increased. The likelihood of the mastery of any specified
goal decreases as the list of goals provided for the student grows
larger.[56] It was at first thought that the decrease in efficiency in the
control of mathemagenic activity was due to the greater density of
goal-relevant information in the text, that is, the ratio of goal-
relevant sentences to the total number of sentences in the passage.[57]
Present evidence, however, suggests that the diminished efficiency in

---

53. Postman, "Short-term Memory and Incidental Learning."

54. Lawrence T. Frase and Valerie S. Kreitzberg, "Effect of Topical and
Indirect Learning Directions on Prose Recall," *Journal of Educational Psychology* 67 (April 1975): 320-24.

55. See, for example, Wayne A. Hershberger and Donald F. Terry, "Typo-
graphical Cuing in Conventional and Programed Texts," *Journal of Applied
Psychology* 49 (February 1965): 55-60.

56. Kaplan and Rothkopf, "Instructional Objectives as Directions to
Learners"; Ernst Z. Rothkopf and Marjorie J. Billington, "Relevance and Similarity of Text Elements to Descriptions of Learning Goals," *Journal of Educational Psychology*, in press.

57. Rothkopf and Kaplan, "An Exploration of the Effect of Density and
Specificity."

control was primarily due to the length of the list of goal descriptions. There are several reasons for thinking so. Among these is the observation that the effectiveness of specific goal descriptions depended on the number of goals and not the length of the passage.[58] This conclusion must obviously be limited to the length range of passages used in the experiments (500-1500 words), since it is not reasonable to expect a single goal to be as effective in a two-sentence passage as in a 1,000-sentence passage. Another reason for suspecting a list length effect is that the fall in efficiency has been observed when goal lists were lengthened by adding descriptions of goals that could not be achieved by reading the experimental passage.[59] Difficulty with longer goal lists is probably not due only to factors associated with the actual inspection of the written goal descriptions. Decreases in the likelihood of mastering any goal as goal lists grow longer have been observed even when the goal list had been memorized prior to the study of the text.

Another limitation in the control of mathemagenic activities by directions appears to be due to differences between the organization of the goal descriptions and the organization of the text. Gagné and Rothkopf have arranged text so that information elements relevant to two components of a goal description were in adjacent locations in the passage or material relevant to other goals was interposed between the two critical elements.[60] In the latter condition recall of information about the second, dispersed goal component was substantially lower than recall of the second component in the adjacent condition. These results suggest that written lists of directions sometimes result in mental bookkeeping problems and a resultant drop in efficiency.

Inductive control. In typical research on inductive control of mathemagenic activities, all subjects read the same text material but some of the experimental groups are asked questions about the text at frequent intervals during the course of the study period. The main experimental evidence about control of mathemagenic ac-

58. Kaplan and Rothkopf, "Instructional Objectives as Directions to Learners."

59. Rothkopf and Billington, "Relevance and Similarity of Text Elements."

60. Ellen D. Gagné and Ernst Z. Rothkopf, "Text Organization and Learning Goals," *Journal of Educational Psychology* 67 (June 1975): 445-50.

tivities by these procedures comes from recall data about information elements in the text that are *not* directly related to the experimental questions. Inferences about mathemagenic activities based on recall of material unrelated to the questions seen during reading is based on the following reasoning. If questions asked during the course of reading affect processing activities, demonstration of knowledge about information relevant to the questions is not sufficient to permit one to infer mathemagenic activities. This is because questions not only influence how question-relevant knowledge is elaborated but may also be in themselves informative. Knowledge relevant to the experimental question therefore reflects information supplied by these questions as well as their shaping effects on mathemagenic activities and processing. These two components cannot be easily disentangled. On the other hand, any performance changes attributable to the questioning in the recall of material unrelated to the experimental questions must be due to processing activities alone. The effect need not necessarily be facilitative. It is conceptually possible that a particular line of questioning may induce substantial processing changes that will *decrease* the likelihood that certain kinds of information are acquired from the experimental text.

Using the experimental approach described above, investigators have been able to provide existential proof that environmental demands made during reading, such as questions, change what is learned from reading a passage and proof, by implication, that these changes were due to modifications in processing activities.[61]

It has also been demonstrated that the topography of mathemagenic activities can be altered by the use of questions requiring restricted classes of answers.[62] For example, questions requiring numerical or quantitative answers have been shown to increase the

61. Roger H. Bruning, "Effects of Review and Test-like Events within the Learning of Prose Materials," *Journal of Educational Psychology* 59 (February 1968): 16-19; Ernst Z. Rothkopf, "Learning from Written Instructive Materials: An Exploration of the Control of Inspection Behavior by Test-like Events," *American Educational Research Journal* 3 (November 1966): 241-49.

62. Edys S. Quellmalz, "Effects of Three Characteristics of Text-Embedded Response Requirements on the Development of a Dominant Focus in Prose Learning" (Ph.D. diss., University of California, Los Angeles, 1971); Ernst Z. Rothkopf and Ethel E. Bisbicos, "Selective Facilitative Effects of Interspersed Questions on Learning from Written Materials," *Journal of Educational Psychology* 58 (February 1967): 56-61.

likelihood of learning other quantitative information in the text—information unrelated to the experimental question. The relevant topography probably involves selective mechanisms, that is, a sentence containing quantitative information is discriminated and processed differently from a sentence that does not contain information of this type. The reason for concluding that inductive rather than deductive control of mathemagenic activities is involved in the use of the restricted-topic questioning procedure was that the treatment effect is obtained only if the questions follow the text segment to which they are relevant and not if the questions precede the relevant text portions. The selection effect appears difficult to demonstrate under circumstances when selective topography would not be expected to be peculiarly efficient—such circumstances as, for example, those in which objects of these restricted questions appear in almost every sentence of the passage.[63]

There are also indications that environmental demands produced by questions increase the persistence of effective processing after the use of the questions has been discontinued.[64] Questions have also been observed to maintain the persistence of positive mathemagenic activities under adverse conditions such as prolonged reading.[65]

Some studies have reported that social factors increase the ability of questions to shape effective mathemagenic activities.[66] Questions relevant to the text, when asked by a teacher-like figure, alter students' processing activities more than questions that are mechanically presented.

63. Rothkopf and Bisbicos, "Selective Facilitative Effects."

64. Evan R. Keislar, "A Descriptive Approach to Classroom Motivation," *Journal of Teacher Education* 11 (June 1960): 310-15; Ernst Z. Rothkopf, "Concerning Parallels between Adaptive Processes in Thinking and Self-Instruction," in *Approaches to Thought*, ed. J. Voss (Columbus, Ohio: Charles E. Merrill Publishing Co., 1969), pp. 299-316.

65. Leonard Carmichael and Walter F. Dearborn, *Reading and Visual Fatigue* (Boston: Houghton Mifflin, 1947). See Rothkopf, "Experiments on Mathemagenic Behavior," for a discussion of these findings.

66. Ernst Z. Rothkopf and Richard D. Bloom, "Effects of Interpersonal Interaction on the Instructional Value of Adjunct Questions in Learning from Written Material," *Journal of Educational Psychology* 61 (December 1970): 417-22; Ernst Z. Rothkopf, "Variable Adjunct Question Schedules, Interpersonal Interaction, and Incidental Learning from Written Material," *Journal of Educational Psychology* 63 (April 1972): 87-92.

The research on inductive control of processing by questions supports the conception of mathemagenic activity as an adaptive mechanism that is responsive to environmental demands. Students respond to any consistencies in the information demands of questions and alter their mathemagenic activities as a consequence. If these alterations are successful, students are able to handle subsequent questions in a satisfactory way. If students are not successful on later questions, further alterations will occur. In this way, questions serve as an environmental pressure that will tend to foster the emergence of adaptive mathemagenic activities. Adaptive, in this context, means that the mathemagenic activities will produce the knowledge required by criterion tests. Positive mathemagenic effects produced by questions can therefore be expected if experimental adjunct questions require knowledge that is obtainable by the same selective and elaborative mechanisms as the knowledge for criterion tests. Furthermore, demonstrable positive mathemagenic effects can only be expected if the students do *not* have or do not exercise effective mathemagenic activities in studying the instructive text.

The latter principle is illustrated by the following findings in an experiment by Rothkopf.[67] Subjects reading an earth science text, photographed on ninety slides, were divided into four groups according to (a) whether their inspection rate increased or not during the first twenty-four slides and (b) whether test performance on information learned from the first twenty-four slides was above or below the group median. Adjunct questions were asked at various intervals *after* slide number 24 and maintained at an average interval of one question every six slides thereafter. It was reasoned that only the group with below-median learning *and* increases in inspection speed had given clear evidence of inappropriate mathemagenic activities. As expected, this group showed the most marked effect of adjunct questions on learning from text slides numbered 25 through 90.

Direct instructive effects of questions. The emergence of adaptive mathemagenic activities that result from questions, as indexed by incidental learning measures, depends on many factors. It therefore requires substantial care in the design of experiments in order to demonstrate these phenomena. The direct instructive effect of

67. Rothkopf, "Variable Adjunct Question Schedules."

questions is much more robust and has been observed in dozens of experiments.[68] Subjects tend to remember more about the information they have been asked about than other text information, and they tend to remember question-relevant information longer. This may be a processing phenomenon, as indicated by the findings of Craik and Tulving.[69] The effect may also be thought of as a repetition phenomenon, that is, another demonstration of the law of exercise. Sufficient data are not at present available to permit an estimate of the relative importance of the processing and the repetition factors. It is clear, however, that the direct instructive effect is substantial and that, if properly used, it has immediate instructional applications.

THE NOMINAL TEXT AND MATHEMAGENIC ACTIVITIES

Rothkopf and Billington have proposed that there is a trade-off between previous general knowledge about the subject matter being studied and the level of mathemagenic activities required for successful outcomes.[70] Thus a text segment that is supposed to inculcate a selected competence requires less extensive and therefore more probable levels of mathemagenic activity for success if the student is familiar with relevant vocabulary and instructional metaphors than if he is not.[71] Rothkopf and Billington [72] suggested that performance resulting from an experimental treatment (P_T) was:

$$P_T = E + (1 - E)m_T$$

In this equation E is a quantitative description of a preexperiment experience factor that determines the ease of acquiring the informa-

68. For a recent review see Richard C. Anderson and William B. Biddle, "On Asking People Questions about What They Are Reading," in *Psychology of Learning and Motivation*, vol. 9, ed. Gordon Bower (New York: Academic Press, 1975), in press.

69. Craik and Tulving, "Depth of Processing."

70. Ernst Z. Rothkopf and Marjorie J. Billington, "A Two-Factor Model of the Effect of Goal-Descriptive Directions on Learning from Text," *Journal of Educational Psychology* 67 (October 1975): 692-704.

71. An implicit assumption that should be noted in this connection is that the law of least effort operates for processing. All other factors being held constant, more "elaborate" mathemagenic activities are less likely.

72. Rothkopf and Billington, "A Two-Factor Model."

tion needed for the test and m_T characterizes the disposition towards mathemagenic processing activities relevant for a given informational item produced by treatment τ. For a control group, in which mathemagenic activity was not systematically manipulated, performance P_c was as follows:

$$P_c = E + (1 - E)m_c$$

Treatment τ involved manipulation of mathemagenic activities by use of goal-descriptive directions. When m_T and m_c were evaluated from P_T and P_c for each of a number of goal-relevant items, the data supported the conclusion that m_T was a constant while m_c varied among items. Goal-descriptive directions produced their biggest effects on items for which m_c was lowest, that is, those aspects of information that the subjects were unlikely to process under usual conditions. This finding was consistent with results reported by Duell.[73] She reported that descriptions of learning goals were most effective for information elements that students would normally judge to be relatively unimportant, that is, aspects of the instructional material that the teacher perceives to be important while students do not.

The exact nature of the equation linking learned performance to E and m is not critical for our present discussion. What is interesting is the conception that when experience relevant to acquisition of a particular information element is small, more elaborate and less probable levels of mathemagenic activities are required for successful learning results. For example, suppose that the instructional goal was to be able to indicate that grasshoppers lay eggs and that they deposit them in holes in the ground. If the student reads: "Grasshoppers lay eggs in small holes in the ground," more probable levels of mathemagenic activity will be required for success than if the student reads: "When Marissa caught the grasshopper, she grabbed the insect too hard, and the ovipositor broke off and remained in the little hole in the ground."

Both statements are sufficient to enable the student to acquire the desired information. More elaborate and less probable levels of

73. Orpha K. Duell, "Effect of Type of Objective, Level of Test Questions, and the Judged Importance of Tested Materials upon Posttest Performance," *Journal of Educational Psychology* 66 (April 1974): 225-32.

mathemagenic functioning will be needed if the student has to acquire the desired competence from the second statement. Even less probable levels are required if the student is not familiar with the term *ovipositor* but knows its Latin roots.

The experience factor E is closely related to characteristics of the nominal stimulus, such as certain aspects of content and the representation and form of the text. Relatively sparse content development, such as weak review of fundamentals or "big instructional steps," require more extensive processing by the student in order to achieve a given set of goals. A large amount of material in the text that is not relevant to instructional goals increases the need for more selective mathemagenic activities in order to achieve acceptable performance levels in an efficient manner. In a given student population, a difficult lexicon, complicated syntax, and inappropriate organization require relatively elaborate mathemagenic activities. These are less probable and require more external supports. It is a simple idea. It says that bad form and exposition (never bad content) can be overcome by stronger environmental supports for mathemagenic activities. Text that is difficult to read is an acceptable (or at least a workable) instructional alternative in many cases if one is willing to create mechanisms for shaping and maintaining the mathemagenic activities needed for these situations. Slipshod work by publishers requires more effort on the part of the schools for a given level of results.

SOME PRACTICAL OPTIONS

The discussion of research on learning from written material has centered on two aspects of the problem: the nominal stimulus characteristics of text and the nature and control of the processing activities required of the learner. Each of these two facets corresponds in some respects to one of two major practical options that are available for the development of written instructional material. Educators who wish to use written material in instruction can either develop materials especially for their particular purpose, or they can select from what is available in the didactic or general literature.

SPECIAL PURPOSE DEVELOPMENT

Special purpose development tends to emphasize the importance

of the nominal stimulus in learning. Two approaches have dominated the special purpose development of stable instructional materials. One sought to find effective expository forms by using
principles from the psychological literature. The early forms of
programmed instruction were products of this spirit. The other
emphasized explicit formulations of goals and the use of empirical
means to assure the effectiveness of the document in achieving the
stated objectives.

Development based on principles. The principles-of-effective-
exposition approach has been used so far with only indifferent
success. Our present knowledge about instructionally important
characteristics of the nominal stimulus is apparently still too incomplete, and the generality of our scientific conceptions of the
nominal stimulus is limited. When intelligent people undertake to
produce a document in a form that is particularly effective, they
tend to do a better job than if only a routine writing assignment
were involved, although the judgment of intelligent people in these
matters is sometimes wrong.[74] The psychological literature serves
mainly to enhance the apperceptive mass of writers and developers
rather than to allow specific useful deductions or generalizations.
This literature and the "golden wisdom" literature on writing probably exerts its influence in subtle and perhaps powerful ways on
writers and developers. It helps them to think and to talk about
their problems. It is difficult, however, to find great successes in
instructional development that were demonstrably due to the use
of expository principles derived from the psychological literature.

Goals and method of successive approximation. The second
approach to the special development of written instructional materials (and the most effective systematic method now available)
is based on a few simple ideas. These ideas are that reproducible
instructional sequences can be tried out on students; that revisions
can be made in the instructional arrangements according to the
measured results of the trial; and that the trial-revision cycle can
be repeated until the instructional sequence consistently produces
the desired instructional effects.

74. Ernst Z. Rothkopf, "Some Observations on Predicting Instructional Effectiveness by Simple Inspection," *Journal of Programmed Instruction* 2
(Summer 1963): 19-20.

These procedures have been called the method of successive approximation. The method has also been called the empirical development technique, the instructional quality control method, and the trial-revision cycle technique.

Two conditions must be met before this simple development technique can be put into practice. First, the goals of instruction must be stated explicitly, clearly, and in great detail. This condition is required in order to construct comprehensive tests to measure whether the stated instructional objectives have been achieved. Second, the instructional sequences or programs must be reproducible, that is, they must have stable, tangible forms. This condition must be met because it is pointless to draw conclusions about the effectiveness of unstable, unreproducible instructional sequences, and because it is difficult to make corrective revisions in instructional sequences that have no tangible, stable form. Written material tends to satisfy these requirements although not perfectly.

The method of successive approximation provides an apparently simple scenario for the development of written instructional materials, that is, the instructional perfection of the nominal stimulus. Instructional materials that have met the requirements described above are tried out on a sample of students who are representative of the target population. Instructional results are measured and revisions are made in the instructional material in order to correct discrepancies between stated objectives and measured results. The trial-revision cycle is then repeated with new samples of students until it can be concluded that the instructional sequence consistently achieves specified instructional goals.

A number of important successes have been claimed for the method of successive approximation. These cannot be documented here. There are convincing indications that the try-out procedures serve useful purposes but that the major impact of the successive approximation method resulted from the reformulation of instructional goals—a refinement of content. Careful determination of what should be taught allows powerful economies of instruction by allowing the evaluation of each potential instructional component in terms of its relevance to goals.

Yet, despite the fact that a remarkably large number of people appear to agree on its merits, the method of successive approximation is not widely used in producing written and other stable instructional materials. There are a number of reasons for this. Not least among them is that the method of successive approximation has proven to be very expensive.

USE OF ADJUNCT PROCEDURES

The best rational method currently available for the development of written material depends on a systematic focus on a carefully chosen number of specified instructional objectives. This creates an unhappy dilemma for publishers. Teachers of the "same" subject matter do not always have the same specific goals. At least they would discover that they did not have identical goals if they had taken the trouble to formulate these goals in explicit and exact language. Publishers wish to sell the largest possible number of copies of a given book. It therefore does not make good economic sense to them to tailor their product to the educational aims of any single group of teachers. Instead they try to produce a book that meets the largest number of educational goals that potential buyers might conceivably have. The needs of the teacher in this way conflict with the needs of the publisher. The teacher should want written materials that are focused on selected educational goals. The publisher wants a book acceptable to teachers whose educational goals may differ from each other.

The research on the control of mathemagenic activities by use of such adjunct devices as questions and directions is very relevant to a resolution of this conflict between teacher and publisher. Providing directions that describe learning goals to students appears to be a method by which teachers can adapt general purpose material to their nonspecific goals. The effective content of a book, rather than being focused through the work of the writer, becomes focused through the selective topography of mathemagenic activities. This allows the school to take advantage of the economies of a centrally produced, general purpose book and adapt it to local purposes by relatively cheap, locally produced, adjunct material. This is, of course, one of the reasons why research on the control of mathemagenic activities is attractive from a practical as well as a purely scientific point of view.

The general framework discussed here sets forth two kinds of determinants of learning from written material. These are the nominal attributes of the text and acts by the readers to create a useful internal representation from the written material. An important feature of this approach is that evaluation of both factors nearly always refers to an external pragmatic criterion and must involve consideration of the state of the other factor. There may be universally negative mathemagenic activities such as falling asleep during reading. Whether a mathemagenic activity is positive, however, depends on the nature of the specific goals of instruction. It is meaningless to inquire whether the use of adjunct questions with text is, in general, instructionally desirable. Similarly the issue of whether a text is effective is not an interesting question without reference to its intended use and the nature of mathemagenic activities that may be supported in the instructional situation. Partial exceptions to the above are the representation and form factors that were described as not being goal-specific in Table 1. These factors may have some use in deciding whether books are likely to invite browsing and whether they are likely to be unsuitable for a particular reader population. There are indications, however, that representation and form are weak nominal stimulus factors compared to content and that their effects can be overcome by suitable mathemagenic activities.[75] However, even if weak, it would not be consistent with the aims of instruction to neglect representation and form factors. For best results, care should be taken not only that students read to learn but also that text has been written to teach.

75. Rothkopf, "Structural Text Features and the Control of Processes."

CHAPTER V

Tutoring

DOUGLAS G. ELLSON

Consider the education of an aristocratic boy, to which one man's whole time is devoted. However excellent might be the results of such a system, no man with a modern outlook would give it serious consideration, because it is arithmetically impossible for every child to absorb the whole time of an adult tutor. The system is therefore one which can only be employed by a privileged caste; in a just world, its existence would be impossible.

—Bertrand Russell, *On Education*

One need not conduct a survey to know that tutoring in American schools today bears little relationship to Russell's "tutorial system." For reasons that Russell suggests, this system was replaced by classroom teaching. More recently, tutoring has reappeared; in fact, it is becoming quite common, especially in the United States, but in quite different form. The new tutor is likely to be a specialist, not a generalist; to be an amateur or a technician rather than a professional; and even if he or she is not a part-time worker, to spend a relatively short time with any one tutee. The function of the tutor has changed so much that Russell's (and still Webster's) definition of a tutor as a "private teacher" no longer seems appropriate. Almost the only remaining common feature is the one-to-one relationship.

Tutoring may be defined as one-to-one instruction. It is sometimes called individualized instruction, but the two terms are not equivalent. Individualized instruction is a broader concept that would include, for example, a method described as "individual diagnosis, group remediation." To qualify as tutoring, the instruction *per se* must be individualized. Ideally, it is based on diagnosis,

130

but the latter may well be a group process. It may utilize paper and
pencil tests to assign people to group categories. It may be mentioned that there is no necessary contradiction in the term "group
tutoring." A classroom teacher can work with several members of
a group, teaching each of them individually on a time-sharing basis.

The Current Status of Tutoring

In 1968, the Federal government's Right to Read program pub-
licized an effort called Ten Million Tutors. This title was less a description of the program than a slogan for a campaign to recruit
volunteers in the absence of adequate financing. The program, perhaps inspired by a Gallup Poll reporting that sixty-five million
Americans said they would volunteer if asked, is now dead. But its
mere conception indicated the extent to which the status of tutoring has changed since Bertrand Russell wrote.

More realistic information is provided by a directory of tutorial
projects compiled in 1968,[1] although its roster of programs is far
from complete. The basis for selection of the sample was not stated;
to judge from the titles of projects and the generally small number
of tutees per tutor, the directory is biased toward volunteer programs. Nonetheless, the results of most of the tabulations are consistent with general knowledge. Project directors for 362 of the 626
projects listed answered a questionnaire. For the answering sample,
the total number of tutors was 35,988, the total number of tutees,
69,600, giving an average tutor/tutee ratio of one to two. Distribu-
tions are shown in table 1.

For the 362 projects reporting, a classification of tutees indicated that 31 percent were white, 50 percent black, 14 percent
Spanish-speaking, and 5 percent other. Table 2 shows the grade
level and subject classification of the tutoring programs in these
projects. The fact that over 77 percent of these programs provided
tutoring at the primary or secondary level, together with other information, suggests that most of the tutoring is aimed at remediation of deficiencies in academic performance. Yet, of the total number of projects reporting content, only 14.9 percent reported their

1. Office of Economic Opportunity, *Directory of Tutorial Projects* (Washington, D.C.: United States National Student Association, Tutorial Assistance
Center, 1968). ERIC: ED 023 728.

TABLE 1

NUMBERS OF TUTORS AND TUTEES IN PROJECTS FOR WHICH
INFORMATION WAS AVAILABLE IN THE
1968 *Directory of Tutorial Projects*

NUMBER	TUTORS		TUTEES	
	N	PERCENT	N	PERCENT
1–20	106	29.3	45	12.4
21–40	59	16.3	55	15.2
41–60	48	13.3	53	14.6
61–80	27	7.5	30	8.3
81–100	32	8.8	31	8.6
101–200	45	12.4	61	16.9
201–300	16	4.4	19	5.2
301–400	8	2.2	21	5.8
401–500	3	0.8	6	1.7
501–750	8	2.2	8	2.2
751–1000	6	1.7	7	1.9
1001–2000			8	2.2
2001–3000			3	0.8
5000*			1	0.3
No information	4	1.1	14	3.9
Totals	362	100.0	362	100.0

*This is not an interval. One location reported 5000 tutees.

SOURCE: Office of Economic Opportunity, *Directory of Tutorial Projects* (Washington, D. C.: United States National Student Association, Tutorial Assistance Center, 1968). ERIC: ED 023 728.

TABLE 2

GRADE LEVEL AND SUBJECT CLASSIFICATIONS
OF 668 TUTORING PROGAMS IN 362 PROJECTS

CLASSIFICATION	PREDOMINANTLY ACADEMIC		PREDOMINANTLY BASIC		OTHER		TOTAL NUMBER OF PROGRAMS, BY GRADE LEVEL	
	N	Pct	N	Pct	N	Pct	N	Pct
Preschool	2	0.3	31	4.6	6	0.9	39	5.8
Kindergarten	1	0.1	17	2.5	5	0.7	23	3.4
Primary	14	2.1	236	35.3	34	5.1	284	42.5
Secondary	22	3.3	188	28.1	23	3.4	233	34.9
College	2	0.3	5	0.7	1	0.1	8	1.2
Adult	9	1.3	63	9.4	9	1.3	81	12.1
Totals	50	7.5	540	80.8	78	11.7	668	100.0

SOURCE: Office of Economic Opportunity, *Directory of Tutorial Projects* (Washington, D.C.: United States National Student Association, Tutorial Assistance Center, 1968). ERIC: ED 023 728.

overall program content to be predominantly academic, while 67 percent described it as predominantly "basic." The apparent discrepancy may be a matter of definition, since remedial work in beginning reading and mathematics is often described as basic rather than academic. Further, there is almost certainly more tutoring at the college level than table 2 suggests, especially if the typical instruction in master's, doctoral, and postdoctoral research is recognized as a form of tutoring.

The result of one tabulation may be questioned, namely, that 162 (45 percent) of the projects reporting indicated "regular evaluation and research." This result may well represent a loose interpretation of the category. If not, there is obviously a large discrepancy between the amount of evaluation and research performed and the amount reported in a form accessible for the present review. During the first eight years of ERIC's existence, only sixty-five evaluation studies of tutoring programs were listed.

The Effectiveness of Tutoring

There is a widespread belief among educators and laymen that individualized instruction, especially in a one-to-one teaching situation, is almost infallibly effective. On occasion it may be conceded that tutoring can fail in achieving certain cognitive learning goals, but in that case tutoring is likely to be justified in terms of its "obviously" favorable effects on affective variables such as attitudes, behavior problems, or the self-concept. Much of this belief is unjustified, as the first systematic review of objective research on tutoring showed.

EFFECTS ON TUTEES

In 1969 Rosenshine and Furst[2] examined thirteen studies in which tutoring procedures had been evaluated objectively in terms of their cognitive and affective consequences for tutors, tutees, or both. Measures of tutee gains in the cognitive area were reported for fourteen tutoring procedures. The reviewers placed these evalu-

2. Barak Rosenshine and Norma Furst, "The Effects of Tutoring upon Pupil Achievement: A Research Review" (Paper read at the annual meeting of the American Educational Research Association, Minneapolis, Minn., February, 1969). ERIC: ED 064 462.

ations in four groups according to (a) the success of the tutoring (statistically significant positive effect of tutoring) and (b) the use of a control group. Eight procedures were classed as successful; of these, six were evaluated in studies that included control groups taught by conventional classroom methods, two in studies without comparison groups. Of the six procedures classified as unsuccessful, one was evaluated without a control group. But three of the studies that Rosenshine and Furst classified as "successful" may be questioned on methodological grounds. In Lundberg's study [3] the tutees were self-selected in such a way that the experimental-control difference could be a consequence of differential motivation rather than of tutoring. In Hassinger and Via's study,[4] which did not include a control group, the results can plausibly be accounted for in terms of the "sawtooth error." This kind of error results when published norms are used for comparison in uncontrolled studies. In Hassinger and Via's study, gains for the tutored group significantly exceeded published norms, but such norms ordinarily (and in this case) cannot substitute for control group data. As Tallmadge and Horst have indicated, all existing published norms have been obtained by interpolation on curves that have been smoothed in such a way as to underestimate the gains normally made between September and June (when gains reported in this study were measured).[5] Some empirical data support Tallmadge and Horst's theoretical point; at least two studies have reported grade-equivalent gains for conventionally taught control groups that were more than twice as great as the gains predicted from national norms.[6]

3. Donald L. V. Lundberg, "Some Evaluations of Tutoring by Peers," *Journal of Secondary Education* 43 (March 1968): 99-103.

4. Jack Hassinger and Murray Via, "How Much Does a Tutor Learn through Teaching Reading?" *Journal of Secondary Education* 44 (January 1969): 42-44.

5. G. K. Tallmadge and D. Horst, "A Procedural Guide for Validating Achievement Gains in Educational Projects," RMC Reports UR-240 (Los Altos, California: RMC Research Corporation, May 1974).

6. R. D. Cloward, "Studies in Tutoring," *Journal of Experimental Education* 36 (Fall 1967): 14-25; Michael J. Wargo, Peggie L. Campeau, and G. Kasten Tallmadge, "Further Examination of Exemplary Programs for Educating Disadvantaged Children" (Palo Alto, California: American Institutes for Research in the Behavioral Sciences, July 1971).

There are two methodological defects in Silver's study,[7] namely, the sawtooth error and the regression error. Both are common in investigations that do not include a comparison group. The regression error occurs because experimental subjects were selected for tutoring on the basis of low scores on the same tests that were used as the baseline for measuring gains. Thus, *there remain only five of fourteen evaluations in which tutoring was clearly shown to be effective in improving cognitive skills.*

In six studies no significant improvement was found. In three of these, at least one experimental-control difference favored the untutored group, and in one case such a negative difference was statistically significant at the .01 level.

In seven of the studies, tutee changes in the affective domain were evaluated with a variety of measures. The results were summarized by Rosenshine and Furst as follows:

The overall results of the objective *affective* measures are far from encouraging. Even though different test instruments were used in different projects, data analysis showed no significant differences from pretest to post-test, *with no exceptions.*

The lack of significant differences becomes even more striking when the identical reports cite subjective evidence from tutors and from teachers indicating strong positive changes in the attitudes of those being tutored. We must conclude this section by noting the strange and irreconcilable difference between the objective measures of pupil attitudes (including a variety of tests) and the subjective reports from those who have engaged in the tutoring process.[8]

In summary, the Rosenshine-Furst review of objective research on the effectiveness of tutoring indicated that some tutoring programs are more effective than conventional instruction for teaching in cognitive areas or for increasing the effectiveness of conventional teaching when used as a supplement to it, but not all programs are effective for the purpose, and, in fact, in some circumstances they are less effective than conventional classroom teaching. (Additional and more favorable information on the effectiveness of tutoring is included in a later section of this chapter entitled "Programmed

7. A. B. Silver, "Extending a Helping Hand Educationally" (Bakersfield, California: Bakersfield College, Office of Institutional Research, 1967). ERIC: ED 017 267 .

8. Rosenshine and Furst, "Effects of Tutoring," pp. 22-23.

Tutoring.") Further, although a variety of instruments were applied to measure changes in the affective domain, there was no statistically significant evidence that tutoring had any effect in this area. Finally, there is considerable anecdotal and subjective evidence that tutoring can improve attitudes, motivation, self-image, and the like, much of it from the developers of the tutoring programs in question, but this evidence was not supported by objective data.

THE SIGNIFICANCE OF INDIVIDUAL ATTENTION

One myth is dispersed and one fact made clear by the data brought together in this review. The success of tutoring can *not* be attributed to individual attention. If individual attention were the critical operating factor, then all tutoring should be successful, but as the review has shown, only some is successful, perhaps less than half. If, as is likely, successful programs are more often reported than unsuccessful ones, the actual proportion of success may be even smaller than the review by Rosenshine and Furst indicated.

One analytic study was aimed directly at the question of individual attention.[9] In this study, carried out in twenty schools, two tutoring procedures were compared under similar conditions, each with comparable untutored controls from the same classrooms. The two tutoring procedures were independently planned by experts with the same terminal objective, namely to improve the first-grade reading achievement of disadvantaged children through the use of tutoring as a supplement to conventional classroom teaching. The treatments were matched in terms of instructional objective, school characteristics, tutor qualifications, and the amount of tutor training and supervision. The two groups of tutors appeared equally motivated. There were no obvious systematic differences in the physical conditions under which the tutoring took place. Scheduling procedures and duration of tutoring were the same, so that the amount of time available for individual attention was equated.

The treatments differed in that, in one case (programmed tutoring), the tutors followed highly structured programs in detail,

9. Douglas G. Ellson, Phillip Harris, and Larry Barber, "A Field Test of Programed and Directed Tutoring," *Reading Research Quarterly* 3 (Spring 1968): 307-64; Phillip Harris, "Experimental Comparison of Two Methods of Tutoring: Programed versus Directed" (Ph.D. diss., Indiana University, June 1967).

while in the other case, which more closely resembled conventional reading instruction, the tutors were allowed considerable freedom to determine details of procedure and interaction with the children. Differences in the degree of individual attention were not obvious, except that the programmed tutors were required to spend more time recording the children's performance during the tutoring sessions.

Although individual attention was effectively equated in the two procedures, a comparison showed significant posttest differences in favor of programmed tutoring in all nine measures of reading achievement. These results clearly agree with those brought together by Rosenshine and Furst: the significant variable in producing effective tutoring is the tutoring program—what the tutors do. There is no magic in individual attention.

EFFECTS ON TUTORS

Rosenshine and Furst also examined the effects of tutoring upon tutors who are themselves students. In five of these studies the tutors were secondary school pupils; in several cases they were underachievers in the subject area tutored. Again no measurable effects were detected in the affective domain. But all five studies reported significant gains for the tutors on at least one test with cognitive content. In two studies the gains were not notable, but of the three remaining, one reported gains of 3.4 years on the Iowa Silent Reading Test after seven months of tutoring, compared with gains of 1.7 years for the controls;[10] a second reported gains of 3.4 years on the same test after seven weeks of tutoring;[11] and a third reported gains of eight months after six weeks of tutoring.[12] Although there were no control groups for the latter two, it is doubtful that the sawtooth error could account for gains of this magnitude. Although some of this research can be questioned on methodological grounds, the findings are important as the first clear

10. Cloward, "Studies in Tutoring."

11. National Commission on Resources for Youth, *Youth Tutoring Youth: It Worked*, Report of an in-school neighborhood youth corps demonstration project (New York: National Commission on Resources for Youth, Inc., 1968). ERIC: ED 030 614.

12. Hassinger and Via, "How Much Does a Tutor Learn?"

indication that tutoring may have greater consequences for the tutor than for the tutee.

Psychological Aspects of Tutoring

THE TEACHING TASK

Tutoring derives from the classroom teachers' task in two ways. First, tutoring is a way of delegating parts of the task. The teaching task, done properly, is difficult and complex, especially for the elementary school teacher. Recent social, educational, and technological developments have increased its difficulty to the point that more is being demanded than most teachers can themselves supply. Second, tutoring is a form of teaching; thus one theory of the teaching process should apply to both. In principle, tutoring differs from classroom teaching only in the number of students taught at one time. In practice, a second important difference is found in the qualifications of the instructor. Classroom teachers are typically professionals, with extensive training and progressively accumulating experience. The tutor is typically a nonprofessional who often (one might say, all too often) is expected to begin tutoring with no specifically relevant training or experience. Insofar as the psychology of tutoring is different from the psychology of teaching, it is primarily a consequence of these two differences.

The problems of classroom teaching became more complex as the objective shifted from education of the few to education for all. When the number of children deemed worthy of education was small, the tutoring system referred to by Bertrand Russell was feasible. As the number increased, considerations of manpower and economics decreed that children be taught in groups. Even for the tutor, the teaching task was not easy, but for the classroom teacher, the problems were multiplied almost in proportion to the number of children in the classroom.

During a period of transition from elitist to universal education, the classroom teachers' task is made still more difficult. During such a period the proportion of educated parents is necessarily smaller than the proportion of children to be educated; as a result, the teacher is faced with many children who get little help from home. Most Western countries are now beyond this stage of educational expansion, but the problem has remained or is increasing as a consequence of other social changes.

One of the more important of these changes is the rural-urban migration that has resulted from industrialization. In the past few years, a large number of disadvantaged children have appeared in urban schools, where the prevalence of objective measurement and the emphasis on accountability have made it impossible to ignore the failures of the schools to teach them adequately. The home background of these children apparently lacks something, perhaps child-oriented conversation in standard English or experience with the printed word, which serves to simplify the teachers' task. Television very likely contributes to this problem, insofar as it replaces conversation and decreases the apparent need for literacy. Whatever analysis of causes may show, it is evident that the presence of disadvantaged children in a classroom complicates the task of the teacher. Recent declines in reading and other test scores at the elementary school level and related symptoms in secondary and higher education indicate that there is a problem and that it is becoming critical.

SOME SOLUTIONS

The classroom teacher's problems are not new, and a number of solutions have been proposed. Many proposed solutions have been tried out and abandoned; others have been retained in spite of the fact that none is clearly successful. One obvious solution is to increase the professional competence of the teacher by improving the art of teaching and the proficiency of the teacher as a creative artist. This solution, supplemented by a number of techniques and technologies designed to increase the teacher's efficiency, is the basic approach of most teacher-training institutions.

A second solution that has been widely adopted is content simplification. At the end of the nineteenth century, when even elementary education was far from universal in the United States, McGuffey's reader was not considered too difficult for the teaching of beginning reading in the classroom. Today McGuffey's reader or others of comparable difficulty are typically preceded by a simpler primer, and that one by as many as four progressively simpler preprimers, which in turn are preceded by "readiness" ma-

terial with almost no reading content. It is perhaps obvious from
recent assessments of reading performance that this device has not
solved the classroom teacher's problem.

A third approach may be called content analysis, which in reading is reflected in wall-size charts containing ordered lists of hun-
dreds of reading skills or objectives, and in beginning mathematics
by equally lengthy and detailed lists of behavioral objectives. Content analyses often appear in the form of teachers' guides that combine a sequential list of content objectives with examples, suggested
schedules, and forms of presentation. These teachers' guides are
reputed to be microscopically detailed sets of instructions for teaching, but examination indicates that most are almost entirely limited
to the stimulus or presentation component of the teaching-learning
situation. Until the recent emphasis on behavioral objectives, few
teachers' guides had much to say about the second component, the
response or performance expected of the pupil. Even less and
sometimes nothing at all is said about the third major component
of instruction, namely, feedback. A few guides suggest praise or
positive reinforcement in cases of success, but they seldom mention
the appropriate treatment in case of failure, although some tell
the teacher to "teach" what the child does not know. This vague
instruction avoids the major problem and emphasizes the fact that
teachers' guides are primarily concerned with content rather than
method. Such guides are unquestionably useful and welcomed by
many teachers, especially the neophyte graduates who find that
their training has been too abstract and that an exhortation to be
creative is insufficient. But content analysis, even combined, as it
often is, with content simplification, has not solved the problems
of the classroom teacher.

A fourth proposal is individualization of instruction. Some children (and adults) learn the same material at different rates than
others. Some learn more easily with one type of material or method
of teaching, while others do better with a different form of task or
presentation. If rate, task, material, and teaching method are the
same for all of the pupils in a classroom, many of them will not be
learning under optimal conditions. The obvious remedy, in principle, is individualization of instruction; but in practice information
handling and administrative problems make full individualization im-

possible. Given thirty children and a five-hour day, one classroom teacher can provide at most an average of ten minutes of fully individualized instruction for each child.

Some teachers have been able to develop workable compromises (for example, individual diagnosis and small group teaching) that increase the classroom teacher's effectiveness; but there is clearly much to be learned about these classroom management techniques.

The problem is basically one of information handling and management. If one takes seriously the notion that each child differs from every other and therefore must be taught differently, there are the problems of (a) diagnosis to determine the nature of the relevant differences, (b) prescription of perhaps thirty different treatments, and (c) administration of each treatment with the skill presumably expected of a professional—in ten minutes per pupil per day. One might also ask what the other twenty-nine children are doing during those ten minutes. The goal of individualized instruction without adequate support may well be the straw that breaks the classroom teacher's back. The teacher who has not been successful in devising one effective program is likely to have difficulty in producing thirty (or even three) different programs for thirty different children.

Small-group teaching increases the time available for working with each child. But the scheduling and organization of groups and the continual reassignment of participants that are necessary for optimal individualization add a very considerable administrative and teaching load. The evidence that small-group assignments tend to be permanent indicates that this compromise breaks down in practice.

A fifth alternative, delegation, is designed to reduce the teacher's load. (The other important form of support, teacher training, does not reduce the load but presumably enables the teacher to carry it more efficiently or effectively.) One or more of the teacher's functions is delegated to other people such as pupils, aides, tutors, administrators, and specialists—or to devices such as books and other teaching materials, diagnostic tests, audio-visual aids, teaching machines, computers, and broadcast media. Every possible function of the teacher—housekeeping (of which no more will be said), planning, subject-matter analysis, classroom management (including information handling and discipline), diagnosis, prescription, remedial teaching, and teaching proper—has been delegated singly and in combination. The use of delegation as a remedy for the inadequacies of classroom instruction is growing rapidly, in part because a growing awareness of the problems coincides with an increased availability of the necessary technologies and funds.

There is increasing evidence that delegation can succeed where other solutions are failing. Recent field evaluations have demonstrated large and significant improvements in objective measures of effectiveness or cost. A search by the author for such studies has so far uncovered twenty-four cases that satisfy two criteria: (a) an improvement factor of two or more (in an objective measure) and (b) adequate and strict, though not necessarily perfect, research design and administration. Such an improvement factor is considered to occur when an innovation is compared with conventional teaching and some objective index or measure of student performance is double or better, or teaching time or some cost factor is reduced by half or more. *In every case*, the entire teaching task or some significant portion of it was delegated. In nineteen of the twenty-four cases, significant teaching responsibilities were delegated to nonprofessionals and in one case to the student (through the use of self-instructional materials). The four cases in which all of the instruction was done by professionals also involved delegation (to other professionals) through use of very low pupil-teacher ratios. The highest ratio was fifteen to one, the lowest five to one.

Other common features of the innovations represented were not obvious. Educational levels ranged from preschool to university. The subject matters included preschool language training, reading, and mathematics at the primary and secondary levels, technical training, and an entire university curriculum. Teaching methods were equally diverse although there may be a common factor of individualization, identified by a variety of terms such as diagnosis, feedback, reinforcement, and tutoring. Eight of the twenty-four programs were primarily tutoring procedures.

THEORY OF TEACHING AND TUTORING

As indicated above, the same basic theory underlies both classroom teaching and tutoring. Since most tutoring today is utilized for the remediation or prevention of failure, the theory presented below will emphasize those aspects of the theory of teaching that are concerned with failure to learn.

Academic failure is accounted for in many ways. Three important groups of factors can be identified, each of which has implications for the nature of tutoring. They are (a) structural factors (including genetic handicaps), (b) affective factors (broadly defined to include not only emotional but attitudinal and motivational factors), and (c) learning or environmental factors.

Structural factors. The structural factors are assumed to be entirely within the pupil and are essentially unchangeable, at least by educational or psychological means—they are physical, chemical, physiological, neurological factors and are sometimes translated as genetic or racial. Since there are no educational remedies for these factors, the related teaching involves either adaptation to them by modifying aspirations or teaching "around" the handicap in special ways. The blind child may be taught Braille as a prosthesis to aid in acquiring intellectual skills, or his goals may be diverted to music or to broom making. The mentally retarded child may be taught by slower, more permissive, or more intensive methods, or his aspirations may be shifted from academic to nonverbal skills. Given the variety of such handicaps and the relatively small numbers of students involved, tutoring is an appropriate method of teaching because of its potential for individualization.

Perhaps because it provides an excuse for failures in teaching, the structural theory of failure is often overapplied. Educators generally estimate dyslexia (a defect defined in structural terms) to be more frequent than do medical researchers. Similarly the diagnosis of learning disability—with implications of structural handicap—is coming to be applied to almost any case of school failure. There is also evidence that mental retardation, with its own implications of structural defect, may be overdiagnosed. Tutoring rather obviously does not change structural factors; yet in a follow-up study of disadvantaged first-grade children who had been tutored in reading, the proportion of tutored children assigned to special education classes (that is, diagnosed as retarded) in the year following tutoring was approximately one fourth of the proportion in a

matched control group that was not tutored.[13] In a follow-up of
a language stimulation program involving small-group instruction
that also resulted in improvement in reading performance, Carter
found a ratio of eight to one between control and experimental
groups in assignments to special education classes.[14]

Structural factors are often combined with affective and environmental factors. Failures due to structural handicaps, especially
if they are severe, may produce emotional, motivational, or attitudinal problems, or they may keep the child out of school or
otherwise limit his opportunities to learn. In such cases tutoring
designed to remedy the effects of emotional or learning factors is
appropriate.

Affective factors. Affective factors as causes of failure presumably reflect undesirable personal and interpersonal relationships,
for example, conflict or inadequate adjustment to home, teacher,
school, or society. The resulting emotional or "behavioral" problems, undesirable attitudes, poor motivation, and so forth, are seen
as obstacles to learning that can be treated independently of more
direct causes of academic failure. In remediation, this leads to an
indirect approach to academic failure; teaching *per se* is considered
to be secondary and is often separated from therapy. This approach
becomes apparent when the problem is delegated to a tutor. As a
nonprofessional therapist, the tutor has the task of providing therapy in the form of extended samples of warm, noncompetitive,
permissive, and supportive human relationships, preferably in a
pleasant environment. Academic tutoring in the area of failure may
be perfunctory or omitted entirely. It is assumed that once the
emotional obstacles are removed the pupil can be returned to the
classroom teacher for instruction.

For tutoring based on this approach, the primary qualifications
of the tutor are largely personal. Concern and the ability to estab-

13. Douglas G. Ellson, "The Effect of Programed Tutoring in Reading on
Assignment to Special Education Classes: A Follow-up of Four Years of
Tutoring in the First Grade," Grant No. OEG 9-242178-4149-032, United
States Office of Education, Bureau of Education for the Handicapped, 1971.

14. J. L. Carter, "Follow-up Study of the Effects of a Language Stimula-
tion Program upon Negro Educationally Disadvantaged First Grade Children:
Final Report" (Houston, Texas: University of Houston, October 1969). ERIC:
ED 035 714.

lish good interpersonal relationships are more important than expertise in subject matter or teaching skills. Since the required qualities are widespread (and perhaps because they are easier to find than to teach), training for tutors in programs based on this approach is often sketchy, limited to indoctrination in the need for an appropriate atmosphere, or omitted entirely.

On first look, much subjective evidence favors the emotional theory of failure, but there is little hard evidence. In their review of five studies in which therapeutic objectives were indicated by attempts to measure affective changes, Rosenshine and Furst found no acceptable evidence for such changes, and among the five reviewed only the Cloward study reported statistically significant improvement in achievement.[15] Nonetheless, a different kind of data may have some bearing. In the "Homework Helper Program" evaluated by Cloward,[16] the tutors were mostly underachieving high school students; the tutees were third to sixth graders, retarded in reading. Gains for the *tutors* were 3.4 grade equivalent years, which was much greater than the gain achieved by a comparable control group that did not tutor; the difference was even greater when tutor gains were compared with tutee gains. In a similar study that used a more highly structured program for tutoring first graders in reading (and had no explicit therapeutic objective), Wells found tutor gains of 2.2 grade equivalent years compared with 0.2 years for a similar group that did not tutor.[17]

The large gains made by the tutors in these and other studies like them may simply be a consequence of practice in the academic subject matter that is incidental to the tutoring, but they may also constitute evidence in favor of the therapeutic approach to tutoring. In this approach, the first qualification of a tutor is to be a warm human being. If so, a first grader may be as well qualified to tutor (therapeutically) as a high school student, and the one-to-one relationship of tutor-tutee should work both ways. In terms of this model we might expect the gains for tutors and tutees to be inde-

15. Rosenshine and Furst, "The Effects of Tutoring upon Pupil Achievement"; Cloward, "Studies in Tutoring."

16. Cloward, "Studies in Tutoring."

17. Jane Wells, personal communication.

pendent of their academic and teaching qualifications but in proportion to the degree of pathology. If, as may well be the case, problems of motivation, attitude, and self-concept are greater for secondary than for elementary students, the data just given fit the therapeutic theory of tutoring very well.

Learning factors. The relationship of learning factors to academic failure and to the teaching necessary to prevent and remedy it has been analyzed more explicitly and in greater detail than is the case for either the structural or affective factors. The term "learning factors" in this context refers to environmental conditions that influence learning. These conditions are defined broadly to include the student's previous stimulus-response history as well as events in the immediate learning and teaching environment. Except for theoretical purposes, the history as such is seldom examined directly; for many practical purposes it is ignored or inferred theoretically from its consequences, states of the organism that are themselves inferred from current behavior such as performance in test situations.

In the introduction and first few chapters of *Preventing Failure in the Primary Grades,* Engelmann presented an impressive but nontechnical summary of a learning theory of failure that he expanded into a theory of teaching.[18] This theory was illustrated with specific applications to the classroom teaching of beginning reading and arithmetic in which the theory and art of teaching are merged. He wrote, "The only facts that are really helpful are facts about performance. Why does the child fail a complex task? Because he hasn't been taught certain skills required by that task."[19]

In his analysis of learning hierarchies, Gagné has expanded a similar proposition in considerable detail to provide the basis for a theory of teaching content, that is, a rational basis for deciding *what* to teach in order to achieve a given instructional objective.[20] Gagné's teaching content theory is complementary to theories of teaching operations that represent more conventional applications

18. Siegfried Engelmann, *Preventing Failure in the Primary Grades* (Chicago: Science Research Associates, Inc., 1969).

19. Ibid., p. 38.

20. Robert M. Gagné, *The Conditions of Learning* (New York: Holt, Rinehart, and Winston, 1965).

of learning theory. In combination, these analyses provide a rational and scientific basis for deciding what to teach in order to achieve a given instructional objective and, within limits, for deciding how to teach it. They are applicable to the three major functions in teaching: subject matter analysis and organization, pupil diagnosis and prescription, and treatment—the latter including the face-to-face interaction of teacher and pupil that is often assumed to be the totality of teaching.

In Gagné's learning-hierarchy theory, intellectual and other skills are ordered in complexity. At the top of the hierarchy are complex skills such as a learning strategy or the "understanding" of a process, concept, or body of knowledge. These skills, defined behaviorally, typically appear in lists of instructional objectives as required terminal behavior. Simpler skills down to the level of S-R connections are identified in the hierarchy as prerequisites for the learning of progressively higher order skills, which in turn are prerequisites for learning the terminal skills.

It follows from learning-hierarchy theory that failure to learn a complex skill results when simpler prerequisites have not been learned (or taught) previously; the remedy for failure is to teach the prerequisite skills or otherwise make sure that they are learned before teaching of the terminal skills is attempted.

Gagné supplements this general theory with a taxonomy of skill types classified in terms of psychological rather than subject-matter characteristics. Examples in ascending order of complexity are: S-R connections and verbal associations, which typically constitute the simplest level; discriminations; chains; rules; and problem solving strategies. The form of the hierarchical tree indicates the order in which skills must be taught. Except for this specification of order, the learning-hierarchy theory is essentially concerned with *what* must be taught.

In determining what must be taught, learning-hierarchy theory requires, first, analysis of the terminal task or skill that is specified by the objective to determine the hierarchy of prerequisites for learning that skill; and second, diagnosis of pupil performance to determine the presence or absence of each prerequisite skill in each pupil to be taught. If the analysis and diagnosis are carried to the level of S-R connections, as Gagné suggests, the result is appropriately described as microanalysis and microdiagnosis.

In the practice of teaching, both analysis and diagnosis *are* carried to the level of S-R connections. For example, reading in some form is a prerequisite for almost all academic skills; decoding is a prerequisite for reading, and the prerequisites for decoding include naming or other appropriate responses to letters, words, numerals, signs, musical notes, and the like. These last are S-R connections.

The task of subject-matter analysis is further complicated by the fact that the optimal learning hierarchies are seldom the same as the logical hierarchies, or structures, of what is to be learned. For example, the synthetic methods for teaching the grapheme-phoneme system that begin by teaching the structural elements (letters) do not necessarily provide the optimal approach to learning the system. It is perhaps obvious that the necessary microanalysis is not something to be undertaken casually. No teacher could expect to develop the optimal learning hierarchy for the grapheme-phoneme system, or for mathematics, in a lifetime. Such an analysis requires the social-cumulative strategies of science.

Once the prerequisite skills are identified, the next step is diagnosis to determine which prerequisites each pupil lacks. This step imposes a further tremendous information-handling task on the teacher. Consider the teaching of reading comprehension at the third grade level (and reading is not the teacher's only instructional objective) in a system that permits "social promotions," that is, one that does not specify prerequisites for admission to the third-grade teacher's classroom. The number of elements in the learning hierarchy for reading at this level is certainly in the thousands; a measure of the information-handling task in diagnosis is this number multiplied by the number of children in the classroom.

Diagnosis is pointless unless it is followed by appropriate prescription and treatment. The principle of prescription is simple: once diagnosis has determined what needs to be taught, teach it. In practice this dictum is complicated by the fact that a complete prescription cannot be written before actual teaching begins. For example, the point at which the teaching of any single skill should stop cannot be determined before teaching begins. This decision, which is properly a part of the teaching prescription, must be based on performance of the pupil, which cannot be predicted in advance of actual teaching. Thus there are two levels of diagnostic prescription. One, a relatively gross prescription of what treatment is needed, is based on a knowledge of what skills a student does or does not possess. This knowledge can be obtained in advance by means such as diagnostic testing. The second, which fills in detail, can be determined only from the successes and failures of the student after the treatment (that is, the face-to-face teaching) has begun.

Treatment is the most public part of the teacher's function, one which is often taken to be the whole of teaching. There is a sense in which this common understanding is correct. Subject matter organization, diagnosis, and prescription are components of a preparatory process; they produce no learning in themselves. Teaching begins only when the results of these preparatory steps are brought into the presence of the pupil as stimuli.

But presentation alone is seldom enough to produce significant learning. Experiments have demonstrated that what psychologists call S-S learning (stimulus-stimulus, rather than stimulus-response)[21] is very difficult to produce. The specialist who brings every conceivable prerequisite to a professional meeting where he functions as a pupil may benefit greatly from a key idea presented by the featured speaker, but such well-prepared and motivated pupils are not typical. Even so, it was only recently recognized that learning is an active process and that, with few exceptions, effective teaching requires more than a clear and logical presentation.

For the associationists of the eighteenth and nineteenth centuries, learning was primarily a result of contiguity of ideas that could be produced by contiguous presentation of stimuli. Ebbinghaus's research on the learning of nonsense syllable lists and Pavlov's research with dogs called attention to the function of the response in learning. But, as the principles of both association and conditioning were understood, the underlying processes were basically passive. Modern theories of active learning derive from a series of experiments reported by E. L. Thorndike in 1898, in which hungry cats learned to manipulate various levers and catches to escape from a "puzzle box" to reach food. Thorndike first called

21. Kenneth W. Spence, *Behavior Theory and Learning: Selected Papers* (Englewood Cliffs, N.J.: Prentice-Hall, 1960).

the underlying principle the "Law of Effect." A more recent term for the same process is "reinforcement," a concept that Skinner adapted to learning and teaching more extensively than did Thorndike. Hull, Mowrer, Premack, and others further investigated the nature of reinforcement and its relation to contiguity in an analysis that is still not complete. Today, reinforcement is generally considered to be a special case of the more general concept of feedback. Most recent applications of learning theory to instructional design and teaching center on what might be called S-R-F (stimulus-response-feedback) theories, which combine contiguity and reinforcement principles in workable if not theoretically pure systems.

The S-R-F system is primarily relevant to the immediate interactions between teacher and pupil that provide the conditions in which learning can take place. The S component in S-R-F refers, of course, to the stimulus. This is defined broadly to include situational factors, lectures, teaching materials and their presentation, learning task instructions, questions, test items, and the like. In some applications of the S-R-F system, especially those that derive from Skinner, the S component is deemphasized or ignored, but this is the exception.

The R component is as diversified as the S. The response or "behavior" may be any activity, from a reflex or the naming of a letter to the solution of a mathematical problem or the performance of a complex skill or strategy. In early versions of the theory associated with Watsonian behaviorism, the response was essentially restricted to "overt" behavior, that is, behavior that was observable without instruments, excluding neural activity for unexpressed reasons. But more recently the definition has been relaxed to include a variety of activities that are generally considered to be covert.

The F component also takes many forms, which have variously been called reward, punishment, satisfying state of affairs, reinforcement, knowledge of results, encouragement, prompting, or information.

Apart from emphasizing the necessity of activity (R) in learning, the S-R-F system or theory has affected the practice and theory of teaching in a number of ways. One important way is to provide an alternative to genetic and racial theories of individual and group differences. By calling attention to environment (stimulus), activity (response), and environmental feedback as causal factors in behavior that are almost independent of structure, it has emphasized the modifiability of individual differences. This emphasis has served to shift responsibility for pupil failures from the pupil's genetic or racial characteristics to the parent and teacher. More directly, it is affecting teaching practice. The change from contiguity theory to feedback theory accompanied and may in part be responsible for a shift from classroom drill to individualized instruction, or at least to a demand for it. A corollary of S-R-F theory is that there must be feedback, and it must be individualized. The teacher must evaluate each response of each pupil and provide the appropriate feedback. In fully individualized instruction, this information-handling (and pupil-handling) task must be added to those imposed by microdiagnosis and subject-matter analysis. The consequence is an excessive load on the classroom teacher—a load that increasingly is being relieved by tutoring and other ways of delegating parts of the teacher's responsibilities.

Programmed Tutoring

Earlier in this chapter the identification of eight unusually successful tutoring programs was mentioned. Each program showed a very large improvement in one or more objective measures obtained in a controlled comparison with conventional classroom teaching. Two of these programs were examples of conventional tutoring, similar to professional classroom teaching in that teaching procedures were improvised by the tutors. The improvisation was based on relatively general principles presented through training and supervisory procedures. However successful such programs may have been, they have the disadvantage of being difficult if not impossible to reproduce.

The remaining six procedures are examples of programmed tutoring. Programmed tutoring is a special case of programmed teaching, a form of programmed instruction that in turn is distinguished from programmed learning (self-instruction) in that teacher activity rather than pupil activity is programmed.

In programmed tutoring, the tutor functions not as a professional teacher "junior grade," but as a technician whose teaching activities are specified in detail by specific instructions or programs. In the ideal case, these programs are developed through a process that closely resembles the engineering of a physical product to satisfy carefully specified objectives. The process involves an initial careful design based on existing knowledge; this design is then refined through one or more cycles of modification based on empirical testing and evaluation. In each of several forms of programmed tutoring that have appeared so far, three types of program (content, lesson, and item) can be identified, each of which performs one of the teaching functions described earlier (subject analysis, prescriptive diagnosis, or teaching treatment).

A *content program* specifies what is to be taught. It is typically presented in the form of teaching materials, or a referenced outline of them, subdivided into lessons and smaller units to accord with a learning hierarchy of the subject matter. The arrangement of this material ordinarily determines the order in which the lessons and other units are initially presented. This order may be modified later on the basis of feedback operating through lesson and item programs. *Lesson programs* perform the primary diagnostic-prescriptive function, utilizing feedback from the student's response to the initial presentation. Remedial loops or bypass programs are used to determine the inclusion, repetition, or omission of lessons or the items of which they are composed. *Item programs* control the treatment, that is, the face-to-face procedures for teaching whatever is specified by the content and lesson programs. They are applied to "items," relatively small units of teaching material that correspond to the "frames" of programmed learning. They typically present a question, a problem, or a task, together with needed teaching material.

Even the simplest item programs are likely to be intricate since they perform many functions. First, they specify the teaching procedures, which in programs based on the S-R-F system include (a) presentation of the item-task, (b) classification of the response, and (c) presentation of differential feedback to the learner based on the acceptability and other characteristics of his response. An acceptable response is ordinarily followed by information in the form of reinforcement; the feedback after an unacceptable response can range from the minimal information that the response was unacceptable to an elaborate remedial teaching sequence determined by the specific nature of the error. The feedback obtained from the student's response is used in three ways: (a) to provide the student with information that is necessary for learning; (b) to provide the tutor with information that is stored for use on the longer-term diagnostic function of the lesson program (in this case the tutoring item doubles as a diagnostic test item); and (c) to provide the tutor with information that determines the next step to be taken within the item program—a secondary, short-term diagnosis.

Although the examples of programmed tutoring summarized below differ in format and other details, it is possible to identify content, lesson, and item programs in all of them. Programmed tutoring has so far taken four general forms, illustrated by George's Tutor Student System, Harrison's Beginning Reading, Rosenbaum's Peer-Mediated Instruction, and Ellson's Programmed Reading Tutorials.

The format of the Tutor Student System[22] is reminiscent of conventional teachers' guides. The basic outline is the content program, a series of items grouped into lessons, with teaching procedures briefly specified for each item and lesson regardless of repetition. Within this form, however, lesson and item programs are easily distinguished. Both are relatively simple. The basic lesson program is a remedial loop that reviews a lesson or part of it until the student answers one or more test items acceptably. Item programs are incorporated into each item in the form of instructions that tell the tutor what to do and say in presenting the item, specify the response, and indicate that he should say "Good" (or an equivalent) after the response, apparently without regard to its acceptability. This last feature suggests that the Tutor Student System is based on a Pavlovian or associationistic model rather than S-R-F theory, since there is no provision for differential feedback to the student. In practice, however, the tutor may provide the student with information concerning the acceptability of his responses, since the general instructions for the system suggest that it is permissible if not desirable for the tutor to improvise.

22. John E. George, "Tutor Student System" (Kansas City, Mo.: National Tutoring Institute, 1974).

The Tutor Student System has been validated as a remedial reading program with a relatively small number of tenth- and eleventh-grade tutees, using eleventh and twelfth graders and college students as tutors.[23] Grade equivalent gains obtained from the Gilmore Oral Reading Test are summarized in table 3.

TABLE 3

GRADE EQUIVALENTS OBTAINED FROM THE GILMORE ORAL READING TEST IN A VALIDATION STUDY OF THE TUTOR STUDENT SYSTEM

MEASURE	TUTORED GROUP (N = 18)			CONTROL GROUP (N = 18)			DIF- FERENCE IN GAIN	P
	PRE	POST	GAIN	PRE	POST	GAIN		
Reading Accuracy.....	3.3	4.6	1.3	3.0	2.9	−0.1*	1.4	< .001
Reading Compre- hension.......	2.8	5.3	2.5	2.8	3.5	0.7	1.8	< .003

*Ten-week gain predicted from norms = 0.25 year.

SOURCE: John E. George, "Dropout Prevention Project: Final Report," Faculty Research Grant Study, University of Missouri (Kansas City), August 1974.

Harrison's Beginning Reading combines features of a typical teacher's guide with programmed tutoring procedures based on the S-R-F system.[24] The content is presented separately, grouped according to type, for example, letters, words, and reading texts. Content, lesson, and item programs can be identified, but they are not consistently separated. They are combined with other material in a sequence of steps that refer as needed to teaching material, testing, and recording procedures and detailed presentations of tutoring procedures. The latter correspond most closely to item programs. The lesson programs utilize bypass, remedial, and review loops that are controlled by written records of student performance and the inclusion and omission of flash cards as the student succeeds or fails on particular items. Item programs are worded differently for use with different teaching materials, but they have the same general form, which reflects the S-R-F system. In the

23. John E. George, "Dropout Prevention Project: Final Report," Faculty Research Grant Study, University of Missouri, August 1974.

24. Grant Von Harrison, *Beginning Reading 1: A Professional Guide for the Lay Tutor* (Provo, Utah: Brigham Young University Press, 1972).

example shown in figure 1, Step 2 will be recognized as an item program, Steps 3 and 4 as a lesson program.

STEP 1	Tell the student that this exercise will help him learn to sound out new words.
STEP 2	Point to the first word and ask the student to *sound* it out.

STEP 1   Tell the student that this exercise will help him learn to sound out new words.
STEP 2   Point to the first word and ask the student to *sound* it out.
     a. If the student reads the word correctly, praise him; then go on to the next word.
     b. If the student is unable to read the word or reads it incorrectly, have him make the individual sounds in the word separately and then assist him in blending the sounds.
    Example:
    Word: "THIN"
    Tutor: Place your finger over the last two letters in the word and ask: "What sound does the *th* make?" If the student answers correctly, praise him and go to the next sound. If he answers incorrectly or fails to answer, tell him the sound and have him repeat it. Follow the same procedure for each sound in the word, and then show him how to blend the separate sounds.
STEP 3   Follow step 2 for each word on the sheet.
    Note: *Acceptable performance is reading each word with no pause or break between the various sounds (e.g., "fan," not "f . . . an"). Do not go to the next step until the student can read every word in a particular decoding exercise without hesitation and with no breaks between the various sounds. If a student has a short attention span, do not have him read every word in the longer decoding exercises in one session.*
STEP 4   At the end of the session, praise the student.
STEP 5   Fill out your tutor log.

FIG. 1. Detail program instructions on procedures to follow when student is reading words in the decoding exercises

Source: Grant Von Harrison, *Beginning Reading 1: A Professional Guide for the Lay Tutor* (Provo, Utah: Brigham Young University Press, 1972), p. 101.

As the last sentence in Step 3 suggests, programming is not complete; however, such instructions, which require the tutor to use professional judgment, are relatively infrequent in Harrison's material.

An early version of this program was evaluated in a study which examined the effect of using tutor-training procedures and professional versus nonprofessional trainers. These variables were compared statistically in terms of the tutors' mastery of the tutoring procedures as measured by observation scales developed especially

for the purpose, and the tutees' performance on a reading achievement test. The effects of both variables were large and statistically
significant at the .01 level. The trained tutors averaged 80 percent
on the tutor observation scales; the untrained control group averaged 13 percent. The mean criterion score for learners tutored by
the trained tutors was 76.5. For untrained tutors the mean was 29.4.
Criterion scores for learners whose tutors were trained by nonprofessionals were higher than for those whose tutors were trained
by professionals, but the difference was not statistically significant.

Rosenbaum has reported several examples of Peer-Mediated Instruction that have been highly successful for tutoring in remedial
reading and mathematics at the secondary level and in other subject areas.[25] Content and operational programs are separated. The
content programs are derived from teaching material developed
by others for classroom purposes, but modified in format to suit
the requirements of the operational programs. Lessons or exercises,
each consisting of a number of items (up to 100), are assembled in
a "teachers' book" that contains answers and a "students' book"
that does not.

One general form of item program has been adapted to the
tutoring of a variety of content. A typical flowchart is shown in
figure 2. In this program, the student is first presented with the item
problem. If he answers correctly, he is reinforced and goes on to
the next item. If he makes a mistake, the error is identified for him
and the problem is presented again. If he succeeds on this second
try, he goes on; if not, the tutor again identifies the error, demonstrates the correct response, and then goes to the next item.

The basic lesson program in Peer-Mediated Instruction utilizes
a remedial loop design. The criterion for passing a lesson typically
permits errors or omissions on ten percent of the items. If the
criterion is met, the student goes on to a more advanced lesson; if
not, the student may repeat the lesson or go to an appropriate
remedial lesson. The judgments on which feedback is based in both
item and lesson programs are maximally objective, and the decisions
based on them are clearly specified so that no professional expertise
is required. As a consequence, the training of tutors is a relatively

25. Peter S. Rosenbaum, *Peer-Mediated Instruction* (New York: Teachers
College Press, 1973).

simple process. If the trainee can read and is willing to follow instructions, training consists chiefly of familiarization with the format of the teaching material and instructions, and providing sufficient practice to minimize error.

Rosenbaum's Peer-Mediated Instruction has yielded substantial improvement in achievement scores in three evaluation studies, each of which involved an application of his operational programs to a different content or student population. The general setting in each case was a remedial classroom in which the students were paired randomly and took the roles of tutor and tutee alternately.

In the first study the tutees were adults, new employees enrolled in a 100-hour remedial class because of poor performance on employee qualifying tests. The controls were a previous class of ethnically similar students with test scores not significantly different from those of the group tutored with Peer-Mediated Instruction. Reading vocabulary scores increased considerably, as did the proportion gaining one year or more grade equivalent in one hundred hours of instruction and in fifty hours. In his summary, Rosenbaum writes that this application of Peer-Mediated Instruction was "roughly twice as effective and four times as efficient as the conventional methodology with which it was compared."[26]

In a large-scale comparison study of remedial reading at the secondary level, Rosenbaum reported mean gains of 0.1 years grade equivalent for twenty-four conventionally taught classes and 0.7 years for twenty-four similar classes in which approximately fifty percent of the conventional instruction was replaced by Peer-Mediated Instruction.[27] In a similar study of remedial mathematics instruction involving approximately one fifth as many students, the mean gain was 0.2 years for the conventionally taught classes and 0.6 years for the Peer-Mediated Instruction classes.

The Programed Reading Tutorial procedures developed by Ellson et al. for tutoring in beginning reading, and adaptations of these developed by Ronshausen for tutoring in beginning mathematics, are similar in principle to those of Rosenbaum's Peer-

26. Ibid., p. 178.

27. Peter S. Rosenbaum, "The Brandeis PMI Reading Project: Mid-year Report," The Peer-Mediated Instruction Project, Horace Mann-Lincoln Institute (New York: Teachers College, Columbia University, April 1974).

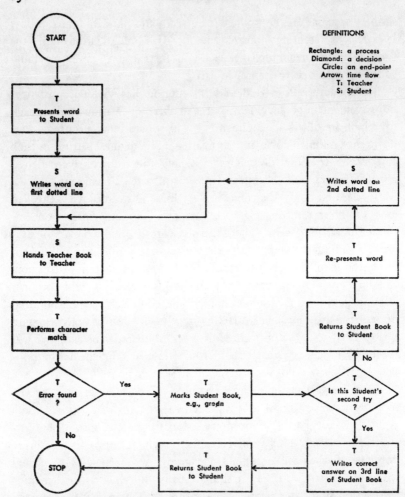

DEFINITIONS

Rectangle: a process
Diamond: a decision
Circle: an end-point
Arrow: time flow
T: Teacher
S: Student

FIG. 2. Item program flowchart for Rosenbaum's Peer-Mediated Instruction
Source: Peter S. Rosenbaum, *Peer-Mediated Instruction* (New York: Teachers College Press, 1973), p. 50.

Mediated Instruction.[28] They differ chiefly in the greater number and complexity of item and lesson programs. As many as eleven item programs may be used for tutoring in reading at one grade

28. Douglas G. Ellson et al., "Programed Tutoring: A Teaching Aid and a Research Tool," *Reading Research Quarterly* 1 (Fall 1965): 77-127; Ellson, Harris, and Barber, "A Field Test"; Nina L. Ronshausen, "Programed Tutoring as a Method for Providing Individualized One-to-one Instruction in First Grade Mathematics," *Improving Human Performance: A Research Quarterly* 3, no. 3 (1974): 118-77; idem, "Programed Tutoring: An Instructional Method for Primary School Mathematics," *Educational Technology* 15 (January 1975): 22-27.

level, and as many as fifteen for tutoring in mathematics. This variety and complexity was made necessary because of the lower grade levels at which the programs are applied and the variety of teaching functions represented. In describing his mathematics program, Rosenbaum says, "The PMI Math program is merely a drill-and-practice adjunct to a math curriculum, and not a replacement for a total program."[29] Although Ellson's programs have ordinarily been used as adjuncts to classroom teaching, there is evidence that they can stand alone.[30] However, because of their complexity (and the obvious limitations of students), these programs are not adapted to peer tutoring at the primary levels where they have been most widely used. Tutors have typically been paid nonprofessionals with a high school diploma, but underachieving students from grades six through twelve have also been successful as tutors.

The reading tutorials use three lesson programs. All of these provide for remedial loops within lessons only, chiefly by recycling students on failed items until they achieve a criterion of mastery. The mathematics tutorials contain two lesson programs, one a within-lesson program taken without change from the reading tutorials, the other a bypass program that assigns or omits entire lessons on the basis of performance on special lessons that also serve as diagnostic placement tests.

The item programs in both the reading and the mathematics tutorials are similar in outline to the basic Peer-Mediated Instruction item program, but they are generally more complex, and the underlying teaching procedure differs. All of the Programed Reading Tutorial item programs use a teaching algorithm called "brightening" to indicate that it is an inverse of the "fading" algorithm commonly used in programmed learning. In brightening, the item-problem is first presented in a relatively difficult form, for example, once, with no supporting prompts. If the learner responds adequately, he is reinforced and goes on. If not, the brightening process begins: a series of prompts are presented that progressively

29. Peter S. Rosenbaum, "The Bushwick PMI Math Project: Mid-year Report," The Peer-Mediated Instruction Project, Horace Mann-Lincoln Institute (New York: Teachers College, Columbia University, April 1974).

30. Ellson et al., "Programed Tutoring"; Leonard C. Kampwerth, "An Experimental Study of Programmed Tutoring for Reading Instruction of Mental Retardates" (Ph.D. diss., Indiana University, September 1970).

increase the probability of an adequate response. For example, if the problem were to point to a picture of Jack in order to demonstrate understanding of an instruction-sentence such as "Point to Jack," which the learner, a beginning reader, had just read, an appropriately cascaded sequence of prompts might be:

From the content program:

1. The printed instruction sentence, "Point to Jack," and a picture in which a boy appears.

From a comprehension item program:

2. Wait (to increase duration of S).
3. "Read it again."
4. "Read it again, faster."
5. "What does it say?"
6. "What does it tell you to do?"
7. "Do what it tells you to do."

For a beginning reader who is very poorly prepared, such a sequence can be extended with further prompts. Such further prompts would be designed to provide him with missing prerequisites, such as the meaning of the word "point", or the notion that a printed sentence can have the same meaning as an oral instruction. For example:

8. "Point to the window."
9. "Point to me."
10. "Point to the book."
11. "Point to the sentence."
12. "Now, what does the sentence tell you to do?"
13. "Do what it tells you to do."

The prompt sequence is designed to increase progressively the likelihood of an acceptable response, terminating with a probability of approximately 1.00. The sequence of prompts is followed until an acceptable response occurs; the response is then reinforced, and the next item presented. The learner is never given a solution to the problem directly (as he is in the fading procedure), but the sequence almost forces him to find a solution, providing whatever help is necessary along the way. Thus the brightening procedure is actually a simple form of the discovery method.

These Programed Reading Tutorials and various applications have been developed over a fifteen-year period on the basis of some fifty formative and evaluative studies. Although conditions have been identified under which the programs are relatively ineffective, most evaluations have shown that, properly administered, they produce significant improvement in reading achievement scores when tutored and untutored children are compared. Effectiveness has also been evaluated in terms of indicators other than test scores. In a number of follow-up studies it has been found that the proportion of nonreaders (children who obtain chance scores or lower on reading achievement tests at the end of the first grade) has been reduced by a factor of twelve, from 9.3 percent to 0.8 percent.[31] Retentions (that is, nonpromotions) have been reduced by as much as 66 percent, from 28.1 percent to 9.5 percent, and assignments to special education classes by a factor of four, from 12.2 percent to 3.0 percent.

Ronshausen's Programed Math Tutorial is an adaptation of the general plan of Ellson's Programed Reading Tutorials to the tutoring of beginning mathematics.[32] Programs have been developed for the kindergarten, first grade, and second grade. Since there is greater uniformity in the beginning mathematics curriculum than in beginning reading, it was possible to devise a single content program that was suitable for use with a number of mathematics textbooks. While the sequence differs from that in some mathematics textbooks (since they differ from each other), the overlap in objectives is large.

One of the lesson programs differs markedly from any of those used in the reading tutorials. Sets of related lessons begin with a test lesson consisting of a sample of the skills included in the remaining lessons of the set. The child's successes and failures on the test lesson determine which of the remaining lessons are presented and which are omitted.

There is relatively little overlap between the specific teaching operations of mathematics and those of reading. There are excep-

31. Ellson, "The Effect of Programed Tutoring."

32. Ronshausen, "Programed Tutoring . . . in First Grade Mathematics"; idem, "Programed Tutoring . . . for Primary School Mathematics."

tions: a program designed to teach a child to read a sentence, if he knows the meaning of the aural words it contains, can also be used to teach mathematical notation to a child who understands and can use the notation in its aural form. Psychologically the two processes are the same, and therefore the teaching procedures can be the same. But, with a few exceptions of this kind, the item programs for mathematics necessarily differ from those developed for the teaching of reading. Ronshausen's list of fifteen item programs includes procedures specifically designed to teach counting, basic addition and subtraction, primary number sentences, place value, and the like, which have no counterpart in the Programed Reading Tutorials.

In many respects, however, the item programs used in the reading and mathematics tutorials are similar. They use the same format, which specifies the objective of the program, the procedure, and the words to be used in presenting the problem or type of problem the item represents. They define acceptable and unacceptable responses and specify the procedure to follow each. Correct responses are praised, and the tutor goes on to the next item. Errors are ostensibly ignored; that is, the tutee is not explicitly told that he has made an error. Instead, the tutor begins a teaching procedure appropriate to the problem and the type of error, using the same brightening process as in the reading programs.

Although performance in mathematics is not directly comparable with that in reading, the effectiveness of the mathematics tutorials appears to be equivalent to that of the reading tutorials. In a terminal evaluation, test score gains were comparable to those achieved with the Programed Reading Tutorials.

Estimates of the Cost-effectiveness of Tutoring

Because of the one-to-one pupil-teacher ratio it involves, tutoring is generally considered to be a luxury, at best an expensive necessity. But some of the data presented above indicate that it can be highly effective as a teaching procedure and that, with recently developed techniques, it can yield excellent results with nonprofessionals (even unpaid students) as tutors. This suggests that the cost-effectiveness of tutoring should be reexamined. Some of the lines such a reexamination might take are suggested below.

For meeting certain clearly definable educational objectives, it appears that some forms of tutoring can be many times as effective as classroom teaching. With measures of effectiveness, such as proportions of nonreaders, retentions, and assignments to special education, ratios of three to twelve have been reported. When the input of teaching or tutoring time is considered, these improvements can become even more significant. For a course in which mean vocabulary score gains for a tutored group were 12.5, as compared with 9.7 for a conventionally taught comparison group, Rosenbaum reported that 74 percent of the tutored students finished in less than half the time allowed for conventional teaching, and none required more time.[33] The duration of Ellson's tutorials is fifteen minutes daily, less than thirty hours per year, compared to two hours daily or 240 hours per year estimated for classroom reading instruction. The corresponding multiplier is eight.

Cost factors resulting from a technology that enables nonprofessionals to teach effectively are also favorable. Salaries for nonprofessional programmed tutors are approximately one-third those for classroom teachers, and nonsalary costs are probably in the same proportion. Thus, given the assumption that teaching salaries are eighty percent of total educational costs, one can calculate that the (nonsalary) costs for *unpaid* tutors are one-fifteenth the total cost for professional teachers.

The cost-effectiveness of tutoring that can be calculated on the basis of some of these figures is impressive, if not spectacular. For example, in achieving the objective of reducing the proportion of nonreaders among disadvantaged first graders, adult nonprofessionals using programmed tutoring were ninety-six times as effective as the classroom teacher (effectiveness-improvement factor: twelve; time-reduction factor: eight). Allowing for the difference in salary (×3) and the fact that the classroom teacher works with thirty children compared with the tutors' one (÷ 30), we estimate that the tutoring was 9.6 times as cost-effective as classroom teaching. If underachieving high school student tutors, unpaid, were as effective as these adult tutors (which, data indicate, they are not, quite), they would be forty-eight times as cost-effective as classroom teachers for achieving the objective in question.

33. Rosenbaum, *Peer-Mediated Instruction.*

Another calculation provides an estimate of the cost-effectiveness that can be achieved by tutoring for a different objective. In one study, assignments to special education classes were reduced by 28.5 years for each 100 pupil-years of tutoring in reading in first-grade classes.[34] In 1974, the cost of regular classroom teaching in the United States was reported to be $1100 per child per year.[35] Assuming that classroom enrollments average thirty, that special education class enrollments average twelve, and that other costs are prorated on the consequent ratio of 2.5 to 1, we estimate the cost of one child-year in a special education class to be $2750. On these assumptions, the saving is $1650 a year for each child not assigned to a special education class, or $47,250 for 28.5 child-years. The 1974 cost of the tutoring required to produce this saving in one representative urban community was $19,600 (salary plus twenty percent). The resulting ratio of cost-reduction to cost is 2.4 to 1.

These calculations are valid, of course, only to the extent that the data on which they are based can be reproduced. Duplication may not be possible since the data were selected. On the other hand, most programs that yielded these data are little more than first attempts, based on limited research and development, and have too short a history to have demonstrated their full potential. Since these programs are reproducible (in ways that the art of a teaching genius is not), it should be possible to apply the knowledge-accumulative methods of science to their refinement. In that case, these data and calculations may betoken far-reaching improvements in education.

Summary

Tutoring is rather generally considered to be an ideal method of teaching for certain objectives, an effective remedy for some of the inadequacies of the more economical classroom method. Recent objective evaluation studies indicate that this faith in the efficacy of one-to-one instruction must be qualified; many, if not most, such evaluations have shown no significant effect on measures of aca-

34. Ellson, "The Effect of Programed Tutoring."

35. National Center for Educational Statistics, *Conditions of Education: 1975* (Washington, D.C.: United States Government Printing Office, 1975).

demic achievement, affect, or other behavior. Other studies, however, indicate that under some conditions tutoring can be extremely effective, even in the hands of tutors with minimal qualifications. In several studies, some objective measure of effectiveness was substantially increased when tutoring was compared with conventional teaching. Examination of these studies suggested that critical conditions for successful tutoring by nonprofessionals are (a) intensive training and supervision by professionals (in unstructured tutoring programs) or (b) highly structured programs that the tutors are required to follow in detail. Since programs that satisfy the first condition are in principle not fully describable (and those that satisfy the second condition have the advantage of being transportable), only examples of the latter are examined in detail.

These examples of structured or programmed tutoring have a number of features in common. All were developed on the basis of clearly conceived and limited objectives, detailed analysis of the subject matter to be taught, and empirical formative evaluation. Although these examples differ greatly in organization and presentational format, three additional common features can be identified: (a) a content program, which determines the systematic arrangement of the subject matter and its presentation in the form of teaching materials; (b) lesson programs, which perform a diagnostic-prescriptive function, controlling presentation, omission, or repetition of items of content on the basis of feedback to the tutor from tutee responses; and (c) item programs, which control actual teaching interactions such as the presentation of particular items, the tutor's classification of tutee responses (basically, as acceptable or unacceptable), and feedback to the tutee contingent upon that classification. Subject matter organization and the diagnostic-prescriptive function are related to Gagné's learning hierarchy theory, and teaching operations are related to stimulus-response-feedback theory.

Tutoring is also discussed as a form of delegation that relieves the overload of individualized instruction imposed on the classroom teacher by recent social-educational changes. Finally, estimates of the cost-effectiveness of programmed tutoring indicate that it is an extremely promising approach to the improvement of certain kinds of achievement without substantial increases in the financial cost of education.

CHAPTER VI

The Discussion Method

MEREDITH D. GALL
and
JOYCE P. GALL

It is coming to be recognized that there is nothing of concern to human beings which may not profitably be discussed in the right spirit, by the right persons, at the right time. This is why the downfall of an effete dogma, the abandonment of an unwise policy, a harmful practice, a vicious custom, or a wasteful process, is prompter now than ever before. . . . It is because that great radical, Discussion, invades every department of life and hurries to a close long-smouldering conflicts, that ours is such a revolutionary epoch.[1]

By the use of such hyperbole Edward Alsworth Ross extolled the discussion method in one of the first textbooks of social psychology, published in 1908. Ross's enthusiasm for the discussion method in American society is shared by contemporary educators. For example, in their manual for teachers, Stanford and Stanford claimed that the discussion method helps students ". . . to solve problems, to air opinions, to find out what others think, to vent feelings, to clarify one's point of view, to re-evaluate one's opinions, and to gain feelings of acceptance and belonging."[2]

This chapter, too, is motivated by enthusiasm for the discussion method. But we realize that classroom discussions are frequently boring, aimless, and even threatening to some participants.[3] Discussions are intended to promote student involvement and thinking about problems and issues, yet researchers have found that discus-

1. Edward A. Ross, *Social Psychology: An Outline and Source Book* (New York: The Macmillan Co., 1908), pp. 309-10.

2. Gene Stanford and Barbara Dodds Stanford, *Learning Discussion Skills through Games* (New York: Citation Press, 1969), p. 15.

3. J. R. Applegate, "Why Don't Pupils Talk in Class Discussions?" *Clearing House* 44 (October 1969): 78-81.

sions in elementary school are characterized by a preponderance of teacher talk and fact questions.[4] At the high school level, researchers have found that teachers without special training in issue-oriented discussions seldom identify the issue under discussion, seldom ask students to substantiate their opinions, and engage only infrequently in other techniques considered desirable.[5] Furthermore, student-to-student interaction is infrequent, even though it is regarded as one of the distinctive attributes of the discussion method.

The purpose of this chapter is to review research on the discussion method, whether conducted in laboratory, business, or school settings. We seek knowledge that can make the discussion method a more reliable and effective tool in the hands of teachers. The knowledge is of three types: (a) knowledge about group processes that facilitate or hinder discussion effectiveness, (b) knowledge about learning outcomes that are effectively promoted by the discussion method, and (c) knowledge about student characteristics that interact with the discussion method to produce positive or negative learning effects. On the basis of available knowledge we offer tentative answers to the questions most likely to be asked by the teacher—Why should I use the discussion method? When? How? And with whom?

The body of the chapter has four sections. First, we describe attributes of the discussion method that distinguish it from other teaching methods. The second section reviews research on group dynamics that affect discussion processes and outcomes. The third section reviews studies in which the discussion method as a whole is compared with other teaching methods. Finally, we consider the few available studies concerning the interaction between student characteristics and effects of the discussion method.

The scope of the review is not limited to particular grade or developmental levels. The discussion method is used from graduate

4. Meredith D. Gall, "The Use of Questions in Teaching," *Review of Educational Research* 40 (December 1970): 707-21.

5. Morris K. Lai et al., *Main Field Test Report, Discussing Controversial Issues*, Report No. A72-12 (San Francisco, Cal.: Far West Laboratory for Educational Research and Development, 1972); Byron G. Massialas and N. F. Sprague, *Dialogue Patterns: Styles of Classroom Discourse in the Teaching of Social Issues* (Ann Arbor, Mich.: University of Michigan, 1970).

school down to the early grade levels, although it may tend to become the recitation method in the latter settings.[6]

The discussion method has been developed in a variety of forms. The range of possible variants is well illustrated by Potter and Andersen.[7] In this chapter we limit our scope to methods in which cognitive outcomes are of primary concern—subject matter mastery discussions, issue-oriented discussions, problem solving by groups, and brainstorming. Encounter groups, sensitivity training, and similar methods also involve the discussion method, but since they are directed primarily at bringing about affective learning, we shall not consider them here.

Attributes of the Discussion Method

Definition of the *discussion method* is a prerequisite to interpretation of the research literature. The term "discussion method" has been used to describe a broad variety of classroom interaction patterns. Later in the chapter we shall note the difficulty in combining and interpreting the results of research on discussion effectiveness because the various studies may have used dissimilar operational definitions of the method. Another reason for stressing the problem of definition springs from the view that the effective teacher is one who makes intelligent decisions about which teaching methods to use in a particular instructional context. Before teachers can select a teaching method, they need to know the attributes that distinguish it from other methods.

The following definition of the discussion method [8] postulates five attributes: The discussion method occurs when (1) a group of persons, usually in the roles of moderator-leader and participant, (2) assembles at a designated time and place, (3) to communicate

6. As we note in this chapter, the discussion method is characterized by student-to-student interaction and educational objectives related to complex thinking processes and attitude change. In contrast, the recitation method is characterized by teacher-student interaction and educational objectives related to recall of curriculum content.

7. David Potter and Martin P. Andersen, *Discussion: A Guide to Effective Practice* (Belmont, Cal.: Wadsworth Publishing Co., Inc., 1963).

8. See ibid., p. 1, for a similar definition: "We define [the discussion] simply and prescriptively as the *purposeful, systematic, oral* exchange of *ideas, facts, and opinions* by a *group* of persons who *share in the group's leadership.*"

interactively, (4) using speaking, nonverbal, and listening processes, (5) in order to achieve instructional objectives.

The five attributes do not provide a simple present-absent basis for deciding whether a particular pattern of interaction is or is not a discussion. Rather, each attribute can be analyzed into variables (for example, size of group, duration of discussion, number of student-student interactions), and any specific occurrence of the discussion method can be described in terms of the level at which each variable exists. We shall consider each attribute from this perspective.

A GROUP OF PERSONS

Learning by discussion occurs in a group, that is, "a collection of interacting persons with some degree of reciprocal influence over one another." [9] The notion of reciprocal influence has several important implications, including the possibility that the learning of each student in a group is affected by the behavior of the other individuals in the group. A series of studies, to be reviewed later, has been concerned with the effect of group composition on discussion processes and outcomes. Also, Peckham, Glass, and Hopkins have stressed the notion of reciprocal influence in arguing that the proper unit for statistical analysis of data from research on instructional methods involving groups is the group, not the individual. [10]

Discussion group members often play different roles. One person may be the designated leader or moderator, while the others are the participants. This pattern can vary, however, as in the leaderless discussion group, in which there is no designated leader and leadership functions are shared among the group members.

ASSEMBLY

The discussion method requires that the group of learners be able to assemble, although this requirement can be circumvented, as in conference phone calls or situations in which homebound

9. Richard A. Schmuck and Patricia A. Schmuck, *Group Processes in the Classroom*, 2nd ed. (Dubuque, Iowa: William C. Brown, 1975), p. 6.

10. Percy D. Peckham, Gene V Glass, and Kenneth D. Hopkins, "The Experimental Unit in Statistical Analysis," *Journal of Special Education* 3 (Winter 1969): 337-49.

students are linked by telephone to a classroom. Once the group is assembled, the discussion can vary in length, from a few minutes (as in a "buzz group") to several hours or longer.

In view of the logistical requirements of discussion groups, the teaching method of choice may be independent study when it is difficult to assemble students. In economic terms, assembly becomes a cost [11] when doing a cost-benefit analysis of the discussion method compared with other teaching methods.

INTERACTIVE COMMUNICATION

The main business of the discussion group members is to communicate with each other—to state one's own ideas and to react to the ideas of others. The communication is interactive in at least three ways. First, the person who has the floor addresses his or her remarks to the entire group. Second, the communication is distributed among group members. Third, the sequence of participation is not highly predetermined.

In practice, classroom discussions tend to be low in interaction. Students customarily address their remarks to the teacher rather than to their peers. The teacher tends to dominate the discussion in terms of talk. Schmuck and Schmuck suggested that some teachers discourage discussions with a high degree of interaction because they believe that such discussions will lead to a disorderly classroom.[12] We prefer to describe patterns of classroom communication in which student-student interaction is low while teacher-student interaction is high as instances of the recitation method.

SPEAKING, OBSERVATIONAL, AND LISTENING PROCESSES

A distinctive attribute of the discussion method is that it provides the learner with the opportunity to assimilate information through the use of listening and observational processes. For example, in reading about an issue, the primary stimulus is the printed word, which may not stimulate the student to think productively about the issue. In discussion, however, the stimulus situation is quite different. As listeners, students are responding to the spoken word

11. The school incurs the costs of providing an instructor and a physical location. Students may incur transportation costs.

12. Schmuck and Schmuck, *Group Processes in the Classroom*, pp. 180-83.

(both the literal word and tone of voice). As observers, they are responding to nonverbal signals, such as facial expressions, gestures, and movement.

In addition to exposure to others' ideas, discussion provides opportunity for students to shape their own ideas. Ideas may be generated in solitary reflection or by composing them in written form; discussion provides a third method—the expression of ideas in speech. Furthermore, discussion provides immediate group feedback that may help the speaker further shape his or her ideas. In contrast, individual reflection and writing only provide feedback from oneself, at least until the learner shares his or her reflections or writing with others.

The modalities of speech, sight, and listening engaged by discussion are critical for conceptualizing the instructional benefits of discussion. As will be noted below, the modality issue is important in designing measurement tools for use in research on discussion effects.

INSTRUCTIONAL OBJECTIVES

Different instructional objectives have been proposed for subject matter mastery discussions, issue-oriented discussions, and problem-solving discussions.

The first type of discussion is focused on subject matter mastery. Usually the teacher has students read or view the curriculum in class and as homework. This activity is preceded or followed by class discussion. In discussion the teaching is focused on higher cognitive processes, whereas in recitation the focus is on "reciting" to the teacher the information that one has read.

In Hill's discussion model for subject matter mastery, students first read curriculum material and then participate in a discussion with approximately the following agenda: terms and concepts in the curriculum selection, the author's message, major themes and subtopics, integration of the material with other knowledge, application of the material, and evaluation of the author's presentation.[13] Discussions of this type are characterized by teacher questions at the comprehension, analysis, application, synthesis, and evaluation

13. William Fawcett Hill, *Learning thru Discussion*, rev. ed. (Beverly Hills, Cal.: SAGE Publications, Inc., 1969).

levels of Bloom's taxonomy of cognitive objectives.[14] Most questions in recitations are at the knowledge level.

Gage and Berliner stated that a broad goal of the second type of discussion, the issue-oriented discussion, is to change student attitudes.[15] Stanford and Stanford suggested that discussion of issues can help students become more aware of their own point of view and of what others think.[16] Joyce and Weil have derived a variety of instructional objectives from the jurisprudential model of Oliver and Shaver for discussing public issues.[17] The main objectives are to help students develop (a) intellectual skills in analyzing and resolving public issues, (b) a commitment to pluralism and social action, and (c) a respect for the point of view and dignity of one's fellow man.

The central concept for organizing the objectives of issue-oriented discussion is *attitude*. Social psychologists generally analyze attitudes into three components: cognitive (ideas, beliefs), affective (feelings), and psychomotor (social action). At the most basic level, the goal of issue-oriented discussion is to increase awareness and understanding of others' attitudes—their beliefs, feelings, and actions. The next goal is to help students analyze critically and evaluate their own and others' attitudes. The third goal is to modify one's attitudes in a way consistent with the results of one's analysis and evaluation. A fourth goal might be to change others' attitudes, particularly if the group is trying to achieve consensus.

The purpose of the third type of discussion is to help a group of persons to solve a problem. The important thing to note in this purpose is the emphasis on a problem that is shared by the discussion group and, as an instructional outcome, on a solution to which the group is committed. Thus, the effectiveness of a problem-solving group should be measured not only by the originality or brilliance

14. Benjamin S. Bloom, ed., *Taxonomy of Educational Objectives: The Classification of Educational Goals, Handbook I: Cognitive Domain* (New York: David McKay Co., 1956).

15. N. L. Gage and David C. Berliner, *Educational Psychology* (Chicago: Rand McNally & Co., 1975), p. 472.

16. Stanford and Stanford, *Learning Discussion Skills through Games*, p. 15.

17. Bruce Joyce and Marsha Weil, *Models of Teaching* (Englewood Cliffs, N.J.: Prentice-Hall, 1972).

of the solution, but also by the degree of the group's commitment to the solution.

Another objective of the discussion method, irrespective of discussion type, is to assist students in improving their discussion skills. As Gage and Berliner observed:

. . . working together in groups requires skills that must be learned. . . . The ability to listen to others, to evaluate their arguments, to formulate one's own views in the heat of give-and-take, to resist the influence on one's reasoning of personal likes and dislikes for others, to continue to focus on the problem at hand despite emotional arguments and influences —these skills require practice in discussion.[18]

It appears then, that discussion effectiveness can be evaluated from two aspects: the level of skill in discussion and what the members have learned. The assumption of many training programs, usually untested, has been that the higher the level of discussion skill that teacher and students display, the more each member will learn from the discussion.

Other objectives for the discussion method relate to its motivational effects. Discussions may motivate students to learn by providing them with an opportunity to satisfy the need to talk and to interact with their peers. This feature of discussion may be particularly important in instructional settings where students tend otherwise to be isolated from each other.

These motivational properties of the discussion method, because they are potentially rewarding, may enhance other learning outcomes, may contribute to class morale and to a positive attitude toward instruction, and may compel students to find out what they do and do not know. A short-answer test or essay test may serve the last-mentioned purpose. But a student may not care as much about this form of feedback as about feedback that reveals to his peers what he knows and does not know. Although students may not be willing to acquire additional information for self-edification, they may want to do so in order to share and demonstrate their knowledge before peers in a group situation.

The discussion method serves an important feedback purpose for the teacher as well. Discussion is an efficient method by which

18. Gage and Berliner, *Educational Psychology*, p. 470.

teachers can evaluate students' entry or exit levels of understanding of a subject matter area. Tests are also useful evaluation techniques, but they are much more time-consuming for the teacher and the students. The discussion method allows learning and the evaluation of learning to occur at the same time.

Discussion Group Dynamics

Social psychology, particularly group dynamics, has made great progress in recent decades in identifying factors that facilitate or hinder group functioning. Although much of the research has occurred in laboratory or industrial settings, the findings are pertinent to use of the discussion method in classroom teaching.

Five major variables from research on group dynamics will be considered: group size, group composition, group cohesiveness, communication patterns, and leadership. Our review will focus on how each of these variables affects interpersonal processes in the group and group performance, that is, subject matter mastery, attitude change, and problem solving.

GROUP SIZE

Probably no variable in social psychology is more obvious and easier to measure than group size; it involves merely counting the number of people in a group or other social unit. Yet no aspect of the group is more critical to its effective functioning.

Gage and Berliner used group size to categorize teaching methods, indicating that the methods of tutoring, programmed instruction, individually prescribed instruction, and independent study are most appropriate in working with one student, the discussion method with a "a small group of perhaps two to twenty students," classroom teaching ("a mixture of the other methods with some characteristics of its own") for groups of twenty to forty students, and the lecture method for groups of forty or more students.[19] Whereas the lecture method tends to minimize the significance of group size (the same lecture can be presented before an audience of one or one thousand), the effects of group size are heightened in the discussion group because of the necessity for member participation and group performance.

19. Ibid., p. 447.

Effects of group size on interpersonal processes. Hare reviewed sociological research on small groups and maintained that the optimum group is five, noting that:

Below this size, members complain that the group is too small . . . (and) above the size of five, members complain that the group is too large, and this may be due to the restriction on the amount of participation.[20]

Hare also emphasized the desirability of an *odd* number of group members. He pointed out that a strict deadlock is not possible in a group with an odd number of members, and, furthermore, that the tendency in a group of five would be to split into a majority of three and a minority of two, so that being in a minority would not isolate a single individual.

The generally higher satisfaction of members in smaller as opposed to larger groups may result, in part, from the increased opportunities for participation that the smaller group provides each member. Studies have shown that as group size increases, the average number of remarks per member and the percentage of members who participate in a discussion decreases.[21] Furthermore, there is a decrease in the average number of ideas volunteered for the solution of a problem.[22]

Stephan and Mishler have shown that as group size increases, the most talkative member (in academic groups, usually the teacher) continues to contribute about 40 percent of the total communication, but the difference between the percentage of his talk and that of each other group member increases.[23] Their data concerning communication curves for groups of four, six, and eight support Hare's conclusion that a group size of five is optimal, since in the groups

20. Alexander Paul Hare, *Handbook of Small Group Research* (New York: Free Press, 1962), p. 243.

21. Helen C. Dawe, "The Influence of Size of Kindergarten Group upon Performance," *Child Development* 5 (December 1934): 295-303; Frederick F. Stephan and Elliott G. Mishler, "The Distribution of Participation in Small Groups: An Experimental Approximation," *American Sociological Review* 17 (October 1952): 598-608.

22. Cecil A. Gibb, "An Experimental Approach to the Study of Leadership," *Occupational Psychology* 25 (October 1951): 233-48.

23. Stephan and Mishler, "The Distribution of Participation in Small Groups."

of six or eight, one or more members contributed less than 10 percent each to the total communication, whereas in the four-member groups even the least talkative member was able to participate over 10 percent of the time.

Effects of group size on performance. Thelen suggested that the ideal group would be the smallest one that contains all the skills required for the accomplishment of the group task.[24] Assuming that the task requirements and the range of relevant skills of potential group members are known, we could then specify an optimal group size for a given task. In a study of the relationship between group size and productivity in creative problem-solving groups, South compared the performance of three-member and six-member groups on concrete problems, such as judging emotions from photographs or rating English compositions, and on abstract problems, such as logical reasoning tasks.[25] The smaller groups were faster and more accurate on the concrete problems, whereas the larger groups were superior in solving the abstract problems.

Research on group size and academic achievement has concentrated upon grades, which are subject to instructor bias and limited to individual rather than group performance. The studies are fairly consistent, however, in finding that students in smaller classes using the discussion method received higher grades or examination scores. But the relationship may hold only in groups whose size varies within a certain range: Cheydleur compared classes ranging in size from nine to thirty-three; Mueller found similar results with classes of twenty and forty students; and Schellenberg worked with discussion groups of four, six, eight, and ten students.[26] In contrast, class size was not found to be related to student achievement by Edmonson and Mulder, who compared classes of forty-five

24. Herbert A. Thelen, "Group Dynamics in Instruction: The Principle of Least Group Size," *School Review* 57 (March 1949): 139-48.

25. Earl B. South, "Some Psychological Aspects of Committee Work," *Journal of Applied Psychology* 11 (December 1927): 437-64.

26. Frederick D. Cheydleur, "Criteria of Effective Teaching in Basic French Courses at the University of Wisconsin," in *Bulletin of the University of Wisconsin* (Madison, Wis.: Bureau of Guidance and Records, University of Wisconsin, 1945); A. D. Mueller, "Class Size as a Factor in Normal School Instruction," *Education* 45 (December 1924): 203-27; J. A. Schellenberg, "Group Size as a Factor in Success of Academic Discussion Groups," *Journal of Educational Sociology* 43 (October 1959): 73-79.

and one hundred nine students, both taught by the discussion method, and by Brown, who taught groups of twenty-five and sixty.[27] Probably the "smaller" class size in these studies was beyond the appropriate range for use of the discussion method, which Gage and Berliner defined as two to twenty students.

Implications. There are perhaps several reasons why increases in group size lessen the effectiveness of the discussion group. First, as noted above, a smaller proportion of the members are able to participate as size increases. Second, diversity of individual needs and personalities in a larger group tends to increase the amount of task-irrelevant behavior, thus slowing progress toward the group's goals. Third, as Drucker pointed out in discussing the optimum size of different business organizations, in both biological organisms and social organizations quantitative increases in size are associated with qualitative changes in complexity of the structure needed to support the organism (or organization) so that it can function.[28] Unless the necessary qualitative changes are made in the structure of a discussion group to accommodate the quantitative increase in size (for example, more explicit procedures governing the expression of minority opinions), the group may reach a size where it cannot function effectively.

Since the total instructional group for whom the teacher is responsible is usually much larger than what has been described as optimum, or even acceptable, for a discussion group, the teacher needs to assemble a smaller group to use the discussion method. One effective approach involves organizing the classroom so that most of the students are engaged in independent study, while the teacher works with a small number of students in a discussion group.[29] Another approach is to divide the entire class into small

27. J. B. Edmonson and F. J. Mulder, "Size of Class as a Factor in University Instruction," *Journal of Educational Research* 9 (January 1924): 1-12; Albert E. Brown, "The Effectiveness of Large Classes at the College Level: An Experimental Study Involving the Size Variable and the Size-Procedure Variable," *University of Iowa Studies in Education* 7, no. 3 (1932): 3.

28. Peter Drucker, *Management: Tasks, Responsibilities, Practices* (New York: Harper & Row, 1974).

29. An example of this approach to classroom organization is found in Beatrice A. Ward, *Minicourse 15, Organizing Independent Learning: Intermediate Level* (New York: Macmillan, 1973).

discussion groups, with one student designated as moderator of each group, if necessary, or else with the groups established as leaderless discussion groups. At the college or university level, large lecture classes may include small sections to permit student discussion of material.

GROUP COMPOSITION

How does group composition affect group functioning? Our analysis focuses on the effects of homogeneity versus heterogeneity of group members on interpersonal processes and group performance. Both personality traits and intellectual abilities have been used as a basis for forming homogeneous and heterogeneous groups.

Effects of group composition on interpersonal processes. A number of researchers have found that greater homogeneity among group members with respect to attitudes and interpersonal orientations is associated with greater group cohesiveness.[30] This finding may be explained in terms of the theory of cognitive balance advanced by Heider, which holds that two people will be more attracted to each other the more similar their evaluations of objects in their common environment.[31] Since group cohesiveness is most commonly assessed by summing the degree of attraction between each pair of group members, greater similarity among all member pairs would be associated with higher cohesiveness.

Further evidence of greater cohesiveness in homogeneous groups is found in research in which interpersonal obstacles to group functioning have been investigated. A number of studies have shown that interpersonal conflicts are less likely to occur in homogeneous groups than in heterogeneous groups.[32] Also, splitting the group

30. Theodore M. Newcomb, "Varieties of Interpersonal Attraction," in *Group Dynamics: Research and Theory*, ed. Dorwin Cartwright and Alvin Zander, 2nd ed. (Evanston, Ill.: Row Peterson and Co., 1960); Leon Festinger, "A Theory of Social Comparison Processes," *Human Relations* 7 (May 1954): 117-40; William A. Haythorn et al., "The Behavior of Authoritarian and Equalitarian Personalities in Groups," *Human Relations* 9 (February 1956): 57-74.

31. Fritz Heider, *The Psychology of Interpersonal Relations* (New York: John Wiley & Sons, 1958).

32. E. Paul Torrance, "Can Grouping Control Social Stress in Creative Activities?" *Elementary School Journal* 62 (December 1961): 139-45; Fred E. Fiedler, Willem Meuwese, and Sophie Oonk, "An Exploratory Study of Group Creativity in Laboratory Tasks," *Acta Psychologia* 18 (1961): 100-119; Haythorn et al., "The Behavior of Authoritarian and Equalitarian Personalities."

into opposing subgroups is less likely to occur in homogeneous groups than in heterogeneous groups.[33]

There are some exceptions to the generalization that group homogeneity is associated with higher cohesiveness, however. Seashore, for example, found no relationship between cohesiveness and homogeneity with respect to the age or educational level of industrial work groups.[34] Cartwright suggested that a relationship between homogeneity and cohesiveness was not observed in this study because age and educational level were not relevant to the group's functioning.[35]

Gross has described a situation in which cohesiveness may be associated with greater group heterogeneity rather than with greater group homogeneity.[36] He distinguished two types of informal groups within the Air Force: a symbiotic group, composed of men with dissimilar characteristics, where attraction is based upon different contributions that one member can make to another, and a consensual group, made up of men with similar characteristics. He concluded that symbiotic relationships provide a more enduring basis for attraction than do consensual ones.

Effects of group composition on performance. Research studies have demonstrated that heterogeneity of member background increases the accuracy of perceptual judgments by a group, probably as a result of the cancellation of random errors.[37] The

33. Leon Festinger and John Thibaut, "Interpersonal Communication in Small Groups," *Journal of Abnormal and Social Psychology* 46 (January 1951): 92-99; Harold B. Gerard, "The Effect of Different Dimensions of Disagreement on the Communication Process in Small Groups," *Human Relations* 6 (August 1953): 249-71; Irwin Altman and Elliott McGinnies, "Interpersonal Perception and Communication in Discussion Groups of Varied Attitudinal Composition," *Journal of Abnormal and Social Psychology* 60, no. 3 (1960): 390-95.

34. Stanley Seashore, *Group Cohesiveness in the Industrial Work Group* (Ann Arbor, Mich.: Institute for Social Research, 1954).

35. Dorwin Cartwright, "The Nature of Group Cohesiveness," in *Group Dynamics: Research and Theory*, ed. Dorwin Cartwright and Alvin Zander, 3rd ed. (New York: Harper & Row, 1968), p. 99.

36. Edward Gross, "Symbiosis and Consensus as Integrative Factors in Small Groups," *American Sociological Review* 21 (April 1956): 174-79.

37. Paul R. Farnsworth and M. F. Williams, "The Accuracy of the Median and Mean of a Group of Judgments," *Journal of Social Psychology* 7 (May 1936): 237-39; Robert C. Ziller, "Scales of Judgment: A Determinant of the Accuracy of Group Decisions," *Human Relations* 8 (May 1955): 153-64.

effects of heterogeneity on the types of outcomes of major concern in a discussion group have been less thoroughly researched. Hoffman conducted a study of problem solving in which he formed groups of college students which were homogeneous or heterogeneous with respect to personality profiles on the Guilford-Zimmerman Temperament Survey.[38] Heterogeneous groups showed superior performance on a problem that required multiple perceptions and cognitive reorganizations. No difference between groups was found in the quality of solutions on a second problem, involving role-playing reactions to a change of work procedure suggested by a foreman to a group of workers.

Using this same "change of work procedure" problem, Hoffman, Harburg, and Maier found that the proportion of creative solutions (that is, integrative solutions in which the group arrived at a solution other than merely continuing the existing procedure or accepting the change recommended by the foreman) produced by the mixed-sex groups was slightly greater than that produced by all-male groups, and substantially greater than the proportion produced by all-female groups.[39] In another study, Hoffman and Maier found that females in mixed-sex groups showed greater and more effective effort in group problem solving than those working in all-female groups.[40] These findings suggest that forming heterogeneous (that is, mixed-sex) groups may lead to higher levels of problem-solving performance by female students, whereas the problem solving of male students may be less affected by the group's sex composition.

Mitnick and McGinnies conducted a study of attitude change in which they formed homogeneous discussion groups of students high or low in racial prejudice.[41] This study will be described in

38. L. Richard Hoffman, "Homogeneity of Member Personality and Its Effect on Group Problem Solving," *Journal of Abnormal and Social Psychology* 58 (January 1959): 27-32.

39. L. Richard Hoffman, Ernest Harburg, and Norman R. F. Maier, "Differences and Disagreement as Factors in Creative Group Problem Solving," *Journal of Abnormal and Social Psychology* 64, no. 3 (1962): 206-14.

40. L. Richard Hoffman and Norman R. F. Maier, "Sex Differences, Sex Composition and Group Problem Solving," *Journal of Abnormal and Social Psychology* 63 (March 1961): 435-56.

41. Leonard L. Mitnick and Elliott McGinnies, "Influencing Ethnocentrism in Small Discussion Groups through a Film Communication," *Journal of Abnormal and Social Psychology* 56 (January 1958): 82-90.

more detail later in the chapter; here, the salient finding is that use of the discussion method with homogeneous groups of highly prejudiced students did not lead to attitude change. Instead, the discussions appeared to reinforce the students' preexisting attitudes. This finding suggests that, for at least certain types of students, group homogeneity may be detrimental to attitude change. Placement of these students in heterogeneous discussion groups may be more effective in helping them examine their own and others' opinions critically.

Implications. In conclusion, there appears to be a positive relationship between group homogeneity and cohesiveness. However, homogeneous groups do not appear to be superior in performance to heterogeneous groups, and perform less well under certain conditions. Therefore, insofar as he is free to select the members of a discussion group, the teacher probably should include students who have a variety of perspectives on the topic, and a range of talents relevant to the group's task (for example, students who are good at critical thinking as well as those with interpersonal skills). While interpersonal obstacles are likely to arise over some of the differences between group members, these can be overcome if they are acknowledged and if the group is helped to cope with them. Moreover, over time, the very process of interaction may serve to increase the attraction among group members and reduce the differences which originally hindered group progress.

GROUP COHESIVENESS

In an introductory essay on group cohesiveness Cartwright and Zander ask:

Why is it that the attendance of one group is so irregular as to result in its slow death, while the attendance of another group with similar activities and leadership remains high? What makes a group "healthy" so that its members work harder, make more sacrifices for the group, more readily extol its virtues, seem happier together, interact more often, and agree with one another more readily that do the members of a dying organization? [42]

Social psychologists usually answer these questions by referring to the concept of group cohesiveness, which can be defined as those

42. Dorwin Cartwright and Alvin Zander, "Group Cohesiveness: Introduction," in *Group Dynamics: Research and Theory*, 2nd ed., p. 69.

forces that operate to keep members in the group and prevent them from leaving the group.

While various approaches to measuring cohesiveness have been advanced by social psychologists,[43] the most common approach is to determine how much the members of the group like or are attracted to one another. Looking specifically at the classroom situation, Schmuck and Schmuck noted that: "A cohesive classroom group is made up of students who are actively involved with one another, who care about one another, and who help one another."[44]

A teacher who believes that cohesiveness is a desirable characteristic in a discussion situation may use two approaches to fostering it. First, he may select members for the discussion group who he knows from previous observation (or by obtaining sociometric ratings) like one another. Or second, once the discussion group is formed, he may take steps to encourage cohesiveness. For example, Back successfully created feelings of high cohesiveness in two-person groups by stressing either the personal attractiveness of the members, the importance of the task, or the prestige of membership.[45] Schmuck and Schmuck identified other techniques that may lead to high group cohesiveness: "Cohesive classes can be created by open discussions of expectations, by dispersion of leadership, by developing several friendship clusters, and by the frequent use of two-way communication."[46]

Effects of cohesiveness on interpersonal processes. Studies have found consistently that group cohesiveness has three positive effects on group functioning: (a) improved maintenance of membership and participation in the group, (b) increased communication, and (c) positive personal feelings of members.

The tendency to remain in the group practically follows from

43. A thorough review of the measurement of cohesiveness can be found in Gardner Lindzey and Donn Byrne, "Measurement of Social Choice and Interpersonal Attractiveness," in *Handbook of Social Psychology*, vol. 2, ed. Gardner Lindzey and Elliott Aronson, 2nd ed. (Reading, Mass.: Addison-Wesley, 1969), ch. 14.

44. Schmuck and Schmuck, *Group Processes in the Classroom*, p. 156.

45. Kurt W. Back, "Influence through Social Communication," *Journal of Abnormal and Social Psychology* 46 (January 1951): 9-23.

46. Schmuck and Schmuck, *Group Processes in the Classroom*, p. 164.

the formal definition of group cohesiveness. As expected, measures of cohesiveness (members' attraction to the group) have been found to be related to such independent measures as turnover,[47] duration of membership,[48] and persistence in working toward difficult goals.[49] Wright found that highly cohesive children's playgroups displayed increased cooperative behavior in response to frustration, whereas less cohesive groups did not.[50]

Concerning the relationship between cohesiveness and communication, Homans proposed that: "If the frequency of interaction between two or more persons increases, the degree of their liking for one another will increase, and vice versa."[51] Empirical support for this proposition has been obtained in several research studies, which found a positive relationship between degree of attraction among members of a group and the extent to which they communicated with each other.[52] Also, Back[53] and Dittes and Kelley[54] found increased interaction among group members as a result of manipulated cohesiveness. Yet, differences in the ways in which cohesiveness is produced may lead to different styles of

47. Barry E. Collins, "An Experimental Study of Satisfaction, Productivity, Turnover, and Comparison Levels" (Ph.D. diss., Northwestern University, 1963).

48. Philip C. Sagi, Donald W. Olmsted, and Frank Atelsek, "Predicting Maintenance of Membership in Small Groups," *Journal of Abnormal and Social Psychology* 51 (September 1955): 308-11.

49. Milton W. Horowitz, Joseph Lyons, and Howard Perlmutter, "Induction of Forces in Discussion Groups," *Human Relations* 4 (February 1951): 57-76.

50. M. Erik Wright, "The Influence of Frustration upon the Social Relations of Young Children," *Character and Personality* 12 (December 1943): 111-22.

51. George C. Homans, *The Human Group* (New York: Harcourt, Brace, and World, 1950), p. 112.

52. Leon Festinger et al., "A Study of Rumor: Its Origin and Spread," *Human Relations* 1 (August 1947): 464-86; Albert J. Lott and Bernice E. Lott, "Group Cohesiveness, Communication Level, and Conformity," *Journal of Abnormal and Social Psychology* 62 (March 1961): 408-12.

53. Back, "Influence through Social Communication."

54. J. E. Dittes and Harold H. Kelley, "Effects of Different Conditions of Acceptance upon Conformity to Group Norms," *Journal of Abnormal and Social Psychology* 53 (July 1956): 100-107.

communication. Back found that when cohesiveness was based on personal attraction among members, a long, pleasant discussion was held, whereas when cohesiveness was based upon effective performance of the task, members quickly and efficiently discussed only those matters pertinent to completing the task.

Marquis, Guetzkow, and Heyns[55] and Exline[56] found group cohesiveness to be related to satisfaction and morale of group members. Group cohesiveness has also been found to be related to the absence of nervous or "jumpy" feelings on the job,[57] heightened self-esteem and lowered anxiety,[58] and greater security[59] in individual members. Schmuck and Schmuck asserted that "students who are accepted members of cohesive classrooms with a dispersed friendship structure have the best chances for achieving high self-esteem and for working up to their intellectual potential."[60]

Effects of cohesiveness on performance. In their review of the literature Collins and Raven found a positive relationship between group cohesiveness and group performance in some studies, but not in others.[61] At least two alternative rationales exist as to why a highly cohesive group would not necessarily be higher in productivity. Davis suggested that high arousal may interfere with some tasks: "To the extent that cohesiveness means proximity and

55. Donald G. Marquis, Harold Guetzkow, and Roger W. Heyns, "A Social-Psychological Study of the Decision-making Conference," in *Groups, Leadership and Men: Research in Human Relations*, ed. Harold Guetzkow (Pittsburgh: Carnegie Press, 1951).

56. Ralph V. Exline, "Group Climate as a Factor in the Relevance and Accuracy of Social Perception," *Journal of Abnormal and Social Psychology* 55 (May 1957); 382-88.

57. Seashore, *Group Cohesiveness in the Industrial Work Group.*

58. James W. Julian, Doyle W. Bishop, and Fred E. Fiedler, "Quasi-therapeutic Effects of Intergroup Competition," *Journal of Personality and Social Psychology* 3 (March 1966): 321-27; Albert E. Myers, "Team Competition, Success, and Adjustment of Group Members," *Journal of Abnormal and Social Psychology* 65, no. 5 (1962): 325-32.

59. Albert Pepitone and George Reichling, "Group Cohesiveness and the Expression of Hostility," *Human Relations* 8 (August 1955): 327-37.

60. Schmuck and Schmuck, *Group Processes in the Classroom*, p. 163.

61. Barry E. Collins and Bertram H. Raven, "Group Structure: Attraction, Coalitions, Communication, and Power," in *Handbook of Social Psychology*, vol. 4, 2nd ed., ed. Lindzey and Aronson, ch. 30 .

distracting interaction, group cohesiveness can contribute to a reduced likelihood of successful goal attainment."[62] A second, more popular explanation relates changes in productivity to the strengthened effect of group norms in highly cohesive groups, which can operate to restrict production[63] as well as to increase it.[64] Seashore, in studying highly cohesive industrial work groups, postulated that a U-shaped curve was indicative of the role played by norms in relation to cohesiveness.[65] Thus, the performance of highly cohesive groups would be either very high or very low (depending on the norms) whereas groups low in cohesiveness would be intermediate in performance. Empirical support for Seashore's U-shaped curve was obtained by Stodgill in his study of industrial work groups.[66] On the basis of this finding, Schmuck and Schmuck have suggested that cohesiveness in instructional groups can support or hinder learning: "Students who share negative attitudes about academic learning and who make up a cohesive class probably would achieve at low levels. Conversely, student groups with positive norms for learning would, especially as they increased in cohesiveness, attain high achievement."[67]

Group cohesiveness and group norms also interact in affecting attitude change. Gerard reported that members of highly cohesive groups show greater resistance to changing an opinion once it becomes a group norm than do members of groups low in cohesiveness.[68] Also, several investigators have found that highly cohesive groups are more likely to reject deviant members who do not share the majority members' norms (in this case, attitudes) than are groups

62. James H. Davis, *Group Performance* (Reading, Mass.: Addison-Wesley, 1969), p. 79.

63. Stanley Schachter et al., "An Experimental Study of Cohesiveness and Productivity," *Human Relations* 4 (August 1951): 229-38.

64. Leonard Berkowitz, "Group Standards, Cohesiveness, and Productivity," *Human Relations* 7 (November 1954): 509-19.

65. Seashore, *Group Cohesiveness in the Industrial Work Group.*

66. Ralph Stodgill, "Group Productivity, Drive, and Cohesiveness," *Organizational Behavior and Human Performance* 8 (February 1972): 26-43.

67. Schmuck and Schmuck, *Group Processes in the Classroom*, p. 159.

68. Harold B. Gerard, "The Anchorage of Opinions in Face-to-Face Groups," *Human Relations* 7 (August 1954): 313-25.

low in cohesiveness.[69] One explanation of these results is that groups that are highly cohesive, that is, highly attracted to each other, are likely to share similar perceptions and attitudes. In this situation group members may use discussions to reinforce preexisting attitudes rather than to analyze them critically. On the other hand, groups that are low in cohesiveness are likely to enter a discussion with opposing attitudes. In this situation, assuming other conditions are favorable, group members can use the discussion process to modify existing attitudes in the light of conflicting attitudes and information.

Implications. From the standpoint of interpersonal processes, high cohesiveness seems to be desirable in a discussion group. Furthermore, if the group members support the task goals established for the discussion group, high cohesiveness should foster an effective discussion. But, as we have noted, there is a danger that members of a highly cohesive group may become concerned primarily with the rewards of interaction, or may collude to oppose actively the task goals of the discussion group. In this event, highly cohesive groups will demonstrate a lower level of performance than groups that are lower in cohesiveness. Enough cohesiveness should exist so that the group members experience some reward from interaction and can establish smooth working relations, yet cohesiveness should not be so high that members holding minority or deviant opinions are rejected or that the task is ignored or actively resisted.

COMMUNICATION PATTERNS

Although the objectives of a discussion group may vary, effective communication is necessary for achieving all of them. Researchers have investigated such complex aspects of communication as the levels of meaning contained in the verbal content, the significance of nonverbal messages, miscommunication arising out of the imbalance of power between teacher and students, and the classification of verbal communication by speaker, sequence, and type of message. Here we shall concentrate upon how spatial ar-

69. Richard M. Emerson, "Deviation and Rejection: An Experimental Replication," *American Sociological Review* 19 (December 1954): 688-93; Schachter et al., "An Experimental Study of Cohesiveness and Productivity"; Stanley Schachter, "Deviation, Rejection and Communication," *Journal of Abnormal and Social Psychology* 46 (April 1951): 190-207.

rangements and communication networks affect discussion group processes and outcomes.

Spatial arrangements. Research on seating patterns and space as they affect small group functioning suggests that the traditional classroom physical arrangement (students in rows facing the instructor) may severely hamper participation in a group discussion. Sommer found that when students sat in rows facing the instructor, students in front participated more than those in the rear and students in the center participated more than those on the sides.[70] In both this arrangement and the seminar arrangement, with students sitting in a circle, students who directly faced the teacher participated more than those on the sides. Sommer claimed that direct visual contact between persons increased communication between them, although in his study position with respect to the teacher appeared to be the sole determiner of differences in participation.

The more general principle that eye contact increases communication among group members was supported in an earlier study by Steinzor, who found that a member of a group is more likely to interact with other members of the group if he or she can see as well as hear them.[71] As to the best location of particular types of individuals, Steinzor recommended that more talkative individuals should be placed opposite quiet ones and those who tend to monopolize discussion should be seated next to each other. Bany and Johnson noted that, in the traditional classroom arrangement, shy students will participate more if they are seated near the front.[72]

Communication networks. The effects of different communication networks upon the interpersonal processes and performance of small groups have received considerable attention from researchers.[73] A communication network may be defined as a system

70. Robert Sommer, "Classroom Ecology," *Journal of Applied Behavioral Science* 3, no. 4 (1967): 489-503.

71. Bernard Steinzor, "The Spatial Factor in Face to Face Discussion Groups," *Journal of Abnormal and Social Psychology* 45 (July 1950): 552-55.

72. Mary A. Bany and Lois V. Johnson, *Classroom Group Behavior: Group Dynamics in Education* (New York: Macmillan, 1964).

73. The communication networks in the studies reviewed in this section were artificially created in that individuals were separated by partitions, and access to other members was possible only by means of slots in the partitions through which written messages could be passed. The main difference be-

of communication barriers and channels between the members of a group. Experimental investigations of communication networks involve the establishment of certain patterns of permissible communication among the members of a group as it works on a task. In the classic study by Leavitt, five-person groups worked either in circle, chain, Y, or wheel networks.[74] In the chain, the only communication links between five people (A, B, C, D, and E) are A-B, B-C, C-D, and D-E, with A and E at the ends of the chain in the most peripheral positions and C in the most central location. If to this network is added a link between A and E, the network becomes a circle. In the wheel network (which may be represented by a large letter X), A, B, D, and E are all located peripherally at the outer four points of the X and can communicate only to C who is in a central position (the intersection of the X), and C can communicate to any other member. Finally, in the five-person Y network, A and E are located at the outer two top points of the Y, C is located at the intersection of the Y, and D lies between C and B on the base of the Y. It should be obvious that these four networks (and a variety of others, of differing member size, which also have been studied) differ in their centrality, that is, the extent to which communications must be channeled through a central person in order to reach the other members. The circle is an example of a decentralized network, whereas the Y, chain, and wheel are all examples of centralized networks.

Three major findings have emerged from the research on communication networks.[75] First, while individual satisfaction was

---

tween decentralized networks (circle and all-channel) and centralized networks (Y, chain, and wheel) was that the slots between most of the members were open in the former networks, whereas some slots were closed in the latter, thereby requiring channeling of messages through central persons. Thus, physical restraints were used to represent the limited communication access that in formal organizations is accomplished by limited distribution of written communications, by differences in position, and by norms and regulations concerning who may communicate with whom.

74. Howard J. Leavitt, "Some Effects of Certain Communication Patterns on Group Performance," *Journal of Abnormal and Social Psychology* 46 (January 1951): 38-50.

75. This research is reviewed by David Krech, Richard S. Crutchfield, and Egerton L. Ballachey, *Individual in Society* (New York: McGraw-Hill, 1962) and by Davis, *Group Performance*.

greatest for those group members in a central position, overall group satisfaction was greater in groups with decentralized networks (that is, where communication channels among more of the members were open) than in groups with centralized networks (that is, where messages must be channeled through persons in one or more central positions). Second, groups with decentralized networks initially took longer to solve problems which required information distribution than groups with centralized networks. Collins inferred that the greater degree of coordination necessary in the decentralized networks created an interpersonal obstacle, thus resulting in decreased efficiency on the early trials.[76] Once these groups had developed a stable pattern of information exchange, however (the most efficient being a centralized pattern where messages were channeled through one or two persons), all of the networks were equally efficient in solving problems. Third, groups with decentralized communication networks were superior in both speed and accuracy to groups with centralized networks in complex tasks, for example, arithmetic, word arrangement, sentence construction, and discussion. On simple tasks (for example, symbol-identification tasks) groups with centralized networks were superior. Shaw suggested that the high-centrality position in a centralized network is likely to become overloaded when the network faces a complex task, a process he termed "saturation."[77]

Implications. It appears that the communication patterns in a discussion group are affected by the spatial arrangement, differences in member status, and the extent to which communication is channeled through particular group members as opposed to flowing freely among all members. Research on spatial arrangements indicates that simply providing students an opportunity to talk is not sufficient to establish an effective discussion. Both the size of the group and the seating arrangement must allow eye contact among students, as well as between students and teacher.

76. Barry E. Collins, *Social Psychology: Social Influence, Attitude Change, Group Processes, and Prejudice* (Reading, Mass.: Addison-Wesley, 1970), p. 211.

77. M. E. Shaw, "Communication Networks," in *Advances in Experimental Social Psychology*, vol. 1, ed. Leonard Berkowitz (New York: Academic Press, 1964).

Even in a small group with good opportunity for eye contact, participation of students with one another will remain low if the teacher uses his high-status role to dominate the discussion or restrict channels of communication. The research findings suggest that discussion group members will be happier and more productive on complex tasks if the teacher creates a decentralized network of communication in which every member feels free to initiate or receive communication from every other member.

LEADERSHIP

In working with discussion groups, the teacher needs to understand the basis and potential effects of his own leadership, and to recognize the group as a source of leadership. Cecil Gibb has defined leadership as follows: "Leadership refers to that aspect of role differentiation by which all or a large number of group members make use of individual contributions which they perceive to have value in moving the group toward its goals."[78] This definition is preferred here because it indicates that leadership acts may be performed by any member of the group, and because it excludes the many acts which the nominal group "head" may perform that do not contribute to goal achievement.[79] Furthermore, this definition stresses the need to examine the group goals to determine which acts of group members represent leadership acts.

Jack Gibb distinguished three types of goals that operate in a classroom group: task goals, group maintenance goals, and individual goals.[80] While it is important to remember that individual

78. Cecil A. Gibb, "Leadership," in *Handbook of Social Psychology*, vol. 4, 2nd ed., ed. Lindzey and Aronson, p. 271.

79. Other definitions define leadership in terms of a single person who is perceived by group members to be the leader (see Jonathan L. Freedman, J. Merrill Carlsmith, and David O. Sears, *Social Psychology* [Eng'ewood Cliffs, N.J.: Prentice-Hall, Inc., 1970], p. 139), or refer to exertion of group influence without regard to its effects upon goal achievement (see David H. Jenkins, "Characteristics and Functions of Leadership in Instructional Groups," in *The Dynamics of Instructional Groups: Sociopsychological Aspects of Teaching and Learning*, Fifty-ninth Yearbook of the National Society for the Study of Education, Part II, ed. Nelson B. Henry [Chicago: University of Chicago Press, 1960], p. 164.)

80. Jack R. Gibb, "Sociopsychological Processes of Group Instruction," in *The Dynamics of Instructional Groups*, ed. Nelson B. Henry, p. 127.

goals do affect member behavior in a discussion group, here we shall consider only group goals, in accordance with our definition of leadership. In a typical discussion group, the group maintenance goals (rarely stated) concern effective interpersonal processes, while the task goals relate to the various types of objectives that the teacher hopes to achieve through discussion—subject matter mastery, attitude change, or problem solving. However, group members are likely to have different perceptions of what the goals are, what they mean in practice, and what behaviors are useful in moving the group toward its goals. Thus leadership is needed both to clarify the goals, and to help move the group toward them.

The teacher's role as leader. In most instructional situations, students assume that the teacher will act as leader, because of the authority he derives from the school organization and the larger community. But since the discussion method is designed to give students increased opportunity to participate and work toward group goals, the teacher must consider carefully the types of leadership in which he should engage so as not to hinder student leadership.

Examining the teacher's responsibilities in a discussion group, McKeachie indicated four duties that the teacher should perform when necessary: (a) calling the meeting to order and introducing the topic for discussion, (b) clarification of goals during the discussion, (c) summarization, and (d) mediation and clarification of differences. Two additional leadership functions that the teacher should ensure are also carried out, whether by himself, by the students, or jointly, are (e) agenda setting, and (f) evaluation of group progress.[81]

Maier and Solem developed a similar set of functions that a democratic discussion leader can perform to improve group problem solving: (a) determining the subject for discussion; (b) causing the group to react constructively by stating the problem in constructive terms; (c) asking stimulating and exploratory questions, providing he is sufficiently skilled; (d) using minority opinions so as to upgrade the quality of a group's thinking.[82] These behaviors resemble those listed by McKeachie. It should be noted that Maier and Solem referred specifically to a democratic discussion leader as performing the above functions. McKeachie also appears to favor a democratic approach to teacher leadership, as described below under the research concerning democratic and authoritarian leadership.

Leaderless group discussion. The above analysis suggests that the teacher, or other appointed leader, is essential to group achievement. But there is evidence that, in groups in which no leader is designated at the outset, one or more leaders will emerge as the situation calls for leadership. Nonetheless, there appear to be important differences between the behavior of emergent leaders in leaderless discussion groups and the outcomes of these groups, on the one hand, and those of groups with appointed leaders, on the other.

The "leaderless group discussion" was originally developed as a situational test of the leadership ability of candidates for military leadership. The method consists of having a group discuss a controversial topic for a designated period, during which observers record the attempted leadership acts and the effectiveness of the leader behavior of each participant.[83] The method has been adapted both for the prediction of leadership in a variety of real-life situations and for research on leadership.

Certain leadership phenomena that are not apparent from examining only groups with appointed leaders become clearer when leaderless discussion groups are investigated as well. For example, Bales assembled five-man leaderless discussion groups that met four times to arrive at a group solution to a human relations problem.[84] After each session members ranked all other members on four scales: Who contributed the best ideas? Who did the most to

82. Norman R. F. Maier and Allen R. Solem, "The Contribution of a Discussion Leader to the Quality of Group Thinking: The Effective Use of Minority Opinions," *Human Relations* 5 (August 1952): 277-88.

83. Krech, Crutchfield, and Ballachey, *Individual in Society*, p. 447.

84. Robert F. Bales, "The Equilibrium Problem in Small Groups," in Talcott Parsons, Robert F. Bales, and Edward A. Shils, *Working Papers in the Theory of Action* (Glencoe, Ill. Free Press, 1953).

guide the discussion? Whom do you like? Whom do you dislike? The highest rank on liking and perceived contribution of ideas and guidance tended to be received by the same man after one session, but by the end of four sessions the rankings diverged, with the most-liked man usually being different from the man chosen as making the greatest contribution. Bales concluded that two different types of leaders tend to emerge in groups: a task specialist, who gives suggestions, opinions, and information directed toward the task goals; and a social-emotional specialist, who makes supportive, encouraging, conciliatory, friendly statements directed toward group maintenance goals.[85] Over time, the task leader tends to engender hostility in other group members, even though he is perceived as contributing most in terms of ideas and guidance.

Maier and Solem studied the performance of problem-solving groups that were leaderless and similar groups that had an appointed leader.[86] College students in a course in psychology were organized into discussion groups, and asked to select a representative. In roughly half the groups, the representative was assigned the role of discussion leader, who was instructed to encourage participation of all members, stimulate group activity by asking questions, and get the group to agree on an answer, but not to express his own views. In the other groups the representative was asked to serve as observer and simply to listen to the discussion. Members recorded their answers individually before and after discussion. The two sets of groups were found to give similar answers before discussion. After discussion, however, the percentage of correct answers in the groups with a leader was significantly higher than that in the leaderless (observer) groups. Analysis of the data showed that the superiority of the leader groups was due mainly to the role of the leader in securing a hearing for correct minority views, which tended in the leaderless groups to be rejected.

85. The task and social-emotional specialist typology corresponds closely to the two types of group goals described above: task goals and group maintenance goals. Two similar dimensions—initiating structure and consideration—have been found with remarkable consistency in factor analytic studies of leadership, causing Gibb to conclude that "these are indeed the major dimensions of leader behavior." See Cecil A. Gibb, "Leadership," p. 232.

86. Maier and Solem, "The Contribution of a Discussion Leader to the Quality of Group Thinking," pp. 277-88.

Leadership styles. The concepts of "authoritarian" and "democratic" leadership are frequently encountered in the research literature. In the classic studies by Lippitt and White, adult leaders were trained to follow three leadership styles: (a) an authoritarian style in which the leader determined all policy, dictated activities and procedures at each step, assigned members to tasks, used personal praise and criticism, and remained aloof from participation; (b) a democratic style in which the leader submitted all policies for group discussion and decision, outlined general goals and suggested alternative procedures, left division of labor up to the group, was objective in praise and criticism, and demonstrated group spirit; or (c) a laissez-faire style in which the leader supplied materials and answered questions, but otherwise remained passive.[87] Leaders alternated leadership style in different boy's clubs engaged in hobby activities. The groups with an authoritarian leader produced a greater quantity of work but were dependent on the leader and lacked a spirit of group friendliness and cooperation, whereas boys led by a democratic leader produced work of higher quality and developed greater independence and a more cohesive group. Laissez-faire was less organized, less efficient, and less satisfying than democracy to the boys, and there is some question whether it can accurately be described as a leadership style, since it involved primarily the absence of leadership acts on the part of the appointed leader.

These classic studies generated a great deal of interest, and numerous researchers have adapted the study of democratic and authoritarian leadership style to the classroom. Anderson reviewed research on authoritarian-democratic teaching styles and concluded that neither democratic nor authoritarian leadership was consistently associated with higher productivity, but that in most situations, democratic leadership was associated with higher morale.[88] On the other hand, Anderson was extremely critical of the methodology of research in this area, pointing out, for example, that the authori-

87. Ronald Lippitt and Ralph White, "The 'Social Climate' of Children's Groups," in *Child Behavior and Development*, ed. R. G. Barker, J. Kounin, and H. Wright (New York: McGraw-Hill, 1943), ch. 28; Ralph White and Ronald Lippitt, *Autocracy and Democracy* (New York: Harper, 1960).

88. Richard C. Anderson, "Learning in Discussions: A Résumé of the Authoritarian-Democratic Studies," *Harvard Education Review* 29 (Summer 1959): 201-15.

tarian leadership style often confounded directiveness and outright hostility on the part of the teacher. Anderson concluded that "the authoritarian-democratic construct provides an inadequate conceptualization of leadership behavior."

McKeachie reviewed thirty-three studies comparing student-centered teaching (comparable to the democratic leadership style) and instructor-centered teaching (comparable to the authoritarian leadership style).[89] He concluded that the two approaches are equally effective with respect to students' acquisition of knowledge, but that in ten studies student-centered teaching was shown to be superior in producing changes in one or more of the following areas of student outcomes: attitudes, motivation, ability to apply concepts, and group membership skills.

Cecil Gibb attempted to clarify research findings on the effects of leadership style by invoking the concept of group members' expectations. He concluded that:

In some respects the democratic technique has decided advantages, but it does have limitations; and there are circumstances and goals which seem to give advantages to authoritarianism. Whatever the group goal, however, the effectiveness of any leadership technique lies in its acceptability to the followers, and whether authoritarian or democratic techniques are more efficient frequently depends on the expectations of the followers, as many studies have now shown.[90]

Implications. The research on leadership indicates, first of all, that leadership is necessary in discussion groups if they are to be effective. But the differentiation between task and social-emotional leadership suggests that no one leader may be able to perform all the necessary leadership functions with a high level of skill, so that unofficial leaders may emerge to take over that function at which the appointed leader is less effective. Furthermore, since research indicates that leaders will emerge in initially leaderless discussion groups, the teacher need not feel that his presence as leader is always required. The teacher should be prepared, however, for the possibility that certain students will become overly dominant in leaderless discussion groups, thereby engendering hostility in other students

89. McKeachie, *Teaching Tips*, p. 40.

90. Cecil A. Gibb, "Leadership," pp. 261-62.

and limiting the opportunities for other students to lead or contribute to the discussion.

Whether the teacher acts as leader, appoints a student leader, or simply lets leadership emerge, research suggests that a student-centered leadership style should be encouraged. Indeed, careful examination of our definition of the discussion method in relation to the description of the democratic or student-centered leadership style suggests that the discussion group requires student-centered leadership in order for the discussion method to be fully implemented. Since the student-centered approach has been found to be equal to the instructor-centered approach in achieving task goals, and better at achieving group maintenance goals, its appropriateness seems clear.

Effectiveness of the Discussion Method

The discussion method has been compared with other teaching methods, especially the lecture, in many research studies. The usual comparison deals with their relative effectiveness in promoting the instructional outcomes of subject matter mastery, attitude change, and problem solving.

Recent critiques suggest that this area of research is particularly subject to methodological problems.[91] In reviewing the studies included in this section, we shall take note of these methodological problems and how they affect interpretation of the findings.

SUBJECT MATTER MASTERY

The discussion method is most often used in schools to help students master curriculum content. Typically the teacher asks students to read a textbook assignment, which is followed by a discussion in which they rehearse, reflect on, and apply their new knowledge.

In many studies of college teaching, this use of the discussion method has been compared in effectiveness with the lecture method. Dubin and Taveggia reviewed thirty-six studies in which the final

91. Michael J. Dunkin and Bruce J. Biddle, *The Study of Teaching* (New York: Holt, Rinehart, and Winston, 1974); Robert W. Heath and Mark A. Nielson, "The Research Basis for Performance-based Teacher Education," *Review of Educational Research* 44 (Fall 1974): 463-84.

course examination scores of students taught by the discussion method were compared with scores of students taught by the lecture method.[92] Of the comparisons, 51 percent favored the lecture method, and 49 percent favored the discussion method, leading Dubin and Taveggia to ". . . feel confident in concluding that the lecture and discussion are equally effective methods of instruction."[93]

We are less sanguine about drawing this conclusion, since Dubin and Taveggia did not critically review the methodology used in each study, for example, how the discussion and lecture methods were operationally defined by each investigator. Since it is likely that the methods varied in form and effectiveness from one study to the next, the reviewers' counts of comparisons favoring discussion or favoring lecture are difficult to interpret. Also, the reviewers did not report whether the researchers collected observational data to determine fidelity of treatment, that is, the extent to which teachers actually used the method which they had been asked to employ.

Other methodological issues pertain to the learning outcomes measured in these studies. Students' performance on the final course examination was the outcome variable used in all of the statistical comparisons. Dubin and Taveggia did not examine the internal reliability or interrater reliability (in the case of essay exams) of the examinations. Test scores which have low reliability will obscure true differences between teaching methods.

It is particularly critical in studies of teaching methods to examine the content validity of the outcome measures to determine how they reflect the content taught in the various treatments. Suppose, for example, that in a particular study, content X was taught in the lecture method, content Y in the discussion method, and content Z in the assigned reading. If the final examination tests students on content X and Z, the comparison will favor the lecture method unfairly. If the examination tests students on content Z only, learning by either teaching method is not measured. Dubin

92. Robert Dubin and Thomas C. Taveggia, *The Teaching-Learning Paradox* (Eugene, Ore.: Center for the Advanced Study of Educational Administration, University of Oregon, 1968).

93. Ibid., p. 31.

and Taveggia did not examine the issue of content validity in their review, and it is doubtful whether the primary sources contain sufficient data for this analysis.

In research on teaching it is important to measure learning in various ways (acquisition, retention, and transfer), and at different cognitive levels, perhaps using Bloom's taxonomy of cognitive objectives[94] as a framework. McKeachie, after analyzing many of the same studies included in Dubin and Taveggia's review from this perspective, reached the following conclusion:

Since discussion offers the opportunity for a good deal of student activity and feedback, it could be (according to theory) and is (according to research results) more effective than typical lectures in developing concepts and problem-solving skills. However, because the rate of transmission of information is slow in discussion classes, we would expect lecture classes to be superior in attaining the objective of teaching knowledge. Research results tend to support this generalization and probably are not more convincing largely because the knowledge tested on course examinations usually can be learned by reading the textbook.[95]

Stovall reached a similar conclusion in his earlier review of the research on lecture versus discussion.[96]

We do not think it fruitful to review the research once again to determine whether real differences between lecture and discussion exist, as McKeachie and Stovall claim, and Dubin and Taveggia deny. Instead, we recommend that efforts be turned to conducting new studies characterized by methodological rigor. Special care should be taken to design discussion treatments which incorporate features of demonstrated effectiveness in previous research (small group size, student-centered leadership style, etc.).

Several recent studies have investigated the effectiveness of the discussion method in elementary school teaching. Gall and his associates conducted two experiments in which sixth-grade students were randomly assigned to an art activity treatment or to various discussion treatments which were designed to investigate the effects of variations in percentage of higher cognitive questions and in

94. Bloom, *Taxonomy of Educational Objectives*.

95. McKeachie, *Teaching Tips*, p. 216.

96. Thomas F. Stovall, "Lecture vs. Discussion," *Phi Delta Kappan* 39 (March 1958): 255-58.

teacher follow-up responses to students' answers.[97] Students in all treatments received the same daily reading assignment for two weeks. After each assignment they either participated in a discussion or in art activity, depending on their treatment assignment. The teachers were trained to follow "semi-programmed" discussion plans so that (a) the parameters of the discussion treatment could be defined precisely, (b) teachers' discussion behavior could be observed and compared to the treatment specifications, (c) students' opportunity to learn the curriculum content in the various treatment groups could be equated, and (d) tests of high content validity could be constructed.

In both experiments, students in the discussion treatments outperformed students in the art activity treatment on measures of knowledge acquisition and retention, and on essay and oral measures of higher cognitive processes, which were observed both with respect to the curriculum content and to different content. There were few achievement differences among student groups assigned to the different discussion treatments. The results also suggested that students made greater achievement gains on the oral measures of higher cognitive thinking than they did on the corresponding written measures. This finding indicates that an oral measure may be more sensitive to the effects of discussion than an essay measure.

The results of the study by Gall et al. indicate that discussion contributes to students' learning beyond the level of achievement obtained by simply reading curriculum material. Studies by Buggey, Savage, and Tyler also demonstrate that highly structured discussion can be used to bring about learning in elementary school students.[98] An interesting finding of Tyler's study was that second-grade students who listened and responded orally to teachers'

97. Meredith D. Gall et al., *The Effects of Teacher Use of Questioning Techniques on Student Achievement and Attitudes* (San Francisco, Cal.: Far West Laboratory for Educational Research and Development, 1975).

98. L. J. Buggey, "A Study of the Relationship of Classroom Questions and Social Studies Achievement of Second Grade Children" (Ph.D. diss., University of Washington, 1971); T. V. Savage, "A Study of the Relationship of Classroom Questions and Social Studies Achievement of Fifth Grade Children" (Ph.D. diss., University of Washington, 1972); J. F. Tyler, "A Study of the Relationship of Two Methods of Question Presentation, Sex, and School Location to the Social Studies Achievement of Second Grade Children" (Ph.D. diss., University of Washington, 1971).

discussion questions performed significantly better on a posttest containing items at each level of Bloom's taxonomy than did students who read and wrote answers to the same questions. This result suggests that discussions may be particularly effective in developing critical thinking ability in students who have not acquired proficiency in reading and independent study. The differences in learning between the discussion and reading treatments might have been even more pronounced had Tyler used an oral posttest, in which students listened and responded orally to test items.

On the basis of research findings, then, it appears that the discussion method is effective in helping students to master curriculum content, especially when cognitive outcomes beyond the level of knowledge are desired. Discussion also may be more effective than the lecture method in promoting higher cognitive outcomes. However, this generalization should be considered tentative until we have the results of further research characterized by more rigorous methodology than has been used previously.

ATTITUDE CHANGE

Is the discussion method effective in bringing about attitude change among the discussion participants? The classic studies relating to this question were done by the social psychologist Kurt Lewin and his associates.[99] In one of their studies they attempted to increase housewive's consumption of meats that they generally rejected. The reason for selecting this attitude for change was to alleviate a meat shortage during World War II. The housewives were formed into groups and exposed to two methods of attitude change. Some groups listened to a lecture concerning the dietary value and economy of these meats. The other groups received the same information within a discussion format. After the discussion, the housewives were asked to indicate by a show of hands their individual decisions about serving these meats. The extent of attitude change was measured by determining whether the housewives later had actually served one of the meats. The follow-up survey

99. Kurt Lewin, "Group Decision and Social Change," in *Readings in Social Psychology*, ed. G. E. Swanson, Theodore M. Newcomb, and E. L. Hartley, 2nd ed. (New York: Henry Holt & Co., 1952).

revealed that 32 percent of the housewives in the discussion groups had served one of the meats, but only 3 percent of the housewives who had listened to the lecture had done so.

The results of Lewin's series of studies were called into question by Bennett, who concluded from her own study that the act of making a decision and the establishment of a group norm through consensus, rather than discussion or lecture per se, were the critical factors in creating attitude change.[100] But a later study by Pennington, Haravey, and Bass found that the act of making a decision and participation in discussion *both* influenced attitude change, and that discussion was the more potent influence.[101] The contradictory results of the two studies may be due, at least in part, to the fact that in Bennett's study the participants were asked to make individual decisions in a group setting, whereas in the study by Pennington et al., they were asked to come to a group consensus. Perhaps discussion is more effective than lecture in inducing attitude change, but only when it is accompanied by attempts to reach group consensus concerning desirable actions to be taken toward the attitude object.

Other research not directly concerned with the lecture-versus-discussion issue has consistently found that the discussion method is effective in inducing attitude change. Group discussion has been successful in causing mothers to give their children orange juice and cod-liver oil,[102] workers to increase their rate of productivity,[103] students to volunteer for experiments,[104] juvenile delinquents to improve their behavior patterns,[105] and parents to change their

100. Edith B. Bennett, "Discussion, Decision, Commitment, and Consensus in 'Group Decision,'" *Human Relations* 8 (August 1955): 251-73.

101. D. F. Pennington, Jr., Francois Haravey, and Bernard M. Bass, "Some Effects of Decision and Discussion on Coalescence, Change, and Effectiveness," *Journal of Applied Psychology* 42 (December 1958): 404-8.

102. Marian Radke and D. Klisurich, "Experiments in Changing Food Habits," *Journal of the American Dietetics Association* 23 (1947): 403-9.

103. Lester Coch and John R. P. French, Jr., "Overcoming Resistance to Change," *Human Relations* 1 (August 1948): 512-32.

104. Stanley Schachter and Robert Hall, "Group-derived Restraints and Audience Persuasion," *Human Relations* 5 (November 1952): 397-406.

105. Irwin G. Sarason and Victor J. Ganzer, "Modeling and Group Discussion in the Rehabilitation of Juvenile Delinquents," *Journal of Counseling Psychology* 20 (September 1973): 442-49.

expressed attitudes toward mental retardation.[106]

Studies in educational settings also have demonstrated the effectiveness of the discussion method in changing attitudes. Fisher conducted an experiment in which fifth-grade students were randomly assigned to (a) read a series of stories designed to promote positive attitudes toward American Indians, (b) read the same stories and, in addition, participate in a discussion after each reading period; or (c) participate in a control condition in which they neither read about nor discussed American Indians.[107] The reading treatment induced more positive changes in attitude than did the control condition. Discussion also had an effect in that reading plus discussion caused significantly more attitude change than reading alone. Similar results were obtained by Gall and his associates, who found that reading supplemented by discussion generally brought about greater change in attitude toward ecological concepts among sixth-grade students than reading supplemented by art activity.[108] At the secondary school level, Miller and Biggs found that students who participated in discussions developed greater expressed tolerance for different racial groups than students not given this opportunity.[109]

These consistently positive effects should not come as a surprise. A variety of processes inherent in the discussion method can be used to induce attitude change. If the student is asked by another student or the teacher to state an opinion on an issue, he is compelled to reflect whether he indeed has an opinion, and if so, what that opinion is. Also, the discussion may confront the student with new data which he may use to form an opinion or to modify one which he already holds. Furthermore, the student simply may be coerced by another student or faction of students to change his expressed opinions, especially where the student holds an opinion

106. James A. Bitter, "Attitude Change by Parents of Trainable Mentally Retarded Children as a Result of Group Discussion," *Exceptional Children* 30 (December 1963): 173-77.

107. Frank L. Fisher, "Influences of Reading and Discussion on the Attitudes of Fifth Graders toward American Indians," *Journal of Educational Research* 62 (November 1968): 130-34.

108. Gall et al., *The Effects of Teacher Use of Questioning Techniques.*

109. K. M. Miller and J. B. Biggs, "Attitude Change through Undirected Group Discussion," *Journal of Educational Psychology* 49 (August 1958): 224-28.

considered deviant. All of these processes may be intensified if, in addition, the teacher or the group presses for group consensus. In fact, just because discussion can have such a powerful effect on attitudes, it should be used judiciously. Some educators have recommended that the teacher or other person in a powerful role not state his or her own opinion, at least in the initial stage of the discussion, to avoid having students adopt that opinion before they have examined others. Another technique calls upon the teacher and other group members to defend a student whose opinion comes under attack before it has been examined rationally.

Research findings are somewhat equivocal concerning the relative effectiveness of lecture and discussion in inducing attitude change. It seems reasonable that if students lack knowledge about the attitude object, a lecture presentation might be sufficient to effect attitude change, simply by filling the need for information concerning the attitude object. On the other hand, if the teacher wants students to reflect on and confront their attitudes, the discussion method may be more effective than the more passive learning environment of the lecture. Support for this notion is provided in studies that found that discussion stimulates more active thinking processes than does the lecture method.[110]

PROBLEM SOLVING

The primary outcome of some discussion groups is the solution to a problem. The problems studied in laboratory research are usually academic (mathematics puzzles are often used), whereas the problems studied in work settings are usually related to real-life work concerns, such as designing a new product or resolving a personnel conflict. Problem-solving groups usually are free to determine their own strategy for solving the problem. In brainstorming, however, the discussion participants use a predetermined strategy in which criticism of ideas is withheld, while "freewheeling" and "piggy-backing" on others' ideas are encouraged.[111]

110. Benjamin S. Bloom, "Thought Processes in Lectures and Discussions," *Journal of General Education* 7 (April 1953): 160-69; C. J. Krauskopf, "The Use of Written Responses in the Stimulated Recall Method" (Ph.D. diss., Ohio State University, 1960).

111. Alexander F. Osborn, *Applied Imagination* (New York: Scribners, 1957).

The effectiveness of problem-solving groups has been a popular research topic among social psychologists. In many of their studies the effectiveness of problem-solving groups was investigated by asking, Are individuals working together as a group able to solve problems better than an individual working alone? The research relating to this question was reviewed by Lorge, Fox, Davitz, and Brenner, who concluded that, in general, "in the evaluation of the relative quality of the products produced by groups in contrast to the products produced by individuals, the group is superior." [112] Groups also have been found to be superior to individuals in the proportion of correct solutions to problems, in reducing the number of errors preceding solution, and in minimizing the time required to reach solution.

In the early 1950s social psychologists began asking a somewhat different question concerning the relative effectiveness of individuals and groups. Suppose that a problem-solving group includes five individuals. Rather than comparing the group's performance with *one* individual working alone, researchers realized that they should compare it with *five* individuals each working alone. The issue then is whether it is more effective to have five individuals solve a problem individually or to have them work together as a group. Taylor, Berry, and Block investigated this problem by forming twelve groups of four individuals each and comparing their problem-solving effectiveness with the problem-solving effectiveness of forty-eight individuals working separately.[113] The groups and individuals were given brainstorming instructions and asked to generate as many solutions as they could to a series of problems, such as how to increase tourist travel in the United States. The solutions of the real four-person groups were compared with the solutions of nominal groups composed by randomly forming four-person groups from the individuals who worked alone. The results clearly showed that the nominal groups outperformed the real groups in number of

112. Irving Lorge et al., "A Survey of Studies Contrasting the Quality of Group Performance and Individual Performance, 1920-1957," *Psychological Bulletin* 55 (November 1958): 337-72.

113. Donald W. Taylor, Paul C. Berry, and Clifford H. Block, "Does Group Participation When Using Brainstorming Facilitate or Inhibit Creative Thinking?" *Administrative Science Quarterly* 3 (June 1958): 23-47.

ideas generated, number of unique ideas generated, and quality of ideas. The nominal groups' productivity per man hour also was better. Similar results have been obtained by other researchers.[114]

The findings of other research studies also suggest that group problem-solving may not be as effective as individual problem-solving. For example, Restle and Davis found that problem-solving groups tend to operate below the level of their best members.[115] They explained this result in terms of their Equalitarian Model, which predicts decrement in group performance because all group members tend to participate equally in the problem-solving process. The less competent problem solvers consume discussion time and provide distractions which interfere with attainment of solutions by the more competent problem solvers in the group.

Maier, as a result of a systematic program of research on problem-solving, has identified a number of other factors which can have an adverse effect on problem-solving groups, especially groups without a designated leader.[116] First, majority opinions tend to be accepted regardless of their soundness, whereas minority opinions, however correct, tend to have little influence on the solution reached. Second, once a certain level of group consensus for a particular solution is reached, the group is likely to reject higher quality solutions suggested later. Another adverse factor, similar to the "problem" of equalitarianism described above, is that a capable individual may not have a chance to influence the group's problem-solving process if another, less capable individual dominates the discussion. The fourth adverse factor identified by Maier is that, as the discussion progresses, group members tend to become

114. William L. Faust, "Group versus Individual Problem Solving," *Journal of Abnormal and Social Psychology* 59, no. 1 (1959): 68-72; Marvin D. Dunnette, John Campbell, and Kay Jaastad, "The Effect of Group Participation on Brainstorming Effectiveness for Two Industrial Samples," *Journal of Applied Psychology* 47 (February 1963): 30-37.

115. James H. Davis and Frank Restle, "The Analysis of Problems and Prediction of Group Problem Solving," *Journal of Abnormal and Social Psychology* 66, no. 1 (1963): 103-116; Frank Restle and James H. Davis, "Success and Speed of Problem Solving by Individuals and Groups," *Psychological Review* 69 (November 1962): 520-36.

116. Norman R. F. Maier, "Assets and Liabilities in Group Problem Solving: The Need for an Integrative Function," *Psychological Review* 74 (July 1967): 239-49.

subverted from their initial goal of solving the problem to the new goal of converting other group members to their own solution, even though it may not be the best solution to the problem.

If we accept the results of the studies reviewed above, we might conclude that, if one has a problem to be solved, the best course of action is either (a) to assign the problem to the most capable problem solver among a collection of individuals, or (b) to have the collection of individuals develop independent solutions rather than forming them into a problem-solving group. However, closer analysis of the studies suggests that their results may be a function of the particular types of problem chosen for investigation.

First, the problems used in the studies reviewed above usually were simple enough so that they could be solved efficiently by an individual working alone or in a group. Thus, they tend to promote duplication, rather than division, of labor among group members. Collins has suggested that group effort might be more effective than individual effort when the problem requires the utilization of the diverse talents present in the group.[117] Support for this notion was provided by Kelley and Thibaut, who reviewed several studies in which group performance was above the level of the most proficient member. They hypothesized that, ". . . these beneficial effects occur only for problems of multiple parts and for group members having noncorrelated (complementary) deficiencies and talents."[118]

The problems used in laboratory research generally have a single correct answer which is obvious to the learner once he has achieved it (called "eureka" problems by Lorge et al.).[119] Yet, many problems do not have a single correct answer. With respect to open-ended problems, the primary outcome variables usually have been quantity and quality of solutions, as in the study by Taylor et al. described above. Although individuals may be superior to groups in generating solutions, it is usually necessary in real-life settings for the individuals then to evaluate the solutions. The reason for

117. Collins, *Social Psychology*.

118. Harold H. Kelley and John W. Thibaut, "Group Problem Solving," in *Handbook of Social Psychology*, vol. 4, 2nd ed., ed. Lindzey and Aronson, p. 69.

119. Lorge et al., "A Survey of Studies."

evaluation is to select one solution, which commits the individuals to a given course of action. Maier suggested that group problem solving may be superior to individual effort under these circumstances:

Many problems require solutions that depend upon the support of others to be effective. Insofar as group problem solving permits participation and influence, it follows that more individuals accept solutions when a group solves the problem than when one person solves it. When one individual solves a problem he still has the task of persuading others. It follows, therefore, that when groups solve such problems, a greater number of persons accept and feel responsible for making the solution work. A low-quality solution that has good acceptance can be more effective than a higher-quality solution that lacks acceptance.[120]

From the perspective of Maier's recommendations, it is apparent that much of the research on problem-solving groups has used objective problems to whose solutions the group members have little commitment. It is quite a different matter when individuals, working either independently or in a group, know that only one solution will be implemented and that it will affect them individually.

What does this review of research suggest for the use of problem-solving groups in classroom teaching? For the sake of variety and student learning, it probably is desirable for the teacher to provide opportunities for students to practice solving problems both individually and in groups. Academic problems which have a single correct answer, such as mathematical puzzles, can probably be solved effectively by individual effort. Problems which require students to draw on the diverse talents of their peers, which have multiple solutions, and which will commit students to a course of action are good candidates for providing students with practice in group problem solving. The teacher will need to exercise or delegate effective leadership, though, to avoid some of the pitfalls of group problem solving described above.

DISCUSSION SKILLS

A frequently mentioned purpose of classroom discussions is to improve the student's skill as a discussion group member. We were

120. Maier, "Assets and Liabilities in Group Problem Solving."

unable to find research relevant to the issue of whether students' performance in discussion groups improves over time with no special training. It appears reasonable, though, that some improvement would occur as a result of practice. Improvement also would be expected as a result of systematic training, and this, in fact, is the case. Training has been demonstrated to improve brainstorming skills[121] and issue-oriented discussion skills[122] of both teachers and students.

There also is evidence that students trained in discussion skills can use the discussion process more effectively as a learning and problem-solving tool than untrained students. Cohen, Whitmyre, and Funk found that groups (actually, pairs of individuals) trained in brainstorming techniques were more effective subsequently in brainstorming sessions than untrained groups.[123] Also, Dunnette, Campbell, and Vaastad found greater individual productivity in brainstorming after a group brainstorming session than after an individual brainstorming session.[124] Hill presented research findings which suggest that, as college students learn and use his "Learning thru Discussion" method, they show gradual improvement in performance on course examinations.[125]

In view of the few existing studies, more research is needed to determine how discussion training affects students' subsequent performance in group and individual situations aimed at promoting subject matter mastery, attitude change, and problem solving. Another unexplored problem is the effect of discussion and discussion training on students' academic motivation. Although motivational

121. Edwenna Werner, *Main Field Test Report, Minicourse 20: Divergent Thinking*, Report No. A72-15 (San Francisco, Cal.: Far West Laboratory for Educational Research and Development, 1972).

122. Donald W. Oliver and James P. Shaver, *Teaching Public Issues in the High School* (Boston: Houghton Mifflin, 1966); Lai et al., *Discussing Controversial Issues*.

123. David Cohen, John W. Whitmyre, and Wilmer H. Funk, "Effect of Group Cohesiveness and Training upon Creative Thinking," *Journal of Applied Psychology* 44 (October 1960): 319-22.

124. Dunnette, Campbell, and Jaastad, "The Effect of Group Participation on Brainstorming Effectiveness."

125. Hill, *Learning thru Discussion*.

effects are frequently claimed, we were not able to find empirical support for them.

Individual Differences

VERBAL PARTICIPATION

The most obvious difference between discussion group members is that some speak more than others. Participation rates are influenced by group characteristics such as size, but they also reflect personal characteristics of the discussants. Black students tend to participate less than white students.[126] The younger students in a group tend to participate less than the older students.[127]

Discussion members' sex is also related to participation behavior. Review of the research literature by Lockheed and Hall led them to state three generalizations concerning sex differences in participation behavior.[128] First, the average male initiates more verbal acts than the average female. This pattern was found even in group discussions among second-grade children. The second generalization is that males are more influential than females. For example, a female is more likely to yield to a male's opinion than vice versa. The third generalization is that males tend to be more task-oriented (for example, inclined to make suggestions and state opinions), whereas females tend to be more socioemotional in their participation (for example, inclined to praise and agree with other discussion members).

The question naturally arises, Is verbal participation important to discussion outcomes? Several studies have found that amount of verbal participation is not related to satisfaction with the group's work. In a study of group problem solving by Hoffman, Burke,

126. Irwin Katz and Lawrence Benjamin, "Effects of White Authoritarianism in Biracial Work Groups," *Journal of Abnormal and Social Psychology* 61 (November 1960): 448-56.

127. T. E. Deal, *Modifying the Effects of Age within Decision-making Groups*, Technical Report No. 4 (Stanford, Cal.: School of Education, Stanford University, 1970).

128. Marlaine E. Lockheed and Katherine P. Hall, "Sex as a Status Characteristic—The Role of Formal Theory in Developing Leadership Training Strategies" (Paper presented at the annual meeting of the American Sociological Association, San Francisco, Cal., August 1975).

and Maier, the amount of verbal participation by individual discussants was unrelated to their degree of satisfaction with the solution finally accepted by the group.[129] However, the extent to which discussants expressed support for the final solution during the discussion process was positively related to their degree of satisfaction with the solution. Porter found only a slight positive correlation ($r = .22$), not statistically significant, between amount of participation in a discussion and stated member satisfaction.[130] However, significant positive correlations were found between stated member satisfaction and amount of group-oriented verbal behaviors.

We were unable to locate studies concerning the relationship between verbal participation and attitude change or subject matter mastery. Concerning the latter outcome variable, Nuthall has observed that individual students spend very little time speaking in classroom discussions.[131] Most of their time is spent in listening to a question-answer dialogue between the teacher and some other student. (Some researchers would use the term "recitation" for such discussions.) Yet Nuthall hypothesizes that covert learning responses evoked by the teacher's questions, not the actual verbal responses, are critical for learning. The teacher's discussion questions can produce learning both in students who respond verbally and those who just listen to the interchange while engaging in covert learning processes.

Some researchers have developed training procedures to increase verbal participation among females, ethnic minority groups, and shy students. But the little evidence available suggests that verbal participation per se may not be important since it does not affect discussion outcomes. Specific verbal behaviors may have effects, though. Therefore, educators are advised to analyze the discussion process carefully to decide which verbal behaviors to reinforce

129. L. Richard Hoffman, Ronald J. Burke, and Norman R. F. Maier, "Participation, Influence, and Satisfaction among Members of Problem-solving Groups," *Psychological Reports* 16, no. 2 (1965): 661-67.

130. Robert M. Porter, "Relationship of Participation to Satisfaction in Small Group Discussions," *Journal of Educational Research* 59 (November 1965): 128-32.

131. Graham Nuthall, "Learning in Classroom Discussion: A Theoretical Explanation" (Unpublished manuscript, Education Department, University of Canterbury, n.d.).

from silent students, rather than reinforcing all attempts at participation indiscriminately.

Perhaps certain students learn more from the discussion method
than other students. To test this hypothesis, Dowaliby and Schumer
conducted an experiment in which college students were randomly
assigned either to a lecture class or to a discussion class for a
semester. Using performance on the course examinations as the
measure of learning, the researchers found that high-anxiety students did better than low-anxiety students in the lecture class; however, low-anxiety students did better than high-anxiety students in
the discussion class.[132] A possible explanation of this finding is provided in an earlier study by McKeachie, who found a positive relationship between degree of structure in teaching method and
school achievement.[133] McKeachie interpreted this finding as follows, "The student's anxiety is heightened or reduced by the instructor's teaching behavior. In general, control of anxiety is easiest
if the student is in a highly controlled situation, where he knows
exactly what he must do." [134] Since discussion is less structured than
lecture, it may provoke anxiety in the predisposed student and
thereby interfere with learning.

Peterson recently conducted an experiment which replicated
certain features of the Dowaliby-Schumer study and added others.[135]
Ninth-grade students were assigned to a two-week curriculum unit

132. Fred J. Dowaliby and Harry Schumer, "Teacher-centered versus Student-centered Mode of College Classroom Instruction as Related to Manifest
Anxiety," *Journal of Educational Psychology* 64 (April 1973): 125-32. A nice
feature of Dowaliby and Schumer's study is that the discussion and lecture
classes covered curriculum material not included in the students' textbook.
Only this material was tested in the course examination. Thus, Dowaliby and
Schumer avoided the problem present in other lecture-versus-discussion studies
in which students could do well on the course examination just by studying
the textbook.

133. Wilbert J. McKeachie, "Anxiety in the College Classroom," *Journal
of Educational Research* 45 (October 1951): 153-60.

134. Ibid., p. 154.

135. Penelope L. Peterson, "Interactive Effects of Student Anxiety, Achievement Orientation, and Teacher Behavior on Student Achievement and Attitude" (Ph.D. diss., Stanford University, in progress).

taught by one of four teaching methods: High Structure/High Participation; High Structure/Low Participation; Low Structure/ Low Participation; and Low Structure/High Participation. "Structure" included teaching techniques such as stating the goal of the lesson and summarizing during the lesson. "Participation" included teaching techniques designed to evoke responses and discussion among students. Peterson found that on a multiple-choice retention test[136] high-anxiety students did better in either the High Structure/ High Participation approach or the Low/Low approach; low-anxiety students did better in the High Structure/Low Participation approach or the Low/High approach. These results do not confirm the Dowaliby-Schumer findings, which would predict that high-anxiety students would do well only under conditions of high structure, or low participation, or both. At this point we can only conclude that student anxiety does interact with the discussion method, but the effects of the interaction are not yet clearly understood.

A study concerning a different type of learner characteristic was conducted by Mitnick and McGinnies.[137] Groups of high school students were randomly assigned to view a film on racial tolerance or to view the film and then participate in discussion. Within each experimental condition, half of the groups consisted solely of highly prejudiced students. The other half of the groups consisted solely of students low in prejudice. The results showed that, for the groups low in prejudice, the film-discussion treatment was more effective in reducing prejudice than the film-alone treatment. However, for the highly prejudiced groups, the film-alone treatment was substantially more effective in reducing prejudice than the film-discussion treatment. Analysis of the discussion transcripts suggests an explanation for this finding: highly prejudiced students spent most of their time expressing their antipathies toward blacks, whereas low prejudice students spent most of their time discussing issues concerning the prejudice shown in the film. It appears, then, that discussion can either promote attitude change

136. As in the Dowaliby-Schumer study, the criterion test in the Peterson study included only information directly taught in the treatment.

137. Mitnick and McGinnies, "Influencing Ethnocentrism in Small Discussion Groups."

or reinforce existing attitudes depending upon the student's entering characteristics.

The few available findings on the interaction between student characteristics and the discussion method provide suggestions rather than prescriptions for teaching. In conducting discussions, the teacher should try to create a nonthreatening discussion environment for the student predisposed to anxiety. If the goal of the discussion is understanding or change of attitudes, the teacher should use techniques that prevent students from simply using discussion time to reinforce each others' existing attitudes. One technique might be to form groups which are heterogeneous with respect to the issue being discussed.

Concluding Remarks

This review has ranged over a substantial body of research pertinent to the discussion method conducted by psychologists in laboratory, industrial, and educational settings. We shall summarize by examining questions of concern to teachers—Why should they use the discussion method? When? How? And with whom?

Why should teachers use the discussion method? They should use it because it is effective in promoting important educational objectives: mastery of subject matter content, especially mastery related to students' use of higher cognitive processes; attitude change, including development of positive attitudes toward concepts taught in the curriculum; solving of complex problems which require group commitment for implementation; and development of discussion skills related to listening, speaking, and group leadership. Furthermore, these positive effects have been observed in a variety of subject matter areas. Although some educators think that the discussion method is more appropriate for teaching the humanities and social sciences than for teaching mathematics and the physical sciences, we find no evidence to support this notion. The nature of the intended learning outcome (for example, attitude change), rather than the curriculum content, determines the effectiveness of the discussion method.

Although we know that the discussion method is effective, further research is needed to determine just how effective it can be when implemented under optimal conditions, for example, with a small group of students led by a well-trained teacher. In doing this type of study, researchers should include performance measures that are sensitive to the various hypothesized effects of the discussion method, in addition to traditional tests of information. Also, we need to learn more about how students perceive the discussion method; for example, do they view it as having the same benefits as those which researchers typically measure? Indeed, students may perceive negative effects of the discussion method which researchers have overlooked.

When should teachers use the discussion method? This is the question that is least well answered by available research. One aspect of this question is the issue of how often the discussion method should be used. Descriptive studies of classroom interaction patterns suggest that it is used infrequently, except perhaps in post-secondary instruction. Probably the discussion method should be used more frequently than is current practice. On the other hand, it is doubtful whether the discussion method should ever be the exclusive vehicle of instruction, particularly since students would become bored by the lack of instructional variety.

Another aspect of this question concerns how the discussion method should be patterned into a sequence of instruction. Research findings reviewed above indicate that a reading assignment followed by discussion is an effective sequence. However, other sequences are possible, such as discussion preceding reading or a pattern of discuss-read-discuss. Investigation of the effects of these sequences and other variations is needed.

The research on group dynamics provides a rich base for answering the third question of concern to teachers, How should the discussion method be used? Five recommendations for implementation of the discussion method emerge from the research findings. First, it appears desirable to limit the size of the discussion group. While two to twenty students represents a reasonable lower and upper limit, the best group size appears to be approximately five members. Although small group size may be difficult to achieve, it probably is the most critical factor in optimal implementation of the discussion method.

The second recommendation is that the teacher form discussion groups in which students are heterogeneous rather than homogeneous with respect to abilities, attitudes, and other characteristics. Although heterogeneity initially may create interpersonal obstacles, time and attention to these obstacles may improve the group's interpersonal processes and allow the variety of perspectives and talents present in the group to foster achievement of the discussion objectives.

The third recommendation is that the teacher should foster moderate rather than high cohesiveness in the discussion group. Although a highly cohesive group may provide greater interpersonal rewards to its members, the possibility of rejecting students with minority views, ignoring the task, or restricting performance if members do not fully support task goals, makes high group cohesiveness a mixed blessing from the standpoint of instructional outcomes.

Fourth, to promote effective communication, the teacher should establish seating arrangements which place students within easy eye contact and hearing range of each other; also, the teacher should place minimal restrictions on the initiation or exchange of communication among students and between teacher and students.

The final recommendation is for the teacher to exercise a democratic rather than an authoritarian leadership style. The use of democratic leadership techniques has several positive effects, such as encouraging student participation in decision making, free expression of viewpoints, and emergence of student leadership.

With whom should the teacher use the discussion method? Positive effects have been found at all grade levels, from elementary pupils to adult learners. The degree of structure, and the range and level of task goals to which the discussion is aimed, may need to be different for students at different age levels, but the discussion method seems adaptable to any age at which students possess sufficient verbal skills for oral exchange. It may be particularly valuable for students whose reading comprehension or independent study skills are weak, since it provides a completely different learning mode (speaking-listening in a group) for achieving subject matter mastery and other educational objectives.

Use of the discussion method with anxious students presents a special problem for the teacher. Research findings indicate that some students are anxious in discussions, and that their anxiety may interfere with learning. We need to know more about how to help such students deal with their anxiety so that they can learn effectively from the discussion method.

Some educators hold the pessimistic view that all teaching methods are equally effective, and thus there is little point in training teachers to use varied methods. Our view, though, is that the findings of research justify at least some of the enthusiasm which educators have expressed for the discussion method. The evidence is persuasive that, properly implemented, this method is more effective than other methods in achieving certain important educational objectives.

CHAPTER VII

Teaching with Simulations and Games

CONSTANCE J. SEIDNER

Socialization Function of Play

Play is a universal phenomenon.[1] Its function in the socialization process may be viewed from several perspectives. Play was seen by the social psychologist George Herbert Mead as essential to the development of the self.[2] Even simple games require that a child deal symbolically with the anticipated actions of other players toward him, or that he see himself as others see him. This process was seen by Mead as the genesis of the social self. Since such anticipation of other's actions is a symbolic task, cognitive processes are involved. Piaget has further explored the place of play in the development of cognitive processes.[3] His work indicates that childhood games play an important role in the evolution of intelligence. Thus, play is viewed by social psychologists and cognitive theorists as an essential element in the social and intellectual development of children.

Since the individual cannot be separated from his environment, play may also be characterized as a process of anticipatory socialization whereby the child learns the norms and mores of his society. The view that a social game provided a means by which the individual could practice, or "play," society was expressed by the sociologist Georg Simmel at the turn of the century.[4] The link

1. Johan Huizinga, *Homo Ludens: A Study of the Play Element in Culture* (Boston: Beacon Press, 1950).

2. George Herbert Mead, *Mind, Self, and Society* (Chicago: University of Chicago Press, 1934).

3. Jean Piaget, *Play, Dreams and Imitation in Childhood* (New York: W. W. Norton, 1962).

4. Georg Simmel, "Sociability: An Example of Pure, or Formal, Sociology," in *The Sociology of Georg Simmel*, ed. Kurt H. Wolff (Glencoe, Ill.: Free Press, 1950), pp. 40-54.

between culture and play forms has been further analyzed by Anderson and Moore, who suggested that various types of play forms, or folk models, mirror analogous processes in society.[5] Noting the inadequacy of traditional folk models as symbolic representations of the complexities of modern society, Moore related the development of simulations to the need for scientific models that would more accurately reflect the dynamics of a world in transition.[6]

If the relationship between play and socialization is generally recognized, and if the primary function of school is to prepare each generation for productive societal membership, one must ponder the relative absence of play activities from school, except as relief—recess—from the real business of learning. It should be pointed out that not all educational theorists have viewed games as an inappropriate learning activity. Dewey noted the link between play and social life and advocated the use of games as an integral part of the curriculum.[7] It is likely that many creative teachers over the years have recognized the fact that any drill can be turned into a game and have proceeded to do so whenever it seemed appropriate. The "spelling bee" is certainly not a recent innovation.

Nonetheless, the current interest in educational games does not represent a gradual acceptance of a long-established teaching technique. Zuckerman and Horn noted a 50 percent increase in the number of readily available games and simulations in a period of two years, from 1970 to 1972.[8] While this increase may not represent a revolutionary landslide, it indicates growing acceptance of a teaching technique that received little attention in educational circles until approximately the last decade.

5. Omar K. Moore and Alan R. Anderson, "Some Principles for the Design of Clarifying Educational Environments," in *Handbook of Socialization Theory and Research*, ed. David A. Goslin (Chicago: Rand McNally, 1969), pp. 571-614.

6. Omar K. Moore, "Autotelic Simulation" (Paper presented at the International Simulation and Gaming Association Conference, West Berlin, May 25, 1974).

7. John Dewey, *Democracy and Education* (New York: Macmillan, 1928).

8. David Zuckerman and Robert E. Horn, *The Guide to Simulations/Games for Education and Training* (Lexington, Mass.: Information Resources Inc., 1973), p. 433.

The increased utilization of educational games may be attributable to many factors, including the coincidence of three trends: (a) the questioning of the traditional socialization function of our educational institutions, (b) the current emphasis on the active learner and discovery learning, and (c) the appearance of a new medium, the simulation game.

Thus the declining utility of the fact-dispensing function of schools and the concomitant increase in the need for providing youth with experiences that will prepare them for the contingencies of contemporary society (trend "a")[9] has coincided nicely with renewed emphasis on the development of problem-solving abilities through involvement of the learner with the structure and content of the learning task (trend "b").[10] The third trend, the development of the simulation game, has become a vehicle that, in theory, may foster achievement of the goals implicit in each of the first two trends.

Before considering the educational objectives that may be achieved through the use of simulation games (or simulations and games) and reviewing the empirical evidence on their effectiveness, we should explain the broad leap negotiated in the preceding few paragraphs. We began with a discussion of play, edged imperceptibly into games, and now have introduced the concept of simulation as either distinct from games, or in some cases related to them. These often confused terms must be distinguished from one another before discussing the rationale underlying the use of simulations and games in education.

Types of Simulations and Games

NONSIMULATION GAMES

Caillois describes play as free, make-believe activity that, although it may be governed by rules, is characterized by uncertainty in that neither the course of the activity nor its final end may be

9. James S. Coleman, "The Children Have Outgrown the Schools," *National Elementary Principal* 52 (October 1972): 17-21.

10. Jerome Bruner, *Toward a Theory of Instruction* (New York: W. W. Norton, 1966).

ascertained before the fact.[11] One distinguishing characteristic of a *game* as opposed to play is that the participants agree upon certain *objectives*, as well as a set of rules that limit the means whereby these objectives may be attained.[12] Games are often competitive, but need not be so.[13]

The number of ways games can be used in education is virtually limitless. Card games may be adapted to educational purposes by requiring students to manipulate factual materials printed on the cards in order to attain some specified objective. The rules of the game are similar to the rules of the card game. While games of this type are commercially available, many teachers construct their own. A useful format for teacher-made games is the frame game, which permits the insertion of different subject matters into a given framework of rules.[14]

An important type of nonsimulation game, developed by Layman E. Allen and his associates, is the resource-allocation game. In this type of game, "the resources to be allocated are symbols representing the fundamental ideas of a field of knowledge." [15] *Equations* and *Wff 'n Proof* are resource-allocation games that deal with mathematics and logic, respectively.[16]

In resource-allocation games, as in other nonsimulation games, students usually work in groups and are actively involved in the learning process. Success, or winning, is related to the degree of subject matter comprehension demonstrated during the game.

11. Roger Caillois, *Man, Play and Games* (New York: Free Press, 1961), pp. 3-10.

12. For an excellent definition of a game see Bernard Suits, "What Is a Game?" *Philosophy of Science* 34 (June 1967): 148-56.

13. For an elaboration of this point see R. Garry Shirts, "Notes on Defining Simulation," *Occasional Newsletter about Simulations and Games No. 15* (La Jolla, Cal.: Western Behavioral Sciences Institute, n.d.), pp. 14-23.

14. See, for example, Gail M. Fennessey and Erling O. Schild, *User's Manual for Information: A Frame Game* (Baltimore: Academic Games Associates, 1974).

15. Layman E. Allen, "RAG-PELT: Resource Allocation Games–Planned Environments for Learning and Thinking," *Simulation and Games* 3 (December 1972): 407.

16. Unless otherwise specified, all simulation/games cited in the chapter are referenced in Zuckerman and Horn, *The Guide to Simulations/Games*.

SIMULATIONS

In the broadest sense, simulation refers to the dynamic execution or manipulation of a model of some object system.[17] In education, simulation entails abstracting certain elements of social or physical reality in such a way that the student can interact with and become a part of that simulated reality.[18]

All-machine simulations. Simulations can be completely computerized. In this case, the parameters that define the referent system are completely contained in the computer program. This type of simulation, although it has some value for learning, does not lend itself to classroom settings, but is more often used in research by planners and theoreticians.

Man-machine simulations. In some simulations, individuals interact with a computerized system by making decisions that affect the functioning of the system. Thus the individual becomes a part of the simulated system by playing the role of a system participant. An example of a man-machine simulation is *Sierra Leone*, an exercise in which students, playing the role of an economic advisor, make decisions that influence the economy of a developing country. Their decisions are transmitted to the computer, which calculates a status report and requests another decision, and so on. Although the instrumentation of man-machine simulations is largely dominated by computers, it should be pointed out that students may also interact with other types of mechanical systems (usually termed simulators), such as a driver-training simulator.

All-man simulations. In all-man simulations the parameters of the referent system are embedded in a set of specifications, or rules, that define the roles and resources of participants. These specifications are devised to reflect the restraints inherent in the referent system so that simulation participants will experience some of the same kinds of pressures and influences that would occur in a real-life setting. As in real life, a number of options are available. Thus

17. Richard F. Barton, *A Primer on Simulation Gaming* (Englewood Cliffs, N.J.: Prentice-Hall, 1970), p. 6.

18. In this discussion, terms used to distinguish different types of simulations are drawn from a classification offered by H. A. Becker in "Levels of Simulation Models" (Paper presented at the International Simulation and Gaming Association Conference, West Berlin, May 25, 1974).

the decisions and subsequent actions of the simulation participants in pursuing their various roles become a part of the system, influencing the behavior of others as well as their own future options.

All-man simulations are the type most frequently used in classroom settings. If access to computers were more readily available, the incidence of man-machine simulations would no doubt increase. Most all-man and man-machine simulations are designed to reflect social rather than physical systems.[19] This fact has led to the use of the term *social simulation* and, when the concept is coupled with the elements of a game, the term *social simulation game*.[20]

One final word should be added about simulations in general. They are abstractions and simplifications of the real world. They focus upon particular aspects of the referent system rather than upon all of its elements.[21] This focusing is especially true of all-

19. One of the earliest publications focusing on simulations was Harold Guetzkow, ed., *Simulation in Social Science: Readings* (Englewood Cliffs, N.J.: Prentice-Hall, 1962). More recent volumes include Michael Inbar and Clarice S. Stoll, eds., *Simulation and Gaming in Social Science* (New York: Free Press, 1972) and Cheryl L. Charles and Ronald Stadsklev, *Learning with Games: An Analysis of Social Studies Educational Games and Simulations* (Boulder, Col.: Social Science Educational Consortium and ERIC Clearinghouse for Social Studies/Social Science Education, 1973). The recent literature, however, indicates increased interest in simulations in such diverse areas as biology (Robert Patterson, T. Custer, and Bayard H. Brattestrom, "Simulation of Natural Selection," *American Biology Teacher* 34 [February 1972]: 95-96); English (James M. Brewbaker, "Simulation Games and the English Teacher," *English Journal* 61 [January 1972]: 104-9); physics (Thomas Liao, "Analog Computer Simulation in High School Science Courses," *Physics Teacher* 10 [May 1972]: 245-48); chemistry (Olaf Rundquist, Rodney Olson, and Bruce Snadeen, "Programmable Calculators: Simulated Experiments," *Journal of Chemical Education* 49 [April 1972]: 256-66); communication (William I. Gordon, "Simulation Review Essay: Simulation Games in the Study of Communication," *Simulation and Games* 6 [June 1975]: 215-24); and dentistry (George W. Gaines, "A Model for Developing Simulation-Performance Tests: Application to Dental Education" [Paper presented at the International Simulation and Gaming Association Conference, West Berlin, May 26, 1974]).

20. James S. Coleman, "Social Processes and Social Simulation Games," in *Simulation Games in Learning*, ed. Sarane S. Boocock and E. O. Schild (Beverly Hills, Cal.: Sage Publications, 1968), pp. 29-52.

21. This poses obvious problems of validity, which have been discussed by Charles F. Hermann, "Validation Problems in Games and Simulations with Special Reference to Models of International Politics," *Behavioral Science* 12, no. 3 (1967): 216-31; John R. Raser, *Simulation and Society: An Exploration of Scientific Gaming* (Boston: Allyn and Bacon, 1969), pp. 137-56; and Sarane S. Boocock, "Validity Testing of an Intergenerational Relations Game," *Simulation and Games* 3 (March 1972): 39-51.

man simulations. The use of a computer, of course, permits the addition of more complex variables, but it also tends to decrease or even eliminate interaction between individuals.

SIMULATION GAMES

Having defined simulations and games, we now consider when a simulation becomes a simulation game. Perhaps the clearest distinction was offered by Coleman, who suggested that, in *simulation games*, success is defined in terms of players' *goals*; there is a prescribed criterion for winning.[22] In simulations that are not games there may be a final position, but a winner is not explicitly determined. Thus, one characteristic that separates play from games, a specified goal or objective, may also be used to distinguish a simulation from a simulation game.[23] As an example, consider a man-machine simulation of a chemical experiment to determine the quantity of an unknown. This simulation would become a simulation game if it were prespecified that the student who made the correct determination first (or with the least amount of computer time) would be the winner.

This example is atypical in that it involves the individual student working with a computer against classmates who are not physically present. Most simulation games involve interaction among a number of students. This characteristic makes them particularly suitable for classroom instruction.

Having traversed the difficult domain of definitions, we shall observe certain conventions in the remainder of the chapter. When referring to simulations and games as a generic class, a type of teaching technique, we shall use the term *simulation/game*. When referring to a particular type, such as a nonsimulation game, we

22. James S. Coleman, "The Role of Modern Technology in Relation to Simulation and Games for Learning" (Washington, D.C.: Academy for Educational Development, 1970). ERIC: ED 039 704. This publication is a support paper for "To Improve Learning: A Report to the President and the Congress of the United States" (Washington, D.C.: Commission on Instructional Technology, 1969), ERIC: ED 034 905.

23. A lack of consensus regarding the distinction between simulations and games is noted in the literature. For alternative criteria, see F. L. Goodman, "Gaming and Simulation," in *Second Handbook of Research on Teaching*, ed. R. M. W. Travers (Chicago: Rand McNally, 1973), p. 929, or Raser, *Simulation and Society*, p. x.

shall use the definitions developed in the foregoing section. Unless otherwise specified, the term *simulation game* will be used to refer to either man-machine or all-man simulations that incorporate a goal-oriented approach.

Relationships of Simulation/Games to Other Teaching Techniques

ROLE PLAYING

The problem of isolating the educational effects of simulation/ games is that such games overlap with other teaching techniques. Take for example a minimum-structure social simulation game that defines the roles of players within a given social context, specifies very broad goals, and then leaves the player largely to his own devices in determining how the role should be articulated.[24] Certainly such exercises involve role playing to a large degree.

Although, as Schild points out,[25] simulation games in general emphasize instrumental rather than expressive behavior, specific simulation games appear to rely heavily on role playing as a means of attaining educational objectives, particularly when these objectives fall within the affective domain. Therefore, variables that influence the effectiveness of role playing as a teaching technique must be considered when planning and evaluating simulation exercises that emphasize expressive identification with assigned roles.[26]

POSTGAME DISCUSSION

Virtually all designers and users of simulation games point to the usefulness of a postgame discussion in clarifying what has transpired during the gaming session. The importance of the postgame

24. James L. Heap, "The Student as Resource: Use of the Minimum Structure Simulation Game in Teaching," *Simulation and Games* 2 (December 1971): 473-87.

25. E. O. Schild, "Interaction in Games," in Boocock and Schild, *Simulation Games in Learning*, pp. 96-97.

26. Boocock noted that the extent to which subjects identified with roles performed in *Life Career* tended to mediate affective outcomes. See Sarane S. Boocock, "An Experimental Study of the Learning Effects of Two Games with Simulated Environments," in Boocock and Schild, *Simulation Games in Learning*, p. 115.

discussion in achieving educational objectives will be considered later. But it should be noted that, if discussion is considered to be part of the simulation game exercise, the skill of the discussion leader is a crucial variable that should not be disregarded.

Finally, simulations or simulation games that utilize computers to represent part of the referent system combine some of the characteristics of computer-assisted instruction and simulation techniques. Computer simulations typically offer the player a choice of strategies, and the best strategy is not always obvious. While a given strategy may be better in terms of the final goal of the player, the "rightness" or "wrongness" of a particular decision within that strategy may not be immediately apparent. Computer-assisted instruction, on the other hand, provides immediate feedback regarding the correctness of any given answer.

This aspect of computer-assisted simulations presents a problem in assessing learning that may result from participation in the simulated environment. In the case of a business simulation, for example, did the player whose correct strategies resulted in monetary gains for his simulated company learn the most, or did the player whose company failed miserably actually learn more?

This question leads to the difficult problem of assessing the effectiveness of simulation/games from a psychological perspective. A tremendously diverse array of educational media has been developed, virtually in a theoretical void. As Boocock and Schild point out, we have a technology that apparently works, at least to some degree, but we are not quite sure why.[27]

Learning from Simulation/Games

NONSIMULATION GAMES

In the case of nonsimulation games, the theoretical rationale is rather straightforward. To play the game, students have to know certain facts, perform certain skills, or demonstrate mastery of certain concepts. Winning depends upon mastery of these cognitive skills. The gaming situation itself, and the social interaction

27. Boocock and Schild, *Simulation Games in Learning*, p. 22.

with peers in an atmosphere that suggests fun rather than classwork, appear to be sufficiently appealing to induce students to devote willingly increased time and energy to learning the requisite skills. (Allen reports that students playing *Wff 'n Proof* asked to be allowed to continue playing rather than go to recess.)[28]

In this type of game, knowledge of results is usually immediate, and repeated plays reinforce learning. Recalling the curvilinear relationship between tension and learning, we consider it possible that gaming situations provide just enough tension in the form of wanting to win, without invoking excessive worry about failure, as in a testing situation.

TRAINING SIMULATIONS

Training simulations appear to present a similar paradigm. Students are provided with the opportunity to practice given skills, as in the case of a driver-training simulator. Results are contingent upon actions, and feedback is immediate.

Training simulations are sometimes distinguished from teaching simulations in that the former stress *how* to do something, while the latter focus on *why*.[29] The difference may be more apparent than real. Is it reasonable to suggest that a prospective businessman who learns how to forecast by participating in a simulation does not know why he acts as he does? The answer here may clarify the somewhat ambiguous research findings on the effects of simulations and simulation games on learning.

SIMULATION GAMES

Simulation games as an instructional model. Coleman has suggested that simulation games involve students in a mode of learning that differs from the traditional information-processing mode. Experiential learning begins with student action, rather than the absorption of information assumed to lead eventually to student ac-

28. Layman E. Allen, Robert W. Allen, and James C. Miller, "Programmed Games and the Learning of Problem-Solving Skills: The *Wff 'n Proof* Example," *Journal of Educational Research* 60 (September 1966): 22-26.

29. Steven J. Kidder and John T. Guthrie, *The Training Effects of a Behavior Modification Game*, Report No. 116 (Baltimore: Center for Social Organization of Schools, Johns Hopkins University, 1971), p. 22.

tion. In a simulation game, the student acts and observes concrete events that result from his action.[30]

Kidder suggested, however, that in analyzing the effects of simulation games, we should focus our attention on *models of teaching* rather than models of learning. Kidder assumed that the mechanisms of learning are similar in both the experiential and information processing modes; some kind of information is processed in either case. What distinguishes simulation games from other modes of instruction is the *type of stimuli* presented, and the *organization* of those stimuli into a teaching sequence.[31] In simulation games, stimuli are generally presented in more than one form (that is, enactive, iconic, and symbolic representations),[32] whereas in other teaching media, one type of representation may predominate. Moreover, the organization of a simulation game has much in common with the organization of a total curriculum sequence. The motivational qualities of simulation games predispose students toward learning. Structure and sequencing of stimuli are embedded in the simulation model, as is the dispensation of rewards.

Role of behavior theory. It has been suggested that the use of simulation games in teaching implies a purposive rather than a positivist orientation toward the origins of behavior.[33] The writer prefers an integrative point of view that recognizes the reciprocal nature of man's relationship to his environment. The degree of motivation evidenced by most (but not all) students engaged in a simulation game suggests the existence of a self-interested individual interacting with his environment in the pursuit of an intrinsically motivating goal. This goal may be winning[34] or some form of role

30. Samuel A. Livingston et al., "The Hopkins Games Program: Final Report," Report No. 155 (Baltimore: Center for Social Organization of Schools, Johns Hopkins University, 1973), pp. 2-9.

31. Steven J. Kidder, "Instruction-Learning-Gaming: Theory" (Paper presented to the American Sociological Association, Montreal, August 1974).

32. Bruner, *Toward a Theory of Instruction*, pp. 10-11.

33. Coleman, "Social Processes and Social Simulation Games," p. 36.

34. While the emphasis on winning is sometimes considered to be a defect of simulation games in general, it is not impossible to define winning in humanistic terms. Tansey notes that simulation/games developed in the United Kingdom generally have less emphasis on competition and winning than do those developed in the United States. See P. J. Tansey, "A Primer of Simula-

support from self or others. Visions of possible extrinsic rewards, such as grades, which might accrue from a successful performance, may also be a motivating factor.

The student engaged in a simulation game is an active learner who, through his experiences with the simulated environment, may discover for himself certain concepts or principles embedded in the simulation model. After participating in a simulation game, students may ask the same kinds of questions that social scientists might pose concerning real social systems, and then experiment with the simulated system by changing the rules to see what might happen if . . . ? [35]

Despite this emphasis on the learner's acting upon his environment, one cannot ignore the response of the environment to the learner. In the case of simulation games, that response has a great deal to do with the design of the learning instrument. For example, let us consider an economic simulation that, among other things, illustrates the relationship between supply and demand. Suppose player X acts in such a way as to bring this principle into operation within the context of the simulation. Did he "learn" this principle? The answer to this question may depend on such factors as:

1. *The degree of impact on the actor:* Was he personally affected or merely an observer of an event that affected his teammates more directly than it affected him?
2. *The contingencies he experienced:* If he was personally affected, did he gain or lose?
3. *The operationalization of contingencies:* Were rewards tangible (such as tokens or play money) or intangible (such as altered status)?
4. *The actor's personal dispositions toward his role:* Was it a role with which he was familiar, felt comfortable?
5. *The character and composition of the group and the actor's position within it.*

---

tion: Its Methods, Models and Application in Educational Processes," in *Educational Aspects of Simulation*, ed. P. J. Tansey (London: McGraw-Hill, 1971), pp. 11-12.

35. For further elaboration on the relationship between simulation games and the inquiry approach to learning, see Samuel A. Livingston and Clarice Stasz Stoll, *Simulation Games: An Introduction for the Social Studies Teacher* (New York: Free Press, 1972), p. 9.

Even if we were able to ascertain what player X learned, what about player Y? Since all the actors in the simulation experienced the same event from their own particular perspectives, it would be fallacious to assume that their learnings were identical. In addition to what happened to each actor, the impact of the event will be influenced by the manner in which the designer operationalized contingencies. Even events over which designers have no control, such as group composition and self-role incongruence, will influence what is learned.

It would appear that the best way to insure learning from simulation games would be to design the game in such a way as to make the desired learning requisite to playing the game, and to provide for at least semicontrolled reinforcement for appropriate player behavior. Reinforcement is derived from the simulated system itself and may take many forms: (a) a computer print-out, (b) the imposition of a game rule, or (c) the reactions of teammates who also comprise an aspect of the simulated system.

It may be argued that man-machine simulation games provide more immediate and controllable feedback than the sometimes capricious actions of peers. This argument cannot be separated from the purposes for which the simulation game is designed. If cognitive skills are the goal, the computer, or a fairly rigid set of game rules, may indeed be a more effective means of providing reinforcement. But if the purpose of the simulation game falls within the affective domain, then interpersonal exchanges may be more appropriate. This leads quite naturally to a discussion of the objectives for which simulation/games may be most appropriate within the classroom context.

Goals for Which Simulation/Games May Be Appropriate

STRUCTURAL AND PROCESS GOALS

The use of simulation/games in the classroom differs sufficiently from more traditional types of teaching techniques, so that it cannot be discussed without reference to the changes in classroom structure and process that such use implies. For some educators, these changes represent goals in and of themselves.

Communication. For those who would like to break the communication barrier associated with the traditional student-teacher relationship, the use of simulation/games offers a viable alternative. Simulation/games in the classroom may also increase interaction among the students themselves. This interaction may be particularly desirable in classes composed of students from divergent ethnic or socio-economic backgrounds.

Motivation. Simulation/games provide a self-motivating type of activity that is gratifying in and of itself and therefore tends to be self-perpetuating. This characteristic of simulation/games would appear to have important implications for student motivation.

Reward structure. It has been suggested by Coleman,[36] Spilerman,[37] and others, that the reward structure of schools that is based on interpersonal competition for grades might well be replaced by interscholastic (or intramural) competition. The work of Julian and Perry [38] suggests that, while individual competition heightens productivity, productivity is also high in groups that work together in a cooperative manner, but compete as a team against another group. Moreover, human relations in this type of "group cooperative-team competitive" situation were described by researchers as more satisfactory than relations in the individual-competitive groups. For educators who subscribe to the goal of decreasing interpersonal competition, simulation/games offer an ideal medium for operationalizing intergroup academic competion, even within the boundaries imposed by the traditional classroom environment.

CONTENT OBJECTIVES

Cognitive objectives. The design of nonsimulation games is particularly appropriate for the teaching of facts and concepts in a given subject-matter area. Many simulations and simulation games also incorporate a body of factual knowledge into the structure and functioning of the game—knowledge that is to be transmitted

36. James S. Coleman, *The Adolescent Society* (New York: Free Press, 1961), pp. 311-29.

37. Seymour Spilerman, "Raising Academic Motivation in Lower Class Adolescents: A Convergence of Two Research Traditions," *Sociology of Education* 44 (Winter 1971): 103-18.

38. James W. Julian and Franklyn A. Perry, "Cooperation Contrasted with Intra-group and Inter-group Competition," *Sociometry* 39 (March 1967): 79-90.

to the student through participation in the simulation. Some of this knowledge reflects higher order concepts and principles embedded in the model of the simulation. Although simulations and simulation games are potentially powerful techniques for teaching complex principles and problem-solving techniques, their effectiveness is highly dependent upon many factors, some of which were enumerated in the previous section. Hence, the potential has yet to be fully realized.

Affective objectives. Objectives in the affective domain appear to be largely limited to simulation games that involve interaction between students. Since some degree of role playing is involved in most simulation games, it might be expected that role empathy may be evoked as a result of the simulated experience.

Simulation games involve the student in a recreated environment, usually a social environment, which reflects the designer's conception of one piece of reality. That reality may, in some cases, differ from the students' preconceived notion of what really goes on in, for example, the Congress of the United States. Thus it is possible that changes in attitude may be induced by participation in a simulation game that mirrors the activities of that legislative body. While it might be assumed that changes in attitude would tend to be in the direction that coincides with the world view reflected in the simulation, when predispositions of the participants are taken into account, this may not always be the case.

Creativity. It has been suggested that simulation/games that encourage divergent solutions may be useful in the nurturance of creativity.[39] In a major address to the International Simulation and Gaming Association, Jungk articulated a similar theme, suggesting that the semireal situation provided by a gaming setting provides a "safe" environment for brainstorming wherein individuals may spin off ideas that, at first blush, may seem preposterous—ideas that might not have been offered in a "real" setting for fear of ridicule.[40]

39. Katherine E. Chapman, *Guidelines for Using Social/Simulation Games* (Boulder, Col.: ERIC Clearinghouse for Social Studies/Social Science Education and Social Science Educational Consortium, Inc., 1973), p. 14.

40. Robert Jungk, "Gaming Alternative Futures" (Paper presented at the International Simulation and Gaming Association Conference, West Berlin, May 25, 1974).

Although Jungk's remarks were addressed to scholars, they appear to be equally applicable to students in school settings.

Many simulation game designers readily admit that the reality they mirror may not reflect the world as they wish it might be, and actively encourage students to redesign the system as they would like it to be. Some of the priming simulation games developed by Goodman, for example, *Policy Negotiations*,[41] are expressly designed to encourage redesign by game participants. This redesign necessarily involves some brainstorming, and sometimes unique solutions evolve in the process.

DEVELOPING COMPETENCE

Categorization is always difficult and sometimes misleading. No doubt there are cognitive as well as affective components of the competencies to be considered here. In reviewing what has been written and researched in the field of simulation/games, one is struck by the convergence of several lines of thought upon the conception of competence articulated by Smith.[42] Smith suggested that one component of competence is a sense of efficacy, a feeling that one's environment is understandable and manageable. This sense of coping with one's environment may be hypothesized to have many components, some of which have been identified with the theory and practice of simulation/gaming. Among them are (a) an emphasis on understanding one's environment and a belief in one's ability to exert some control over that environment, and (b) the development of those interpersonal and technical strategies that increase one's coping abilities.

Control beliefs. Noting the association between a sense of control of one's destiny and academic achievement, particularly for black students,[43] a group of scholars at Johns Hopkins University who developed a number of simulation games were particularly

41. For a description of *Policy Negotiations* see Frederick L. Goodman, "An Introduction to the Virtues of Gaming," in Tansey, *Educational Aspects of Simulation*, pp. 34-35.

42. M. Brewster Smith, "Competence and Socialization," in *Socialization and Society*, ed. John Clausen (Boston: Little, Brown, 1968), pp. 271-319.

43. James S. Coleman et al., *Equality of Educational Opportunity* (Washington, D.C.: United States Government Printing Office, 1966), p. 23.

concerned with the potential of educational gaming for fostering control beliefs. Their thesis was that children who exhibit a low sense of control may have had insufficient experience in situations characterized by clear, actual contingencies.[44] For these children, the outcomes of their behavior may have too often depended not on their own actions but on the actions of others, or the felt pressures of an unseen and uncontrollable environment.

It was hypothesized that simulated environments where contingencies could be clearly linked to behavior might encourage a sense of efficacy. That sense, in turn, might increase an individual's confidence in his ability to cope with "real world" situations. Implicit in this approach is the participation in experiences designed to give the student practice in performing roles, such as parent, consumer, or legislator, that he will perform or encounter in the future.

Perhaps it should be emphasized that although a simulation game is *not* a real family, or business, or legislature, it does represent a *real social experience* for the child—one where the consequences of his actions among a group of his peers have real meaning in terms of his own self-appraisal. Success in simulation games, like any success experience, tends to have positive effects on the self-concept. These effects generalize to other situations. Unfortunately, success opportunities in school may not be as readily attainable to the child who needs them most; hence his already low sense of control may be further depressed by his inability to cope with school. As will be pointed out later, success in simulation games is not as dependent upon those factors that affect success in other types of school activities. Thus simulation games tend to provide success opportunities for more kinds of children, including those whose control beliefs may be the most tenuous.

Technical strategies. An obvious corollary of increasing control beliefs would be the development of strategies that do in fact enable the individual to cope better with his environment. Simulations have long been used outside the field of education for develop-

44. Sarane S. Boocock, E. O. Schild, and Clarice Stoll, *Simulation Games and Control Beliefs*, Report No. 10 (Baltimore: Center for the Social Organization of Schools, Johns Hopkins University, 1967).

ing technical competencies,[45] and, as advocated by Gagné,[46] are now slowly infiltrating the educational scene. Simulations are used in professional schools of education in the training of teachers, and to some extent in secondary schools.

Interpersonal strategies. Another type of strategy that may be related to participation in simulation games is the ability to deal effectively with people. This type of interpersonal strategy is more subtle but nevertheless is represented in many if not most simulation games, particularly all-man simulation games. Since the principles of exchange theory are reflected in many simulation games, it seems plausible that through participating in these games students may develop rational strategies for dealing with people: how to bargain, how to persuade, how to compromise. Interpersonal competence is a lofty goal long advocated among educators. Simulation games may be an underutilized technique in helping to attain this goal.

Effectiveness of Simulation/Games

STRUCTURAL AND PROCESS GOALS

Communication. The evidence to support the hypothesis that simulation/games may alter the pattern of communication within the classroom is almost wholly anecdotal. Indications of some changes in the authority relationship between students and teachers may be noted in student comments after playing simulation games: "the class led itself . . . no interference from teachers," "puts you in the driver's seat." [47] Similarly, teachers happily note the development of rapport with students as a result of gaming experiences.[48]

Few studies have sought to examine what actually happens to the social relationship between students during the play of simula-

45. See, for example, the uses of simulation described in *Instructional Simulation: A Research and Development and Dissemination Activity*, ed. Paul A. Twelker (Monmouth, Ore.: Teaching Research Division, Oregon State System of Higher Education, 1969).

46. Robert M. Gagné, "Simulators," in *Training Research and Education*, ed. Robert Glaser (New York: Wiley, 1962), pp. 223-46.

47. Hall T. Sprague and R. Garry Shirts, *Exploring Classroom Uses of Simulations* (La Jolla, Cal.: Western Behavioral Sciences Institute, 1966).

48. Heap, "The Student as Resource."

tion/games. One careful study by DeVries and Edwards using *Equations* in a team setting reported increased peer tutoring, which resulted in students' perceiving the learning task to be more satisfying and less difficult.[49]

An unexpected finding of a study of the task performance of black and white third-grade boys from integrated and segregated environments suggests that a gaming approach has important implications for improving relations between children from varying social and ethnic backgrounds. While a gaming setting was used in this case simply to provide a laboratory setting in which interaction could be observed, the setting itself appeared to alter behavior. After the sessions, which consisted of playing cooperative games, with group rewards administered after each game, the derogatory racial remarks that occasionally cropped up before the gaming session were replaced by friendly conversation as the boys were returned to their respective schools. More striking than these anecdotal observations was the lack of racial patterns in sociograms completed after the gaming session, although some of the boys, all previously unacquainted, had come from segregated home and school environments.[50] Apparently a setting that encouraged and then rewarded cooperative interaction in a gaming context had the effect of reducing barriers based on status characteristics. Further support for this assertion is provided by a subsequent study by DeVries and Edwards, who reported that the use of student teams helped reduce racial barriers to student interaction.[51]

Motivation. In summarizing the work of the Johns Hopkins Games Program, Livingston stated that the most consistent finding of research with games in the classroom is "that students prefer games to other classroom activities. This finding holds true for stu-

49. David L. DeVries and Keith J. Edwards, "Learning Games and Student Teams: Their Effects on Classroom Process," *American Educational Research Journal* 10 (Fall 1973): 307-18.

50. Jeanne K. Seidner, "Effects of Integrated School Experience on Interaction in Small Bi-Racial Groups" (Ph.D. diss., University of Southern California, 1971), pp. 125, 160-69.

51. David L. DeVries and Keith J. Edwards, "Student Teams: Integrating Desegregated Classrooms," *Proceedings of the Eighty-first Annual Convention of the American Psychological Association*, Montreal, Canada (1973), pp. 647-48.

dents from elementary school through high school and for both simulation and nonsimulation games." [52] This finding is substantiated by a number of additional studies. Not only do students report that they prefer gaming activities,[53] even when compared to other innovative teaching techniques,[54] but behavioral indicators indicate that they mean what they say.[55] In an interesting comparison between simulation and case studies at the college level, Anderson and his colleagues found that, although the case studies were more successful in eliciting student interest as measured by student's perceptions, measures of behavior (that is, attendance in class, prolonged discussions after class, participation in laboratory sessions) indicated that simulations were more successful in eliciting student involvement.[56]

Several researchers reported that simulation/games were particularly effective in motivating students who normally were uninterested in school, or who tended not to work up to their capabilities.[57]

52. Livingston et al., "The Hopkins Games Program," p. 26.

53. Jerry L. Fletcher, "Evaluation of Learning in Two Social Studies Simulation Games," *Simulation and Games* 2 (September 1971): 259-86; Cleo H. Cherryholmes, "Developing in Simulation of International Relations in High School Teaching," *Phi Delta Kappan* 47 (January 1965): 227-31; Robert S. Lee and Arlene O'Leary, "Attitude and Personality Effects of a Three-Day Simulation," *Simulation and Games* 2 (September 1971): 309-48.

54. Everett T. Keach, Jr. and David A. Pierfy, "The Effects of a Simulation Game on Learning of Geography Information at the Fifth Grade Level: Final Report" (Washington, D.C.: National Center for Educational Research and Development, 1972). ERIC: ED 068 889.

55. Lower absence rates were noted by Karen C. Cohen, *Effects of the Consumer Game on Learning and Attitudes of Selected Seventh Grade Students in a Target-Area School*, Report No. 65 (Baltimore: Center for the Social Organization of Schools, Johns Hopkins University, 1970). No dropouts were noted by Allen in a summer program normally characterized by a 14 percent dropout rate (Allen, Allen, and Miller, "Programmed Games and Learning").

56. Lee F. Anderson et al., "A Comparison of Simulation, Case Studies, and Problem Papers in Teaching Decision-making: Final Report" (Evanston, Ill.: Northwestern University Cooperative Research Project No. 1568, 1964). ERIC: ED 001 231.

57. Dale C. Farran, "Competition and Learning for Underachievers," in Boocock and Schild, *Simulation Games in Learning*, pp. 191-204; Paul F. Magnelia, "The *Inter-Nation Simulation* and Secondary Education," *Journal of Creative Behavior* 3 (Spring 1969): 115-21; Clark C. Abt, *Serious Games* (New York: Viking Press, 1970).

Reward structure. Evidence is beginning to accumulate in support of the hypothesis that intergroup competition within classrooms promotes better interpersonal relationships. DeVries and Edwards, using the nonsimulation game *Equations* in seventh-grade mathematics classes, found that the use of teams increased mutual concern among team members, and when rewards were based on team performance, even more helping relationships were noted.[58]

Cognitive objectives. Students can learn from simulation/games. The clearest evidence comes from research with nonsimulation games. In the field of language, Entwisle noted small increases in word performance tests after playing a word game.[59] Seventh-grade students who played *Equations* in team situations scored significantly higher than a control group taught by traditional methods on achievement tests designed to measure skills specific to the game as well as general arithmetic skills.[60] Convincing evidence that participation in nonsimulation games can increase cognitive skills is provided by two studies that indicated significant gains in scores on a nonlanguage test of intelligence for students who played *Wff 'n Proof* for relatively short periods of time.[61]

The evidence of learning from participation in simulation games is less convincing. In studies utilizing no-treatment control groups, it has been demonstrated that students can learn factual knowledge about such diverse subjects as international relations,[62] business,[63]

58. DeVries and Edwards, "Learning Games and Student Teams."

59. Doris R. Entwisle et al., *Giant Steps: A Game to Enhance Semantic Development of Verbs*, Report No. 81 (Baltimore: Center for the Social Organization of Schools, Johns Hopkins University, 1970).

60. Keith J. Edwards, David L. DeVries, and John P. Snyder, "Games and Teams: A Winning Combination," *Simulation and Games* 3 (September 1972): 247-70.

61. Alien, Allen, and Miller, "Programmed Games and Learning"; Layman W. Allen, Robert W. Allen, and Joan Ross, "The Virtues of Non-Simulation Games," *Simulation and Games* 1 (September 1970): 319-26.

62. Magnelia, "*Inter-Nation Simulation* and Secondary Education."

63. Samuel A. Livingston, *Two Types of Learning in a Business Simulation*, Report No. 104 (Baltimore: Center for the Social Organization of Schools, Johns Hopkins University, 1971).

physics,[64] and careers.[65] Students playing *Caribou Hunting*, a simulation game that is part of a larger social studies unit, not only learned facts but acquired understanding of certain analogies between the game and life situations, as well as strategies related to game play.[66]

Yet, when simulation games are compared with other teaching techniques, the overwhelming pattern of evidence suggests that they are about as effective as other techniques for teaching cognitive skills, but not necessarily any better. Such a judgment was made by Cherryholmes in his review in 1966 of six studies.[67] The evidence accumulated since then only serves to reinforce his conclusion. While Baker found that students learned more from a pre-Civil War simulation than did students taught by traditional methods,[68] a number of studies, again involving diverse subject matter (politics and government,[69] economics,[70] consumer education,[71] en-

64. John M. Boblick, "The Use of Computer-Based Simulations and Problem Drills to Teach the Gas Laws," *Science Education* 56 (January-March 1972): 17-22.

65. Sarane S. Boocock, "An Experimental Study of the Learning Effects of Two Games with Simulated Environments," in Boocock and Schild, *Simulation Games in Learning*, pp. 107-34; Sverker Lindb'ad, "Simulations and Guidance: Teaching Career Decision-Making Skills in the Swedish Compulsory School," *Simulation and Games* 4 (December 1973): 429-39.

66. Fletcher, "Two Social Studies Simulation Games."

67. Cleo H. Cherryholmes, "Some Current Research on Effectiveness of Educational Simu'ations: Implications for Alternative Strategies," *American Behavioral Scientist* 10 (October 1966): 4-7.

68. Eugene H. Baker, "A Pre-Civil War Simulation for Teaching American History," in Boocock and Schild, *Simulation Games in Learning*, pp. 135-42.

69. Otto A. Heinkel, "Evaluation of Simulation as a Teaching Device," *Journal of Experimental Education* 38 (Spring 1970): 32-36; William K. Hart, "An Analysis of the Usefulness of Simulation Games in Affecting Attitudinal Changes and Skill-Type Learning: Final Report" (Washington, D.C.: United States Office of Education, Bureau of Research, 1970). ERIC: ED 039 615.

70. Richard L. Wing, "Two Computer-Based Economics Games for Sixth Graders," in Boocock and Schild, *Simulation Games in Learning*, pp. 155-65.

71. C. Raymond Anderson, *Measuring Behavioral Learning: A Study in Consumer Credit*, Report No. 67 (Baltimore: Center for the Social Organization of Schools, Johns Hopkins University, 1970).

vironmental problems,[72] and career information)[73] indicated either no difference, or only slight differences in amount of comprehension of subject matter between experimental and control groups.

Some evidence does support Coleman's contention that better retention may result from action-oriented learning environments.[74] The delayed retest scores from two studies, both using the simulation game *Life Career*, indicated that students retained more of what they learned from participation in the simulation than did students taught by traditional methods.[75] A study by Keach and Pierfy, utilizing a geography simulation, produced similar results.[76] Attempting to control for the Hawthorne Effect by using another innovative teaching technique, a programmed text, for the control group, Keach and Pierfy found no significant difference on the posttest, but did find a significant difference on delayed posttests, indicating that students who played the simulation retained more of what they had learned. It is interesting to note that this particular geography simulation was designed so that students received continual feedback from their decisions and were required to use that feedback in subsequent decisions. Thus the material had to be learned in order to play the game—a design that, in theory and evidently in practice, facilitates learning and retention.

Affective objectives. Empirical evidence suggests that changes may occur in the affective domain as a result of playing simulation games. In some instances more role empathy appears to be evoked, as in the case of boys who took a more liberal view of women's

72. Gail M. Fennessey et al., *Simulation Gaming and Conventional Instruction: An Experimental Comparison,* Report No. 128 (Baltimore: Center for the Social Organization of Schools, Johns Hopkins University, 1972).

73. John F. Curry and Robert L. Brooks, "A Comparison of Two Methods of Teaching Life Career Planning to Junior High School Students: Final Report" (Washington, D.C.: United States Office of Education, 1971), ERIC: ED 059 401; Richard J. Johnson and Delores E. Euler, "Effect of the *Life Career* Game on Learning and Retention of Educational-Occupational Information," *School Counselor* 19 (January 1972): 155-59.

74. Livingston et al., "The Hopkins Games Program," p. 9.

75. Curry and Brooks, "Two Methods of Teaching Life Career Planning"; Johnson and Euler, "Effect of the *Life Career* Game."

76. Keach and Pierfy, "Effects of a Simulation Game."

roles after playing a girl in *Life Career*.[77] Similar changes can be noted in Livingston's finding that students exhibited a more positive attitude toward poor people after playing *Ghetto* [78] and DeKock's finding of higher tolerance scores after playing *Sunshine*.[79] The stability of these as well as other changes in the affective domain are called into question by Livingston's subsequent finding that, after a period of four months, initial changes produced from playing *Ghetto* had disappeared.[80]

Other studies have indicated that students' feelings about the way a system works may be altered by participation in a simulation game. In general, as Cherryholmes points out, these changes tend to be in the direction of forming more "realistic" attitudes about the referent system.[81] For example, students are more willing to accept the logrolling tactics of Congressmen after participating in *Democracy*.[82] While Baker found simulation games to be more effective in changing attitudes than conventional instruction,[83] Fennessey found no difference between a simulation game, a simulation exercise, and conventional instruction in inducing attitude change.[84]

A comparison of two studies, both using political simulations, points to the fallacy of generalizing the results of playing one simulation to other simulation experiences because of the diversity

77. Boocock, "Learning Effects of Two Games with Simulated Environments," p. 129.

78. Samuel A. Livingston, *Simulation Games and Attitude Change: Attitudes Toward the Poor*, Report No. 63 (Baltimore: Center for the Social Organization of Schools, Johns Hopkins University, 1970).

79. Paul DeKock, "Simulations and Changes in Racial Attitudes," *Social Education* 33 (February 1969): 181-83.

80. Samuel A. Livingston, *Simulation Games and Attitudes Toward the Poor: Three Questionnaire Studies*, Report No. 118 (Baltimore: Center for the Social Organization of Schools, Johns Hopkins University, 1971).

81. Cherryholmes, "Some Current Research."

82. Samuel A. Livingston, "Effects of a Legislative Simulation Game on the Political Attitudes of Junior High School Students," *Simulation and Games* 3 (March 1972): 41-51; Samuel A. Livingston and Steven J. Kidder, "Role Identification and Game Structure: Effects on Political Attitudes," *Simulation and Games* 4 (June 1973): 131-44.

83. Baker, "A Pre-Civil War Simulation."

84. Fennessey et al., *Simulation Gaming and Conventional Instruction*.

among simulation instruments. Lee and O'Leary reported no significant differences in beliefs or perspectives related to international affairs after playing *Inter-Nation Simulation*, a reasonably complex man-machine simulation. But they did note an increased tolerance for ambiguity as a result of the simulation experience.[85] On the other hand, Heinkel reported that students formed more extreme attitudes toward the government as the result of playing a relatively less complex all-man simulation game, *Napoli*.[86]

Even though changes in the affective domain as a result of playing simulation games are diverse and sometimes ambiguous, they illustrate the fact that attitudes and values are inextricably tied to simulation games that reflect societal institutions. Thus social simulation games may be used by the skillful teacher in the study of values by pointing out those values that are inherent in given social structures and encouraging students to examine their personal orientations as they participate in these simulated social situations.

Creativity. The creativity-inducing potential of self-motivating environments has been noted by Moore,[87] and Landau reported the extensive use of games in the Young Person's Institute for the Promotion of Arts and Science.[88] Yet this is a potential of simulation/games that remains relatively unexplored.

DEVELOPING COMPETENCE

Control beliefs. The empirical evidence to support the hypothesis that participation in simulation games will increase a student's sense of control of his environment is as yet meager. While some trends toward increased control beliefs have been observed,[89] gains

85. Lee and O'Leary, "Attitude and Personality Effects of a Three-Day Simulation."

86. Heinkel, "Simulation as a Teaching Device."

87. Omar K. Moore and Linda K. Burns, *A Clarifying Environment Approach to Creativity* (Pittsburgh: The Clarifying Environments Program, Sociology Department, University of Pittsburgh, and the Responsive Environments Foundation, Inc., 1973).

88. Erika Landau, "Psychological and Educational Meanings of Creativity" (Tel-Aviv, Israel: The Young Person's Institute for the Promotion of Arts and Science, n.d.).

89. Sarane S. Boocock and James S. Coleman, "Games with Simulated Environments in Learning," *Sociology of Education* 39 (Summer 1966): 215-36;

are usually slight. In some cases no gains were noted as a result of the simulated experience.[90] Lee and O'Leary's finding that gains in efficacy were related to subjects' initial feelings of trust emphasized the differential impact of simulation games on students with different predispositions.[91]

A true assessment of the impact of simulation games on control beliefs must await the results of studies that consider not only the individual predispositions of students, but also the consequences of the gaming session for the individual. Do "losers" feel as efficacious as "winners"? Moreover, one-shot exposures are not likely to have much effect on personal orientations that have been built up as a result of many past experiences. If we are serious about increasing control beliefs, students need frequent exposure to experiences in which they can be successful. Lee and O'Leary found that those students whose initial feelings of trust were lowest became the most optimistic about the influence of the average person on public affairs after playing *Inter-Nation Simulation*.[92] This finding suggests that we may be on the right track, and simply have not pursued it with sufficient conviction or rigor.

Technical strategies. The results of using simulations in teacher training, while not always consistent or statistically significant, appear to be encouraging.[93] At the secondary level, few studies have focused on developing technical competencies, but those studies are also encouraging. Finch and O'Reilly found that a troubleshooting simulation in an auto mechanics course made the experimental group perform significantly better than the control group on four criterion measures that indicated proficiency in task procedures.

Rex Vogel, "The Effect of a Simulation Game on the Attitude of Political Efficacy," *Simulation and Games* 4 (March 1973): 71-78; Nancy H. Roberts, "A Dynamic Feedback System Approach to Elementary Social Studies: A Prototye Gaming Unit" (Ed.D. diss., Boston University, 1975).

90. Boocock, Schild, and Stoll, *Simulation Games and Control Beliefs.*

91. Lee and O'Leary, "Attitude and Personality Effects of a Three-Day Simulation."

92. Ibid.

93. For a review of results see P. J. Tansey, "Simulation Techniques in the Training of Teachers," *Simulation and Games* 1 (September 1970): 281-303; or Donald R. Cruikshank, "Teacher Education Looks at Simulation: A Review of Selected Uses and Research Results," in Tansey, *Educational Aspects of Simulation.*

The authors viewed their results as supportive of the usefulness of simulations in teaching appropriate technical strategies.[94] In a different kind of study, Anderson found that experimental and control groups did not differ in factual knowledge about consumer economics. But students who had played *Consumer* engaged in more comparative shopping in a posttest simulation of a car buying experience than did students who had been taught by traditional methods.[95] Yet another study emphasized the appropriateness of performance-based criteria in evaluating the effectiveness of training simulations. Kidder and Guthrie noted that, although students who had participated in a behavior modification simulation did no better on a written test measuring knowledge of behavior modification techniques than did controls who had been taught by traditional methods, the experimental group did better on a performance test that involved the ability to apply behavior modification techniques.[96]

The implications are clear. If simulations and simulation games are intended to promote experiential learning, performance-based tests may be one appropriate measure of their effectivenss. This does not mean that the verbal transfer of principles from such experiential learning should not be measured. The crucial question is, Which types of simulation/games produce which type of learning for which kinds of students? The answer requires the use of several criterion measures.

Interpersonal strategies. Both Schild[97] and McFarlane[98] have noted the development of rational strategies by participants in the *Parent-Child Game* (now called *Generation Gap*), a dyadic simulation game aimed at the development of such strategies of exchange between parent and child. McFarlane's sample was comprised of fifth-grade boys from inner-city schools. He noted that, although

94. Curtis R. Finch and Patrick A. O'Reilly, "The Effects of Simulation on Problem-Solving Development," *Simulation and Games* 5 (March 1974): 47-71.

95. Anderson, *Measuring Behavioral Learning.*

96. Kidder and Guthrie, *Training Effects of a Behavior Modification Game.*

97. E. O. Schild, "The Shaping of Strategies," in Boocock and Schild, *Simulation Games in Learning*, pp. 143-54.

98. Paul T. McFarlane, *Pilot Studies of Role Behavior in a Parent-Child Simulation Game*, Report No. 39 (Baltimore: Center for the Social Organization of Schools, Johns Hopkins University, 1969).

some students exhibited quite sophisticated strategies during game play, they were unable to explain their strategies to the experimenter when asked to do so. Perhaps herein lies at least a partial answer to the question posed earlier in the chapter: Are the training and teaching functions of simulations distinct, in that an individual can learn how to do something without symbolic understanding of why? The previously cited studies of the development of both technical and interpersonal strategies suggest the answer may be yes, at least in some situations for some individuals.

Again we see the need to identify the kinds of learnings that may be fostered by any simulation instrument as well as the kinds of stimuli used to bring about the learning. Moreover, we should be aware that individual students' cognitive styles and personality characteristics must be compatible with the requisites of effective game play.

Correlates of the Effectiveness of Simulation/Games

STUDENT CHARACTERISTICS

Ability. One student characteristic often considered in research with simulation/games is academic ability. Some studies have indicated a relationship between academic ability and learning from simulation/games.[99] Other studies show little or no relationship between learning with simulation/games and learning in conventional settings.[100] This apparent contradiction may be clarified by Edwards' finding that scores on standard achievement tests were nonsignificantly correlated with students' understanding of the mechanics and strategies of game play.[101] However, achievement scores were related to students' ability to make analogies between the game model and real life situations. As Fletcher has suggested, per-

99. Magnelia, *"Inter-Nation Simulation* and Secondary Education"; Keach and Pierfy, "Effects of a Simulation Game."

100. Fletcher, "Two Social Studies Simulation Games"; Lee and O'Leary, "Attitude and Personality Effects of a Three-Day Simulation"; Larry A. Braskamp and Richard M. Hodgett, "The Role of an Objective Evaluation Model in Simulation Gaming," *Simulation and Games* 2 (June 1971): 197-212.

101. Keith J. Edwards, *The Effects of Ability, Achievement, and Number of Plays on Learning from a Simulation Game,* Report No. 115 (Baltimore: Center for the Social Organization of Schools, Johns Hopkins University, 1971).

haps "the thing a game teaches best to all students, regardless of ability, is how to play it. Other kinds of learning which involve reflecting on, or making inferences from, experiences in the games are not independent of ability."[102] But the question remains only partially answered: Are the performance skills involved in learning to play the game transferable to *real life behavior*, regardless of whether or not their significance can be dealt with symbolically?

One unique finding regarding student ability runs counter to other studies. This is the finding that lower-ability students who played *Equations* exhibited the greatest gains in tests of divergent solutions and content relevant items.[103] But this finding cannot be separated from the team aspect of this particular treatment, since students of higher ability were encouraged to help lower-ability students. In any event, this significant finding supports the effectiveness of the teams-games-tournament approach.[104]

Sex and personality variables. Differences in attitude change,[105] learning,[106] and game strategy[107] have been linked to sex of subject. Interesting interactions have also been noted between sex, personality variables, and cognitive style.[108] Yet not enough studies of these variables have been done to permit generalizations. It seems safe to say that these differences do exist and therefore have implications for the assignment of roles in simulation games, particularly since there are indications that self-role incongruence has an adverse affect on game performance.[109]

102. Fletcher, "Two Social Studies Simulation Games," p. 277.

103. Edwards, DeVries, and Snyder, "Games and Teams."

104. David L. DeVries, Keith J. Edwards, and Gail M. Fennessey, *Using Teams-Games-Tournament in the Classroom* (Baltimore: Center for the Social Organization of Schools, Johns Hopkins University, 1974).

105. Boocock, "Learning Effects of Two Games with Simulated Environments," p. 129.

106. Allen, Allen, and Miller, "Programmed Games and Learning."

107. Clarice S. Stoll and Paul T. McFarlane, "Player Characteristics and Interaction in a Parent-Child Simulation Game," *Sociometry* 32 (September 1969): 259-71.

108. Anderson et al., "Simulation, Case Studies, and Problem Papers."

109. Richard L. Dukes and Constance J. Seidner, "Self-Role Incongruence and Role Enactment in Simulation Games," *Simulation and Games* 4 (June 1973): 159-73.

246 TEACHING WITH SIMULATIONS AND GAMES

CHARACTERISTICS OF THE GAMING SESSION

One of the important correlates of the effectiveness of a simulation game experience is group enjoyment.[110] In general, those students who are most interested,[111] and those who participate most in the simulation,[112] learn most. Thus it is important to attempt to maximize group and individual enjoyment through careful planning and administration of the gaming session.

Most users of simulation games advocate the use of a postgame discussion, but its effectiveness in enhancing attitude change and learning must be reexamined in the light of two studies that indicated no difference between groups who participated in postgame discussions and those who did not.[113] In another study, however, a game-discussion-game sequence proved to be the most useful in promoting learning.[114]

TEACHER CHARACTERISTICS

The teacher who administers the simulation/game may significantly affect the learning,[115] attitude change,[116] and enjoyment[117] of students. Unfortunately, the kinds of behaviors that bring about these variations have not been systematically examined.

110. Michael Inbar, "Individual and Group Effects on Enjoyment and Learning in a Game Simulating a Community Disaster," in Boocock and Schild, *Simulation Games in Learning*, pp. 169-90.

111. Johnson and Euler, "Effect of the *Life Career* Game"; Marianne Bonds, "A Quasi-Experimental Study Using Games and Simulations at the College Level" (Paper presented at the National Gaming Council, Pittsburgh, October 1974).

112. Gerald Zaltman, "Degree of Participation and Learning in a Consumer Economics Game," in Boocock and Schild, *Simulation Games in Learning*, pp. 205-15.

113. Samuel A. Livingston, *Simulation Games in the Classroom: How Important Is the Post-Game Discussion?*, Report No. 150 (Baltimore: Center for the Social Organization of Schools, Johns Hopkins University, 1973); Myron Chartier, "Learning Effects: An Experimental Study of a Simulation Game and Instrumented Discussion," *Simulation and Games* 3 (June 1972): 203-18.

114. Kidder and Guthrie, *Training Effects of a Behavior Modification Game.*

115. Baker, "A Pre-Civil War Simulation."

116. Livingston, *Simulation Games and Attitude Change.*

117. Inbar, "Individual and Group Effects on Enjoyment and Learning."

Research Issues

Findings concerning the motivational aspects of simulation/ games may be criticized because few studies have attempted to control for the novel effect of a new teaching technique. Yet the selection of educational objectives may be an even more serious problem. The preceding review of research clearly indicates that most studies have dealt with simulation games, rather than non-simulation games, and have focused on an outcome—factual knowledge—for which simulation games appear to be least effective. This focus may be partially due to the need among researchers in this relatively new field to make simulation games appear respectable as a teaching technique. It is also easier to construct paper and pencil tests of the achievement of cognitive objectives than to assess the kinds of performance learning that may result from participation in simulation games.[118] Yet it is in the area of performance that simulation games may make their most unique contribution to the educational process.

But even in research focused on cognitive objectives, studies that attempt to link propositions derived from learning theory to the dependent variables are conspicuously lacking. Researchers in the field of simulation/games have largely come from sociology, business, economics, and international relations rather than from psychology or professional education. It is the present author's view that Gagné's formulations, which deal with both types and sequencing of learning, may provide a particularly useful framework for researchers in simulation/games.[119]

The same inattention to theory is evidenced in studies that focus on attitude change. Knowledge concerning the variables related to attitude change has largely been neglected by researchers in simulation/games. Only recently have some studies begun to consider

118. The sophisticated mathematical techniques that have been developed to measure the evolution of strategy over repeated plays of a game should be helpful toward this end. See Andrew Z. Jankowicz, "Feedback for Learning in a Business Game," *Simulation and Games* 4 (June 1973): 175-203.

119. Robert M. Gagné, *The Conditions of Learning*, 2d ed. (New York: Holt, Rinehart & Winston, 1970).

such variables as emotional arousal[120] and role taking[121] in effecting attitude change.

Other criticisms of research design may help improve the quality of research in simulation/games.[122] The most important step, however, has already been taken. With the recognition of simulation/games as a legitimate and useful teaching technique, researchers are assuming a less defensive stance and are attempting to classify simulation/games in terms of level of learning objectives[123] and effectiveness in bringing about attainment of these objectives by specific individuals.[124] Perhaps the recognition among educators of the similarities between simulation/games and other teaching techniques will facilitate this process.[125]

120. Steven J. Kidder, *Emotional Arousal and Attitude Change During Simulation Games*, Report No. 111 (Baltimore: Center for the Social Organization of Schools, Johns Hopkins University, 1971).

121. Agnes Jean Groome, "Interaction Effects of Personological Variables of Grade Eleven Participants in Simulation *Life Career* upon Role-Taking and Career Maturity" (Paper presented at the National Gaming Council, Pittsburgh, October 1974).

122. Jerry L. Fletcher, "The Effectiveness of Simulations/Games as Learning Environments: A Proposed Program of Research," *Simulation and Games* 2 (December 1971): 425-54; Cathy S. Greenblat, "Teaching with Simulation Games: A Review of Claims and Evidence," *Teaching Sociology* 1 (October 1973): 63-83.

123. Steps in the right direction are the typologies offered by Paul A. Twelker and Kent Layden, "A Basic Reference Shelf on Simulation and Gaming," in Zuckerman and Horn, *The Guide to Simulations/Games*, pp. 448-49, and by Katherine Chapman, James E. Cavis, and Andrea Meier, *Simulation/Games in Social Studies: What Do We Know?* (Boulder, Col.: ERIC Clearinghouse for Social Studies/Social Science Education and Social Science Educational Consortium, Inc., 1973), p. 42. What is now needed is more empirical evidence to substantiate these various typologies.

124. A recent research effort toward this end measured learning that resulted from playing a simulation game adapted from the *World 3* model. Results indicated significant differences in fifth and sixth graders' understanding of dynamic feedback systems from pretest to posttest, as measured by items designed to reflect all levels of Bloom's taxonomy of cognitive objectives. However, since the simulation game was part of a total curriculum unit, at the present time it is impossible to separate the learning effects of the game from learning effects that derive from other methods incorporated into the total unit. Roberts, "A Dynamic Feedback System Approach."

125. Umpleby, for example, suggests the usefulness of cooperation between researchers in computer-assisted instruction and simulation/games. Stuart Umpleby, "The Teaching Computer as a Gaming Laboratory," *Simulation and Games* 2 (March 1971): 5-25.

Role of the Teacher in Using Simulation/Games

It has already been suggested that changes in student-teacher relationships occur when simulation/games are used in the classroom. The teacher is not primarily a purveyor of information and judge of competencies, but a coach or a director of a complex learning environment. Students learn not so much from interacting with the teacher, but from interacting with the medium itself. Reinforcement comes directly from the medium or from peers who themselves are part of the educational context.

This does not mean that the teacher's role is unimportant in this type of activity; in some ways it may be even more demanding. In response to the growing use of simulation/games in the classroom, a number of publications intended to help the teacher use this technique have appeared.[126]

SELECTION

It is important that the teacher be a selective consumer. The first task is to choose a simulation/game that is appropriate to one's educational objectives. This is not an easy task, since some simulation/games may have several goals.[127] It is also important to sift from the many commercially available simulation games those that have been biased by the values of the designer. Cues that indicate possible biasing effects include rules that tell players how they should behave or roles that have been assigned "loaded" labels, such as "peace negotiator."[128]

---

126. For example, see Livingston and Stoll, *Simulation Games*; Chapman, *Guidelines for Using Social/Simulation Games*; Harry Lindy, *Using Simulation Games in the Classroom*, Report No. 44 (Baltimore: Center for the Social Organization of Schools, Johns Hopkins University, 1969); Alice Kaplan Gordon, *Games for Growth* (Chicago: Science Research Associates, 1972); John L. Taylor and Rex Walford, *Simulation in the Classroom* (Baltimore: Penguin Books, 1972); Armand Lauffer, *The Aim of the Game* (Ann Arbor, Mich.: Gamed Simulations, 1973).

127. It has been suggested that games designed for too many goals may achieve none because student behavior required for one goal may be incompatible with behavior conducive to achieving other goals. For a discussion of this point see Marilyn Clayton and Richard Rosenbloom, "Goals and Designs," in Boocock and Schild, *Simulation Games in Learning*, pp. 85-92.

128. Coleman, "The Role of Modern Technology."

MANAGEMENT

It is crucial that the teacher be thoroughly familiar with the simulation/game to be used in class so that appropriate time, space, and equipment arrangements can be made prior to the gaming session. It has been suggested by some teachers that one effective way to introduce a simulation/game is to assign a group of students the task of learning the game and then demonstrating it to the class.[129] Nothing is so deadly as a long reading of the rules, particularly, as Farran notes, for underachievers who may become frustrated by complexities that prevent their immediate involvement in the game.[130]

The teacher's role during the actual gaming session will depend on the type of simulation/game used. Fletcher's research indicated that teachers can play a vital role in making the game work by encouraging students to use information and plan strategies.[131] Teachers should not, however, suggest which strategies students should use, or students will respond to the teacher rather than to the demands of the simulation, thus negating the value of the technique.[132] Some simulation games, such as *Sim-Soc*, require a game administrator to handle resources or compute status reports. Such roles may be filled by the teacher. Whatever role the teacher may take during the gaming session, the role of unobtrusive observer should not be overlooked. Students actively engaged in a game may not be aware of the subtleties of interaction that may provide an excellent basis for a productive postgame discussion.

Although the postgame discussion may not be as useful in promoting learning as simulation/gamers might like to believe, most teachers attest to its usefulness in pulling together loose ends and correcting misconceptions. For example, in *Star Power*, a uniquely effective simulation game about class, status, and power, the group

129. Clarice Stoll, "Games Students Play," *Media and Methods* 7 (October 1970): 37-41; Barbara Orris, "Simulation Review: The Game of Empire," *Simulation and Games* 6 (March 1975): 95-98.

130. Farran, "Competition and Learning for Underachievers."

131. Fletcher, "Two Social Studies Simulation Games."

132. For a more detailed discussion of this point see John D. Baldwin, "Influences Detrimental to Simulation-Gaming," *American Behavioral Scientist* 12 (July-August 1969): 14-20.

designated as "triangles" (translate: lower class) often tends to lose interest, largely (I am told by my students) because they see no way to win. They may express the sentiment that it is not a very good game. It is important to point out at the end of the session that the triangles were responding to the constraints of the simulation and that their "dropping out" of the simulated society may be analogous to what has been called the "apathy of the lower classes." A rousing discussion often ensues.

INTEGRATION INTO THE CURRICULUM

How can simulation/games be integrated into the total curriculum? This issue is related to the purpose for which the experience is intended: a sensitizing experience to prepare students for a forthcoming unit, a means of conveying a major portion of the content, or a final experience to put previous learnings into perspective. On the last purpose, Farran noted that students attributed learning not found in the particular simulation game they played to the gaming experience. She suggested that simulations may provide a conceptual framework that infuses previously acquired learnings with new meaning.[133]

THE SELF-FULFILLING PROPHECY

One final word should perhaps be said about the self-fulfilling prophecy. Since simulation/games apparently can "turn on" students who may not be enchanted with regular school work, teachers experience the pleasant sensation of viewing these particular students in a new light. Perhaps a whole new pattern of interaction will be initiated by the game.

Teachers not only are perpetuators of the self-fulfilling prophecy, but also can become its subjects. Perhaps the advocacy of simulation/games may result from a massive experimenter effect involving the teacher as subject. If students do respond positively, for whatever reason, to a gaming experience, a teacher cannot help but be gratified and impressed with his or her own effectiveness. Perhaps the most humanizing effect of simulation/games is on the teacher, and as a teacher, the present author views that effect as a pleasant prospect.

133. Farran, "Competition and Learning for Underachievers."

CHAPTER VIII

The Lecture Method

JOHN MC LEISH

Introduction

ORIGIN AND PURPOSES OF THE LECTURE METHOD

The lecture has been used for many centuries as the method of choice in higher education. We can trace it to the fifth century pre-Christian Academy, the public pleasure-gardens in Athens where Plato and his students foregathered. In medieval times, manuscripts being scarce and expensive, it became established as the prime method in university teaching. The word itself means "a reading."

The lecture has numerous virtues as a mode of communication. This accounts for its survival in the contemporary world when books are readily available and inexpensive, and when newer methods of communication carry the word and the visual image to mass audiences with the speed of light. In earlier times, in a more limited way, the lecture served the same function; it made it possible to communicate with large audiences in the most economical fashion.

In origin the lecture was contemporaneous with the rise of the theatre. Like the theatre, it developed in the social context of the Greek democratic process where the training of the citizen in oratory was a major component of the educational curriculum. It was incumbent on the teacher working in this tradition to present his materials in the most interesting form. His delivery was expected to conform to the standards of a stage presentation or a Senate oration. The living personality and the trained artistry of the teacher constituted the medium by which materials of human interest were presented to a highly receptive, but at the same time perceptive, critical, and thoughtful audience. The lecture was a carefully prepared, probably rehearsed, but seemingly improvised performance. The model we have in mind is the later books of

Plato's *Republic* where Socrates, abandoning the dialectic technique
with which his name is always associated, proceeds to outline a
general philosophy as a framework for living. Similarly, the works
of Aristotle were almost certainly delivered as lecture-courses in
the first instance.

In these sources we see the traditional virtues of the lecture
made manifest. As a teaching device, it is undoubtedly the most
economical method by which the individual can present in a per-
sonalized and continuous argument the general framework for understanding the fundamentals of a particular subject, emphasizing
the key concepts and involving the audience in reflective thought
that moves in time with the on-going performance. An air of
studied improvisation gives the lecture its salient character, that is,
an extended conversation that has developed into a monologue
because of the intensity of student interest in the thoughtful contribution of the master.

As practiced in medieval Europe, not to speak of the universities of the Muslim East, the lecture developed into a *system* wherein
this lively conversation took the form of the reading of, and commentary on, a book. As it happened, the lecturer had the only
available copy. The dogmatic and *a priori* tone of the aged Plato of
the *Laws* set the pattern for the formal university system of instruction.

By this time, university education was closely tied to the professional training of the theologian, the physician, and the lawyer.
The main disadvantage of the lecture then became apparent; it does
not necessarily engage the attention or the active participation of
the auditor. In spite of the worst excesses of the pedagogues of this
period, however, the lecture survived. This was probably due to
the fact that knowledge was regarded as a closed system whose
essential elements were believed to have been handed down in the
theological, philosophical, medical, and other treatises inherited
from antiquity. These works were, of course, not generally available to the student body.

There was no question of adapting instruction to the needs of
the individual student in those far-off days. It was the function of
the auditor to sit at the feet of the master and to reproduce the
artificial pearls of his wisdom when called upon to do so. With the

invention of printing, the fact that the lecture system was uneconomic and inefficient was not apparent because the system of professional training had developed its own inertia and its own set of vested interests.

In modern times, the main defense and purpose of the lecture in higher education has been stated by Paulsen, as follows: (a) it provides a survey of a whole field of knowledge through the medium of a living personality; (b) it relates this body of knowledge to the primary aims of human life; (c) it arouses an active interest, leading to an independent comprehension of the subject on the part of the listener.[1]

THE ATTACK ON THE LECTURE SYSTEM

On the other hand, it may be said that the main defect of the lecture system is that there is no guarantee that these stated objectives are achieved even by the generality of performers. If we take these declared purposes seriously, it can be asserted with confidence that the number of teachers capable of getting even some way towards achieving them at the established lecture hour every day for a considerable period of time must be decidedly small. If Paulsen's declaration is accepted as a serious statement of intent, and not mere rhetoric, several consequences follow. It is surely implied that lecturing is an *art* that requires special study and training; that probably few people are really capable of lecturing at all; that no one should attempt to use the method over any length of time as an all-purpose vehicle. It implies that a system of evaluation must seek to discover if, and under what conditions, failure to achieve the declared objectives takes place, and when some other teaching method could usefully be employed.

Lacking the basic training in oratory, under present-day conditions of the restricted availability of the best models in theatre and lecture-room for imitation, it is indeed surprising that the average untrained lecturer is capable of performing at the level we find today in institutions of higher learning. It is not, however, surprising that the lecture system has come under fire from the student body. During the reappraisal of educational resources that followed

1. Friedrich Paulsen, *Die deutschen Universitäten und das Universitätsstudium* (Berlin: A. Asher & Co., 1902), pp. 240-41.

the Second World War, many voices inside universities were critical of the teaching methods used. It is a historical fact that it was faculty, in advance of the student body, who adopted a posture hostile to formal instruction. As higher education became more generally available, with larger and larger classes and the consequent need to appoint greater numbers of inexperienced and untrained lecturers, criticism of university teaching mounted until it reached the scale of student riots in India, Britain, the United States and other places. Voices were raised to proclaim the need for student-faculty "conferences" on the model of the Soviet and Chinese systems, where academics are encouraged to engage in "self-criticism" and to give pledges of amendment.

The so-called "knowledge explosion," associated with the fact that the most recent developments in science and the arts are available in the mass media, provides students with evidence that many lecturers are using out-of-date materials. The examination pressures on students; the new social groupings now being educated in institutions of higher learning; the new orientation of the universities themselves towards technology and modern science—all these create doubts about the efficiency of the transmission of academic materials by the traditional method of an uninterrupted discourse. Students express their resentment that many lectures are without benefit of rest pause, of variety of presentation and pace, of visual materials and sometimes that they are devoid even of human warmth and intelligibility. Critics find fault with the impersonality of the lecture system, the large classes involved in using the method, and the fact that the materials communicated could be learned more efficiently from a textbook, a programmed text, or a teaching machine. Concepts of efficiency and productivity are more and more being applied to higher education. This application is conceptualized on the model of an industrial process with a determinable and measurable product. These factors generate an attitude in the face of which it is difficult to justify traditional scholarship and its techniques of communication.

ATTACK AND DEFENSE: THE HISTORICAL SOURCES

The criticism and defense of university teaching can be traced at least as far back as the Middle Ages. Rabelais mocked the *cog-*

noscenti of the University of Paris. The students who flocked to
hear Abelard were voting with their feet against the dreary and
turgid commentators of the Sorbonne. In more modern times criticism is linked to that same questioning radicalism that gave birth
to the French Revolution. Fichte, in his *Vorlesungen über die
Bestimmung des Gelehrten* (1794), criticized the "reading off" of
lectures and the anachronism of a system that had survived the
invention of printing (*circa* 1440).[2] These criticisms were echoed
by Schleiermacher in 1808 and by many since then. Even conservative rectors of continental universities, such as Bernheim
(Berlin)—not to mention radicals such as von Hartmann and Eugen
Duhring—sought to persuade professors to devise a more modern
and efficient technique of communication of the fruits of their
scholarship. In 1898 Bernheim stated (*Der Universitätsunterricht
und die Erfordernisse der Gegenwart*) all of the objections now
current: the listener is passive; the lecture system limits his auto-
didactic activities to the taking down of notes to which he seldom
subsequently refers; the system is self-defeating in that the student
is completely buried under a mass of courses and can only save
himself (and his sanity) by an equally systematic cutting of
courses.[3] Bernheim's positive suggestions have a ring of familiarity:
the independent use of sources by the student, the setting of exercises which introduce these materials, a *few* orientation lectures,
private reading, and compulsory seminars. These should be the
major teaching and learning activities, with written work as the
main degree-qualifying activity.

Paulsen defended the lecture system against these criticisms in
terms already outlined. He provided further counsel, accepting a
great deal of the criticism outlined above: "The lecture cannot, and
the lecturer should not, aim at transmitting to the hearer the entire
material of the study, nor should he attempt to place before him
all the facts and problems, all the opinions and controversies, the
complete history and literature of the subject. This material should
rather be the object of a systematic manual."[4] His most compelling

2. Ibid., p. 239.

3. Ibid., p. 238.

4. Ibid., p. 241.

argument in favor of the lecture, as far as the contemporary critic of the lecture system is concerned, is that the *professor* learns from having to prepare and deliver his courses year after year!

It would be tedious to trace systematically the arguments against the lecture system. These basic criticisms have been restated with greater or less vehemence, with no novel additional points. One or two highlights of attack and defense in English-speaking countries may be mentioned, although they add little to our understanding of process. It has to be said about these critics and defenders of the lecture system that they use the old-fashioned techniques of subjective evaluation and exaggerated statement of a one-sided viewpoint. Doctor Samuel Johnson set the tone against the lecture by his blunt assertion: "Lectures were once useful; but now, when all can read, and books are so numerous, lectures are unnecessary. . . . I cannot see that lectures can do so much good as reading the books from which lectures are taken."[5]

The views of this English pedant were developed at some length by Quiller-Couch, although he determinedly refused to practice what he was preaching.[6] The moralist Sidgwick had already come out strongly, in a lecture, against the system of lecturing.[7] These diatribes changed nothing in the accepted pattern.

In 1943, Bruce Truscot (E. Alison Peers) published his knowledgeable criticisms of university education in Britain.[8] His major attack was on the narrowness of university courses and the out-of-date conception of the educated person then prevalent. While defending the lecture system against all comers, he castigated the dreariness of courses arising from "spoon-feeding" of the undergraduate and the dogmatism of professors. Truscot's study, *Red Brick University*, was in a genre that had a certain popularity—a wry Voltairean type of criticism of an extremely general character based on a one-sided interpretation of students' reactions embodied

5. James Boswell, *Life of Samuel Johnson* (London: J. M. Dent and Company, 1906).

6. Sir Arthur Quiller-Couch, *A Lecture on Lectures* (London: Hogarth Press, 1927).

7. Henry A. Sidgwick, "A Lecture Against Lecturing," in *Miscellaneous Essays and Addresses* (London: Macmillan, 1904), pp. 340-51.

8. Bruce Truscot, *Red Brick University* (London: Faber, 1943).

in printed reports. As has been said, defense and criticism of university teaching continue to use this rather old-fashioned methodology.[9]

In Britain, the Hale Committee on University Teaching Methods reported in 1964.[10] Providing a great deal of factual material based on questionnaires, the Committee adopted a strong stand on particular issues, including a defense of the lecture system. They reported an overwhelming weight of opinion in British universities that the lecture performed an essential function and was, in fact, an indispensable teaching method. Two-thirds of the university teachers who replied to the questionnaire were satisfied with the amount of lecturing given to their students; another nine percent believed there should be more. Various arguments were brought forward to justify the lecture: students are too immature to learn effectively by reading; the lecture opens up the subject for them; the lecturer can go back over the same materials in different words, whereas books are restricted to one form of explanation; in science, complex materials, not yet in text-books, can be introduced; visual aids can be built up gradually; the lecture gives a framework, an outline, a critical point of view; it provides aesthetic pleasure and communicates enthusiasm; the lecture is better prepared, more profound, and better thought out than the impromptu answers to students during a discussion; it reaches larger numbers and brings the student into contact with many minds and points of view; the lecture can release the student from thraldom to an uncongenial tutor; finally, it is the most economical in terms of staff time.

The influential Robbins Committee on Higher Education, on the other hand, could see no virtue in formal lectures delivered to small audiences.[11] The Committee agreed with the point made by

9. Gilbert Highet, *The Art of Teaching* (London: Methuen, 1951); "The Use of Lectures," *Universities Quarterly* 4 (May 1950): 237-65; A. D. C. Peterson, *Techniques of Teaching*, vol. 3 (London: Pergamon Press, 1965).

10. Edward Hale (Chairman), *University Teaching Methods*. Report of the Committee on University Teaching Methods, Great Britain Parliament (London: Her Majesty's Stationery Office, 1964).

11. Lionel Charles Robbins (Chairman), *Report of the Committee on Higher Education*, Great Britain Parliament (London: Her Majesty's Stationery Office, 1961-63).

Paulsen that, in spite of everything that could be said against it, at least the professor learned something from delivering a course of lectures. For the professor, the lecture performs two essential functions: it clears the mind and is a half-way house to publication. Of the various justifications of the lecture system outlined above, three are taken by the Committee as particularly compelling: the lecture gives a framework; it can provide a point of view and information not otherwise available; it may kindle enthusiasm for a subject and stimulate original thinking.

IMPROVING THE LECTURE: GENERALIZED SUGGESTIONS

The lecture is a staple teaching technique in the Soviet system of higher education. Even here, however, there is criticism of this method. The problem as seen by Nekrasova is how to activate the students in the direction of independent thinking that connects with social life and productive labor.[12] She discussed ways in which the theoretical content of the lecture can be related to practical activity during the course of the lecture. For this, two basic conditions are necessary. First, the lecture itself must be the result of creative thinking by the lecturer. Secondly, the students must be actively involved in this creative thinking. On the basis of an analysis of successful and unsuccessful lectures, Nekrasova lays down eight basic rules useful for activating reflective thinking by students participating in a lecture session. These are that: (a) finished conclusions should not be presented by the lecturer but rather problems and rules or indications of methods for solving them; (b) controversial subjects should be introduced and debated, the lecturer at the appropriate stage indicating his own viewpoint; (c) the lecturer presents his materials in accordance with the established psychological principles that describe how concepts are actually developed and their relationships to things; (d) the living significance of the materials being dealt with is made clear to the auditors by demonstrating the close relation of theory to practice; (e) significant questions are posed by the lecturer either to himself or directly to the students (a dialogue may develop in place of the traditional

12. K. A. Nekrasova, "On the Activation of Thinking in Students in the Process of Teaching by Lecture," *Voprosy Psikhologii* 6, no. 6 (1960): 166-71 (in Russian).

monologue); (f) experiments and demonstrations should be cited in support of particular viewpoints by the lecturer and by his students; (g) the students are presented with problems arising from the lecture or text-book materials, but which require independent thought for solution; (h) the students are actively encouraged to pose problems and questions to the lecturer, these being dealt with in the concluding section of the discourse.

These recommendations in effect translate the lecture into a totally different dimension or category. We are talking about a method to which the present writer has assigned the description of "step-by-step lecture-discussion."[13]

Ivashchenko discussed the defects of the lecture in maintaining the interest of large classes in psychology (100 to 200 students in the group) and described a method of holding their attention.[14] Around such themes as "the moral and intellectual qualities of humans" and "the motives for activity," he organizes experiments using, for example, photographs of expressions and emotional reactions. The students are invited to interpret these photographs and other materials in relation to problems that are posed during the lecture. Ivashchenko records an increase of interest and motivation as a result of this technique. This is shown by improvement in examination results.

The place of the lecture in higher education was discussed in a series of articles in the *Soviet Journal of Higher Education* in 1965, 1966, and 1967. Chanbarisov pointed out that for something like thirty years, in the Soviet system of higher education, the lecture has been regarded as a preliminary to independent work by the student.[15] It is a preparation for group study by means of the seminar in the sciences. Chanbarisov defended the lecture against charges of inefficiency by suggesting that a well organized lecture course is the most economical way to organize instruction. The lecture gives the possibility of providing a significant sum of basic

13. John McLeish, Wayne Matheson, and James Park, *The Psychology of the Learning Group* (London: Hutchinson, 1973).

14. F. I. Ivashchenko, "Solving Psychological Problems as a Method of Teaching Students," *Voprosy Psikhologii* 12, no. 6 (1966): 172-75 (in Russian).

15. Sh. Kh. Chanbarisov, "Once More, on the Lecture," *Vestnik vysshei Shkoly* 25, no. 3 (1967): 7-10 (in Russian).

knowledge of the subject for a large group of students. It is the most productive of all techniques of instruction. This is true even today when programmed instruction is used to rationalize the learning and teaching processes, making them maximally efficient. On the other hand, Parisi, on the basis of his work at the University of Illinois, pointed out that the development of programmed texts and the new emphasis on the need for the utmost clarity about one's teaching objectives draws attention to the obligation to consider the individual character of learning and to plan for individualized instruction.[16]

On the basis of the behavior and the reports of the "consumer" of lectures, it is possible to work out what can be regarded as the normal sequence of reactions by auditors. Introspective material is supported by empirical evidence derived from studies of fatigue, boredom, and monotony in an industrial or work situation. There are also objective signs of student reaction that can be pieced together to provide a synthetic picture of the normal or typical situation. Observation of student behavior (using a time-sampling technique), analysis of student notes taken during the lecture, discussion with students, and the comments of an informed observer following on a lecture or lecture series provide some objective data. The pattern probably varies from student group to student group, and from lecturer to lecturer. But differences are mainly in the duration of particular sequences rather than in the basic pattern.

The principal independent variable that operates over all such work sessions is, of course, time. In this case time is measured from the beginning of the lecture hour. Lloyd suggested that there is a close parallel, or a complementary relationship, between various stages in the lecturer's output and the receptivity and assimilation of his material by the class group.[17] Industrial psychologists and ergonomics experts have long recognized the sequence in work performance: (a) an initial spurt, or period of high output or performance, which comes at the beginning of the defined work-period;

16. D. Parisi, "Insegnamento individualizzato e istruzione programmata," *Securitas* 51 (January 1966): 87-110.

17. D. H. Lloyd, "Communication in the University Lecture," *Staff Journal* (University of Reading) 1 (February 1967): 14-22.

(b) a middle sag, which follows the initial high level of perform-ance and results from a combination of boredom and fatigue; (c) an end-spurt, where the output or measured performance climbs back to a level approximating the initial stage. This over-all pattern of "spurt-sag-spurt" is to be recognized not only over the whole work-period but, if this should be of long duration, the pattern may be repeated a number of times within a total context of an over-all decrement in performance.

This sequence can be recognized in the lecturer's output during a fifty-minute lecture work-period. It also appears in parallel sequences in the pattern of student intake, that is, the assimilation of lecture materials by the student. This pattern corresponds to the work-performance of the student auditor. Lloyd claimed that he had recognized these various intake-patterns in students' notes taken during lectures.[18] We are talking here of the traditional lecture in the sense of a (relatively) uninterrupted discourse. There is a short initial "warming-up" period, which lasts perhaps five or more min-utes. Efficiency is then at a maximum. There follows a decline in student and lecturer efficiency that continues over a long period to produce a deep trough. This decline probably reaches its lowest point after approximately forty minutes. Both lecturer and student then begin slowly to find their way back toward their initial rela-tively high level of achievement. The students continue to improve to the end of the lecture period but do not succeed in reaching their initial level. The lecturer is in worse case. After something like five to ten minutes of improvement during this final end-spurt, he suffers a set-back, which can be identified as the "winding-down" or tapering-off period, signaling to the student the end of the lec-ture hour. (See figure 1a.) As regards the student work-decrement curve, these sequences have been confirmed by Thomas in an in-genious experiment.[19] (See figure 1b.)

Individual lecturers and students will depart from this typical pattern, but not radically. Contributing to these individual differ-ences are such factors as the fatigability of the students, the level

18. Ibid.

19. E. J. Thomas, "The Variation of Memory with Time for Information Appearing during a Lecture," *Studies in Adult Education* 4 (April 1972): 57-62.

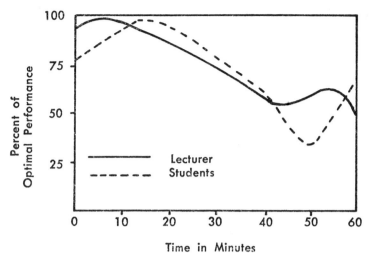

FIG. 1a. Decrement in lecturer and student performance during a lecture

Source: John McLeish, *The Lecture Method* (Cambridge, Eng.: Cambridge Institute of Education, 1968), p. 36.

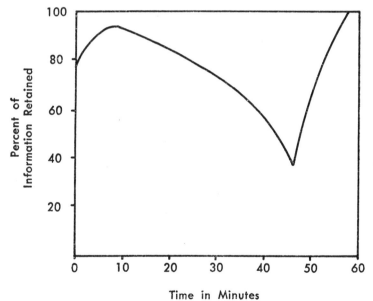

FIG. 1b. Decrement in student retention of a lecture

Source: E. J. Thomas, "The Variation of Memory with Time for Information Appearing during a Lecture," *Studies in Adult Education* 1 (April 1972): 60.

of difficulty of the lecture materials, the rapport or lack of it between lecturer and class group, the amount and quality of feedback

from students to lecturer, and his sensitivity and appropriate reaction to their psychological condition.

The basic capacity of the lecturer, which can be defined as his
output per unit of time, appears to be a relatively fixed value,
depending on various personality constants and the teaching objectives aimed at, largely unawares. On the other hand, the receptivity
of the student group appears to be more variable. Receptivity seems
to be more sensitive to (a) factors of the physical environment,
such as the size, acoustics, illumination, and ventilation of the classroom, and (b) psychological conditions, such as fatigue and alert-
ness, which vary with mood, time of day, and the nature and duration of any preceding mental and physical work. We can visualize
the kind of mathematical relation that would express the causal
connection between the receptivity of the students and other variables, as follows:

$$i = k \frac{r \times a}{f}$$

where i represents the intake of the student group per unit of time,
k is a constant, r is the amount of rapport established during the
class hour, a is the lecturer's adaptive reaction to feedback from the
class, and f stands for various items covered by the blanket terms
fatigue and boredom. Receptivity will fluctuate throughout the
class period in terms of some complex function of these variables.

The main lesson to be drawn from this discursive account of
what we may regard as the typical lecture sequence is that, to improve the lecture, the time available must be diversified by a variety
of materials, teaching aids, pauses, and varied activities by lecturer
and students. These act to maximize rapport and to minimize
monotony and fatigue. The lecturer must be sensitive to the effect
of a monotonous stimulus applied over a lengthy period. Overt
signs of boredom and inattention should act as a cue to digress
along a prepared line—visual aids, a change of pace or of theme,
a diversion introduced by a question to the class or a problem-
exercise bearing on the matter in hand. These are some of the techniques that experience suggests as ways to reverse the otherwise
inevitable process of deepening depression, apathy, and boredom.

The conflict of views to be discovered among armchair critics
and defenders of the lecture system is probably attributable to the

fact that student auditors fall into various types in terms of their reaction to the teaching methods to which they are subjected.[20] "Rebels" are in marked contrast to "enthusiasts," "oracular" students to "participatory" students, "group-oriented" students to "individually-oriented" students, not only in their attitudes toward instruction but also in their basic personality traits, political attitudes, and educational values. Indeed, it is probable that the reactions of a group of students to a *particular* lecture, or to a lecture-series, are even more individualized than the typology suggests. In evaluating criticisms and defenses of the lecture system, we should surely adopt the principle that the onus of proof is on the shoulders of the defenders of the lecture system. "He who asserts must prove." They must be prepared to demonstrate that what they assert to be true of the lecture system *in general* is true of specific cases.

Stories are told of lecturers whose particular style or personality so impressed itself on the auditors that it remained a constant stimulus through a lifetime of work. Several things must be said in this connection. The experience is relatively uncommon when we call to mind the considerable numbers who actually lecture as their professional activity. Again, maybe it was the *personality* of the teacher rather than the lecture method that created the effect. The great lecturer might have been even more impressive had he used a different method of teaching altogether. It is usually the lecturer, his idiosyncracies, his character, or perhaps only the rosy glow he communicated to his auditors that are remembered, rather than his message. We must offset the hour's delight experienced in one lecture with the dreary wastelands of time endured in compulsory lectures by vast multitudes of students.

Like the sermon in religious life, the lecture no doubt has a prescriptive right of entry into higher education wherever provided. But the evangelicals discovered that, without catechizing, the sermon was in a sense wasted and thrown away on congregations.[21] It tended to dry up the religious feelings, especially where it was

20. John McLeish, *The Lecture Method* (Cambridge, England: Cambridge Institute of Education, 1968).

21. John McLeish, *Evangelical Religion and Popular Education* (London: Methuen, 1969).

the practice to read the sermon. The congregation failed to learn the intellectual content of Christianity, never mind its affective message, even when subjected to two or three sermons on Sundays. This is the testimony of a man who was regarded as probably the second greatest preacher of his generation (Griffith Jones).

A similar lesson still needs to be learned in many institutions of higher learning, namely, that there is a need to diversify the techniques of communication. Students learn in a great variety of styles.

Systematic Experiments on the Lecture Method

EFFECTIVENESS OF THE LECTURE

Student recall. Jones carried out one of the first systematic studies of the lecture method.[22] As subjects, he used the students in his psychology courses. He managed to involve 782 students in a total of thirty lectures, asking 5,000 questions to test their retention of lecture materials. Immediate memory for lecture materials was assessed by administering a test immediately after the lecture. He discovered considerable individual differences in the amounts assimilated. The ratio of the best to the worst score was of the order of six to one. On the average, about 62 percent was retained. Following Ebbinghaus,[23] he verified that the forgetting of lecture material was of a lawful character. The curve of retention dropped from about 60 percent on immediate recall to about 20 percent after eight weeks.

In a series of experiments designed to discover ways of improving the effectiveness of the lecture, Jones found that note-taking made no substantial difference in amounts retained. On the other hand, the technique of giving a short multiple-choice test five minutes before the end of the lecture facilitated retention over an eight-week period. Retention was also improved by increasing the forcefulness, dramatic appeal, and quality of the lecture; by reducing the number of points presented and going at a slower pace; by increasing the concreteness and the number of illustrations used.

22. Harold E. Jones, "Experimental Studies of College Teaching," *Archives of Psychology*, no. 68 (November 1923): entire issue.

23. Hermann Ebbinghaus, *Memory*, trans. Henry A. Ruger (New York: Teachers College, Columbia University, 1913).

The general conclusion was that the large range of individual differences in retention (from zero to just under 100 percent) indicated that the lecture system suited only a relatively small proportion of the student group. Jones recommended that the lecture system be supplanted by projects and discussions. In spite of its general excellence, Jones's work failed to stimulate any continuing interest in empirical research on the lecture. Nor did his findings have any impact on the traditional system.

Although not using the lecture situation in his investigations, Bartlett's work on "remembering" is of considerable relevance.[24] In a laboratory situation, he demonstrated the rapidity with which connected verbal materials were forgotten by highly intelligent subjects. More important, he showed in detail how these and other materials were transformed into something quite different as the result of the subject's preconceptions and habitual ways of thinking.

In a number of studies in the early 1950s, Trenaman attempted to discover possible differences between various groups in their assimilation of recorded broadcast talks, originally presented by the British Broadcasting Corporation. The general outcome of his work was the discovery that the assimilation and retention of "talks" material was minimal, even in the case of interested and educated groups. With increasing length of recorded talk, the amount assimilated decreased to the vanishing point. These conclusions were based on a well-designed and systematic enquiry.[25] Matched samples of listening groups were used and three different media (television, radio, and print) were compared.[26] Some of the other conclusions from these extensive studies are worth noting: the three media communicate with roughly equivalent efficiency; the intellectual differences of auditors or viewers are much more significant for the understanding and retention of materials than are any differences due to the medium employed; visual materials with sound yield a significantly better outcome than radio or print alone; television is

24. Frederic C. Bartlett, *Remembering* (Cambridge, England: Cambridge University Press, 1932).

25. Joseph M. Trenaman, "The Length of a Talk," unpublished paper (London: British Broadcasting Corporation Research Unit, 1951).

26. Joseph M. Trenaman, *Communication and Comprehension* (London: Longmans, Green, 1967).

more effective in holding attention during periods when the interest in the content of a program begins to flag; those who already know a lot about the subject learn more than those who know only a little.

Nichols identified various components of effective listening. His analysis tends to support the other studies quoted.[27] Ten variables promote effective assimilation: previous experience with the material; interest in the topic; adjustment to the speaker; the amount of energy expended by the listener; his degree of adjustment to the listening situation, to emotion-laden words, and emotion-arousing points; ability to recognize the central ideas of the discourse; efficiency in note taking; the reconciliation of the speed of reflective thinking by the listener with the speed of delivery by the lecturer. In an elaborate experimental study, Rogers identified a general factor of listening ability in a group of students as well as an independent factor of self-reliant, or independent, thinking.[28] These skills were not related directly to age or sex. There was only a moderate relationship between ability to listen to a lecture and academic achievement in general.

Another interesting finding was that by McClendon. He studied the note-taking practices of 678 students in relation to their comprehension of lectures.[29] Contrary to expectation, it appeared that note taking had no effect on the comprehension of a lecture. Comprehension was not affected either by taking notes or by not taking notes. Where students recorded only the main points, in contrast to making detailed notes, their comprehension of the lecture was not impaired.

The next question is, of course, whether note taking affects retention. McClendon's finding about note taking was supported by the work of Freyberg, who found that students who merely listened

27. Ralph G. Nichols, "Ten Components of Effective Listening," *Education* 75 (January 1955): 292-302.

28. George W. Rogers, "Lecture Listening Skills: Their Nature and Relation to Achievement," *Dissertation Abstracts* 20 (April 1960): 4165.

29. Paul I. McClendon, "An Experimental Study of the Relationship between the Note-taking Practices and Listening Comprehension of College Freshmen during Expository Lectures," *Speech Monograph* 25 (August 1958): 222-28.

did better on a recall test immediately afterwards than did groups who took detailed notes, and others who took only outline notes.[30] They also did better than the other two groups on a retest after two weeks. After an eight-week interval, however, when opportunities for review were provided all groups, those who took no notes scored lower than the other groups. They were also overtaken by a fourth group, which had been given a duplicated summary of the lecture.

A number of experiments were carried out by the present writer to answer certain specific questions about student retention: (a) Does retroactive inhibition operate during the lecture period so that as time progresses the amount assimilated by the student falls off progressively to zero? (b) How much of the lecture material is actually available to the student either by recall or by the use of notes immediately after the lecture is over? (c) Are students capable of deriving as much from the printed text of a lecture as from the same lecture delivered by an experienced practitioner? (d) If students are motivated by telling them that the materials referred to in the lecture will be used in practical exercises within a relatively short period, do they assimilate more? [31]

The experiments conformed to a single research design. The same lecturer operated in various experimental contexts. Single classes were used as the basic unit. Each class was divided at random into experimental and control groups that were subjected to different treatments. The control groups were made up by randomly assigning students within the class to subgroups. A criterion test was carefully devised in advance to assess the amounts assimilated immediately after the students had heard the lecture. After an interval, usually of a week, sometimes a month, and always without prior warning, the students were retested to discover the amount retained. In the retest, the same criterion test was used as in the initial test. These experiments took their starting point from the work of Trenaman.[32] In his experiments, broadcast talks of forty-

30. P. S. Freyberg, "The Effectiveness of Note-Taking," *Education for Teaching* 39 (February 1956): 17-24.

31. McLeish, *The Lecture Method.*

32. Trenaman, "The Length of a Talk."

five minutes duration by distinguished speakers were played over to volunteers—groups of adult students, high school students, and others. Some heard only fifteen minutes, some thirty minutes, and some the whole forty-five minutes of the recorded talk. They were tested immediately with recognition, free recall, and true-false tests to discover how much they had assimilated. Trenaman discovered that with the increase in the duration of the talk the amount remembered thinned out. In the typical case, assimilation diminished seriously after fifteen minutes. At thirty minutes, most listeners were approaching the point where the total taken in was zero. In some cases there was, in fact, a loss of material previously learned. This is, of course, the phenomenon known as retroactive inhibition.

The present writer failed to replicate Trenaman's findings, using a face-to-face lecture situation and an immediate test of recall.[33] It was discovered, however, that students could recall less than half (40 percent) of the ideas in the lecture materials as measured by the tests, even when using their notes and a prepared blackboard summary. A week later they had forgotten half of this material. Great individual differences were found: the scores varied from 28 percent recall to 70 percent.

The experiment was repeated by the present writer, with certain variations, using sixty architectural students randomly assigned to one of three groups. The members of Group I, the motivated reading group, were informed that they would spend an hour in studying the verbatim text of a lecture entitled "Synectics: A Method of Developing Potential Creativity," written by a distinguished authority. They were told that it was intended to use this material almost at once in synectic-type exercises on the design process. Having studied the lecture transcript for fifty minutes, they joined other students in the lecture room for testing. Group II, the motivated lecture group, was told that they would hear a one-hour lecture on synectics, which is a special method of group work used to develop originality and creativity. They were told to listen critically, to think of ways of testing out the method in their school of architecture because they would be taking part in synectics exercises very soon. Hence they were to try to learn what

33. John McLeish, "Student Retention of Lecture Material," *Cambridge Institute of Education Bulletin* 3 (July 1966): 2-11.

it is all about, perhaps taking some notes, while attending actively to what is being said. Group III, an unmotivated lecture group, was directed into the lecture theatre, having been told only that they would be hearing a lecture. The speaker was introduced to Groups II and III, mentioning only the lecturer's name, place of work, and the title of the lecture. The third group knew only that a lecture, not in the general context of architectural studies, was being delivered.

The results of this experiment were similar to the previous one. Precisely the same score (40 percent) on a test on the lecture was obtained by both lecture groups (Groups II and III) on an immediate posttest (see table 1). The reading group learned about ten percent more than either of the lecture groups. They were also more strongly motivated to use the materials than were the lecture groups.

TABLE 1

ROUNDED SCORES (IN PERCENTS) OF THREE GROUPS ON THE TEST ON SYNECTICS

Test	Group I Motivated Reading	Group II Motivated Lecture	Group III Unmotivated Lecture
Immediate Recall......	50	40	40
Interest Level.........	45	40	35
Delayed Recall........	35	35	35

These groups had been using techniques similar to those described by the lecturer ("synectics") in the interval between testing and retesting a month later. They were all given a copy of the text of the lecture on completion of the examination. Their delayed recall of the lecture content was therefore much better than the subjects in the previous experiment. The experiment clearly elicits what McLeish has called the "equalization effect". This is described as follows:

. . . irrespective of differences due to the teaching methods used, the work which students do for themselves in preparation for an examination will tend to bring their scores close to equality. This will vitiate any long-term comparison of the relative efficiency of the various "treatments" to which they have been subjected.[34]

34. McLeish, *The Lecture Method.*

The most interesting result of this study was that it was the initially high-scoring students whose scores deteriorated, whereas the scores of the low-scoring students remained virtually the same.

Hartley and Cameron compared the notes taken by students with what the lecturer had actually said.[35] A transcript of the lecture was divided by the authors into "informational units" and the students' notes were then checked for the number of units recorded. Approximately one-third of what the lecturer said was noted by the students. The content agreement with a set of "ideal notes" prepared by the lecturer varied from about 70 percent during the first ten-minute period to 20 percent during the final period.

To complete the general picture on note taking at lectures, Eisner and Rohde, in a carefully designed experiment, found no significant difference between one group that took notes during a lecture and another that wrote out summary notes after the lecture.[36] This was true of immediate as well as delayed recall. The design called for the two groups to try both methods in succession. Although students became upset when not allowed to take notes, the experiment demonstrated that note taking made virtually no difference to recall.

Comparisons with other methods. If students do not benefit much from taking notes on lectures, it is conceivable that they do not benefit much from *attending* them. This possibility occurred to Milton, who found that 188 students in psychology, without having attended the classes, did as well on written tests as 173 other students who did attend.[37] He also found that attendance or nonattendance made no difference in the percent of students withdrawing from courses or taking further psychology courses.

A similar study by Marr et al. established that students who attended a course of lectures scored higher in the final examination than did other students who attended question-and-answer sessions

35. James Hartley and A. Cameron, "Some Observations on the Efficiency of Lecturing," *Education Review* 20 (November 1967): 30-37.

36. Sigmund Eisner and Kermit Rohde, "Note Taking during or after the Lecture," *Journal of Educational Psychology* 50 (December 1959): 301-4.

37. Ohmer Milton, "Two-year Follow-up: Objective Data after Learning without Class Attendance," *Psychological Reports* 11 (December 1962): 833-36.

with the same instructors (no discussion allowed).[38] The authors concluded that lectures make a significant contribution to a college student's education. But the actual differences between the groups were so small (about 10 percent in aggregate) that we must conclude that a more economical and effective method for teaching students, replacing the lecture, could easily be devised.

A problem that regularly recurs is whether there is an optimum size of group for lecturing purposes. Interest in this problem has revived in recent years because of the increasing use of closed-circuit television at the college level. Most studies indicate that students seem to remember as much, and can use the knowledge acquired as well, whether they are taught in very large or very small groups, whether these are numbered in tens or in thousands.[39] Nonetheless, students consistently say that they benefit more when the class is small.

Criticisms made earlier of comparative studies (nonrandomization, students' work as a confounding variable, inappropriate criteria) apply to a large proportion of these investigations of class size. An interesting experiment by de Cecco throws some light on this question.[40] Eighteen course groups, ranging in size from 18 to 127 students, were provided with instruction in introductory psychology. Students were randomly assigned to the normal course instructors in groups of various sizes. A number of criteria for evaluation were used, covering a variety of teaching objectives. In logical thinking and information about the subject, there were no differences between the large and small groups. Since student work for the examination was not controlled, the conclusion must be expressed in the form that there is no evidence that students were *disadvantaged* by being taught in large lecture classes in this experiment. As for the students' opinions about their groups, however, significant differences were found in favor of the small

38. John N. Marr et al., "The Contribution of the Lecture to College Teaching," *Journal of Educational Psychology* 51 (October 1960): 277-84.

39. Wilbert J. McKeachie, "Research on College Teaching: A Review," Report 6 (Washington, D.C.: Clearinghouse on Higher Education, 1970). ERIC: 043 789.

40. John P. de Cecco, "Class Size and Co-ordinated Instruction," *British Journal of Educational Psychology* 34 (February 1964): 65-74.

groups, since the students rated the small groups higher in assisting them to compose critical reports in an experimental project, and in promoting general gain. De Cecco concluded that the students' declared preference for being taught in small groups, and the belief that they benefit more, are inconsistent with the facts. He posited a "halo effect" based on stereotyped thinking about teaching methods. Alternatively, the students' view may refer to the greater "warmth" that can develop in small classes.

In an earlier experiment, Churchill and John compared small lecture-discussion groups with a large lecture class.[41] Instruction in mathematics was supplemented by a laboratory course, in the first case conducted by the instructor, in the second case by a student assistant. The student groups were equated for initial ability. The primary object of the experiment was to discover if the time of the teaching staff could be conserved by having them lecture to large audiences, handing over the task of detailed explanation to student demonstrators. The two groups in this experiment did equally well on the multiple-choice test and on the essay used for evaluation. As one could have predicted, however, the large lecture class expressed themselves as less satisfied with the course, while valuing the student-led laboratory as providing an opportunity to clarify the lecture for themselves.

These experiments suffer from the methodological weakness that students are not tested *immediately* to discover what part of the increment in knowledge, skill, or desirable attitude is to be attributed to the method and what to later work by the student preparatory to his final examination. It is tempting to suggest that there is no evidence that teaching at the university level really conveys any lasting benefit to the student. If he does benefit from higher education, the benefit appears only in the form of learning how to work independently, and this benefit is one which the lecturing system can hardly provide. In exceptional cases, perhaps, and against the stream of organized talk, the student may work out for himself what needs to be done to make an original contribution. Students cultivate an intuitive awareness of how much they need to

41. Ruth Churchill and Paula John, "Conservation of Teaching Time through the Use of Lecture Classes and Student Assistants," *Journal of Educational Psychology* 49 (December 1958): 324-27.

do to make up for the inadequacies of the provision made for teaching them so that, at least, they perform creditably in their examination. An interesting problem for empirical research is: to what sort of signals do students respond so as to ensure that a fairly uniform standard is achieved?

Teaching in small groups does make a difference, but the effects are masked by the "equalization phenomenon" previously referred to.[42] This appears rather convincingly in a study by Nachman and Opochinsky.[43] They compared the scores made by matched groups of students, both groups attending a lecture course. The small group consisted of a single class of twenty-one. The matching students were in a different group, being "embedded" in a class of 150. The definitive comparison was that between the scores made at two examinations. One examination was given a week after the course had ended and revealed no difference between the two groups. The other examination consisted of two "spot-quizzes" inserted immediately after the second and fourth lectures, and here the small class performed significantly better. But it should be noted that there were individual differences such that, although thirteen students in the small group did better than their matched student in the larger group, five scored the same, and three scored less well. Also, the actual difference between the groups was quite small.

Holloway has verified that attendance at lectures adds only slightly to student gain on multiple-choice tests.[44] For those not attending the lecture, a duplicated hand-out distributed at the lecture was available. The students were first- or third-year dental students attending clinical lectures dealing with subjects of a practical nature.

In a carefully designed investigation, where special concern was shown for controlling the "Hawthorne effect," Keeling and Lenz found that students preferred the lecture method to a programmed

42. John McLeish, "Lecture, Tutorial, Seminar: The Student's View," *Education for Teaching* 75 (Spring 1968): 21-27.

43. Marvin Nachman and Seymour Opochinsky, "The Effects of Different Teaching Methods: A Methodological Study," *Journal of Educational Psychology* 49 (October 1958): 245-49.

44. Philip J. Holloway, "The Effect of Lecture Time on Learning," *British Journal of Educational Psychology* 36 (November 1966): 255-58.

text in statistics by a two-thirds majority.[45] There was, however, no perceptible difference in effectiveness. This finding is contrary to the results of previous comparisons.

Tistaert compared lecture and discussion methods in geography.[46] Students, in matched groups of twenty-three, were taught by the same instructor. Discussion was superior in developing "reflective thinking" and retention of subject matter. The advantage in knowledge and attitude toward the subject, associated with the discussion method, persisted over four months and was demonstrable both with very bright students and the more ordinary ones.

On the other hand, Eyestone discovered that there was nothing to choose between the effectiveness of a lecture (with and without discussion), a bulletin, or a film in conveying factual information about research findings, except that subjects did better where there was *no* discussion.[47] Neither was there an advantage in any of the three methods in terms of desirable changes in attitude in the 513 experimental subjects employed in his experiments.

In a similar study, Ruja, comparing lecture and discussion methods in three college courses, discovered no differences so far as gains in subject matter are concerned.[48] The same applied to gains in emotional and social adjustment. The main differences seemed to be that students in discussion groups knew a greater number of each other's names and graded their instructors more favorably than did the lecture groups.

This result must not be taken as implying that students will inevitably prefer discussion methods, or some other innovation in teaching. There are a number of variables at work. Chief among these is the maturity of the students and the amount of examination pressure to which they are subjected. Wispe found that most

45. B. Keeling and E. O. Lenz, "The Efficiency of and Attitudes towards Two Methods of Teaching Elementary Statistics," *New Zealand Journal of Educational Studies* 1 (November 1966): 89-101.

46. G. Tistaert, "A Classroom Experiment on Lecture and Discussion Methods," *Paedagogica Europaea* 1 (1965): 125-35.

47. Merle L. Eyestone, "A Comparison of the Effectiveness of Bulletin, Film, and Lecture, with and without Discussion, in Presenting Research Information," *Dissertation Abstracts* 27A (October 1966): 922-23.

48. Harry Ruja, "Outcomes of Lecture and Discussion Procedures in Three College Courses," *Journal of Experimental Education* 22 (June 1954): 385-94.

students preferred directive to nondirective teaching.[49] They enjoyed the latter, but did not consider nondirective courses of much value. The bright students did equally well under both types of teaching: the duller ones benefited more from directive teaching. The criterion here was examination results.

Ward also compared group study methods with lecture demonstrations.[50] He found that the group method resulted in improved retention, better understanding, and greater expression of individual differences, in the case of academically superior students. On the other hand, the lecture-demonstration method produced better results with the least capable students.

Joyce and Weatherall, on the basis of controlled experiments, discussed the economics of various methods of teaching students in medical school.[51] They demonstrated that discussion groups were superior in that they resulted in greater knowledge of subject matter than did lecture or practical methods of instruction. The least effective method was unsupervised reading. Since lectures were only slightly inferior to discussion, and considerably less time-consuming and more economical in the use of faculty, they concluded that the efficiency of the lecture, in terms of results obtained for equal amounts of work, is highest. In a second experiment, matched groups in a course on the pharmacology of the nervous system showed no difference in knowledge when subjected to lectures with demonstrations, or lectures with practical classes, or conventional seminars.[52] Using similar arguments about the economical use of staff time, they concluded that demonstrations and discussion should be used in preference to seminars and practical classes. Nonetheless, they conceded that their criteria covered only

49. Lauren G. Wispe, "Evaluating Section Teaching Methods in the Introductory Course," *Journal of Educational Research* 45 (November 1951): 161-86.

50. John N. Ward, "Group-study versus Lecture-demonstration Method in Physical Science Instruction for General Education College Students," *Journal of Experimental Education* 24 (March 1956): 197-210.

51. C. R. B. Joyce and M. Weatherall, "Controlled Experiments in Teaching," *Lancet* 6992 (31 August 1957): 402-7.

52. C. R. B. Joyce and M. Weatherall, "Effective Use of Teaching Time," *Lancet* 7072 (14 March 1959): 568-71.

a narrow range of teaching objectives. The students favored demonstrations and seminars.

Joyce and Weatherall also used the interesting technique of playing back tape recordings in the discussion groups, in the absence of the lecturer.[53] In a similar experiment in teacher education, Popham randomly assigned thirty-six students to two matched groups.[54] One group was taught by a standard lecture-discussion method; the other listened to hour-long taped lectures and then discussed these with a student-leader. The various tests used at the end of the course showed that there were no differences of any significance between the two groups.

Webb introduced a completely new dimension into the argument about the effectiveness of the lecture as a teaching method.[55] His technique consisted of having students prepare tape-recorded lectures in four psychology courses. Control groups were subjected to traditional lectures as a basis for comparison. The enthusiasm and the improved grades achieved by students in the experimental group might be explained in terms of the Hawthorne effect and variables other than teaching method employed. The technique shows considerable promise, however, as it is clear that instructional objectives of a diversity of types could be achieved by these procedures, objectives that the traditional lecture system might fail to encompass.

Several studies reported the superiority of independent study over the lecture. McCullough and van Atta have shown that flexible students benefit more from independent study than do those with rigid personality structures.[56] Gruber and Weitman have demonstrated the superior results of independent study in helping students become able to make difficult applications of the materials learned,

53. Joyce and Weatherall, "Controlled Experiments."

54. W. James Popham, "Tape Recorded Lectures in the College Classroom: II," *Audiovisual Communication Review* 10 (March-April 1962): 94-101.

55. Neill J. Webb, "Student Preparation and Tape Recording of Course Lectures as a Method of Instruction," *Psychological Reports* 16 (February 1965): 67-72.

56. Celeste McCullough and E. L. van Atta, *Experimental Evaluation of Teaching Programs Utilizing a Block of Independent Work* (Oberlin, Ohio: Oberlin College, 1960).

to learn new materials, and manifest curiosity about the subject.[57] These results are probably to be explained in the light of the classic studies of "completed" and "uncompleted" tasks carried out by Lewin and his co-workers in the 1930s in Germany. Students who were deliberately interrupted before they had completed certain laboratory problems returned surreptitiously to them and seemed to suffer from a kind of intellectual "hunger" for "closure." This phenomenon may be related to the report by Thistlethwaite of a negative correlation between the degree to which a college provided "directive" teaching (as indicated by students' reports) and the number of doctorates awarded to students of the college in biological sciences in the United States.[58] The implication of this finding, at first sight at any rate, seems to be that "directive" teaching (the lecture method being a prime example of this kind of teaching) fails to encourage initiative and originality in students.

Summarizing the advances in our understanding brought about by research in the areas of teaching materials, programmed learning, lecture, discussion, and independent study, Ryan asserted that this work had resulted in no major change in established procedures in the period 1928 to 1968.[59] She pointed out that the effectiveness of the lecture compared to discussion is a function of the lecturer, his objectives, and the type of student. The lecture seems to be superior to discussion for the purpose of transmitting information, but underachievers require supplementary methods that involve immediate feedback and an emphasis on student activity (for example, through programmed instruction). As Bloom has shown, discussion is better than a lecture in facilitating creative or reflective thinking.[60] Similarly, Baskin has shown that independent study results in greater learning resourcefulness in students, compared to

57. H. E. Gruber and M. Weitman, "Self-directed Study: Experiments in Higher Education," Report No. 19 (Boulder: University of Colorado, Behavior Research Laboratory, 1960).

58. Donald L. Thistlethwaite, "College Environments and the Development of Talent," *Science* 130 (10 July 1959): 71-76.

59. T. Antoinette Ryan, "Research: Guide for Teaching Improvement," *Improving College and University Teaching* 17 (Autumn 1968): 270-76.

60. Benjamin S. Bloom, "Thought-Processes in Lectures and Discussions," *Journal of General Education* 7 (April 1953): 160-69.

those taught by small group discussion or lecture.[61] In this regard, personality factors appear to be more important than academic ability, according to the work of Chickering and of Dearing.[62] The importance of considering student characteristics as well as teaching method is emphasized in Ryan's survey article. Her work has shown that students seem to be quite capable of selecting the special pattern of teaching methods suited to their academic needs and they are also capable of achieving a high level of performance in the method of their choice.[63] The methods themselves produce no differences of any significance as between the various student groups. Thus, an important factor in college teaching would seem to be the interaction between student personality and teaching method.

MacManaway formed three randomly chosen groups of forty-five, forty-four, and twenty students.[64] One group was given the typescript of three lectures on educational sociology, and instructed to take notes on these; the second group attended the three lectures in question and were instructed to take notes in the usual way; the third group attended the lectures without taking notes. Without warning, all three groups were given a test designed to measure factual knowledge and the main arguments used. The author concluded that the private reading of lecture scripts as a substitute for lectures resulted in more efficient note taking and was slightly more time-consuming, but resulted in a greater understanding of the material. The results of the experiment in note taking are summarized in table 2.

MacManaway concluded that much faculty time could be saved without loss in student learning by the use of lecture scripts that would replace the formal lecture. The time saved could be used in

61. Samuel Baskin, "Experiment in Independent Study (1956-1960)," *Journal of Experimental Education* 31 (December 1962): 183-85.

62. Arthur W. Chickering, "Dimensions of Independence," *Journal of Experimental Education* 32 (Spring 1964): 313-16; and Bruce Dearing, "The Student on His Own: Independent Study," in *Higher Education: Some Newer Developments*, ed. Samuel Baskin (New York: McGraw-Hill, 1965), pp. 49-77.

63. T. Antoinette Ryan, "Testing Instructional Approaches for Increased Learning," *Phi Delta Kappan* 46 (June 1965): 534-536.

64. Lancelot A. MacManaway, "Using Lecture Scripts," *Universities Quarterly* 22 (June 1968): 327-36.

TABLE 2

RESULTS OF AN EXPERIMENT ON NOTE TAKING

Group	N	Time Utilized (in minutes)	Score on test	Range of Scores	Efficiency Index (Score/Time)
Lecture with notes	45	135	17	9–23	0.1260
Typescripts with notes	44	166	20	11–35	0.1205
Lecture without notes	20	188	19	9–25	0.1010

tutorials and seminars where the students assumed a more active role. Students could be encouraged to read and study independently.

In a monograph summarizing the results of research to 1968, Dubin and Taveggia employed the novel procedure of combining the data from the available studies.[65] This provided a high precision measure of, among other things, a comparison of the lecture method with other teaching techniques. Reporting the results of this re-analysis of ninety-one studies conducted between 1924 and 1965, they concluded that there was no evidence for the superiority of one teaching method over another when these are evaluated by student performance on final examinations. The most significant suggestion they make is that research needs to move into the area of "teaching-learning" linkages and that a Skinnerian model is appropriate for this purpose. In the examination of outcomes in relation to process, the present author, with a team of collaborators, has been doing precisely this in an ongoing analysis of small group teaching.[66] As yet, we have not applied these techniques to the lecture situation.

Comparisons between methods are too global in character—attention must be paid not only to the formal description of a class

65. Robert Dubin and Thomas C. Taveggia, *The Teaching-Learning Paradox: A Comparative Analysis of College Teaching Methods* (Eugene, Ore.: Center for the Advanced Study of Educational Administration, University of Oregon, 1968).

66. McLeish, Matheson, and Park, *The Psychology of the Learning Group;* and John McLeish and Jack Martin, "Verbal Behavior: A Review and Experimental Analysis," *Journal of General Psychology* 93 (July 1975): 3-66.

as a "lecture course," or "discussion forum" or "independent study" but, more important, to the actualities of the educational processes in the face-to-face situation of instructor and students. Group dynamics must be related to outcomes in a much more sophisticated and intensive study of the teaching-learning encounter.

Pascal, in a well-designed study, demonstrated that students allowed to choose between a lecture, a lecture with discussion, and independent study differed in their basic need structures but not in their final grades in the course.[67] Lecture and lecture-discussion students, however, were better at recall of course material whereas independent study students were significantly better at evaluating *new* materials. These students reported that this option allowed them to pursue their individual goals and promoted creativity more than did lectures or discussion.

In a comparison of formal lectures and programmed instruction in histology and embryology with dental school students, McCrea and Swanson concluded that lectures were neither needed nor wanted by the students.[68] The programs involved only about half the time of the lecture courses and resulted in much better student performance. In fact, the students in the programmed learning group were awarded ten times as many "A" grades in the theoretical examinations (226 *vs.* 22) and twice as many (124 *vs.* 56) in the practical tests as the students in the lecture-discussion class.

Pikas offered the qualification, however, that comparisons between programmed instruction and traditional teaching must take account of two variables usually ignored.[69] He claimed that *transfer* is better from traditional instruction and that *retention* of factual information persists over a longer period. As a general hypothesis, he claimed, the greater the dissimilarity between the

67. Charles E. Pascal, "Offering Course Options: Personality, Option Preference, and Course Outcomes," *Dissertation Abstracts International* 31A (November 1970): 2194.

68. Marion W. McCrea and Ernest A. Swanson, Jr., "Are Formal Lectures Really Necessary?" *Journal of Dental Education* 33, no. 4 (1969): 424-31.

69. Anatol Pikas, "Comparisons between Traditional and Programmed Learning as a Function of Passive Performance and Active Application and Time till Application," *Programmed Learning and Educational Technology* 6 (January 1969): 20-25.

learning and the task situations, the greater is the superiority of traditional teaching over programmed learning. Using three groups of eighty to ninety students each, Pikas found limited but consistent evidence for the advantage of *active* teaching (question-and-answer interaction) over both programmed instruction and a passive lecturing technique. This applies to application and delayed recall. It does not apply to scores on a multiple-choice test given as an immediate posttest of factual knowledge. Here the results consistently favored programmed instruction as a method.

A contribution in this area by Jamieson, James, Leytham, and Tozer also indicated that programmed instruction is superior to lectures and to lectures augmented with audio-visual materials.[70] After five months, the programmed instruction group retained their superiority in retention of the tested materials. But the authors hypothesized that the differences were due to the similarity of the test materials and the learning activities. Intelligence test scores had no value for predicting the amounts learned. Nearly 200 graduate students in educational psychology were used in these experiments and a well-known program, Stones's *Learning and Teaching*, provided the learning materials for the experiment.[71] The pretest and posttest, like the lectures and augmented lectures, were drawn from this text. An additional finding was that the perceptual aids used to enrich one of the augmented lecture courses seemed to have no long-term value, as the scores of the experimental and control lecture groups became equal over a period of five months.

Carlson compared the large-group discussion method ($N = 71$) with the lecture method ($N = 60$) in teaching earth science.[72] The lecture was found to be superior, but there was no significant difference between the two methods in changing students' attitudes toward the subject.

70. G. H. Jamieson et al., "Comparisons between Teaching Methods at the Post-graduate Level," *Programmed Learning and Educational Technology* 6 (October 1969): 243-49.

71. Edgar Stones, *Learning and Teaching* (London: John Wiley & Sons, 1968).

72. Roger L. Carlson, "A Comparison between the Teaching Effectiveness of a Large-Group Lecture and a Large-Group Discussion When Evaluating the Cognitive and Affective Domains," *Dissertation Abstracts International* 31A (October 1970): 1642-43.

After devising an unusual combination of simulation exercises
and audio-tutorial instruction, Stuck and Manatt attempted to compare this technique with the traditional lecture method in teaching
about law in relation to schools to student-teachers.[73] Seven hours
of formal lectures were provided for one randomly assigned group;
a second group of students was given a one-week assignment, complete with audio-tapes, working through simulations of particular
school situations. Half of each group received one or the other of
these treatments before, and the other half after, their practice
teaching experience. The lecture group spent almost 40 percent
more time on the unit of instruction; they also scored significantly
lower than the audio-tutorial group. But the difference in scores
was small, representing only about 10 percent of the average gain
score.

MacManaway in Belfast and Gallagher in Boston experimented
with the abandonment of the lecture method, substituting for it the
provision of printed materials for discussion in class.[74] Eliminating
the lecture did not significantly alter student achievement. Both
research workers, one teaching sociology to student teachers, the
other teaching the preclinical course in prosthodontics to dental
students, decided that presenting course content by means of a
printed substitute was more effective and more efficient than lecturing. Greater or equivalent achievement in less instructional time
indicated that perhaps up to 25 percent of available time is wasted
in formal lecturing.

Fletcher and Knott came to an opposite conclusion. They
adopted the radical approach, abolishing the lecture altogether, substituting small-group discussion in a course in the history of education.[75] They reported that students took on greater responsibility

73. Dean L. Stuck and Richard P. Manatt, "A Comparison of Audio-
tutorial and Lecture Methods of Teaching," *Journal of Educational Research*
63 (May-June 1970): 414-18.

74. Lancelot A. MacManaway, "Teaching Methods in Higher Education:
Innovation and Research," *Universities Quarterly* 24 (Summer 1970): 321-29;
and James B. Gallagher, Jr., "An Evaluation of the Transfer of Information
by Printed Materials without a Formal Lecture," *Journal of Dental Education*
34 (December 1970): 59-66.

75. John Fletcher and Tom Knott, "Abolishing the Lecture," *Universities
Quarterly* 26 (Winter 1971): 96-101.

and the more demanding work that goes with preparation for discussion in a course concerned with analysis and evaluation instead
of with specific factual materials. Students' essays and examination papers were better informed and better argued than under the
lecture system. But the experimental design leaves the result in
doubt.

Using a cross-over research design involving two classes, Barnes
and Holloway directly compared lecture and small-group teaching
in a course on children's dentistry.[76] Factual recall, and the application of facts in the treatment situation, were assessed by a multiple-
choice examination. Two groups of thirty students were involved in
consecutive years. The small groups, which received essentially
step-by-step lectures with questions and answers, consisted of approximately six students. As the lectures were not compulsory, the
analysis of responses to topics in the multiple-choice test could compare three kinds of treatments (on the same subjects): lecture, small
group, and no formal teaching. The authors discovered no significant differences between these three treatment groups. Comparison
of the students who attended all the lectures but one with the students who attended less than four out of eleven lectures also revealed
no differences. The frequent lecture attenders did not perform any
better on small-group topics than did the poor lecture attenders. It
was concluded that formal teaching has little advantage over a
system where university students are left to find out the facts for
themselves (under guidance), and that small-group informal lectures
providing informational materials constitute a misuse of staff time.

The audio-tutorial method, developed by Postlethwait, Novak,
and Murray, focuses on individualized student activity, the careful
analysis of objectives, and the use of the most appropriate combination of media for presentation of material.[77] Welser, Lewis, and
Stockton compared this system with the lecture method in a school

76. D. S. Barnes and Philip J. Holloway, "Small and Large Group Teaching in Clinical Dentistry," *British Dental Journal* 129 (1 September 1970):
201-4.

77. S. N. Postlethwait, K. Novak, and H. T. Murray, Jr., *An Integrated
Experience Approach to Learning* (Minneapolis: Burgess Publishing Company,
1964).

of veterinary science.[78] No significant differences were found between randomly assigned groups of students. But students spent almost 50 percent more time in the audio-tutorial system. The lecture method in this experiment could therefore be regarded as more efficient, although taking up more *staff* time than the new method. The authors held, however, that the time required of students could be reduced by various means that would have the effect of making the audio-tutorial system more effective than the lecture system. The attitude of the students was more favorable to audio-tutorial instruction.

Assigned readings, duplicated notes, and question-answer sessions were substituted for a series of seven one-hour lectures on gastrointestinal pathology by Kent and Spivey.[79] Two multiple-choice examinations were given, one of which was administered two months after the course ended. The nonlecture group scored higher on easy, factual questions; the lecture group was superior on difficult factual questions and problem-solving questions. The lecture group scored about one standard deviation higher on the immediate recall test, but the two groups did about equally well after the two-month interval. This result appeared because the lecture group dropped about two standard deviations and the nonlecture group dropped only one. An interesting comparison between these 120 undergraduate students and 22 graduates in the same department (including six faculty members)—the graduates having no instruction before the test—revealed that the undergraduates scored at about the same level as the graduate students, the lecture group indeed doing significantly better on the immediate recall test. Students preferred the lecture method in a ratio of six to one. The authors emphasized the fact that, after two months, there was no difference in score between the two groups.

Lecture, discussion, and independent study were compared by

78. J. R. Welser, R. E. Lewis, and J. J. Stockton, "Audio-tutorial vs. Lecture-recitation: A Comparative Trial in the Teaching of Canine Radiographic Anatomy," *British Journal of Medical Education* 4 (December 1970): 316-22.

79. Thomas H. Kent and Bruce E. Spivey, "Lecture versus Nonlecture in Teaching Gastrointestinal Pathology," *Journal of Medical Education* 46 (June 1971): 525-31.

Atherton.[80] Fictional case study materials in the area of social welfare were used to control for previous learnings. The independent study group did better on the test as a whole. But, once again, it was demonstrated that there were no real differences across the three methods in recall, understanding, and ability to apply the knowledge gained. Nor did students in the lecture and discussion classes differ in the time they spent in study or in learning strategies.

Atherton concluded that, although the method of teaching may not be crucial, it is important that teaching be done to ensure contact between teacher and student. If the rules of the experiment had not been bent a little, well over half of the "independent study" group, those with minimal teacher contact, would have to be counted as learning nothing at all. Twenty-two students who did not deal with the material in any way were discarded when comparisons were made. In other words, two-thirds of the "independents" dropped out. The present writer would add to Atherton's recommendation that teaching should take place, that it is crucial that the teachers, and the institution within which the teaching is provided, be concerned and knowledgeable about their objectives, especially in relation to the values and attitudes they seek to cultivate. In general, classes provide a more favorable climate for learning than do minimal teaching strategies. The *amount* of teacher-student contact is probably related to student learning, although the most effective form of the contact is still undetermined by research evidence.

A comparison by Siegel of lecture-discussion with group counseling, involving seventy-two (three randomly assigned groups of twenty-four each) parents of mentally retarded children, revealed no end-of-course differences between the groups in anxiety level, self-concept, congruency, and knowledge of mental retardation.[81] The control group, which did not participate in the lecture course or the group counseling, was not more anxious, but *was* more con-

80. Charles R. Atherton, "College Teaching Methods: A Comparison of Three Common Strategies," *Dissertation Abstracts International* 32A (April 1972): 5603.

81. Edward M. Siegel, "The Effects of Lecture-Discussion and Group-Centered Counseling on Parents of Moderately Mentally Retarded Children," *Dissertation Abstracts International* 33A (September 1972): 978.

gruent, than either of the experimental groups. In other words, it appeared that neither lecture-discussion nor group counseling fostered achievement of any of the objectives defined for this kind of client.

A four-week unit on atomic theory and chemical bonding in a chemistry course for freshmen was presented to separate groups, each consisting of fifty students, in three forms: film program only, lecture with films, and lecture only.[82] Five full-length and ten single-concept films were specially chosen by a panel of professors. In the lecture-film treatment, only the full-length films were used, the single-concept films being omitted. In the films-only treatment, the additional single-concept films were presented in a programmed sequence along with the full-length films. A sixty-six item multiple-choice test was devised to cover the content of instruction. Of these items, thirty were administered halfway through to determine how much learning took place without special preparation for the test by the students. The remaining items were given as a posttest. The group was tested for retention ten weeks after the teaching was completed. A significant difference was found in favor of the self-instruction group, which had been given the films-only treatment, on both the posttest and the retention test. Attitude and posttest achievement were positively related; the films-only group had a more favorable attitude toward the subject.

This experiment seems to demonstrate the superiority of a programmed-learning based presentation of materials over the lecture method, rather than of films per se as instructional materials. Unfortunately, the design of the experiment does not allow us to discover the effect of the ten single-concept films by themselves and in combination with the lectures.

A direct comparison between self-instruction based on a programmed text and a lecture-course based on the traditional text from which the program was made was carried out by Himmel, using two groups of thirty-four students in an introductory psy-

82. Henry Zimmerman, "A Comparison of the Effectiveness of Using Single-Concept and Multi-Concept Films in a Self-Instructional Program with Lectures Reinforced by Full-Length Films and Lectures Only in Teaching a Unit in Introductory Chemistry in Community College," *Dissertation Abstracts International* 33A (October 1972): 1545.

chology course.[83] The self-instruction group had access to a learning center where additional materials were available and received a careful "briefing" about the method of self-directed study and the materials to be covered. At the end of the semester, the self-instruction group had an advantage of five points (half a standard deviation) over the lecture group. The difference disappeared, however, over a period of three months. The programmed text group also gave about the same favorable rating for subject matter, but a much more favorable rating (3.82 vs. 2.83 on a five-point scale) for the teaching method used, than the lecture group. But these differences also seemed to vanish over the three-month interval. The time spent on the course materials was about equal. There seemed also to be no differences between the groups on follow-up over twelve months on other measures of academic achievement.

A similar comparison of an open learning method, involving students themselves in deciding how much small-group teaching and/or independent study suited them in learning foundation mathematics, was carried out by King.[84] The forty-nine students who used this method were compared with two groups of forty-three students in the same course taught by the lecture method. Pre- and posttests were administered to measure gain in knowledge of real number theory and probability, as well as changes in attitude, self-concept, anxiety, and interest. The methods were found to be more or less equivalent in bringing about cognitive and affective changes. Cognitive gains in the lecture courses were associated with responsibility, sociability, socialization, and femininity (California Psychological Inventory); cognitive gains in the "open" method were associated with self-control. Negative correlations were found in the latter method with social presence and self-acceptance. Similar relationships were found between affective changes and personality traits in *both* methods. The great majority of students on the "open" plan favored this method.

83. Clark E. Himmel, "College Learning With and Without Formal Classroom Instruction: A Comparison," *Psychology in the Schools* 9 (July 1972): 272-77.

84. Estelle M. King, "Open Learning and Lecture Methods of Teaching College Mathematics," *Dissertation Asbstracts International* 33A (February 1973): 4122-23.

Smith and Pearn found that rote learning tasks presented by lecture were more effective in teaching easy tasks to poorly educated immigrant bus drivers in England than were discovery methods.[85] The training was concerned with "road sense." They attribute this result to the poor early education of a passive nature to which these immigrants had been subjected in their homelands. For nonimmigrant bus driver trainees, discovery methods were found to be more efficient. On difficult items the training method did not appear to influence performance at all. The sample consisted of 56 immigrants from Africa, India, Pakistan, and the Caribbean with a control group of 64 British trainees. Simulations were used in both lecture and discovery methods.

Adapting Bloom's technique of "stimulated recall," Schoen compared the effectiveness of seven teaching methods in terms of the student's attention.[86] Schoen improved on the method by signaling to the subjects at appropriate points and having them record the content of consciousness at the time. Such "consciousness sampling" revealed that not more than two-thirds of the students were paying attention during a lecture, and not much better attention was manifested in other methods. Most effective in maintaining attention were problem-solving and films; least effective were panel discussions and student-led exercises.

McWilliams canvassed 450 college students to ascertain their perceptions of their special academic needs and also with a view to discovering what would happen if changes were made to cater to those perceived needs.[87] Two simple principles were declared to cover the needs of students as they perceived them: to relate to others, and to be free within the area of their involvement. Two radically different situations were then set up—a control group of randomly selected students (N = 53) in a traditional classroom situation, and an experimental group (N = 29) seeking to create an

85. M. C. Smith and M. A. Pearn, "Conventional Lecture versus Discovery Training Methods in the Preparation of Immigrant Bus Conductors," *Journal of Cross Cultural Psychology* 3 (December 1972): 407-12.

86. James R. Schoen, "Use of Consciousness Sampling to Study Teaching Methods," *Journal of Educational Research* 63 (May-June 1970): 387-90.

87. Perry McWilliams, "Involvement: Is This What Students Really Want?" *College Student Journal* 6 (April-May 1972): 78-86.

"open," personal atmosphere of "total student involvement." Complete freedom, lack of structure, and student need-centered activities were the basic principles in this group. In fact, the experimental group chose to study the same materials as the control group. It was therefore possible to compare their expressed attitude toward the method, and their achievement on the course materials, with the compulsory lecture, standard text, examination-oriented group. The students' evaluations revealed that both groups reported enjoying the course almost equally well on the average. But the experimental group, which used an "encounter" group method, was sporadic in its progress and frustrating for many of the members. Only the leaders were satisfied with the course objectives. The lack of structure placed increased responsibility on the student. McWilliams concluded that, although these students were able to envisage desired changes, they were not, as a group, prepared to accept the consequences of the changes they desired.

STUDENTS' ATTITUDES TOWARD THE LECTURE

Comparisons with other methods. Beach attempted to discover what kind of student benefits most from which kind of instruction.[88] Five different teaching "treatments" were used. He established a lecture group of thirty-six, a discussion group of thirteen, five autonomous groups of five students who met without an instructor, an independent study group of twenty-four students who did not meet at all, and a control group of fifty-two students who submitted to the pre- and posttesting without any other "treatment." A test of extraversion-introversion was used as well as a sixty-item achievement test as criterion. The lecture group performed significantly better than the other three kinds of groups. In round figures, the gains in test scores were as follows: lecture, 8; independent study, 7; autonomous groups, 6; discussion, 5.5. But more salient was the discovery that (in terms of their group norm) introverts benefited more than extraverts in the lecture and class discussion groups (instructor present) whereas the reverse was true in the autonomous groups (instructor absent). There was no difference

88. Leslie R. Beach, "Sociability and Academic Achievement in Various Types of Learning Situations," *Journal of Educational Psychology* 51 (August 1960): 208-12.

at all between introverts and extraverts in the independent study group.

This experiment opens up a very wide field for inquiry. It should be replicated, using larger samples and allowing students to choose the kind of teaching method they preferred. In Beach's study the instructors chose the method congenial to them, but the students were not given an option. Another improvement would consist of including other kinds of course objectives in the evaluation process, in addition to factual recall. Dimensions of personality in addition to extraversion-introversion, as well as cognitive styles and study habits, should be studied as independent variables.

Using the same technique, Koenig and McKeachie compared a traditional lecture-discussion method with a lecture-small-discussion and a lecture-independent-study method.[89] In a mixed group of thirty-five men and eighty-nine women, they discovered that women students high in need-achievement preferred independent study and small-group discussion to the lecture and large-group discussion. The other women preferred the lecture method. Various puzzling findings of this study (such as the finding that women high in need-achievement participated *less* in group discussion than did the others) may be explained by the fact that the innovations of private study and small-group discussion only happened once each, replacing the traditional method. The hypothesis that students high in affiliation-need would prefer small-group discussion was not supported. The main recommendation was that students need special training and supervision in respect of study habits. This investigation could bear to be repeated over a much longer period, using both men and women lecturers.

Using a questionnaire, the present author elicited students' and professors' attitudes to three methods—lecture, tutorial, and seminar.[90] The three-part questionnaire revealed that, on equivalent scales, the lecture was strongly *disfavored* by all the student and

89. Kathryn E. Koenig and Wilbert J. McKeachie, "Personality and Independent Study," *Journal of Educational Psychology* 50 (June 1959): 132-34.

90. McLeish, *The Lecture Method*; idem, "Students' Attitudes to Teaching Methods," *Alberta Journal of Educational Research* 16 (September 1970): 179-87; idem, *Students' Attitudes and College Environments* (Cambridge, England: Cambridge Institute of Education, 1970).

lecturer groups whereas a verbal preference was expressed for the
tutorial and seminar methods (see table 3).

TABLE 3

AVERAGE OF SCORES EXPRESSING PREFERENCES FOR LECTURE,
TUTORIAL, AND SEMINAR METHODS

Group	N	Lecture	Tutorial	Seminar
Student Teachers..............	1246	13.15	20.01	20.00
Undergraduates..............	208	13.71	20.66	18.63
Mature Students..............	157	14.91	20.87	19.83
Commonwealth Teachers.......	126	14.75	21.96	20.62
Lecturers...................	131	11.66	21.77	20.78
Dentists...................	17	14.41	20.30	18.60
S.U.N.Y. Graduates..........	49	11.96	19.37	22.41

The figures in table 3 may merely indicate that the lecture,
being still the method of choice in higher education, is the target of
student discontent. They may simply be requesting a change. If
tutorial and seminar methods were to be used as widely as the lecture is now (implementing the same academic standards by requiring students *to prepare* in depth for discussion), experience
suggests that many students would express just as unfavorable attitudes to the tutorial and seminar as they now do to the lecture
method.

Some evidence for this interpretation is derived from the author's study, which indicated that the *older* students were more
favorably disposed to the lecture than younger students ($p < .0003$)
and that Conservatives were more favorable than Liberals or Radicals ($p < .001$).[91] Various other kinds of association were found
with personality and other differences (see the following section
on "Student Typologies"). As already indicated (see page 290)
McWilliams found that students subjected to a self-chosen "freedom and involvement" curriculum express more frustration, and a
greater sense of futility and purposelessness, than a control group
taught by the lecture method and standard text. McWilliams concluded that students are not prepared to accept the consequences
of the changes they demand.

Tillerson revealed the development of a similar negative attitude
toward the innovation of a "learning center" in comparison with a

91. McLeish, "Students' Attitudes to Teaching Methods."

control group (in a different college) taught by lecture.[92] The learning center consisted of one of the largest and most modern remote access and information retrieval systems available.

Student typologies. The present writer devised a classification of students on the basis of their favorable or unfavorable attitudes toward the lecture, tutorial, and seminar methods.[93] Nine basic types were recognized, each being associated with particular personality variables (such as neuroticism, extraversion, tendermindedness), need systems (power, security, recognition, submission), value systems (religious, scholastic, aesthetic, physical, utilitarian) and political and social attitudes (radicalism, conservatism, and so forth). "Oraculars," characterized by a highly favorable attitude to the lecture and a highly unfavorable attitude to the other two methods, were found to be relatively anxious and neurotic conservatives with a high power need, interested in scholastic values. The "student-centered" type, rejecting the lecture and tutorial methods, consisted of radical atheists who value scholastic standards and who are strongly opposed to corporal punishment and formal instruction in schools. These two types accounted respectively for nineteen percent and thirteen percent of the undergraduate population of a university. Striking differences were found between students and instructors from different departments in terms of their attitudes toward the lecture method and other variables in the areas described previously.[94]

Pascal allowed 200 students to choose between lecture, lecture-discussion and independent study methods and related their choices to personality and need structures.[95] The three option groups were on a continuum, with lecture-discussion students in the middle. Those who chose the lecture option were found to be less flexible and autonomous, with a lower tolerance for ambiguity and a greater disinclination toward abstract and scientific thinking, than those

92. Charles W. Tillerson, "Effects of a Learning Center Method versus Lecture Method of Teaching as Related to Achievement, Self-Concept, and Attitudes of College Freshmen," *Dissertation Abstracts International* 33A (May 1973): 6142.

93. McLeish, *The Lecture Method*; idem, "Students' Attitudes to Teaching Methods."

94. McLeish, "Students' Attitudes to Teaching Methods."

95. Pascal, "Offering Course Options."

who chose independent study. They were better at recall of course content. No differences with regard to grades or application of course materials were found, but independent study students were better at evaluating new material and reported that this method was superior in facilitating their creative powers. Students who were placed in their first choice of option group had a more positive attitude toward psychology.

Joyce and Hudson, using the convergent-divergent classification of thinking, studied the success of four instructors with 150 medical students in the teaching of statistics by lecture.[96] They found neither the convergent nor the divergent style of problem solving to be necessarily better. Academic learning, as measured by examination results, would seem at first glance to be influenced by similarities between the intellectual styles of the student and the teacher. It is not necessarily true, however, that "convergent" students learn best from "convergent" teachers, and vice-versa. Convergence-divergence seems to be unrelated to effectiveness in teaching.[97] The authors concluded that students should be exposed to both types.

In a similar study, Menges discovered that there was no relationship between cognitive compatibility between students ($N = 153$) and a single professor and the students' scores on an achievement test in educational psychology.[98] However, there was a relationship between cognitive compatibility and the students' expressed attitude toward the course. Cognitive compatibility was defined as similarity in orientation to the subject matter as measured by five attitudinal-value statements.

A study at Strathclyde University in Scotland confirmed the findings of the present author that there are considerable subject differences in preference for the lecture method.[99] Impromptu

96. C. R. B. Joyce and Liam Hudson, "Student Style and Teacher Style: An Experimental Study," *British Journal of Medical Education* 2, no. 1 (1968): 28-32.

97. Liam Hudson, *Contrary Imaginations* (London: Methuen, 1966).

98. Robert J. Menges, "Student-Instructor Cognitive Compatibility in the Large Lecture Class," *Journal of Personality* 37 (September 1969): 444-59.

99. Jean Reid, "Survey Throws Light on Lectures—and Lecturers," *Times Educational Supplement* 2861 (20 March 1970): 13; McLeish, "Students' Attitudes to Teaching Methods."

lectures, using notes only as a guide, were the most popular form
of lecture method in all schools of the university. The percent
choosing this option was twice as high in arts as in engineering.
Television lectures were much less popular than conventional lectures; most students expressed a desire to see the lecturer in the
flesh every once in a while.

The hypothesis that effective instruction is a resultant of an interaction between learners and the instructional method rather than
of the method as such was tested by Haskell, using 145 students
enrolled in industrial education classes in two senior high schools
in Indiana.[100] Linear programmed instruction was compared with
lecture-discussion in relation to ten personality variables. "General
Activity" and "Friendliness" were found to interact significantly
with method of instruction. The programmed learning method
worked better with those who were relatively slow and methodical
or with those who could be described as agreeable. The more aggressive students performed better under conventional instruction.
"Restraint" and "Emotionality" were found to be significant predictors of achievement on either method. In other words, serious-
minded and persistent students who were cheerful and reasonably
well-composed did well with either programmed instruction or
lectures.

Improving the Lecture

It is clear from the review of research that the lecture is open
to serious criticism if used as an all-purpose teaching method. It has
to be noted that it continues to be used in this way in a great number of institutions of higher learning. The reasons for criticism are
manifold. Among the objectives of higher education about which
there can be no dispute we can recognize (a) the training of students in defined cognitive and manipulative skills, (b) the transformation of certain basic attitudes toward reality, society, and
knowledge, and (c), the transmission of factual content in relation
to a particular subject. These changes form the basis of the student's
future professional life. The lecture system is not capable of carry-

100. Roger W. Haskell, "Effect of Certain Individual Learner Personality
Differences on Instructional Methods," *AV Communication Review* 19 (Fall
1971): 287-97.

ing the enormous weight imposed by these educational objectives. We have seen too that it pays little regard to individual differences among the students.

The lecture has its own specific virtues as a teaching method. These must be duly emphasized. By means of this technique the scholar can readily inspire an audience with his own enthusiasm; he can capture the imagination of his auditors by relating his special field to human destiny and human purposes; he can communicate research results and relate these to the practical and theoretical problems that bear on man's estate. The lecture method enables him to achieve these ends with the utmost economy of means. This accounts for its survival over two thousand years of higher education.

Defined thus, however, the art of lecturing is a difficult one. To achieve the required standard of performance it seems obvious that both training and practice are essential. The lecturer needs to have at his disposal a variety of skills that do not come together as a result of natural endowment, except perhaps in exceptional cases.

What has been said of the virtues of the lecture *method* cannot be taken as a justification of the lecture *system*—that is, compulsory daily lectures unleavened by tutorial discussion, seminars, workshops, and the like. There is little to be said in favor of this system once it has been noted that it can provide extremely effective training in passing examinations. The highly questionable side effect of this training is that it encourages undesirable attitudes toward the subject. Where there are compulsory lectures buttressed by examination pressures, it is more or less inevitable that students, and to some extent their teachers, come to regard knowledge as a closed system. Where the object of education is to develop conformity to declared truths, especially where the totality of knowledge is believed to be embodied in an accepted text, the lecture system is clearly the preferred instrument, as in the medieval universities. Yet, even under the most favorable conditions, this system fails to engage the attention and goodwill of the auditors. They must compensate for the deficiencies of the technique, and the instructor, by private study. They must supplement the lecture with the printed word.

There are, of course, ways of enlivening the lecture and of improving its efficiency. These are referred to below and need not detain us at this stage. It is even possible to humanize the system of compulsory lectures by incorporating ancillary techniques. Valuable training in reflective thinking about the lecture content and in how this is related to first-hand experience can be gained from individual and group tutorials, case discussions, group projects, and workshops. Where students prepare for the lecture by assigned readings and private study beforehand, the way is paved for the transformation of the lecture system into a dialogue in place of an oracular monologue.

Gage and Berliner, in a text that has two units devoted to the objectives and techniques of the lecture method, provided a step-by-step breakdown of the lecture sequence with the object of making recommendations for improving the performance of the lecturer.[101] They provided a rationale as well as advice based on experience and research. Our analysis of the literature supports and complements their suggestions and advice.

The choice of method should be based on prior apprehension of his objectives by the teacher.[102] These objectives must be stated in terms of anticipated changes in student behavior that can be detected if they happen and, equally important, can be detected *not* to be present if they fail to happen. It is not enough for the vague aspirations of the instructor to be declared in ambiguous abstractions that permit no terminal evaluation. In the absence of clear, operationally defined aims, feedback from the student body can serve as one, possibly biased but still fruitful, source of evaluation.

If the stimulation of reflective thinking by the student is taken to be a prime objective of the lecture method, the students' views of what kinds of lecture have this effect would appear to be useful data. Musella and Rusch attempted to obtain such data, asking students at the State University of New York (Albany) to name two professors who had done most to improve their thinking, to describe the behavior of those professors, and to select, from a list of ten, three qualities that were of greatest importance in this re-

101. N. L. Gage and David C. Berliner, *Educational Psychology* (Chicago: Rand McNally, 1975).

102. Benjamin S. Bloom et al., *Taxonomy of Educational Objectives, Handbook 1: The Cognitive Domain* (New York: David McKay Co., 1956).

gard.[103] Almost 400 responses were obtained from a sample of nearly 700 students in five faculties. This study was a replication of one made by Riley and others at Rutgers University.[104] Differences were found between the sciences, where "systematic organization" and "ability to explain clearly" were among the top three qualities, and the arts and social sciences, where the three top qualities selected were "ability to encourage thought," "enthusiastic attitude to the subject," and "expert knowledge." In the two groups of students taken together, these were the five qualities most frequently selected. Considered least important were qualities of personality, namely, fairness, tolerance, sympathetic attitude, speaking ability, and pleasing personality. In other words, these students regarded effective teaching as being the result of *knowledge* of the subject, *organization* and method in presenting it, and *commitment* to the area of specialization.

The results of this investigation were independently confirmed by Smithers at the University of Bradford, England.[105] Slight differences were found between the views of extroverts and introverts and between relatively neurotic and relatively stable students. Authoritarian students (high scorers on Rokeach's dogmatism scale) had different expectations of the ideal lecturer from those of non-authoritarian students. Yet Smithers' main conclusion is that, regardless of personality, students tend to use similar criteria in judging lectures: whether the lecturer knows his subject, is able to expound it lucidly, structures his presentation, and places the material in an appropriate context.

Globig and Touhey found that angry, depressed, or elated presentations of the same material in a lecture did not result in differences in student recall of the content.[106]

103. Donald Musella and Reuben Rusch, "Student Opinion on College Teaching," *Improving College and University Teaching* 16 (Spring 1968): 137-40.

104. J. W. Riley, B. F. Ryan, and Marcia Lifshitz, *The Student Looks at His Teacher* (New Brunswick, N.J.: Rutgers University Press, 1950).

105. Alan Smithers, "What Do Students Expect of Lectures?" *Universities Quarterly* 24 (Summer 1970): 330-36.

106. Linda Globig and John C. Touhey, "Sex and Affective Determinants of Lecture Content Retention," *Psychological Reports* 29 (October 1971): 538.

Cantrell made a pilot study of thirty lectures delivered as "celebrity" talks by visiting professors at Makerere Medical College, Uganda.[107] A four-point rating scale was used to assess each of sixteen individual aspects of the lecturing method used. A bimodal distribution was found, with over one-third of these experienced lecturers placed in the category "poor." Professional status, age, and qualifications were not associated with good lecturing. Many of the faults observed—in matters such as method of presentation, engaging the motivation of the auditors for further study of the subject, the use of visual aids, and the provision of memory aids—were correctable. The author suggested the desirability of a training program for lecturers and regular evaluation of their performance.

The question of whether it is better to provide students with a summary of the lecture (a "handout") before or after the lecture was tested experimentally by McDougall, Gray, and McNicol.[108] Those given the handout before the lecture did significantly better in the immediate post-course examination, but this difference disappeared over a period of seven weeks (presumably because of student study for the end-of-term examination). The authors concluded (incorrectly in the view of the present author) that the timing of the distribution of the handout may safely be left to the wishes of the individual teacher.

Zillman and Cantor compared lectures delivered in two versions: one containing rhetorical question-and-answer sequences, the other without the questions.[109] Student learning and recall were significantly enhanced by ten question-and-answer sequences, but only under conditions of artifically induced boredom or distraction.

Petrie and Thompson in earlier reviews of informative speaking and public address and communication pointed to the following variables as being significant: meaningfulness, informal style, verbal

107. E. G. Cantrell, "Thirty Lectures," *British Journal of Medical Education* 5 (December 1971): 309-19.

108. I. R. McDougall, H. W. Gray, and G. P. McNicol, "The Effect of Timing of Distribution of Handouts on Improvement of Student Performance," *British Journal of Medical Education* 6 (September 1972): 155-57.

109. Dolf Zillmann and Joanne Cantor, "Induction of Curiosity via Rhetorical Questions and Its Effect on the Learning of Factual Materials," *British Journal of Educational Psychology* 43 (June 1973): 172-80.

emphasis, development of ideas, visible action, eye contact, the speaker's intelligence and scholastic achievement, and the students' expectation of a test or a monetary reward.[110]

Several professors in Great Britain and the U.S.S.R. have used a method of periodically interrupting their continuing discourse with prearranged questions with multiple-choice answers. Students press one of several buttons to indicate what they think is the correct answer. Each student's response causes a light to go on in a public display panel. In this way, students and professor can see at a glance the effectiveness of the teaching process at these particular points. Jones's studies suggest strongly that this may be the most cogent way of maintaining motivation and improving recall and understanding.[111] As yet, this technique does not appear to have been properly evaluated.

The work of Lloyd and Thomas revealed the great variation of students' recall in relation to the time, counted from the start of the lecture, at which the topic was dealt with.[112] This has been referred to previously, the results being shown in figures 1a and 1b. The "middle sag" in attention and recall points to the need for a diversification of activities during the lecture period so that it ceases to be an uninterrupted discourse by one person, performed face-to-face with a passive audience. The principles of programmed learning, and learning theory in general, suggest that the best way to improve the lecture is to convert it into a step-by-step presentation with perhaps half-a-dozen intervals of recapitulation and informal testing of the students' assimilation and ability to apply the materials presented.

110. Charles R. Petrie, Jr., "Informative Speaking: A Summary and Bibliography of Related Research," *Speech Monographs* 30 (June 1963): 79-91; and W. N. Thompson, *Quantitative Research in Public Address and Communication* (New York: Random House, 1967).

111. Jones, "Experimental Studies of College Teaching."

112. Lloyd, "Communication in the University Lecture"; Thomas, "The Variation of Memory with Time."

CHAPTER IX

Teaching with Television and Film

AIMÉE DORR LEIFER

Introduction

We assert nothing new when we state that television and film can teach and that they are capable of serving as substitutes for, or supplements to, more traditional modes of teaching. Nonetheless the search continues for criteria concerning when teaching with television or film should be chosen over live teaching, for guidelines to the selection or production of appropriate programs or series, and for techniques for integrating television or film most effectively into the educational experience of the student. This chapter will review the information we have obtained thus far and demonstrate again that, as with all decisions about teaching, there is no substitute for careful, sensitive consideration of the characteristics of the students, the teaching goals, and the variety of available teaching techniques.

In much of this chapter television and film will be treated as though they are equivalent media. Many researchers have done so when they have investigated the ability of one or the other to communicate information, compared live and mediated instruction, and examined ways to integrate television or film into an educational environment. It is worth noting, however, that television and film are not fully interchangeable media. The artistic formulas differ; for instance, film makers are much freer to present wide panoramas and crowd scenes than are television producers. Economies of scale cannot be as easily or completely achieved with film as they can be with television by increasing the audience size.[1] Scheduling of

1. General Learning Corporation, *Cost Study of Educational Media Systems and Their Equipment*, 3 vols. (Washington, D.C.: General Learning Corporation, 1968).

television and film differs in that television is most often broadcast at a specified time to a presumably large audience, while film is most often shown to a small audience at a time the teacher chooses. Finally, the technical means for producing the images differs between the two media, and this may produce differences in the information processing skills required of the user.[2] Where appropriate in this chapter, these differences will be considered, but for the most part television and film will be considered as equivalent, alternative delivery systems.

The chapter is divided into six sections. The first presents five types of content, or messages, that television and film convey and evaluates their effectiveness in conveying them. The second discusses the processes by which students learn from television and film. The third relates these processes to the evaluation of existing programming or the production of new material. The fourth considers the utility of television and film in teaching, and the fifth discusses the ways in which television and film may be most effectively integrated into ongoing educational activities. The sixth section summarizes the chapter.

Content That Television and Film May Convey

Television and film are most often given the explicit educational goal of conveying cognitive information to students. Recently they have occasionally been used intentionally to teach social and emotional content. There is a growing recognition that television and film can also be explicitly used to convey visual and cognitive processes, that television and film programs carry with them effective implicit as well as explicit content, and that choosing either of these media as an educational agent communicates to students ideas about appropriate and useful modes of learning. This section reviews what is known about the educational impact of television and film in these five content areas.

TEACHING COGNITIVE CONTENT

The earliest—and still most prevalent—use of television and film in education was in the communication of cognitive content to

2. Marshall McLuhan, *Understanding Media: The Extensions of Man* (New York: Signet Books, 1964), pp. 36-44, 248-58, 268-93.

students. Current cognitive programming encompasses a wide range of topics and intended audiences. Individual programs and series are available in nearly all, if not all, the traditional areas in which we educate children from preschool to high school graduation: mathematics, history, science, art, social science, government, and so on. Material for college students and adults does not span all the areas in which they may wish to be educated, but nonetheless a wide range of material exists. Most television and film material is apparently geared for "the average student." Generally this means a middle-class white student in an urban or suburban community. Recently, however, there has been some programming for more specialized audiences, such as inner-city blacks, Hispanic groups throughout the United States, and Appalachian whites. I expect that this trend toward production for both general and more specialized audiences will continue.

Much educational television has been produced by local and state agencies intimately linked with the school system, while most educational film has been produced by commercial organizations. Educational television particularly is considered to be low budget, low quality, minimally entertaining fare. The introduction of "Sesame Street" (a television series for preschool children) in the late 1960s did more to change this view of educational television than did any of the other excellent television and film material produced either before or after "Sesame Street." At present, educational television and film for every age group range from the groovy to the gruesome and from informed to ignorant.

Whatever their merits as entertainment or information, educational television and film can communicate their messages to students. Evaluations of instructional programs viewed in class have repeatedly indicated that children, adolescents, and adults learn the cognitive content that is presented.[3] Evaluations of the first and second years of "Sesame Street" indicate that programs viewed at

3. Ronald W. Henderson et al., *Televised Cognitive Skill Instruction for Papago Native American Children*, First year report on Children's Bureau Grant No. OCD-CB-479 (Tucson, Ariz.: Arizona Center for Educational Research and Development, College of Education, University of Arizona, 1974); Wilbur Schramm, *Big Media, Little Media* (Stanford, Cal.: Institute for Communication Research, Stanford University, 1973), pp. 44-50, 52.

home or in class teach preschoolers a variety of cognitive content,[4] and evaluations of "The Electric Company" indicate that programs viewed in class can increase the reading skills of some elementary school children.[5] None of these evaluations is, however, free from criticism and counterinterpretations. For example, the evaluations of the Educational Testing Service (ETS) of "Sesame Street" have been roundly criticized by a number of researchers who conclude that the gains from viewing that program are considerably less than those reported by ETS and that "Sesame Street" may widen, rather than narrow, the gap between the educationally advantaged and disadvantaged.[6] Nonetheless, there is overwhelming support for the conclusion that a teacher can use television and film with relative assurance to communicate cognitive information.

The teacher may also be assured that, on the average, television and film will impart information as well as the average live teacher does. Innumerable studies support this assertion. In 1967, Chu and Schramm reviewed more than 400 comparisons of live and television teaching at all grade levels and in 1969 Dubin and Hedley reviewed nearly 400 comparisons of live and television teaching at the college level, including many of those reviewed by Chu and Schramm.[7]

4. Samuel Ball and Gerry Ann Bogatz, *The First Year of "Sesame Street": An Evaluation* (Princeton, N.J.: Educational Testing Service, 1970); Gerry Ann Bogatz and Samuel Ball, *The Second Year of "Sesame Street": A Continuing Evaluation*, 2 vols. (Princeton, N.J.: Educational Testing Service, 1971).

5. Samuel Ball and Gerry Ann Bogatz, *Reading with Television: An Evaluation of "The Electric Company"* (Princeton, N.J.: Educational Testing Service, 1973); Samuel Ball et al., *Reading with Television: A Follow-up Evaluation of "The Electric Company"* (Princeton, N.J.: Educational Testing Service, 1974).

6. Thomas D. Cook et al., *"Sesame Street" Revisited: A Case Study in Evaluation Research* (New York: Russell Sage Foundation, 1975); *Down "Sesame Street": A Study of Instructional Technology*, Notebook No. Six (New York: The Network Project, 1973), pp. 27-30, 44-49.

7. Godwin C. Chu and Wilbur Schramm, *Learning from Television: What Research Says*, Final report, Contract OE 4-7-0071123, U.S. Office of Education (Stanford, Cal.: Institute for Communication Research, Stanford University, 1967), pp. 1-22; R. Dubin and R. A. Hedley, *The Medium May Be Related to the Message: College Instruction by TV* (Eugene, Ore.: University of Oregon Press, 1969); Dean Jamison, Patrick Suppes, and Stuart Wells, "The Effectiveness of Alternative Instructional Media: A Survey" (Stanford, Cal.: Institute for Communication Research, Stanford University, 1973), pp. 26-28; Schramm, *Big Media, Little Media*, pp. 44-50.

Although these reviews deal for the most part with students in secondary school and college and with mathematics and science curricula, all grade levels and traditional areas of instruction are adequately represented so that broad conclusions may be drawn from the data. The evidence clearly supports the conclusion that television and film are as effective at teaching students from kindergarten through college as are live teachers. This conclusion is based upon summary comparisons of the results of all studies reviewed and upon comparisons of the many fewer studies researchers consider to be unambiguous comparisons of live and mediated teaching.[8] There is a slight indication that television teaching may be relatively more effective with elementary school students than with older students, but there is no indication that television teaching is more effective in some curriculum areas than in others.[9]

All comparisons of live versus television and film teaching run into problems. Experimentally, the cleanest comparison is one between the same teaching format and the same content presented by a live teacher and by television or film. In this situation the stimuli obviously differ only in the channel of communication. Thus, conclusions may clearly be drawn about the differential impact of these two modes of teaching. Such comparisons, however, restrict each medium to a limited range of teaching techniques; the live teacher cannot engage in an animated, responsive discussion with the students, and television and film cannot resort to slow motion, instant replay, or animation. The more nearly unique capabilities of each medium are not brought into play in presenting the curriculum.

Researchers have not yet characterized educational tasks and medium capabilities precisely enough to permit conclusions about which medium is better suited to which educational goal. In the late 1960s Allen rated the ability of various modes of instruction to teach various educational tasks,[10] and Briggs, Campeau, Gagné, and May proposed a set of procedures by which educators could

8. D. W. Stickell, "A Critical Review of the Methodology and Results of Research Comparing Televised and Face-to-Face Instruction" (Ph.D. diss., Pennsylvania State University, 1963).

9. Chu and Schramm, Learning from Television, pp. 12-18.

10. William H. Allen, "Media Stimulus and Types of Learning," Audio-Visual Instruction 12 (January 1967): 27-31.

decide which medium to use for which educational goal.[11] More recently such divergent thinkers as Salomon, Olson and Bruner, and Lesser have also sought to characterize media-specific capabilities.[12] None of these efforts has been supported by abundant research, nor has any yet led to a clear specification of curriculum goals for which television and film are better, worse, or equally well-suited when compared with live teachers. As Schramm concluded after a thorough review of the efforts of the 1960s, teaching media may be interchangeable for most educational tasks. Until better information is available, prospective users of television and film must content themselves with the consideration of such commonsense questions as the extent to which achieving a curriculum goal depends upon dynamic visual images, student-paced instruction, verbal interchange, active manipulation of materials, or uncommon material or occurrences. Answers to questions such as these should help an educator decide whether to find a good classroom teacher or to look for television or film materials and evaluate the feasibility of delivering them to students.

TEACHING SOCIAL AND EMOTIONAL CONTENT

While the bulk of instructional television material deals with topics traditionally classified as cognitive or intellectual, some recent series have dealt with social and emotional content. Such production no doubt proceeds from the increasing concern with social and emotional, as well as intellectual, education in school.[13] Examples

11. Leslie J. Briggs et al., *Instructional Media* (Pittsburgh: American Institutes for Research, 1967), pp. 28-34.

12. Gerald S. Lesser, *Children and Television: Lessons from "Sesame Street"* (New York: Random House, 1974), pp. 19-31; McLuhan, *Understanding Media*; David R. Olson and Jerome S. Bruner, "Learning through Experience and Learning through Media," in *Media and Symbols: The Forms of Expression, Communication, and Education*, ed. David R. Olson, Seventy-third Yearbook of the National Society for the Study of Education, Part I (Chicago: University of Chicago Press, 1974), pp. 125-50; Gavriel Salomon, "What Is Learned and How It Is Taught: The Interaction between Media, Message, Task, and Learner," in Olson, *Media and Symbols*, pp. 383-406.

13. This is not to say that social and emotional development have not always been within the purview of traditional education. Rather it acknowledges the more explicit awareness of and focus on these areas by the community control, free school, and radical movements of the 1960s and 1970s and the ways in which more traditional educational institutions have incorporated some of the concerns of these movements into their curricula.

of such series include "Ripples" (a perspective-giving series on urban children's lives) and the Emmy award-winning "Inside/Out" (a mental health series). Both of these were created for older elementary school children by the Agency for Instructional Television. "Sesame Street" includes segments designed to teach prosocial behavior and recognition of emotions to preschoolers. "Mr. Rogers' Neighborhood" focuses on preschoolers' social and emotional development. Several series for children between preschool and junior high, funded by the Emergency School Aid Act, deal with racial stereotyping and integration. The goals of these programs differ somewhat from those with more traditional cognitive content in that producers often intend the programs to be instigators of classroom discussion or influencers of social behavior rather than simple communicators of information.

Social and emotional programming has undergone considerably less evaluation than has cognitive programming. Evaluation of the prosocial behavior segments of "Sesame Street" indicates that they can promote preschoolers' understanding of the concept of cooperation,[14] recognition of pictorial instances of cooperation,[15] and prosocial behavior similar to that portrayed in the program and tested in situations similar to those portrayed in the segments.[16] Preliminary evaluations of the emotional segments indicate that preschool children can recognize simple emotions when they are presented (for example, happy, sad, and mad) and may increase their ability to recognize them in other contexts.[17] Recent evaluations of "Mr. Rogers' Neighborhood" indicate that viewing the program as part of a preschool program can increase children's sharing, self-control,

---

14. F. Leon Paulson, D. L. McDonald, and S. L. Whittemore, "An Evaluation of 'Sesame Street' Programming Designed to Teach Cooperative Behavior," Unpublished report to the Children's Television Workshop (Monmouth, Ore.: Teaching Research, 1972).

15. Ibid.

16. Aimeé Dorr Leifer, "The Use of Television to Encourage Socially Valued Behaviors in Preschoolers," Unpublished manuscript, Harvard University, 1974; Paulson, McDonald, and Whittemore, "An Evaluation of 'Sesame Street.'"

17. Harry Lasker and Naomi Bernath, "Status of Comprehension Study of 'Sesame Street' Affect Bits," Unpublished report to the Children's Television Workshop (Cambridge, Mass.: Harvard University, 1974), pp. 1-12.

and positive interpersonal interaction.[18] Informal evaluations of series such as "Inside/Out" indicate that students and teachers in the upper elementary school grades like the programs, identify with the interpersonal and individual dilemmas they present, and find themselves provoked into challenging class discussions after viewing.[19] More formal evaluations of the effects of these series have not, to my knowledge, been conducted, nor have comparisons of effectiveness been made between television or film teaching of these topics and more traditional teaching either in or out of class.

TEACHING INFORMATION PROCESSING SKILLS

Recently the visual and time-dependent aspects of television and film have been recognized as potential teachers of visual and information processing skills. Carpenter and McLuhan were early and notable exponents of this concept.[20] McLuhan categorized media as "hot" (for example, film), extending a single sensory modality, well-filled with data, and requiring low participation, and "cold" (for example, television), low in data and requiring high participation. American culture was viewed as logical, linear, literary, hot, and troubled by its encounter with the cool world of television. McLuhan's ideas were presented with all the razzmatazz of modern life, perhaps overshadowing the important point that different experiential modes required different human skills and energies. His ideas excited the populace, but educators and psychologists originally did little to pursue them.

18. Brian Coates, H. Ellison Pusser, and Irene Goodman, "The Influence of 'Sesame Street' and 'Mr. Rogers' Neighborhood' on Children's Social Behavior in the Preschool," *Child Development* 47 (March 1976): in press; Lynette K. Friedrich and Aletha Huston Stein, "Prosocial Television and Young Children: The Effects of Verbal Labeling and Role Playing on Learning and Behavior," *Child Development* 46 (March 1975): 27-38; Kenneth Shirley, "Prosocial Effects of Publicly Broadcast Prosocial Television," Unpublished manuscript, Stanford University, 1975; Aletha Huston Stein and Lynette K. Friedrich, "Television Content and Young Children's Behavior," in *Television and Social Behavior*, vol. 2, *Television and Social Learning*, ed. John P. Murray, Eli A. Rubinstein, and George A. Comstock (Rockville, Md.: National Institute of Mental Health, 1972), pp. 202-317.

19. *"Inside/Out": A Guide for Teachers* (Bloomington, Ind.: National Instructional Television Center, 1973), pp. 1-9.

20. Edmund Carpenter, "The New Languages," in *Explorations in Communication*, ed. Edmund Carpenter and Marshall McLuhan (Boston: Beacon Press, 1960), 162-79; McLuhan, *Understanding Media*.

Unlike most of us who have remained locked into our literary view of television and film as communicators of intellectual, social, and emotional content, Bruner, Olson, and Salomon have each explored the information-processing skills required by various modes of experience.[21] None of them has differentiated television and film as McLuhan did, but they have differentiated visual media, print media, and individual activity. Olson and Bruner, for instance, make a major distinction between "knowledge" and "skills" (or abilities).[22] For them knowledge about objects and events is constituted by the "set of features that are more or less invariant across different activities," and skills are "the set of operations or constituent acts that are invariant when performed across different objects and events." These authors suggest that educators must be concerned with the acquisition of both knowledge and skills, for without skills children cannot easily acquire knowledge from teachers nor can they educate themselves.

Salomon has provided some experimental evidence that television and film do indeed promote information-processing skills. Films that explicitly modeled operations such as focusing on details and laying out solid objects could increase such skills in eighth and ninth graders who were initially less skilled, and films that required viewers to focus on details or mentally to lay out solid objects could increase such skills in eighth and ninth graders who were initially more skilled.[23] Evidence for similar effects was found in a field study of the effects of "Sesame Street" on Israeli children between the ages of five and eight.[24] There is also some evidence that live and film models can encourage more reflective or more impulsive

21. Jerome S. Bruner, "The Course of Cognitive Growth," *American Psychologist* 19 (January 1964): 1-15; David R. Olson, "Mass Media Versus Schoolmen: The Role of the *Means* of Instruction in the Attainment of Educational Goals" (Paper presented at the biennial meeting of the International Society for the Study of Behavioral Development, Ann Arbor, Mich., 1973), pp. 1-19; Gavriel Salomon, "Can We Affect Cognitive Skills through Visual Media? An Hypothesis and Initial Findings," *AV Communication Review* 20 (Winter 1972): 401-22.

22. Olson and Bruner, "Learning through Experience."

23. Salomon, "Can We Affect Cognitive Skills?"

24. Gavriel Salomon, "Cognitive Effects of Media: The Case of 'Sesame Street' in Israel" (Paper presented at the biennial meeting of the International Society for the Study of Behavioral Development, Ann Arbor, Mich., 1973).

approaches to intellectual tasks by elementary school children.[25]

Developmental studies of children's understanding of television and film programs indicate that there are age-related changes in their ability to process plot-line information correctly. Of course, one cannot know whether these changes result from general intellectual development or from the additional practice in decoding television and film presentation that comes with increasing age. The changes found, which could be due to acquiring skill in utilizing the medium, are in the ability to sequence main events in the plot,[26] to retain plot-line connections that are interrupted by commercials,[27] to understand both the main plot and subplots without confusing the two,[28] to acquire the expectation that information will be presented linearly,[29] to anticipate the next event in the plot,[30] and to understand the depicted motivations and consequences for characters' actions.[31]

We have some evidence that television and film can influence the

25. S. Cohen and C. Przybycien, "Modifications in Children's Cognitive Styles: Some Effects of Peer Modeling" (Paper presented at the biennial meeting of the Society for Research in Child Development, Philadelphia, Pa., 1973); Ray L. Debus, "Effects of Brief Observation of Model Behavior on Conceptual Tempo of Impulsive Children," *Developmental Psychology* 2 (January 1970): 22-32; Eugene H. Ridberg, Ross D. Parke, and E. Mavis Hetherington, "Modification of Impulsive and Reflective Cognitive Styles through Observation of Film-Mediated Models," *Developmental Psychology* 5 (November 1971): 369-77.

26. Aimée Dorr Leifer et al., "Developmental Aspects of Variables Relevant to Observational Learning," *Child Development* 42 (November 1971): 1509-16.

27. W. Andrew Collins, "Effect of Temporal Separation between Motivation, Aggression, and Consequences: A Developmental Study," *Developmental Psychology* 8 (March 1973): 215-21.

28. W. Andrew Collins and Sally Driscoll Westby, "Children's Processing of Social Information from Televised Dramatic Programs" (Paper presented at the biennial meeting of the Society for Research in Child Development, Denver, Col., 1975).

29. Ibid.

30. Ibid.

31. W. Andrew Collins, Thomas J. Berndt, and Valerie L. Hess, "Observational Learning of Motives and Consequences for Television Aggression: A Developmental Study," *Child Development* 45 (September 1974): 799-802; Leifer et al., "Developmental Aspects of Variables"; Aimée Dorr Leifer and Donald F. Roberts, "Children's Responses to Television Violence," in *Television and Social Behavior*, vol. 2, *Television and Social Learning*, pp. 43-180.

information-processing skills of children and the suggestion that there are particular decoding skills that children learn when they use these media. We have no information yet about the relative impact of mediated versus live experience in influencing certain skills required by both, nor do we have a clear delineation of the different skills each requires. In the future we can expect more information on the ability of television and film to promote information-processing skills in children as researchers such as Salomon, Olson, and O'Bryan develop their current lines of work.[32] For the present educators should be aware of the fact that television and film require and promote information-processing skills that differ somewhat from the skills required by conversation, lecture, and reading.

IMPLICIT TEACHING

One factor that most students of instructional television and film overlook and that most students of entertainment television and film explore is the implicit curriculum of a program. The usual issues here are the social characteristics of the live, puppet, or animated people presented in a program and the ways in which these people interact with each other. In general, programs are much more likely to feature males than females and to portray males as sources of authority and expertise.[33] Similar statements can be made for comparisons between whites and minority groups.[34] For ex-

32. These three men are all actively engaged in research in this area: Gavriel Salomon, at The Hebrew University of Jerusalem, Israel; David R. Olson, at the Ontario Institute for Studies in Education, Toronto, Canada; and Kenneth O'Bryan, also at the Ontario Institute for Studies in Education, Toronto, Canada.

33. Judith L. Lemon, "A Content Analysis of Male and Female Dominance Patterns on Prime Time Television," Unpublished manuscript, Harvard University, 1975; Sarah Hall Sternglanz and Lisa A. Serbin, "Sex Role Stereotyping in Children's Television Programs," *Developmental Psychology* 10 (September 1974): 710-15; Helen White Streicher, "The Girls in the Cartoons," *Journal of Communication* 24 (Spring 1974): 125-29; Nancy S. Tedesco, "Patterns of Prime Time," *Journal of Communication* 24 (Spring 1974): 119-24; Joseph Turow, "Advising and Ordering: Daytime, Prime Time," *Journal of Communication* 24 (Spring 1974): 138-41.

34. Judith L. Lemon, "A Content Analysis of Black and White Dominance Patterns on Prime Time Television" (Master's thesis, San Francisco State University, 1975); Gilbert Mendelson and Morissa Young, "A Content Analysis of Black and Minority Treatment on Children's Television," Report to Action

ample, a recent film strip designed to facilitate growth in moral judgments featured a black male youth group leader and a white male boat captain. No women were visible or active in this world. The social interaction of the two men conveyed additional information in that the black youth group leader repeatedly deferred to the "wisdom" of the white boat captain in making decisions about the activities of the children, even when these decisions had nothing to do with the boat. There is evidence from studies of entertainment programs and commercials that such portrayals influence children's opinions about men and women of various racial and ethnic groups, even when there has been no explicit intention on the part of the producers to impart "information" about social roles.[35]

The evidence from studies of entertainment television and film is fairly consistent. Programs made solely to entertain children and adults influence viewers' antisocial and prosocial behavior, their reactions to violence, and their attitudes and ideas about national groups, American racial groups, sex roles, occupational roles, interpersonal interactions, and the American social system and its place within the world.[36] If entertainment television and film can communicate these messages to viewers between the ages of three and

for Children's Television (Washington, D.C.: Black Efforts for Soul Television, 1972); Linda H. Ormiston and Sally Williams, "Saturday Children's Programming in San Francisco, California: An Analysis of the Presentation of Racial and Cultural Groups on Three Network Affiliated San Francisco Television Stations," Paper presented at hearings on children's television before the Federal Communications Commission, January 8-10, 1973 (San Francisco, Cal.: Committee on Children's Television, Inc., 1973).

35. Terry Freuh and Paul E. McGhee, "Traditional Sex Role Development and Amount of Time Spent Watching Television," Developmental Psychology 11 (January 1975): 109; Sherryl Browne Graves, "Racial Diversity in Children's Television: Its Impact on Racial Attitudes and Stated Program Preferences in Young Children" (Ph.D. diss., Harvard University, 1975); R. C. Peterson and L. L. Thurstone, Motion Pictures and the Social Attitudes of Children (New York: Macmillan, 1933); Suzanne Pingree, "A Developmental Study of the Attitudinal Effects of Nonsexist Television Commercials Under Varied Conditions of Perceived Reality" (Ph.D. diss., Stanford University, 1975).

36. For recent summaries see George Comstock, Television and Human Behavior: The Key Studies (Santa Monica, Cal.: The Rand Corporation, 1975); Aimée Dorr Leifer, Neal J. Gordon, and Sherryl Browne Graves, "Children's Television: More Than Mere Entertainment," Harvard Educational Review 44 (May 1974): 213-45; Robert M. Liebert, John M. Neale, and Emily S. Davidson, The Early Window: Effects of Television on Children and Youth (New York: Pergamon Press, 1973).

314 TEACHING WITH TELEVISION AND FILM

forty, there is every reason to expect similar effects from educational television and film. It is up to researchers to provide evidence of the effects of educational television and film and to compare the influence of live and mediated experience on social attitudes and behavior. Still, a sensitive educator should expect a program or series to convey unintended, usually social, messages as well as intended intellectual or social information and should evaluate programs on these bases as well as the more usual ones.

TEACHING ABOUT MODES OF LEARNING

The final type of message that television and film can convey is one about appropriate and useful modes of learning. When we use television and film to teach, we are also saying something to students about how we think they can or should learn. As yet we have very little research evidence about what this means to a learner. There are indications that students from elementary school through college like being taught by television, although college students prefer seminars to televised courses, and that teachers are less enthusiastic about television than are students.[37] Teachers also worry that the current generation is deficient in speaking, listening, reading, and writing skills—those traditionally fostered in school—precisely because it has been acquiring the skills required for extracting information from television.[38] But we do not yet have good evidence for whether students who have more television teachers have different skills and opinions of themselves as learners and of the learning process than do students who have more live teachers.

Educators must decide how much they want to suggest to students that less personal, active, and interactive processes are appropriate learning modes. This·issue certainly encompasses more than television and film, since many forms of face-to-face teaching also require students to sit passively and absorb information given by another. Nonetheless it is an issue that is largely endemic in current television and film programs. To the extent that television and film embrace commercial standards of excellence, educators must also

37. Chu and Schramm, *Learning from Television*, pp. 110-31.

38. S. I. Hayakawa, "Mass Media and Family Communications" (Paper presented at the annual meeting of the American Psychological Association, San Francisco, September 1968), pp. 1-7.

ask how much they want to convey to students the impression that learning comes slickly packaged in entertaining, fast-paced modules. Such packaging may make education more palatable to the current generation of students, but it may not be the message that educators would like to reinforce.

Processes of Learning from Television and Film

Over the years we have acquired a great deal of information about the ways in which people learn from television and film and about program characteristics that influence their learning. In general, different variables have been assessed by researchers interested in educational programming and researchers interested in entertainment programming, although there is some commonality in the conclusions one can draw from this material. In this section I shall review what is known about how people learn from both educational and entertainment programming, because I believe that the processes identified in one area will ultimately be shown to apply in the other as well.

OBSERVATIONAL LEARNING

The first and most obvious point is that television and film learning results from relatively passive consumption of content chosen by someone else and presented at a predetermined pace. Increments in learning or performance may result from student activity during or after the presentation or from variations in the way in which content is presented. Still the principal form of learning must be visual and auditory encoding of material presented on a two-dimensional screen. Observational learning is the current popular theory that deals most directly with this phenomenon, although contiguity and associationist theories are also able to account for such learning.[39]

Observational learning theory states that individuals learn by watching and listening to others in either live or mediated form.[40]

39. Albert Bandura, "Vicarious Processes: A Case of No-Trial Learning," in *Advances in Experimental Social Psychology*, ed. Leonard Berkowitz (New York: Academic Press, 1965), vol. 2, pp. 1-55; Edwin R. Guthrie, *The Psychology of Learning*, 2d ed. (New York: Harper, 1952); Edward C. Tolman, *Collected Papers in Psychology* (Berkeley, California: University of California Press, 1951).

40. Bandura, "Vicarious Processes."

Furthermore, variables that traditional learning theory has identified as affecting learning when they are experienced directly also affect learning when they are experienced vicariously.[41] In analyses of learning from television and film there is indisputable evidence for this position from studies of learning cognitive content from instructional television and film,[42] cognitive content from public and commercial television,[43] aggressive behavior from commercial entertainment television and film,[44] prosocial behavior from "Sesame Street" and "Mr. Rogers,"[45] "facts" from Hollywood-made entertainment films in the 1930s,[46] and racial and sex-role attitudes from entertainment television and film.[47] Except for learning cognitive content from instructional television and film and aggressive behavior from entertainment television and film, none of these areas has been explored with viewers from preschool through adulthood. Nonetheless, the obtained effects so consistently demonstrate the phenomenon of observational learning that there is no reason to doubt that they would also be found if viewers of all ages were studied in all content areas.

It is important to note, however, that the effects of viewing televised or filmed information may not be as unidirectional as most summaries would lead one to believe. Scattered throughout the

41. Ibid.

42. Schramm, *Big Media, Little Media*, pp. 44-50, 52.

43. S. William Alper and Thomas R. Leidy, "The Impact of Information Transmission through Television," *Public Opinion Quarterly* 33 (Winter 1969-70): 556-62; Ball and Bogatz, *The First Year of "Sesame Street"*; Bogatz and Ball, *The Second Year of "Sesame Street"*.

44. Leifer, Gordon, and Graves, "Children's Television," pp. 214-17; Liebert, Neale, and Davidson, *The Early Window*, pp. 34-88.

45. Aimée Dorr Leifer, "An Examination of the Socializing Influence of Television in the United States," in *Television and Processes of Socialization within the Family* (tentative title) (Munich: Internationales Zentralinstitut für das Jugend- und Bildungsfernsehen, in press); Liebert, Neale, and Davidson, *The Early Window*, pp. 89-96.

46. P. W. Holaday and G. D. Stoddard, *Getting Ideas from the Movies* (New York: Macmillan, 1933).

47. Frueh and McGhee, "Traditional Sex Role Development"; Graves, "Racial Diversity in Children's Television"; Peterson and Thurstone, *Motion Pictures and the Social Attitudes of Children*; Pingree, "Attitudinal Effects of Nonsexist Television Commercials."

literature are indications that some presentations elicit from some viewers effects opposite to those one would predict from examining the content. For instance, examples of nontraditional roles for women led third and fifth grade boys and girls and eighth grade girls to endorse less traditional roles for women, while it led eighth grade boys (who presumably are most concerned about their own masculinity) to a stronger endorsement of traditional roles for women.[48] Similarly, viewing aggressive material can lead to increases in prosocial behavior in middle class preschool children,[49] even though it also leads to more aggression in most preschoolers.[50] In angered adult males, viewing aggression sometimes leads to decreased rather than increased aggression, apparently because it recalls to them sanctions against aggressive retaliations.[51] Thus, material can occasionally lead to behavioral and attitudinal effects opposite to those predicted by a simple, unidirectional stimulus-response model. There is no ready explanation for this phenomenon, but the best guess is that it occurs when the intended message is received by an individual with a vital investment in a behavioral or attitudinal stance opposite to that suggested by the presentation. Most students, however, learn or accept what is presented, so that the old saw "What you see is what you get" is worth remembering in choosing or producing television and film materials.

CONTENT VARIABLES AFFECTING LEARNING

A number of content variables—other than simply what messages are presented—influence learning. The effects of most of these variables on learning from instructional television and film have been tested with only a limited range of subject matter and a limited age range of potential learners. Schramm has provided a very com-

48. Pingree, "Attitudinal Effects of Nonsexist Television Commercials."

49. Stein and Friedrich, "Television Content and Young Children's Behavior," pp. 250-56.

50. Leifer, Gordon, and Graves, "Children's Television," pp. 214-17; Liebert, Neale, and Davidson, *The Early Window*, pp. 34-88.

51. Leonard Berkowitz, Ronald Corwin, and Mark Heironimus, "Film Violence and Subsequent Aggressive Tendencies," *Public Opinion Quarterly* 27 (Summer 1963): 217-29; Leonard Berkowitz, John P. Lepinski, and Eddy J. Angulo, "Awareness of Own Anger Level and Subsequent Aggression," *Journal of Personality and Social Psychology* 11 (March 1969): 293-300.

prehensive review of this work, including about 150 experiments using instructional television or film.[52] He indicates that fully 31 percent of the experiments were conducted with college students, another 28 percent with military personnel, and only 41 percent with elementary and secondary school students and adults.[53] In terms of subject matter, 26 percent dealt with science, 16 percent with military skills, 12 percent with applied or practical science, and the remaining 44 percent in decreasing percentages with psychological and social sciences, miscellaneous topics, language and literature, professional and semiprofessional skills, and motor skills.[54] Schramm's review indicates that active practice and repetition of content most consistently lead to improved learning. The salutary effects of repetition have also been demonstrated in evaluations of "Sesame Street."[55] Schramm finds other content variables that generally increase learning such as (a) feedback on correct and incorrect practice; (b) material that is clearly and sequentially structured; (c) relatively simple material without irrelevant, attention-getting features; and (d) material that is made easily encodable by being written below the viewer's reading level, by being delivered at relatively slow rates, or by being overtly labeled on the sound track.

Some of these content variables have also been found to influence learning and performance from entertainment television and films. Repetition of the same or similar content increases learning or performance of aggression by viewers from preschool through junior high school[56] and of social attitudes by children from seventh to

52. Wilbur Schramm, "What the Research Says," in *Quality in Instructional Television*, ed. Wilbur Schramm (Honolulu: The University Press of Hawaii, 1972), pp. 44-79.

53. Ibid., p. 45.

54. Ibid., pp. 45-46.

55. Samuel Ball and Gerry Ann Bogatz, *A Summary of the Major Findings in "The First Year of 'Sesame Street': An Evaluation"* (Princeton, N.J.: Educational Testing Service, 1970), p. 3.

56. Leifer and Roberts, "Children's Responses to Television Violence," pp. 84-87; Faye B. Steuer, James M. Applefield, and Rodney Smith, "Televised Aggression and the Interpersonal Aggression of Preschool Children," *Journal of Experimental Child Psychology* 11 (June 1971): 442-47.

twelfth grade.[57] Clearly organized, sequentially presented plot lines
are better understood, especially by younger elementary school
children.[58] Irrelevant, attention-getting aspects of a presentation will
be learned by children, especially prior to adolescence,[59] and may
interfere with learning by fourth graders.[60] Finally, codability influences adults' retention of complex patterns of movements,[61] and
children between four and eight remember social material better
when they are helped to encode verbally as they view.[62]

Other content variables have been found to influence learning
of behavior or of information through entertainment programming.
Although they have not been examined in instructional programming, it is reasonable to assume that they would also be effective
there. These variables include (a) the depiction of positive and
negative consequences for an event, (b) mild arousal, (c) characters who are similar to viewers, (d) situations that are familiar to
the viewers, and (e) more realistic portrayals. Studies of the first
of these, that is, the effects of vicarious consequences on learning and performance, have recently been reviewed by Thelen and
Rennie.[63] From their summary and other work, there is ample evi-

57. Peterson and Thurstone, *Motion Pictures and the Social Attitudes of Children.*

58. Collins and Westby, "Children's Processing of Social Information."

59. W. Andrew Collins, "Learning of Media Content: A Developmental Study," *Child Development* 41 (December 1970): 1133-42; Gordon A. Hale, Leon K. Miller, and Harold W. Stevenson, "Incidental Learning of Film Content: A Development Study," *Child Development* 39 (March 1968): 69-77; Robert P. Hawkins, "Learning of Peripheral Content in Films: A Developmental Study," *Child Development* 44 (March 1973): 214-17.

60. Lance Kirkpatrick Canon, "Motivational State, Stimulus Selection, and Distractibility," *Child Development* 38 (June 1967): 589-96.

61. Marvin S. Gerst, "Symbolic Coding Operations in Observational Learn-ing" (Ph.D. diss., Stanford University, 1968).

62. Albert Bandura, Joan E. Grusec, and Frances L. Menlove, "Observa-tional Learning as a Function of Symbolization and Incentive Set," *Child De-velopment* 37 (September 1966): 499-506; Brian Coates and Willard W. Hartup, "Age and Verbalization in Observational Learning," *Developmental Psychology* 1 (September 1969): 556-62.

63. Mark H. Thelen and D. L. Rennie, "The Effect of Vicarious Reinforce-ment on Imitation: A Review of the Literature," in *Progress in Experimental Personality Research*, ed. Brendan A. Maher (New York: Academic Press, 1972).

dence for the influence of vicarious consequences, including influence on (a) the performance of aggression by viewers between the ages of three and about eleven,[64] (b) game playing strategies used by boys between the ages of eleven and fourteen,[65] (c) strategies for leading groups used by children between the ages of nine and thirteen,[66] (d) commodity preferences of six- and seven-year-old girls,[67] and (e) recall of behavior by first to third graders.[68]

There is less evidence for the utility of the other four variables, but there is enough to warrant mentioning them here. Moderate arousal has been shown to facilitate observational learning of aggression and attitudes by elementary and secondary school children.[69] Material filmed in familiar environments is better remembered by children between second and tenth grades than is less familiar material,[70] and the actions of characters who are more similar (and hence also more familiar and relevant) to children between the ages of eleven and fourteen may be better remembered than those of less similar characters.[71] Finally, there is some indica-

64. Leifer and Roberts, "Children's Responses to Television Violence," pp. 91-100; Mary A. Rosekrans and Willard W. Hartup, "Imitative Influences of Consistent and Inconsistent Response Consequences to a Model on Aggressive Behavior in Children," *Journal of Personality and Social Psychology* 7 (December 1967): 429-34.

65. Mary A. Rosekrans, "Imitation in Children as a Function of Perceived Similarity to a Social Model and Vicarious Reinforcement," *Journal of Personality and Social Psychology* 7 (November 1967): 307-15.

66. Robert B. Zajonc, "Some Effects of the 'Space' Serials," *Public Opinion Quarterly* 18 (Winter 1954-55): 367-74.

67. Robert M. Liebert and Luis E. Fernandez, "Effects of Vicarious Consequences on Imitative Performance," *Child Development* 41 (September 1970): 847-52.

68. Mark H. Thelen et al., "Effect of Model-Reward on the Observer's Recall of the Modeled Behavior," *Journal of Personality and Social Psychology* 29 (January 1974): 140-44.

69. Albert Bandura and Richard H. Walters, *Social Learning and Personality Development* (New York: Holt, Rinehart and Winston, 1963), pp. 86-89; Donald P. Hartmann, "Influence of Symbolically Modeled Instrumental Aggression and Pain Cues on Aggressive Behavior," *Journal of Personality and Social Psychology* 11 (March 1969): 280-88.

70. Holaday and Stoddard, *Getting Ideas from the Movies.*

71. Eleanor E. Maccoby and William Cody Wilson, "Identification and Observational Learning from Films," *Journal of Abnormal and Social Psychology* 55 (July 1957): 76-87; Rosekrans, "Imitation in Children," pp. 307-15.

tion that children from preschool through adolescence learn, perform, or react more to material that is labeled as real than to material that is labeled as fantasy. These results have been found to occur for emotional responses to aggressive programming[72] and for aggressive behavior subsequent to viewing "real" or "fantasy" violence,[73] but the latter finding should not obscure the fact that "fantasy" material also teaches.

PRODUCTION TECHNIQUES AFFECTING LEARNING

A number of production variables do not seem to affect the amount of learning of cognitive content that results from viewing instructional programming. Again, Schramm has provided a thorough summary of these variables based on the same set of studies that were described at the beginning of the preceding section.[74] Variables that he found not to matter, unless they impair the clarity of the presentation, include focus and size of the picture. Variables that matter only when they are relevant to the content being presented include color, subjective camera angle, animation, and special pictorial treatments. Finally, some variables are never consistently related to learning: eye contact, background music, a multiplicity of camera angles or film techniques (these may even

72. W. S. Dysinger and C. A. Ruckmick, *The Emotional Responses of Children to the Motion Picture Situation* (New York: Macmillan, 1933); Hilde Himmelweit, A. Oppenheim, and P. Vince, *Television and the Child* (London: Oxford University Press, 1958); D. K. Osborn and R. C. Endsley, "Emotional Reactions of Young Children to TV Violence," *Child Development* 42 (March 1971): 321-31.

73. Albert Bandura, Dorothea Ross, and Sheila A. Ross, "Imitation of Film-Mediated Aggressive Models," *Journal of Abnormal and Social Psychology* 66, no. 1 (1963): 3-11; Leonard Berkowitz and Joseph T. Alioto, "The Meaning of an Observed Event as a Determinant of Its Aggressive Consequences," *Journal of Personality and Social Psychology* 28 (November 1973): 206-17; Seymour Feshbach, "Reality and Fantasy in Filmed Violence," in *Television and Social Behavior*, vol. 2, *Television and Social Learning*, pp. 318-45; Jack McLeod, Charles K. Atkin, and Steven Chaffee, "Adolescents, Parents, and Television Use: Adolescent Self-Report Measures from Maryland and Wisconsin Samples," in *Television and Social Behavior*, vol. 3, *Television and Adolescent Aggressiveness*, ed. George A. Comstock and Eli A. Rubinstein (Rockville, Md.: National Institute of Mental Health, 1972), pp. 173-238; Grant Noble, "Effects of Different Forms of Filmed Aggression on Children's Constructive and Destructive Play," *Journal of Personality and Social Psychology* 26 (April 1973): 54-59.

74. Schramm, "What the Research Says."

detract from learning), elaborate visual aids, professional production techniques, dramatic rather than expository styles, and humor.

While these conclusions are warranted from existing research, there are a number of reservations that educators should have about them. First of all, they are often based on one or two studies of viewers within a particular age group. One cannot be certain that the conclusion would be supported by future studies of the same age group and the same content, nor can one be certain that the conclusion would apply to age groups or content other than that studied. There are good reasons to believe that preschool and early elementary-school age children may learn differently than older students who again may learn differently than adults. Thus, age- and content-specific results are necessary before one can be certain of an effect. Second, nearly all of the studies upon which these conclusions are based were conducted in laboratory or classroom settings, both of which increase attention to and retention of stimulus material. Consequently, some of the variables, such as commercial production techniques, humor, and animation, that do not affect cognitive learning in these settings might affect it in other settings where students are freer to reject unattractive material. The final caveat is that almost any variable can be shown to influence learning when it is applied in ways that are relevant to the desired and measured learning outcome. Once again educators need to decide upon educational goals before they can decide what variables will help programming achieve these goals.

Designing or Evaluating Programming

The preceding section has summarized much of what is known about content and production variables that seem to influence learning from educational and entertainment programming. This knowledge can be put to use in selecting programming to fulfill an educational goal or in producing new television or film material. In the discussion that follows, I shall apply the information to the selection of programming, but the principles apply equally well to program production.

An educator's first responsibilities are to know the characteristics of the intended audience and the goals of the curriculum. Looking first at the way in which the curriculum is presented, we have suggested in the preceding section that an educator should select programming that covers the curriculum goals, omits undesired content of any type, focuses on reality rather than fantasy, avoids irrelevant, distracting information, repeats curriculum content exactly and with variations, elicits rehearsal of the content, provides feedback on the correctness of what is rehearsed, shows positive outcomes for acquisition or use of the content, produces moderate arousal in viewers, and presents information in a manner that is easily encoded by the viewers.

Some of these evaluations cannot be made without a clear understanding of the characteristics of the individuals who will be viewing the programming. For example, younger children seem to have more trouble than older children in deciding what content is relevant and avoiding irrelevant content. Consequently, the amount of material that should be considered irrelevant and distracting will certainly vary with the age and expertise of the viewers. Likewise, decisions about the amount of repetition, appropriate ways to elicit practice, what will produce moderate arousal, and what makes a presentation easily encodable must all be made with the target audience firmly in mind.

The social characteristics and experience of the intended audience should also be considered in evaluating programming. If it is generally true that individuals learn more or accept more information from people more like themselves or remember more of what happens in familiar environments, then curriculum—of whatever type—presented by people with whom viewers can identify, in places and events familiar to them, is more likely to be remembered than is curriculum that is unfamiliar. Thus, the inner-city child profits from numbers, letters, and shapes presented in a ghetto environment by blacks, whites, and hispanics who might live there, but the Navajo child profits more from the same material presented by Navajos and a few western whites and chicanos in a desert environment dotted with hogans.

As stated in the preceding section, certain production techniques are not reliably associated with greater learning. Thus, on the surface, it seems that an educator need pay little attention to the way in which the program was made. For a number of reasons, such a conclusion may be fallacious. First, since there is reason to believe

324   TEACHING WITH TELEVISION AND FILM

that "production techniques" can influence information-processing
skills, an educator should choose programming that will encourage
appropriate information-processing skills. Second, there are indications that different cultural groups within the United States have
different behaviors and rhythms in social encounters,[75] may have
different learning styles,[76] and do produce qualitatively different
television and film programs.[77] Hence, an educator must relate
audience characteristics to such production variables as the pace at
which material is presented, the ways in which the camera is used,
the editing, and the sequencing of material. Finally, since at least
a modicum of attention must be directed at a presentation if it is
to be learned, production techniques that make a program more
attractive decrease the need for a teacher to encourage attention
to the program.

With the advent of "Sesame Street" has come increased knowledge about what makes a program appealing, at least to a preschool-
age viewer. Researchers have used attention ratings of children
watching "Sesame Street" in small groups in a naturalistic setting
and of children watching in a laboratory with a slide show dis-
tractor. From these ratings, the research staff has concluded that
young American children are attracted by other children, animals,
short and self-contained segments, catch-and-get-caught rhythms,
change, slapstick humor, the familiar, animation, and pixilation.[78]

75. Paul Byers, "From Biological Rhythm to Cultural Pattern: A Study of
Minimal Units" (Ph.D. diss., Columbia University, 1972); Paul Byers and Hap-
pie Byers, "Nonverbal Communication and the Education of Children," in
Functions of Language in the Classroom, ed. Courtney Cazden, Vera John,
and Dell Hymes (New York: Teachers College Press, 1972), pp. 3-31; Fred-
erick Erickson et al., "Inter-ethnic Relations in Urban Institutional Settings,"
Final technical report, Projects MH 18230, MH 21460, National Institute of
Mental Health (Cambridge, Mass.: Graduate School of Education, Harvard
University, 1973).

76. Cazden, John, and Hymes, *Functions of Language.* See especially the
articles by Philips, John, and Dumont.

77. Sol Worth and John Adair, *Through Navajo Eyes: An Exploration of
Film Communication and Anthropology* (Bloomington: Indiana University
Press, 1972).

78. Pixilation is an editing technique that results in a syncopated visual display rather like early silent movies.

They do not like adults, talking, abstract argumentation, nonsense or ambiguity, and low key material.[79]

Our knowledge of the preferences of older children, adolescents, and adults is limited to program characteristics such as action, humor, characters with whom they can identify, and moderate familiarity.[80] We may not need as much information about these older viewers, since it is much easier for adults to predict what they will like than it is to predict what young children will like.[81]

Educators can obtain sufficient information to begin to make some reasonable choices about programming appropriate for the students for whom they are responsible. One additional step is highly advisable: trying out material with a representative target audience. There is no substitute for the information obtainable from watching children watch a program and talking to them afterwards. This procedure has been followed recently by groups responsible for the production of "Sesame Street," "The Electric Company," "Carroscolendas," "Fat Albert," "Cozmics," and a few other commercial, public, and instructional programs. In all cases it has led to some beneficial revisions of material.[82] Of course, teachers, network and station executives, and parents also attend on a more informal basis to the opinions of the students, audiences, or chil-

79. Lesser, *Children and Television*, pp. 102-31; Barbara F. Reeves, "The First Year of 'Sesame Street': The Formative Research" (Report to the Children's Television Workshop, 1970). ERIC: ED 047 822.

80. Leonard A. LoSciuto, "A National Inventory of Television Viewing Behavior," in *Television and Social Behavior*, vol. 4, *Television in Day-to-Day Life: Patterns of Use*, ed. Eli A. Rubinstein, George A. Comstock, and John P. Murray (Rockville, Md.: National Institute of Mental Health, 1972), pp. 33-86; Jack Lyle and Heidi R. Hoffman, "Children's Use of Television and Other Media," ibid., pp. 129-256; Wilbur Schramm, Jack Lyle, and Edwin Parker, *Television in the Lives of Our Children* (Stanford: Stanford University Press, 1961), pp. 24-56; Gary Steiner, *The People Look at Television* (New York: Knopf, 1963).

81. Samuel L. Becker and Glenn Joseph Wolfe, "Can Adults Predict Children's Interest in a Television Program?" in *The Impact of Educational Television*, ed. Wilbur Schramm (Urbana: University of Illinois Press, 1960), pp. 195-213.

82. Chu and Schramm, *Learning from Television*, pp. 90-91; Lesser, *Children and Television*, pp. 132-43, 152-63; Edward L. Palmer, "Formative Research in Educational Television Production: The Experience of the Children's Television Workshop," in *Quality in Instructional Television*, pp. 165-88.

dren they wish to influence. Still, such tryout is worth recommending explicitly, since the information that can be gained from such a procedure can help educators adapt their program choices so that they better fit the interests and needs of their students.

Utility of Television and Film Teaching

As has already been demonstrated, television and film can successfully teach a variety of content and skills, and students from preschool through college can find television an acceptable and attractive teacher. Therefore an evaluation of the utility of television and film as teaching devices must be based on criteria such as the expertise with which they can present a particular curriculum area, ease of delivery, and cost per pupil. The ease with which these media can be transported to a wide variety of educational environments and the economies of cost that may result from broadcasting television, but not film, programs to a large audience no doubt account for the fact that television and film are most often considered to be effective tools for teaching large groups of students.

Television and film are often thought of as replacements for more traditional classroom teaching. The comparisons of the effectiveness of live and television or film teaching in the second section above, reflect just such a view. They overlook, however, the fact that each teaching method has particular advantages and is peculiarly able to communicate certain information or skills. Television and film can (a) capture the uncommon or hard to duplicate and make it available to everyone; (b) present static and moving visual information easily; (c) alter visual, auditory, and temporal characteristics of material and phenomena; (d) resort to animation; (e) reach a very large audience; and (f) be repeated endlessly. On the other hand, television and film cannot as easily (a) respond to students as they are learning the lesson; (b) foster practice of reading, writing, and speaking skills; (c) oversee students learning through their own activity; and (d) take the idiosyncrasies of each student into account.

Thus the question "Which medium is better?" is probably better rephrased as "Which medium is better for what?" Separate decisions must be made for each educational goal.

At another level, the choice of teaching medium must be based on decisions about the feasibility and cost of delivery by that medium. This is the point at which television and film become more nearly uniquely appropriate for large groups. Both television and film programs are educational packages that are easily transportable *in toto* to a wide range of students and locales. In this way they differ significantly from more traditional teaching methods. A curriculum or a master teacher can go wherever there is equipment for showing a film or receiving a television program. While this mobility has the advantage of making more unusual experiences available to a wide range of students, it has the disadvantages of requiring relatively expensive equipment for broadcasting and of tying students and educational systems into relatively inflexible times for receiving a television broadcast or viewing a film. For this reason, many classroom teachers find television and film considerably less desirable than they would if these media could be viewed at times chosen to match individual classroom schedules.

The costs of television and film vary considerably depending upon the type of production and reception hardware, the type and quality of programs produced, the delivery system, and the audience size. Production costs for both media are relatively high and cannot be reduced without significant reductions in the quality of the program. In those situations where programs are viewed by highly motivated or well-supervised students, simple productions made with a low budget may be perfectly adequate, but in situations where programs must compete for viewers (for example, "Sesame Street"), high quality programs and the attendant higher costs are essential. Thus, reductions in per pupil costs most often come from economies in the delivery system and increases in the audience size.

In the last decade at least four separate studies have been made of the costs of various means of instruction and the factors that most influence these costs.[83] Each of them indicates the extreme

83. General Learning Corporation, *Cost Study of Educational Media Systems*; J. G. Miller, "Deciding Whether and How to Use Educational Technology in the Light of Cost-Effectiveness Evaluation," Unpublished manuscript, Cleveland State University, 1969; Schramm, *Big Media, Little Media*, pp. 77-110; Sidney G. Tickton and Sherwood Davidson Kohn, *The New Instructional Technologies: Are They Worth It?* (Washington, D.C.: Academy for Educational Development, 1971).

variation in per pupil costs that may result from differences in production equipment and quality, delivery system, instructional use
of the medium, and audience size. For example, a poll of educational
television stations across the country found that estimates of per
student costs for inschool programs during the 1970-1971 season
varied from $0.006 to $7.00 per week, with the average for thirty-
three stations being $0.43 per student per week.[84] In 1969 Miller
estimated that the cost of live closed-circuit or broadcast instructional television ranged from $0.02 to $10.00 per user-hour, while
the cost of taped closed-circuit or broadcast instructional television
ranged from $0.01 to $5.00 per user-hour.[85] As a comparison, Miller
estimated that the cost of classroom lectures ranged from $0.15 to
$3.00 per user-hour, and the cost of small discussion groups ranged
from $0.50 to $15.00 per user-hour.[86] Neither of these studies provided estimates of the cost of using films.

In 1968 the General Learning Corporation published a major
summary of the costs of instructional media. Estimates were based
on 1,000 hours of production per year per school system, which
would represent heavy reliance on instructional media. The study
concludes that instructional television broadcast only locally (about
15,000 students) would cost between $30 and $40 per student per
year. When the broadcasting was to a city or metropolitan area
(at least 150,000 students) costs fell to approximately $10 per stu-
dent per year.[87] On the other hand, "Sesame Street," with an estimated audience of about seven million, cost approximately $0.65
per viewer for its first season.[88] Instructional films cost about $50
per student per year regardless of the size of the student population
utilizing them.[89] Greater economy cannot be achieved with film

84. Tickton and Kohn, *The New Instructional Technologies*, p. 80.

85. Miller, "Deciding Whether and How to Use Educational Technology,"
p. 71.

86. Ibid., p. 71.

87. General Learning Corporation, *Cost Study of Educational Media Systems*, pp. 40 ff.

88. Tickton and Kohn, *The New Instructional Technologies*, p. 34.

89. General Learning Corporation, *Cost Study of Educational Media Systems*, pp. 40 ff.

because of current duplication and distribution systems. Thus, while television and film have been viewed as equivalent educational systems throughout most of this chapter, they are very unequivalent systems when cost is considered.

All of this ignores the fact that most instructional television is viewed by students in a traditional classroom with a teacher present. The teacher must still be paid and so his or her costs must be added to those for the television program. This does not mean that television teaching is always costly or that it is always necessary to have a live teacher present for television to be an effective teacher. "Sesame Street" is a prime example of the benefits obtainable from unsupervised viewing of educational programming, and many other examples are available at the college and adult education level.[90] Thus, television may profitably substitute for a traditional classroom teacher. It is also useful as a supplement to traditional classroom teaching, because it can provide a different learning experience and relatively unusual material.

Integrating Television and Film Teaching with Classroom Teaching

TEACHER FACILITATION OF TELEVISION AND FILM TEACHING

We have some knowledge about ways in which classroom teachers can facilitate learning from television or film presentations. These are perhaps most easily divided into activities prior to, during, and after viewing. Each strategy asks teachers to help students learn better from televised or filmed material. The alternatives of asking television and film to help students learn better from live teachers and of combining teaching modes to produce maximum learning have not to my knowledge been explored, although they seem equally legitimate goals. We need to know how to use each teaching medium to facilitate the work of the others and how to put them all together to bring about the maximum learning of which each student is capable.

Prior to viewing a television or film program, a teacher can either motivate students to learn the content that will be presented

90. Ball and Bogatz, *A Summary of the Major Findings*, p. 4; Chu and Schramm, *Learning from Television*, pp. 77-82.

or provide them with structures for assimilating that content. Either of these activities should increase the likelihood of learning from the presentation. A teacher may motivate students by promising a monetary reward for learning, praising or criticizing their learning, or promising a related activity subsequent to viewing. All three of these strategies have been shown to increase learning of television or film content by military recruits and junior high school, high school, and college students.[91] High school students who are intrinsically more interested in the content, and therefore self-motivated, will also learn more than students who are not.[92] Providing introductions for students prior to viewing has been recommended by Chu and Schramm in their extensive review of learning from television and by Chen in his exploration of ways to increase active participation by viewers of "The Electric Company."[93] Neither of these recommendations is supported by strong research evidence, but it is reasonable to assume that introductions would increase learning by increasing codability of material, providing a little learning prior to viewing, and increasing the availability of structures within which to assimilate the information.

During viewing, a teacher may increase learning by insuring attention to the program, eliciting rehearsal of the content, providing feedback on the correctness of the rehearsal, and commenting positively on those aspects of the program the teacher would like remembered or performed. We have clear evidence for the utility of rehearsal and feedback from a number of studies of junior high school students.[94] For example, Michael and Maccoby found that stopping a film and asking students to rehearse what they had just seen increased learning over that which occurred when students watched the film straight through.[95] Feedback on the correctness

91. Ibid., pp. 83-87.

92. Ibid., pp. 85-86.

93. Milton Chen, "Verbal Response to 'The Electric Company': Qualities of Program Material and the Viewing Conditions Which Affect Verbalization" (Report to the Children's Television Workshop, 1972), pp. 15-20; Chu and Schramm, Learning from Television, pp. 26-28.

94. Chu and Schramm, Learning from Television, pp. 26-28, 94-97, 101-107.

95. Donald N. Michael and Nathan Maccoby, "Factors Influencing Verbal Learning from Films under Varying Conditions of Audience Participation," Journal of Experimental Psychology 46 (December 1953): 411-18.

of what was rehearsed also improved learning; Michael and Maccoby concluded that this activity improved learning more than any of the other three variables they studied (participation, overt and covert practice, and extrinsic motivation).[96]

There is also evidence that adult commentary on the social acceptability of material, while it is being viewed, influences children's later performance of what they have seen. For example, if children see an aggressive performance and an adult expresses approval of it, the children are much more likely to be aggressive in subsequent test situations than are children who have heard an adult disapprove of the action.[97] Interestingly, the impact of such comments apparently varies with the age of the child. Preschoolers will show the influence of an adult's commentary only in test situations where that adult is present, while seven-year-olds will show that influence whether or not the adult is present in the test situation.[98]

Subsequent to viewing a program, a teacher may facilitate learning and performance of the content by providing practice and feedback, by differential reinforcement, and by integrating the content into other material and activities in the class. The utility of practice and feedback has been amply demonstrated throughout this chapter, but it is perhaps worth noting that music, jingles, slogans, doggerel, and the like from a program are particularly easy for students to practice—and something they enjoy practicing. This fact is most often applied to teaching young children and to teaching foreign languages, but it applies equally well to older students and other subject matter. Reinforcement effects have been demonstrated for learning and performance of all kinds of intellectual and social information and behaviors. Thus it is no surprise that reinforcement can affect retention and performance of what has been seen on television.[99] There is scant evidence for the utility of inte-

96. Ibid.

97. Joan E. Grusec, "Effects of Co-Observer Evaluations on Imitation: A Developmental Study," *Developmental Psychology* 8 (January 1973): 141; David J. Hicks, "Effects of Co-Observer's Sanctions and Adult Presence on Imitative Aggression," *Child Development* 39 (March 1968): 303-9.

98. Grusec, "Effects of Co-Observer Evaluations," p. 141.

99. Albert Bandura, "Influence of Models' Reinforcement Contingencies on the Acquisition of Imitative Responses," *Journal of Personality and Social*

grating television or film content into other material, although it is a common suggestion to teachers. In fact, many programs put out teacher guides that contain a plethora of suggestions about how to integrate ideas from the program (or series) into other classroom activities. This piece of folk wisdom would undoubtedly be borne out in more refined experimental tests of its utility, but we now have little experimental support for it.

Most of these strategies for increasing learning from television and film are familiar to classroom teachers and utilized by them. Reviewing them only serves to emphasize the benefits that may be derived from a teacher's acceptance of television or film teaching and integration of it into the entire educational experience of the student. Teachers who are most comfortable with television and film often depart from these more usual teacher-directed uses of television and film and use the media in more individualized, innovative ways.

UNCOMMON USES OF TELEVISION AND FILM

Some teachers have capitalized on children's extensive attraction to television and film by piggybacking other learning onto involvement with television programs or film production. Most of these activities are enthusiastically received, but their usefulness has not often been evaluated. Teachers in Philadelphia who used scripts from television programs to teach reading report improved reading scores and much more interest in reading.[100] Television scripts were even stolen from a classroom—the first known theft of reading material in that school. Borton has added a second audio track to popular children's television programs and demonstrated that children who listen on an FM station while they view the program learn the vocabulary and concepts it presents.[101] Others have used

Psychology 1 (June 1965): 589-95; James P. Flanders, "A Review of Research on Imitative Behavior," *Psychological Bulletin* 69, no. 5 (1968): 316-37; Olga Linne, "Reactions of Children to Violence on TV" (Stockholm: Swedish Broadcasting Corporation, 1971).

100. Craig R. Waters, "Thank God Something Has Finally Reached Him," *TV Guide* (19 January 1974): 6-9.

101. Terry Borton, "Dual Audio Television," *Harvard Educational Review* 41 (February 1971): 64-78; Terry Borton, Leonard Belasco, and Steven Baskerville, "Broadcasting Dual Audio TV Instruction," in *Mass Communications and American Education*, ed. P. Klinge and A. Bluem (New York: Hastings House, in press).

film making as a vehicle for practicing reading and writing, as well as planning, skills. Still others have asked students to view particular programs at home because they present information relevant to class curriculum.[102] There is every indication that learning results from home viewing of such programs by pre-schoolers, elementary school students, high school students, and adults.[103] Finally, some teachers have used entertainment programs as material for discussions about social issues, for concept formation, and for teaching the ordering of events in time.

Relatively inexpensive videotape equipment has been used to teach performance and role-taking skills, again with little or no formal evaluation of its utility. Videotape records provide excellent feedback to a student. For example, programs in such areas as speech, dramatics, and athletics have used videotaped records of students to give them more feedback on their performance. Others have used videotape to document social interactions so that participants can analyze their roles without the distortions that arise when one attempts to remember such interactions. Finally, videotape has been used to foster role-taking skills by providing students with an opportunity to act out a variety of roles and to receive feedback on their performance. One such experimental program with adolescent delinquent boys resulted in increased role-taking skill as measured experimentally and in decreased arrests over a one-year period.[104] Of course, the boys may simply have learned enough role-taking skills to avoid being caught rather than learning to empathize with their victims. The experimental evaluation was not fine-grained enough to rule out this possibility.

The last-mentioned uses of television and film are appropriate

---

102. A useful reference for programs broadcast commercially is *Teachers Guide to Television*, published twice a year by the Television Information Office, Broadcasting Association, P.O. Box 564, Lenox Hill Station, New York 10021.

103. Alper and Leidy, "The Impact of Information Transmission through Television"; Ball and Bogatz, *The First Year of "Sesame Street"*; Bogatz and Ball, *The Second Year of "Sesame Street"*; Ball and Bogatz, *A Summary of the Major Findings*; Chu and Schramm, *Learning from Television*.

104. Michael J. Chandler, "Egocentrism and Antisocial Behavior: The Assessment and Training of Social Perspective-Taking Skills," *Developmental Psychology* 9 (November 1973): 326-32.

for small groups of students, but not for large. Each of them demands supervision by a classroom teacher. In them television and film become useful tools for arousing interest in the actual curriculum area or for providing feedback to students. Thus, one can begin to think of television and film not as simple substitutes for a lecture, but also as instruments for increasing interest, for eliciting practice of particular skills, and for providing elaborate, realistic feedback on a learner's performance.

Conclusion

Television and film can certainly be used to teach cognitive, social, and emotional content and information-processing skills to students who range in age from preschoolers to adults. In doing so television—but not film—can be cost-effective when the student population it serves is relatively large. Thus an educator need not worry about whether or not to use television or film; rather the teacher must decide when to use them, how to produce or evaluate a program, and how best to integrate them into an entire educational experience.

Television and film are most likely to be successful teachers when educators participate in careful planning of the material, select material that conforms to our present knowledge about the more successful ways of presenting curriculum content, and actively work to integrate television or film material into the entire educational experience of the student. The most useful strategies for increasing learning, either within a program or through classroom activities, are active participation by students, feedback of student responses, and repetition. As with all education, these strategies must be evaluated within the context of student characteristics. It is up to the educator and the producer, with little help from existing research, to find the correct blend of curriculum content, of effective means of presenting it on television and film, and of consideration for the unique characteristics of the target audience—no mean job for any of us.

CHAPTER X

Classroom Instruction

BARAK ROSENSHINE

This chapter describes some of the major recent studies in the area of classroom instruction and their results. It begins with a summary of major publications in this area since 1970, and proceeds with a review of results on six variables of interest: time spent, content covered, work groupings, teacher questions, child responses, and adult feedback. Particular attention is given to recent studies on instruction for primary-grade pupils from low socioeconomic backgrounds, and from these studies an instructional pattern labeled "direct instruction" is described.

Summary Publications Since 1970

Since 1970, a number of summary books, chapters, and articles on classroom interaction have appeared. Most of these publications contain detailed reviews of research, descriptions of the construction and use of observation instruments, and suggestions for future research.

REVIEWS OF RESEARCH ON CLASSROOM TEACHING

Brophy and Good summarized research on a number of areas concerning individual differences in teacher-student interaction patterns.[1] The topics covered included teacher expectations, teacher attitudes toward students, and the influence of such characteristics of students as social class, sex, prior achievement, and race upon teacher behavior, teacher attitudes, and student achievement. The book by Flanders summarized developmental work on his inter-

1. Jere E. Brophy and Thomas L. Good, *Teacher-Student Relationships: Causes and Consequences* (New York: Holt, Rinehart and Winston, 1974).

action analysis instrument and presented detailed results of studies using that instrument.[2]

A special issue of the *International Review of Education* was devoted to the classroom behavior of teachers.[3] The major sections dealt with the history of this research, its conceptual framework, the collection and analysis of data, teaching behavior and measures of pupil growth, and the application of research results.

A monograph of the American Educational Research Association entitled *Classroom Observation* contained a review by Nuthall of research in this area, a presentation by Gallagher of his Topic Category System and the results of studies using this instrument, and a paper by Rosenshine on the evaluation of observational instruments.[4]

The text by Dunkin and Biddle provided the most detailed coverage to date of studies with category instruments, that is, instruments that yield frequency counts of classroom events.[5] In addition to an overview and critique of this area of research, they presented detailed summaries of research on relationships (a) between teacher characteristics and classroom processes, (b) between classroom processes of one kind and those of another kind, and (c) between classroom processes and student achievement and attitude. Rosenshine's volume summarized research with both category and rating instruments on relationships between teacher behavior and student achievement.[6] Gage and Berliner presented a unit categorizing the major results cited by Dunkin and Biddle and by Rosenshine under three headings: teacher structuring, teacher soliciting or questioning, and teacher reaction to pupils.[7]

2. Ned A. Flanders, *Analyzing Classroom Behavior* (New York: Addison-Wesley, 1970).

3. Ned A. Flanders and Graham Nuthall, eds., *The Classroom Behavior of Teachers*, in *International Review of Education* 18 (1972): entire issue.

4. James J. Gallagher et al., *Classroom Observation*, American Educational Research Association Evaluation Monograph No. 6 (Chicago: Rand McNally, 1970).

5. Michael J. Dunkin and Bruce J. Biddle, *The Study of Teaching* (New York: Holt, Rinehart and Winston, 1974).

6. Barak Rosenshine, *Teaching Behaviors and Student Achievement* (Slough, Eng.: National Foundation for Educational Research in England and Wales, 1971).

7. Nathaniel L. Gage and David C. Berliner, *Educational Psychology* (Chicago: Rand McNally, 1975.)

Overviews of observation procedures are contained in the volumes by Flanders, Brophy and Good, Dunkin and Biddle, and Rosenshine.[8] Rosenshine and Rosenshine and Furst also presented overviews of observational instruments and research.[9]

Gage presented a revision of thirteen of his papers on research on teacher effectiveness and on teacher education.[10] Similarly, seven authors presented papers on future directions in the study of teaching in a symposium entitled *How Teachers Make a Difference*.[11]

TEACHING MODELS

A teaching model might be described as a teaching pattern that is comprised of, and gives focus to, a number of discrete behaviors. Such models are frequently discussed in research on classroom teaching, and recent publications have continued this discussion. Joyce and Weil described sixteen such models in the areas of information processing, social development, and personal development, together with observational approaches used to study a number of these models.[12] Nuthall and Snook reviewed the research on three such models: behavior control, discovery learning, and rational teaching.[13] The same conception of model pervades the chapters in the catalogue of teaching skills edited by Turner, in that the authors of the chapters on various subject areas tended to

8. Flanders, *Analyzing Classroom Behavior*; Brophy and Good, *Teacher-Student Relationhips*; Dunkin and Biddle, *The Study of Teaching*; Rosenshine, *Teaching Behaviors and Student Achievement*.

9. Barak Rosenshine, "Evaluation of Classroom Instruction," *Review of Educational Research* 40 (June 1970): 279-301; Barak Rosenshine and Norma F. Furst, "The Use of Direct Observation to Study Teaching," in *Second Handbook of Research on Teaching*, ed. Robert M. W. Travers (Chicago: Rand McNally, 1973), pp. 122-83.

10. Nathaniel L. Gage, *Teacher Effectiveness and Teacher Education* (Palo Alto, Cal.: Pacific Books, 1972).

11. U.S. Office of Education, Bureau of Educational Personnel Development, *How Teachers Make a Difference* (Washington, D.C.: U.S. Government Printing Office, 1971). The papers were presented by Ned A. Flanders, Nathaniel L. Gage, Philip W. Jackson, Dan C. Lortie, Alexander Mood, Barak Rosenshine, and Lawrence M. Stolurow.

12. Bruce Joyce and Marsha Weil, *Models of Teaching* (Englewood Cliffs, N.J.: Prentice-Hall, 1972).

13. Graham Nuthall and Ivan Snook, "Contemporary Models of Teaching," in *Second Handbook of Research on Teaching*, pp. 47-76.

organize teaching skills around general models or approaches.[14] Two foci characterize all the model-oriented ideas. One kind of model might be labeled behavior-analytic, detail-specific, and structured, in that the learner proceeds through small, prespecified steps toward each goal. The other kind of model might be labeled inquiry-oriented, learner-centered, and learner-choice, in that the learner has greater choice of the means to be employed toward reaching the goal. As we shall see, these two general approaches also occur in the Follow Through and Planned Variation programs to be discussed below.

It is difficult to assess the product or promise of the research to date. Different reviewers, looking at the same studies, have assessed some results as "holding up" over a variety of contexts[15] and as inherently trivial.[16] But all reviewers agree that the methodology and conceptual base of most of the studies to date have been inadequate. Studies currently under way appear to offer some improvement, and we eagerly await their results and the comparison of results across studies.

Reviews of Selected Instructional Variables

Many variables in classroom instruction have been studied. Each of the three major studies discussed below—those by Stallings and Kaskowitz, Soar, and Brophy and Evertson—examined more than 300 variables.[17] Although many of these variables represent combi-

14. Richard E. Turner, ed., *A General Catalogue of Teaching Skills* (Bloomington, Ind.: College of Education, Indiana University, 1973).

15. Nathaniel L. Gage, "Evaluating Ways to Help Teachers Behave Desirably," in *Competency Assessment, Research, and Evaluation: A Report of a National Conference, March 12-15, 1974* (Washington, D.C.: American Association of Colleges for Teacher Education, 1974), pp. 173-85.

16. Robert S. Heath and Mark Nielson, "The Research Basis for Performance-Based Teacher Education," *Review of Educational Research* 44 (Fall 1974): 463-84.

17. Jane A. Stallings and David H. Kaskowitz, *Follow Through Classroom Observation Evaluation—1972-1973* (Menlo Park, Cal.: Stanford Research Institute, 1974); Robert S. Soar, *Follow Through Classroom Process Measurement and Pupil Growth (1970-71): Final Report* (Gainesville, Fla.: College of Education, University of Florida, 1973); Jere E. Brophy and C. M. Evertson, *Process-Product Correlations in the Texas Teacher Effectiveness Study: Final Report* (Austin, Tex.: University of Texas, 1974).

nations of simpler variables (for example, "teacher asks a small group a direct question on academic matters"), the total number of possible variables is extremely large. Thus, selection of variables for review has become an increasingly difficult task.

This section contains short reviews of recent research on six variables in classroom instruction. Three variables—content covered, time spent, and child work groupings—were selected because they appear to be important and useful variables that are frequently overlooked in classroom research. Three variables that fit together —teacher questions, child responses, and teacher reactions—were selected because they have frequently been studied in classroom research. Finally, there is an attempt to tie the current findings together in a "Direct Instruction Model."

The scope of this review is deliberately limited to primary-grade instruction in reading and mathematics for children of low socioeconomic status. This delimitation of scope is intended to achieve a sharper focus, at the acknowledged expense of a broader scope. Studies in other contexts are included whenever possible, however, in order to probe the generality of findings obtained within this limited focus.

OVERVIEW OF MAJOR RECENT STUDIES

The three classroom studies, all completed in 1974, that receive special consideration in this chapter were selected because of their size and breadth. The setting for the studies by Stallings and Kaskowitz and by Soar was the Follow Through and Planned Variation programs. Follow Through is a federally supported program aimed at providing special instruction for children from low-income families. Planned Variation is the concomitant attempt to determine which of the different Follow Through programs are most effective for various ends. Several Follow Through programs represent the existing range of well-formulated approaches to early childhood education[18] and were selected from a larger group of possible models. Each program was first developed in a laboratory-like setting and then tested in regular classrooms before being implemented

18. Joan S. Bissell, "Implementation of Planned Variation in Head Start," mimeographed (Washington, D.C.: U.S. Department of Health, Education, and Welfare, Office of Child Development, 1971), p. 5.

on a larger scale. Each program has a "sponsor" located at a university or a research organization. The sponsors are responsible for training teachers, supervising the installation and implementation of their program, and modifying the program. The programs began in 1969 and have continued since then. Currently, each sponsor is carrying out its program in five to twenty sites around the country. Each site usually contains two to five schools.

The Planned Variation programs are usually divided into at least two types: structured and flexible programs. Examples of structured programs are those in Kansas, Oregon, and Pittsburgh. These programs have a highly organized, small-step, teacher-directed instructional format in which children proceed through a series of specified tasks and receive fairly immediate feedback on the correctness of their responses.

Examples of flexible programs are those sponsored by the University of Arizona, the Bank Street College of Education, and the Far West Laboratory for Educational Research and Development. Although these programs vary, they are characterized by a greater concern with the child's expressed interests and needs. They allow more time for the child to make choices and to explore and manipulate his environment. The two types of Follow Through programs represent the two dominant approaches to education: direct instruction and inquiry. Indeed, these two and only these two recur in ancient and modern educational thought.[19]

Follow Through classrooms have been subjected to intensive observational study. One purpose of such study has been to assess implementation of the program, that is, to determine whether these programs reflect, in practice, the intentions of the sponsors. The level of implementation appears to be improving as the sponsors apply their experience. The results presented by Soar, and those on the 1972-73 programs presented by Stallings and Kaskowitz, suggest that the programs are being implemented in ways that are close to the intentions of the sponsors. A second purpose of observation has been to determine the relationship between observed classroom behaviors and pupil achievement, and the results of those analyses are given special attention in this chapter.

19. Harry S. Broudy, "Historic Exemplars of Teaching Method," in *Handbook of Research on Teaching*, ed. Nathaniel L. Gage (Chicago: Rand McNally, 1963), pp. 1-43; Turner, *A General Catalogue*.

The study by Stallings and Kaskowitz was based on observations made in 108 first-grade and 58 third-grade classrooms during 1972-73. Three full days of observation took place in each classroom. The programs observed represented six sponsor models plus non-Follow Through classrooms used for purposes of comparison. More than one-half of the classrooms were those of the sponsors of flexible approaches, one-quarter were those of sponsors of structured approaches, and one-quarter were non-Follow Through, or control, classrooms. Both cognitive and affective outcome scores were adjusted for entering characteristics. Only the results on reading and mathematics achievement are discussed here. Almost 350 process measures were derived from the observation instrument, and the part correlations between process and outcome (adjusted for entry scores) were presented in the report. These results were given for each of four contexts: first- and third-grade mathematics and first- and third-grade reading.

The study by Soar was based on observations in 150 Follow Through classrooms in 1970. Four low-inference instruments and one high-inference rating instrument were used. The results for each of these instruments were factor analyzed and then correlated with achievement scores in mathematics and reading. Separate analyses were presented for kindergarten, first-grade, and second-grade classrooms.

The Brophy and Evertson study did not examine Follow Through classrooms, but it is similar to the two studies mentioned above in that it is also based on observations of primary-grade classrooms with low socioeconomic status children, using outcome measures in reading and mathematics. Brophy and Evertson spent two years studying primary-grade teachers who had been identified as consistent in their effects upon student achievement across four years. Thirty-one teachers were observed four times during the first year of the study, and twenty-eight teachers were observed fourteen times during the second year. Of these teachers, nineteen were common to both years. In addition to analyses conducted across the entire sample, separate analyses were made for teachers in high and low socioeconomic status classrooms. There were thirteen teachers with low socioeconomic status classrooms in each year of the study; there were eighteen teachers with high socioeconomic status classrooms the first year and fifteen such teachers the second year. Information was collected on 163 high-inference and 208 low-inference classroom process variables, or a total of 371 variables. Correlations were then computed between scores on each of these measures and the average residual gain scores of each teacher's pupils for the previous four years. Most of the discussion centered upon results within each socioeconomic status context. The .10 level of significance was applied to the results.

TIME

The investigators in all three studies gave attention to the amount of time spent on academic activities. But first we examine total time in school, a related variable that has been discussed in contexts other than the three major studies just described.

Total time in school. In their study of time as a factor in educational achievement in the Detroit metropolitan area, Wiley and Harnischfeger found that the average number of hours of schooling provided in a particular school (computed from figures on average daily attendance, length of school day, and length of school year) was positively related to achievement in verbal ability, reading comprehension, and mathematics.[20]

Similarly, in the study by Harris and associates, teacher reports on the length of the school day were positively correlated with all four adjusted reading outcome measures, and the results were significant in two cases ($r = .40$ and .49).[21] Yet an apparently similar variable—length of school week—yielded inconclusive and inconsistent results in an international study of achievement in mathematics.[22]

20. David E. Wiley and Annegrete Harnischfeger, "Explosion of a Myth: Quantity of Schooling and Exposure to Instruction, Major Educational Vehicles," *Educational Researcher* 3 (April 1974): 7-12.

21. Arthur J. Harris et al., *A Continuation of the CRAFT Project: Comparing Reading Approaches with Disadvantaged Urban Negro Children in Primary Grades*, United States Office of Education Project No. 5-0570-2-12-1 (New York: Division of Teacher Education of the City University of New York, 1968). ERIC: ED 010 297.

22. Torsten Husén, ed. *International Study of Achievement in Mathematics: A Comparison of Twelve Countries*, vol. 2 (New York: John Wiley & Sons, 1967).

In other studies reviewed by Rosenshine[23] (see table 1), both days of student absence and days of teacher absence were usually negatively correlated with achievement, although the magnitude of these correlations seldom exceed $-.20$. Such results support the importance of total time in school.

TABLE 1

CORRELATIONS OF STUDENT ACHIEVEMENT WITH STUDENT ABSENCE
AND TEACHER ABSENCE

Study	Number of Teachers	Grade Level	CORRELATIONS WITH STUDENT ACHIEVEMENT	
			Student Absence	Teacher Absence
Bond and Dykstra	187	First	$-.08$	$-.04$
Harris et al.	30	First	$-.12$	$-.17$
Harris et al.	38	Second	$.10$	$-.32$
Harris et al.	26	Second	$-.66$	$-.12$
Harris and Serwer	48	First	——	$-.04$

SOURCES: Guy L. Bond and Robert Dykstra, "The Cooperative Research Program in First-grade Reading Instruction," *Reading Research Quarterly* 2 (Summer 1967): 1-42; Arthur J. Harris et al., *A Continuation of the CRAFT Project: Comparing Reading Approaches with Disadvantaged Urban Negro Children in Primary Grades*, U.S. Office of Education Project No. 5-0570-2-12-1 (New York: Division of Teacher Education of the City University of New York, 1968); Arthur J. Harris and B.L. Serwer, *Comparison of Reading Approaches in First-Grade Teaching with Disadvantaged Children*, U.S. Office of Education Cooperative Research Project No. 2677 (New York: City University of New York, 1966).

Time on academic activities. Stallings and Kaskowitz used two procedures to assess ways in which school time was used. When coding teacher-student interactions, they used a "modifier" code to give a more precise description of each interaction. This modifier code contained categories for describing the topic of the interaction, and these topics included "academic" (that is, concerning either reading or mathematics) and "behavior." The results for academic interactions in table 2 show consistent, significant, and positive correlations for activities involving academic topics.

Stallings and Kaskowitz also took a "snapshot" every fifteen minutes, one in which they recorded the activities of each child and also recorded the materials being used. Again the results as shown in table 2 are clear, straight-forward, and dramatic. Time spent in mathematics or reading, and time spent on academic texts, yielded positive, significant, and consistent correlations of about .40, whereas time spent in other activities almost always yielded negative correlations. In all four contexts, the less academic ac-

23. Rosenshine, *Teaching Behaviors and Student Achievement.*

TABLE 2

Correlations between (a) Time Spent, Activities, and
Materials and (b) Student Achievement in Mathematics
and Reading in Grades One and Three

Variables	Grade One (N = 108)		Grade Three (N = 58)	
	Mathematics	Reading	Mathematics	Reading
Time spent in academic interactions				
Approximate number of children involved in mathematics	.35	.29	.60	.31
Approximate number of children involved in reading	.32	.40	.50	.32
Percent instances in which an academic activity occurs	.21	.35	.59	.42
Total academic *verbal* interactions	.41	.42	.50	.29
Activities				
Numbers, mathematics, arithmetic	.29	.26	.59	.33
Reading, alphabet, language development	.18	.40	.40	.23
Group time	−.21	−.30	−.43	−.23
Arts, crafts	−.23	−.29	−.26	−.03
Story, music, dancing	−.03	−.16	−.52	−.39
Active play	−.26	−.23	−.29	−.10
Wide variety of activities over one day	−.13	−.30	−.45	−.36
Child selection of seating and work groups	−.09	−.26	−.33	−.30
Classroom management	−.33	−.23	−.10	−.17
Materials				
Texts, workbooks/academic activities	.09	.24	.38	.13
Instructional materials used	.21	.21	−.02	.11
Puzzles, games/academic	−.15	−.04	−.30	−.34
Games, toys, present	−.15	−.32	−.46	−.29
Different resource categories coded	−.03	−.19	−.30	−.23

Source: Jane A. Stallings and David H. Kaskowitz, *Follow Through Classroom Observation Evaluation, 1972-1973* (Menlo Park, Cal.: Stanford Research Institute, 1974).

tivities—such as arts and crafts, stories, music, dancing, blocks, and active play—yielded negative and usually significant results. Similarly, there were negative correlations for use of games, toys, audiovisual equipment, and the total number of different resources used. The item "wide variety of activities over one day" is a count of the number of different activities that appeared in the snapshots. Most of these activities were not in reading and mathematics, suggesting that a variety of nonacademic activities was dysfunctional.

The message of this section seems clear. The stronger the academic emphasis, the stronger the academic results. Time spent on reading and numbers is associated with growth in those areas, whereas time spent in other areas appears to detract from growth in reading and mathematics. Furthermore, there was *no* nonacademic activity that yielded positive correlations with reading and mathematics achievement. This finding is somewhat surprising, since it has frequently been argued that some of these other activities contribute to reading achievement by motivating students or by providing additional stimulation or practice. Such indirect enhancement was not evident in this study.

Soar found that children's ability to name pictures or objects correlated quite negatively with achievement in the second grade. This result suggested that time spent on areas the children have already covered is not functional.

Other studies on how time was used were reviewed by Rosenshine.[24] These reports, summarized in table 3, showed no consistent relationship between the total amount of time spent on instruction and student achievement. In four studies by Harris and his associates, teacher reports on time spent were further subdivided into direct and supportive reading activities. Again, as shown in table 4, the correlations were inconsistent in sign and usually low. The results obtained by Harris are particularly surprising because the students were from families of low socioeconomic status comparable to those in the Follow Through studies.

Why were the results on time spent clear and consistent only in the Stalling and Kaskowitz study, when we would expect similar results in all studies? In the studies by Harris and associates, we note that the time estimates came from teacher reports and that

24. Ibid.

TABLE 3

RESULTS OF SELECTED STUDIES ON RELATIONSHIP BETWEEN TIME
SPENT ON INSTRUCTION AND STUDENT ACHIEVEMENT

Study	Number of Teachers	Grade Level	Result (Means of Correlations)
Harris and Serwer	48	First	.06
Harris et al.	30	First	.07
Harris et al.	38	Second	−.21
Harris et al.	26	Second	−.01
Husén	a	13 - and 17 year-olds	.03
Welch and Bridgham	41	Eleventh	−.08

SOURCES: Harris and Serwer, *Comparison of Reading Approaches;* Harris et al., *A Continuation of the CRAFT Project;* Torsten Husén, ed., *International Study of Achievement in Mathematics: A Comparison of Twelve Countries,* vol. 2 (New York: John Wiley & Sons, 1967); W. W. Welch and Robert G. Bridgham, "Physics Achievement Gains as a Function of Teaching Duration," *School Science and Mathematics* 68 (May 1968): 449-54.

a The International Study of Educational Achievement does not report the number of teachers involved. The result reported here was based on data obtained in ten countries.

TABLE 4

CORRELATIONS OF STUDENT ACHIEVEMENT WITH TIME ON TWO KINDS OF
READING ACTIVITIES

Study	Number of Teachers	Grade Level	Correlation of Achievement with Time on Direct and Supportive Reading Activities	
			Direct	Supportive
Harris and Serwer	48	First	.40	.06
Harris et al.	30	First	.07	−.18
Harris et al.	38	Second	.00	−.23
Harris et al.	26	Second	−.22	.10

SOURCES: Harris and Serwer, *Comparison of Reading Approaches;* Harris et al., *A Continuation of the CRAFT Project.*

teachers who are busy interacting with a class may not be accurate estimators of time spent. Yet, in other studies in which observers rather than teachers estimated time spent, similarly inconsistent results were obtained.[25] Perhaps the observation instrument used by Stallings and Kaskowitz is particularly useful; but perhaps their results reflect the variation across the Follow Through programs in other factors associated with time more than they reflect the significance of time itself. Further research on time, using instruments such as that used by Stallings and Kaskowitz, is urgently needed.

25. Brophy and Evertson, *Process-Product Correlations;* Wayne W. Welch and Robert G. Bridgham, "Physics Achievement Gains as a Function of Teaching Duration," *School Science and Mathematics* 68 (May 1968): 449-54.

Ways of spending direct instructional time. Brophy and Evert-son also found that, for low socioeconomic status classrooms, time spent on seatwork or on individually prescribed learning activities was positively related to achievement, whereas time spent on oral responding was negatively related. For the high socioeconomic status classrooms, the opposite result was obtained: time spent on oral responding was positively related to achievement. These findings suggest that some uses of academic time are more productive than others. In this case, time spent on workbook exercises was most productive for low socioeconomic status classrooms, whereas time spent on oral responding was most productive for high socioeconomic status classrooms. Such a finding seems sensible but needs replication. In his study of fourth- and fifth-grade children of high socioeconomic status who were studying mathematics, Good found that time spent on workbooks was most productive,[26] a result that is the opposite of that of Brophy and Evertson. At any rate, the content of academic time seems to be a promising research area.

Brophy and Evertson also presented evidence that noncurricular interactions were negatively related to achievement. Within the high socioeconomic status classrooms, significant negative correlations with achievement were obtained for (a) frequency of teacher questions about self, (b) procedural contacts, as compared to substantive contacts, and (c) student initiated contacts involving personal concerns. For these three variables negative but nonsignificant correlations were also found for the students of low socioeconomic status.

Summary. Measures of total time spent in school, and supportive measures such as student absence and teacher absence, have yielded fairly consistent results suggesting that increased time in school is related to increased achievement. There is also the possibility that, for students of low socioeconomic status, too much time may be dysfunctional.

Stallings and Kaskowitz found that time spent by teachers on interactions regarding reading or mathematics materials was consistently and usually significantly related to achievement. Such clear

26. Thomas L. Good et al., *Teacher Behavior and Student Outcomes in the Missouri Teacher Effectiveness Study* (Columbia, Mo.: College of Education, University of Missouri, 1975).

results were not always replicated in other studies, even when the students also came from low socioeconomic backgrounds. Perhaps the other studies were deficient in the procedures for coding time spent; perhaps the results of Stallings and Kaskowitz are artifacts of the Planned Variations setting. More research is needed.

Finally, Brophy and Evertson presented data to suggest that some forms of direct instructional time are more functional than others and show differences between groups of different socioeconomic status on these measures of direct instructional time.

CONTENT COVERED

A variable closely related to time is the amount of content covered in school. This factor has also been called "student opportunity to learn." [27] It would appear, intuitively, that the amount of content taught would be strongly related to achievement. Despite the obviousness of this idea, there has been relatively little research on the topic and a good deal of research that did not take it into account. Although many studies have been conducted relating teacher behaviors and student achievement, only a few of these have attempted to measure the amount of content taught and to use such a measure as a predictor of achievement. Likewise, items on content covered do not appear on teacher evaluation checklists.

Measures of content covered were not reported in the three major recent studies already mentioned that dealt with low socioeconomic classrooms in the primary grades. In these cases, we have only the data on time to support the importance of content covered. In two prior studies of instruction for students of low socioeconomic status in the primary grades, however, the thirty-eight and twenty-six teachers computed the mean number of books read by their students during the individualized reading period.[28] This variable yielded positive results in both studies (mean $r = .27$ and .31) and was significantly correlated with one of the four criterion measures in reading in each year ($r = .37$ and .41). Estimates of the number of books partially read yielded inconsistent results.

In a review relevant to this topic, Walker and Schaffarzick surveyed twenty-three studies that compared new and traditional cur-

27. John B. Carroll, "A Model of School Learning," *Teachers College Record* 64 (May 1963): 723-33.

28. Harris et al., *A Continuation of the CRAFT Project.*

riculums.[29] They concluded that the outcomes of different curriculums were strongly determined by what content was emphasized by the curriculums. In general, the new curriculums were more effective than traditional ones when the posttest measured content relevant to the new curriculum, and the traditional curriculums were slightly superior when traditional posttests were used. Each curriculum seemed to be most effective when the posttest included the type of content emphasized in that curriculum. Further, because different curriculums emphasize different content, one does not gain much by comparing these curriculums. Walker and Schaffarzick also noted that, although the above conclusions appear obvious, such obviousness is *not* reflected in decisions about curriculum packages and textbooks.

Perhaps the most dramatic study of the importance of content was conducted by Pidgeon.[30] He compared the mathematics achievement of 3,000 eleven-year-old students in California with that of a similarly stratified sample of 3,000 eleven-year-old students in England. Of the 3,000 English students, 2,000 achieved a score above thirty-five on the seventy-five-item test, while only fifty-four of the 3,000 California students achieved a score above thirty-five. Pidgeon then inspected the mathematics textbooks used in the two countries and concluded that the material in the English textbooks was one to two years in advance of that in the California textbooks. He concluded that the English students were able to learn more mathematics because the teachers expected more learning from them, and these teacher expectations were reflected in the content covered.

Additional evidence on the importance of content comes from two studies conducted by the International Association for the Evaluation of Educational Achievement (IEA). In two cross-national studies, one in mathematics[31] and one in science,[32] the teachers were asked to look at the items on the test and to indicate

29. Decker F. Walker and Jon Schaffarzick, "Comparing Curricula," *Review of Educational Research* 44 (Winter 1974): 83-111.

30. Douglas A. Pidgeon, *Expectation and Pupil Performance* (Slough, Eng.: National Foundation for Educational Research in England and Wales, 1970).

31. Husén, *International Study of Achievement in Mathematics.*

32. L. C. Comber and John P. Keeves, *Science Education in Nineteen Counties* (New York: John Wiley & Sons, 1973).

the percent of students in the class who had had the opportunity to learn the material covered by each item. In both studies, there were strong positive correlations between opportunity to learn and student achievement when the results were aggregated by country. When results were aggregated by school, within country, only a few significant results were obtained in each study. The results within country are hard to understand, however, because the school, not the teacher, was the unit of analysis.

In the science study, correlations between opportunity to learn and science achievement (adjusted for home background variables) were computed within participating countries, first using schools as the unit and then using individual pupils. (Analyses were not made with teachers as the unit.) With schools as the unit, for fourteen-year-old students, significant positive correlations, ranging from .09 to .30, were reported for six of the fourteen participating countries.[33] In the United States, the correlation was .15. For students at the terminal grade level, significant results were not reported and presumably were not obtained. With students as the unit, "clear relationships" were also reported between opportunity to learn and adjusted achievement scores for about a third of the participating countries; most of these correlations, however, ranged from .04 to .06. Overall, there is some support for the correlational importance of opportunity to learn in the IEA science study,[34] particularly for fourteen-year-old students, but the overall results are not strong.

It is also possible to note the importance of content, and emphasis upon learning the content, by looking at studies within a curriculum or a course of study. Armento, Chang and Raths, Rosenshine, and Shutes all found significant relationships between their assessment of the content covered and student achievement.[35] In

33. Ibid., p. 221.

34. Ibid., p. 161.

35. Beverly Armento, "Correlates of Teacher Effectiveness in Social Studies" (Ph.D. diss., Indiana University, 1975); Sunnyich Shin Chang and James P. Raths, "The Schools' Contribution to the Cumulating Deficit," *Journal of Educational Research* 64 (February 1971): 272-76; Barak Rosenshine, "Objectively Measured Predictors of Effectiveness in Explaining," in *The Ability to Explain*, Technical Report No. 4 (Stanford, Cal.: Stanford Center for Research and Development in Teaching, 1968), ERIC ED 028 147; Robert E. Shutes,

the Armento study and the Rosenshine study, the correlations between content covered and achievement were larger than those
obtained for any of the observed teacher behavior variables. Similarly, the correlations between time and mathematics achievement
(or time and reading achievement) obtained by Stallings and
Kaskowitz were the highest correlations in their study.

Another approach to the importance of content and teacher
ability to cover appropriate content might be derived from the
study by Pellegrini and Hicks.[36] In this study, tutors worked individually with elementary school children. Three groups could be
compared to assess the expectancy effect. One group of tutors was
told that their tutees were of high ability and would make dramatic
gains in academic areas in the next few months, a second group
was told their students were of average ability, and a third group
was told their children were below average in ability. After seven-
teen weeks of tutoring, the children were retested on the Peabody
Picture Vocabulary Test (PPVT) and the Similarities Test of the
Wechsler Intelligence Scale for Children (WISC). There were no
significant differences between the three groups. A fourth group
of tutors was also told that their students were of high ability, and
these tutors were shown sample items from the PPVT and the
WISC Similarities Test. The children tutored by this group scored
significantly higher on the PPVT than the children in the three
other tutor groups, probably because the tutors' familiarity with
the instrument resulted in instruction in the specific skills necessary
for successful test performance. But this group did not perform
better than the others on the WISC, probably because the tutors
did not possess sufficient skills to teach the more complex reasoning
required by the items on this test.

A series of studies of trainees tutoring pupils for periods of
thirty minutes or less has also yielded mixed results. In these studies
the tutors were given fictitious information about their tutees—
information designed to induce a set for a low-achieving or a high-

---

"Verbal Behaviors and Instructional Effectiveness" (Ph.D. diss., Stanford University, 1969).

36. Robert J. Pellegrini and Robert A. Hicks, "Prophecy Effects and Tutorial Instruction for the Disadvantaged Child," *American Educational Research Journal* 9 (Summer 1972): 413-19.

achieving pupil.[37] In the studies by Beez, by Carter, and by Brown, the teachers attempted to teach more words to the "high-achieving pupils." In the Panada and Guskin study, there was no difference in the number of words taught. The results on the number of words learned were fairly consistent. Students learned more words in two of the three studies (those by Beez and Carter) in which they were taught more words.

In summary, the results of some of the above studies suggest that content covered, opportunity to learn, and a teacher's emphasis upon student achievement are important variables that merit continued study.

Walker and Schaffarzick went further and claimed that, against such powerful variables as content and emphasis, other variations such as teaching procedures have relatively less influence on outcomes.[38] A similar conclusion was reached by Dubin and Taveggia, who reviewed almost one hundred studies of methods used in teaching college courses. Over all studies, they found no consistent differences in the effects of the methods. They concluded that the similarities in content and textbooks among differently taught courses are too powerful to be washed out by the methods of instruction (lecture, discussion, independent study, and so on).[39]

The educational implications of the results on content covered and time spent are that what is taught and how long it is taught are at least as powerful as how something is taught. The power of these factors appears to emerge in situations in which they vary

37. W. Victor Beez, "Influence of Biased Psychological Reports on Teacher Behavior and Pupil Performance," *Proceedings of the Seventy-sixth Annual Convention of the American Psychological Association* (1968), pp. 605-6; Ronald M. Carter, "Locus of Control and Teacher Expectancy as Related to Achievement of Young School Children" (Ed.D. diss., Indiana University, 1969); Karen Panda and Samuel Guskin, "Effect of Social Reinforcement, Locus of Control, and Cognitive Style on Concept Learning among Retarded Children," mimeographed (Bloomington, Ind.: Center for Educational Research and Development for Handicapped Children, Indiana University, 1970); William E. Brown, "The Influence of Student Information on the Formulation of Teacher Expectancy" (Ph.D. diss., Indiana University, 1969).

38. Walker and Schaffarzick, "Comparing Curricula."

39. Robert Dubin and Thomas C. Taveggia, *The Teaching-learning Paradox: A Comparative Analysis of College Teaching Methods* (Eugene, Ore.: Center for the Advanced Study of Educational Administration, University of Oregon, 1968).

widely, as in different curriculums or the different models used in Planned Variation. In Planned Variation, for example, the percent of time that different models devoted to reading in the first grade ranged from 28 to 59 percent.

WORK GROUPINGS

There has been relatively little study of the relationship between the size of work groups and student achievement, although two of the three recent major studies have data on this topic. For Stallings and Kaskowitz, the results on children's work groups are rather consistent and somewhat surprising (see table 5).[40] Consistent, negative, and usually significant correlations with achievement were obtained for children working alone (singly or in an unsupervised group) and for the teacher working with one child or two. The only positive correlations occurred for teachers working with small groups (three to seven children) or large groups (eight or more children). In the first grade, either small or large groups yielded similar correlations; in the third grade, the results were positive and high only for teachers working with large groups. In the most successful programs in the third grade, children were spending about 45 percent of their time in large groups.

The results obtained by Soar on work groupings tended to parallel those of Stalling and Kaskowitz, although the number of significant results was not as high. Soar found that, for occasions when students were working in a group under the supervision of an adult, the correlations were positive and frequently significant; for occasions when students were working without the teacher, the correlations were negative and frequently significant.[41]

Thus, across two studies, one can conclude that the amount of time children eligible for Follow Through spend working independently of adult supervision will be negatively related to achievement. Such results clearly argue against having children engage in a variety of different activities at the same time. The results do not support "individualizing" and provide support, particularly in the

40. Stallings and Kaskowitz, *Follow Through Classroom Observation Evaluation.*

41. Soar, *Follow Through Classroom Process Measurement.*

TABLE 5

CORRELATIONS BETWEEN WORK GROUPS AND MEAN CLASSROOM
ACHIEVEMENT IN MATHEMATICS AND READING IN GRADES ONE AND THREE

Work Groupings	GRADE ONE		GRADE THREE	
	Mathematics	Reading	Mathematics	Reading
Two children working independently	−.22	−.28	−.36	−.32
Small group of children working independently	−.36	−.31	−.33	−.33
Small group of children working independently in mathematics	−.14	−.22	−.46	−.41
Small group of children working independently in reading	−.26	−.19	−.23	−.23
Teacher with one child	−.29	−.31	−.13	−.12
One child with any adult	−.20	−.26	−.15	−.16
Teacher with two children	−.26	−.30	−.38	−.37
Two children with any adult	−.19	−.21	−.32	−.21
Teacher with small group	.16	.23	−.30	−.39
Small group of children with any adult	.14	.19	−.41	−.41
Teacher with large group	.07	.15	.47	.54
Large group of children with any adult	.10	.09	.42	.48
Child self-instruction	.10	.29	.30	.17
Child self-instruction, academic	.26	.42	.37	.24
Child self-instruction, nonacademic	−.26	−.10	−.27	−.28

SOURCE: Stallings and Kaskowitz, *Follow Through Classroom Observation Evaluation.*

third grade, for the use of large groups. One possible explanation is that children at this age are more likely to attend to their task when they are being supervised. While teachers are with one or two children, they are unable to provide sufficient supervision for the remaining children. Thus, use of larger groups allows for more supervision.

An alternative explanation is that these results are artifacts of the types of programs in Follow Through. When program means are studied, there is a strong correlation between variables such as time on instruction, use of direct academic questions, and use of groups of eight or more. The tendency of these variables to correlate positively suggests that programs using the direct instruction approach tend to use all three of these major variables. Thus, the more intensive programs, which are also the most successful in reading and mathematics, also use large groups more than the other programs. Therefore, the success of large groups may reflect the effectiveness of the intensive, direct instruction approach, and it is possible that the direction instruction approach could also be successful using a more individualized approach. One critical variable appears to be development of procedures for maintaining student attention in the unsupervised work situation. At present, it would seem that, other things being equal, it is easier in the primary grades to maintain student attention in the large group setting than in the individualized setting.

TEACHER QUESTIONS

In the study by Stallings and Kaskowitz, positive and significant correlations with achievement were obtained for only one type of interaction: adult commands, requests, and direct questions that had an academic focus (see table 6).[42] In the third grade, such questions appeared most effective when directed at groups of eight or more children; in the first grade, direct academic questions were equally effective with all types of groupings. All other types of questions yielded consistently negative correlations with achievement. These included open-ended questions and direct questions that were not academic in focus.

Similarly, in the study by Soar, factors that had high loadings (.70 to .90) for convergent questions, drill, or questions with a single answer, usually correlated significantly with achievement.[43] Divergent and open-ended questions were never positively related to achievement.

Brophy and Evertson categorized academic questions into three types—choice, product, and process[44]—and these three appear to

42. Stallings and Kaskowitz, *Follow Through Classroom Observation Evaluation.*

43. Soar, *Follow Through Classroom Process Measurement.*

44. Brophy and Evertson, *Process-Product Correlations.*

TABLE 6

CORRELATIONS BETWEEN ADULT QUESTIONING AND STUDENT ACHIEVEMENT
IN MATHEMATICS AND READING IN GRADES ONE AND THREE

Forms of Adult Questioning	GRADE ONE		GRADE THREE	
	Mathematics	Reading	Mathematics	Reading
Adult academic commands, requests and direct questions—as received by children	.32	.44	.57	.35
Adult academic commands, requests, and direct questions to groups of children	.10	.29	.54	.51
Adult academic commands, requests, and direct questions to individual children	.23	.29	.30	.10
Adult nonacademic commands, requests, and direct questions to individual children	−.31	−.25	−.47	−.37
Adult open-ended questions to children	−.03	−.11	−.35	−.31
Adult open-ended questions to children, nonacademic	−.15	−.20	−.42	−.36

SOURCE: Stallings and Kaskowitz, *Follow Through Classroom Observation Evaluation.*

resemble the categorization of direct and open-ended questions studied by Stallings and Kaskowitz. Their analyses of these three types of questions yielded "mixed and conflicting findings." As Brophy and Evertson note, however, the procedure they used for classifying questions may have been a poor choice. Another indicator of type of question is their result on the percent of questions answered correctly, partly correct, or incorrectly. For low socioeconomic status classes, the percentage of correct answers usually correlated positively and significantly with achievement, whereas the percentage of wrong answers yielded significant negative correlations. If one assumes that the correct answers were usually responses to factual, direct questions, then their results match those of Stallings and Kaskowitz and of Soar.

Previous correlational studies on direct questions reviewed by Rosenshine and by Dunkin and Biddle have usually yielded nonsignificant results with a trend toward positive correlations.[45] In

45. Rosenshine, *Teaching Behaviors and Student Achievement*; Dunkin and Biddle, *The Study of Teaching.*

previous studies there were usually nonsignificant correlations for higher-level cognitive questions, and a trend toward negative (and some significant) results for questions on personal opinion or personal experience. Such results were consistent across different grade levels and types of tests. Thus previous results have not been as dramatic as those obtained by Stallings and Kaskowitz or by Soar, perhaps because there was more variation across the Follow Through settings than is found in regular classrooms.

Frequency of questions. Investigators of classroom instruction have usually gathered data on the importance of frequencies of questions. As noted above, Brophy and Evertson found that workbook activities were more functional than questions for classes of students of low socioeconomic status, and oral interactions were more functional in classrooms of students of high socioeconomic status.[46] Unfortunately, in his study of fourth- and fifth-grade classrooms of students with high socioeconomic status, Good found that workbook activities were more functional,[47] a result that is the opposite of that obtained by Brophy and Evertson.

The above pattern of inconsistent results across studies on the frequency of questions mirrors that of fifteen previous studies. Previous reviewers have noted that counts of the frequency of questions, and interchanges, have not shown consistent relationships to student achievement.[48] In sum, the overall pattern of questioning and seatwork need further investigation.

Experimental studies of questioning. In experimental studies, the usual question is whether some mixture of higher- and lower-level questions will yield improved achievement. In most of these studies, no significant results were obtained. Two recent studies on questions, formulated on the basis of reviews of the literature, were designed to avoid many of the criticisms of previous studies. In both studies the teachers were "semiscripted," in that they learned and practiced a script containing different proportions of higher- and lower-order questions.

46. Brophy and Evertson, *Process-Product Correlations.*

47. Good et al., *Teacher Behavior.*

48. Dunkin and Biddle, *The Study of Teaching*; Rosenshine, *Teaching Behaviors and Student Achievement.*

In the first study three conditions were used: 25, 50, and 75 percent lower-order questions with the remainder in each case being higher-order questions.[49] Significant results were obtained only for the factual tests, that is, no significant results were obtained for essay tests and multiple-choice tests of higher-level learning. For the factual tests, both the conditions with 25 percent and 75 percent factual questions were significantly superior to the 50 percent condition. Such a confusing result suggests that training teachers to use a higher percentage of higher-order questions will not provide any better results than leaving them alone. In the second study students of teachers asking 85 percent lower-order questions were superior to students of teachers asking 40 percent lower-order questions in terms of achievement on lower-order test items; the two groups did not differ in terms of student achievement on higher-order test items.[50]

Summary on teacher questions. The research on types of questions and student achievement remains confusing even after one reads recent studies that incorporated improved design features. The effects of higher-order questions are nowhere to be seen, nor are the effects of lower-order questions as clear as one would wish. And the few studies on ratios of higher- to lower-order questions have not been any more revealing.

The results are best stated as trends: lower-order questions tend to be positively related to achievement, higher-order questions tend to be unrelated, and personal questions tend to be negatively related.

We are left, as usual, with many suggestions for future studies and the unsettling realization that, when previous suggestions have been incorporated into new studies, the results have not been particularly productive. One suggestion would be that simply dividing questions into two types is inadequate and that more complex questioning typologies should be used in future studies. Another suggestion is that we also code the appropriateness of questions.

49. Meredith D. Gall et al., *The Effects of Teacher Use of Questioning Techniques on Student Achievement and Attitudes* (San Francisco, Cal.: Far West Laboratory for Educational Research and Development, 1975).

50. Stanford Program on Teaching Effectiveness, "A Factorially Designed Experiment on Teacher Structuring, Soliciting, and Reacting," multilith (Stanford, Cal.: Stanford Center for Research and Development in Teaching, 1975).

People who have observed instruction are frequently struck by a single higher-order question that appears appropriate, or by a series of higher-order questions that seem inept and perfunctory. This suggests that in future research a rating of appropriateness should be obtained along with the counting of types of questions. And the rating of appropriateness should be based on explicitly formulated rules.[51]

One must be impressed with the consistent and significant results obtained by Stallings and Kaskowitz and by Soar for the value of direct questions, and the fact that those studies were conducted within the Follow Through and Planned Variation programs. Those programs insured a wide variation in educational practice, and therefore the results are more trustworthy than those obtained in traditional classrooms where the variation across teachers is not as great as the variation across Follow Through models. But such optimism is heavily tempered by the results of the experimental studies of Gall et al. and of the Stanford Program on Teaching Effectiveness. These investigators also obtained a wide variation of behavior through the use of semiscripted teachers. Therefore, their apparently inconsistent results on the optimal proportion of higher-order questions is disheartening. One can argue that these two experimental studies were conducted over shorter time periods, used different criteria, and considered different types of students than did the Follow Through studies. It remains a puzzle, particularly because the results obtained by Stallings and Kaskowitz and by Soar are so intuitively appealing.

Another emerging issue is that of the proper role of teacher questioning in a lesson. Questioning as we usually conceive it—a central teacher interacting with a whole class—may not occupy much time in schools today. Calfee and Hoover found that the mean percentage of time spent on directed discussion ranged from only 9 to 14 percent in second- and fifth-grade classrooms. In contrast, the mean time spent on seatwork ranged from 42 to 62 percent.[52] Seatwork, of course, also provides questions on paper, but

51. David C. Berliner, *Impediments to the Study of Teacher Effectiveness* (San Francisco, Cal.: Far West Laboratory for Educational Research and Development, 1975).

52. Robert Calfee and Kathryn Hoover, "Reading and Mathematics Ob-

such questions are seldom, if ever, considered in the study of classroom instruction. Thus the role of teacher questioning and the role of seatwork questions need to be considered more fully in subsequent studies.

CHILD RESPONSES

In the study by Stallings and Kaskowitz the correlations of child responses with achievement correspond to those obtained for adult questions (see table 7). Child responses to direct academic questions had consistent and significant positive correlations with achievement. Other forms of child responses—nonacademic responses and responses to open-ended questions—had negative relationships. For third-grade students, the correlations for direct questions were highest when pupils were in large groups; for first-grade students, the correlations were equally high in small or large groups.

TABLE 7

CORRELATIONS BETWEEN CHILD RESPONSES AND MEAN CLASS ACHIEVEMENT IN MATHEMATICS AND READING IN GRADES ONE AND THREE

Forms of Response	GRADE ONE		GRADE THREE	
	Mathematics	Reading	Mathematics	Reading
Child responds, academic	.39	.38	.42	.15
Child extended responses, academic	.29	.21	.34	.27
Responds to open-ended questions	−.03	−.11	−.30	−.08
Child responds, nonacademic	−.26	−.19	−.41	−.30
Group responds to direct academic	.14	.22	.52	.34
Child responds to direct academic	.28	.21	.18	−.01

SOURCE: Stallings and Kaskowitz, *Follow Through Classroom Observation Evaluation.*

No other studies on *type* of child answer were found, but Brophy and Evertson coded the *correctness* of children's answers. They found that, for children of low socioeconomic status, the percent of correct answers had significant positive correlations with achievement and other correlations were weak or negative. In contrast, for children of high socioeconomic status, the percent

servation System: Description and Analysis of Time Expenditures," in *Beginning Teacher Evaluation Study: Phase II,* vol. 3, ed. Frederick J. McDonald (Princeton, N.J.: Educational Testing Service, in press), ch. 2.

of wrong answers yielded strong positive correlations, with other correlations being weak or negative. These results suggest that the difficulty of questions should be near the child's level of ability in classrooms with children of low socioeconomic status, whereas it is better to ask questions slightly above the child's level of ability in classrooms with children of high socioeconomic status. The classification used by Brophy and Evertson for coding the difficulty level of questions answered did not yield the same pattern.

No other studies were found in which the correctness of child answers was coded. Because of the significant findings and the strong social class differences obtained on this type of variable, the coding of the correctness of children's answers might well be pursued in future studies.

ADULT FEEDBACK

Stallings and Kaskowitz divided adult feedback into such types as praise and negative corrective feedback. Each type was further subdivided as to topic (for example, academic, behavior, other-task related). The results on adult feedback from all four contexts in the study by Stallings and Kaskowitz are shown in table 8.

There is a heartening consistency in these results. When the topic was academic (that is, involved reading or mathematics) nineteen of the twenty correlations were positive, and thirteen were significant. This positive correlation held regardless of the type of feedback, that is, even for negative feedback. Similarly, when the topic was "other tasks" (that is, tasks in other areas such as music, art, dance, or science), the correlations were almost always negative regardless of type of feedback. Feedback regarding behavior yielded mixed results.

Such results suggest that the *topic* of feedback (for example, academic or behavioral) is more important than the *type* of feedback (for example, positive or negative). They also suggest that, when time is spent on tasks other than reading or mathematics, whatever feedback is used will not be positively related to reading or mathematics achievement.

These results are also different from those usually obtained. In their reviews, Rosenshine and Dunkin and Biddle noted that most studies had shown no clear relationship between praise and achieve-

TABLE 8

CORRELATIONS BETWEEN ADULT FEEDBACK AND MEAN CLASS ACHIEVEMENT IN MATHEMATICS AND READING IN GRADES ONE AND THREE

Forms of Adult Feedback	Grade One		Grade Three	
	Mathematics	Reading	Mathematics	Reading
All adult acknowledgment to children	.28	.20	−.16	−.10
Academic acknowledgment...........	.34	.29	−.05	.14
Acknowledgment of behavior.........	a			
Other task acknowledgment..........		−.13		−.42
All adult praise......................	.36	.39	−.01	.25
Academic praise....................	.33	.37	.13	.36
Praise for behavior.................	.27	.36	.10	.16
Praise for other tasks..............	.12	−.06	−.33	−.30
All adult positive corrective feedback......		.38		.14
Positive corrective feedback, academic	.21	.44	.08	.34
Positive corrective feedback, for behavior.....................		−.04		−.27
Positive corrective feedback for other tasks......................	−.20		−.21	
All neutral corrective feedback..........	a			
Neutral corrective feedback, academic......................	.23	.23	.10	.30
Neutral corrective feedback, for behavior.....................	−.23		.19	
Neutral corrective feedback for other tasks.....................	−.34		−.22	
All adult negative corrective feedback......	a			
Negative corrective feedback, academic......................	.16	.15	.30	.38

SOURCE: Stallings and Kaskowitz, *Follow Through Classroom Observation Evaluation.*

[a] Results are reported only for rows in which at least one significant correlation was obtained. Blank rows mean that the correlations were lower than ±.19.

ment, that criticism was usually negatively related to achievement, and that acknowledgement or acceptance of responses was usually positively related to achievement.[53] Thus the results obtained by Stallings and Kaskowitz differed from the usual results on both praise and criticism.

Brophy and Evertson also coded teacher reactions to child responses. In contrast, they did *not* find that praise, criticism, or process feedback were significantly related to achievement for stu-

53. Rosenshine, *Teaching Behaviors and Student Achievement;* Dunkin and Biddle, *The Study of Teaching.*

dents of low socioeconomic status. But using unique observational categories, they found that each type of student answer had its optimal type of teacher response. Thus, for the low socioeconomic status classes, if the student answer was correct, the best teacher response was to ask a new question; if the answer was part correct, the best response was to give the answer. These results suggest a drill pattern containing little feedback and asking questions the students can answer. Such a drill pattern seems similar to that implied by the results obtained by Stallings and Kaskowitz and by Soar with similar samples. The identification of such a common drill pattern across these three studies may be more important than the noted differences in teacher use of praise or the differences among teachers in the level of difficulty of their questions.

Brophy and Evertson found a different optimal pattern for high socioeconomic classrooms. There, if the pupil's answer was correct, the best teacher response was to give process feedback (that is, show how the answer was found). If the answer was partly correct, the best response was to give the answer. And if the answer was wrong, the best response was to give criticism. Such criticism usually consisted of saying "wrong" and following this with an admonishing sentence such as "you should have gotten that." In contrast to the results for the low socioeconomic status classes, these results suggest that the high socioeconomic pupils benefited from a more demanding pattern with harder questions and feedback on how the answer could be found.

An interesting socioeconomic status difference emerged for all instances in which the student was unable to give the correct answer. For low socioeconomic status classrooms, calling on another student correlated negatively and significantly with achievement, whereas for high socioeconomic status classrooms it correlated significantly and positively. One explanation might be that pupils of higher verbal ability are better able to process information coming from more than once source, whereas for the pupils lower in verbal ability a structured small-step format controlled by the teacher is most beneficial.

In short, the value of different teacher reactions, such as praise or criticism, was not consistent across studies, perhaps because of differences in the coding categories. Nonetheless, it appears that a drill pattern is most functional for pupils of low socioeconomic status. Such a pattern contains questions a student can answer followed by short acknowledgement of correctness.

The Direct Instruction Model

As one looks over the findings on time, content covered, work groupings, teacher questions, student responses, and adult feedback, one sees a general pattern of results that might be labeled the direct instruction model (sometimes called a structured approach). In discussing this model, we shall limit our generalizations to teaching aimed at fostering reading and mathematics achievement in primary grade classes of children who are low in verbal ability and in socioeconomic status. The extent to which these generalizations need to be modified as one moves to other grade levels and contexts remains to be determined.

STRUCTURED LEARNING

Behaviors that might comprise direct instruction, or a structured approach, are measured in each of the observation instruments used by Soar. Factors on which direct instruction variables had high positive loadings usually had significant positive correlations with student achievement. In contexts where significant correlations were not obtained (notably, the entering first-grade classrooms), Soar noted that mean classroom scores on structuring tended to be higher than those of classrooms in other contexts. Thus, as Soar concluded, structuring tended to be significantly and positively related to achievement except for contexts in which it was already high.

The variables listed in the left-hand column of table 9 are those that appeared on the factors described as representing structured teaching. The description of structured teaching given below is based on these items. This description is intended to be merely suggestive. (One should note that each item that loads on a factor significantly related to student achievement is not itself necessarily significantly related to student achievement, and also that items in different factors may not be related to each other. Thus the description given below suggests a general picture for future research, rather than a list of significant and intercorrelated variables).

In direct instruction, the lessons and workbook activities are supervised by the teacher, and there is little free time or unsuper-

TABLE 9
STRUCTURING BEHAVIORS

Structuring	Opposite Pole
Percent time structured by teacher Formal physical arrangement	Pupil freedom Gamelike activities Art work Number of interest centers
Hours of structured learning with teacher	Hours of structured learning without teacher Hours of unstructured time
Teacher central Teacher directs without giving reason Pupil given no choice	Pupil free choice Pupil limited choice Pupil uses play object as itself Free work groups Frequent socializations
Teacher occupies center of attention Teacher expects pupil to come up with answer teacher has in mind Teacher expects pupil to know rather than to guess answer Teacher immediately reinforces answer as right or wrong Teacher asks another pupil to give answer if one pupil fails to answer quickly Teacher organizes learning around questions posed by teacher Teacher collects and analyzes subject matter for pupil Teacher approaches subject matter in a direct, businesslike way	Teacher makes pupil center of attention Teacher joins or participates in pupil's activities Teacher organizes learning around pupil's own problem Teacher approaches subject matter in an indirect, informal way Teacher encourages pupil to ex- press himself freely Teacher permits pupil to suggest additional or alternative answers
Teacher asks narrow question Drill Teacher elicits	Silence Pupil initiation

SOURCE: Robert S. Soar, *Follow Through Classroom Process Measurement and Pupil Growth, 1970-71, Final Report* (Gainesville, Fla.: College of Education, University of Florida, 1973).

vised desk work. The teacher is the dominant leader of the activities, decides what activities will take place, and directs without giving reasons. Teacher questions tend to be narrow, pupils are expected to know rather than to guess answer, and the teacher immediately reinforces an answer as right or wrong. The learning is organized around questions posed by the teacher or materials provided by the teacher, and it is approached in a direct and businesslike way.

At the opposite pole, that might be called "unstructured teaching," there are more pupil freedoms, gamelike activities, and art work. Play can be an object in itself. Pupils have free choice, free work groups, and frequent socialization. The teacher approaches learning in an informal manner, organizes learning around a pupil's own problem, encourages pupils to express themselves freely, and joins in pupil's activities.

In their study of Follow Through classrooms, Stallings and Kaskowitz obtained similar results relating to direct instruction. Their results are summarized in table 10. They found that, in the classrooms that achieved more in reading and mathematics, there were more teacher academic commands and direct questions, pupil academic responses, and teacher feedback on academic matters. The teacher also occupied the central directing role, and more class time was devoted to academic learning. One overall conclusion would be that, for the children of low socioeconomic status in these classrooms, academic learning is facilitated by direct, academic instruction. Moreover, both for Soar and for Stallings and Kaskowitz, none of the indirect activities (for example, arts and crafts, focus on child interests, or student and teacher discussion of how time will be used) had a positive relationship to student achievement.

In the study by Brophy and Evertson, three results, taken together, illustrate the importance of proceeding in small steps and using direct instruction for low socioeconomic status classrooms. What is also notable is that, for each variable, the results for children of high socioeconomic status were almost the opposite. These results indicated that (a) a high percentage of correct answers correlated positively with gain, suggesting the need for moving in small steps; (b) seatwork, individualized teaching, and teacher demonstrations were more functional than public questioning or focused discussions; (c) giving the student the answer when he did not know or giving him a phonics clue in reading was more functional than giving him feedback on how to solve something or giving him praise; and (d) when a student knew the answer, the best response was to ask another question rather than give detailed feedback or elaboration.

These results, and similar results throughout the report, suggest the importance for children of low socioeconomic status of moving in small steps through fairly structured materials with an emphasis upon supervised seatwork.

TABLE 10
Summary of Results Obtained by Stallings and Kaskowitz

Area	Positive Correlations with Achievement	Negative Correlations with Achievement
Materials	Textbooks and academic workbooks	Puzzles, games, toys, variety of different materials
Activities	Number and reading activities	Arts, crafts, stories, active play
Time spent	Time spent in mathematics, reading, and academic verbal interactions	
Groupings	Groupings of eight or more pupils with a teacher (grade three)	Children working alone
Child questioning		Child open-ended questions Child nonacademic comments
Adult questioning	Adult commands, requests, or direct questions that had an academic focus	Adult nonacademic commands, requests, or direct questions
Child responses	Child academic responses Child extended academic responses	Child nonacademic responses Child responses to open-ended questions
Adult feedback	All types of adult feedback that had an academic focus (i.e., acknowledgment, praise, positive corrective feedback, negative corrective feedback)	Adult feedback concerning other tasks (e.g., play, music, regardless of type)
Child self-instruction	Child self-instruction in academic areas	Child self-instruction in nonacademic areas
Conversation		Child general comments to adults or among children
Child behavior	Child task persistence	Child movement Child cooperation with another child

Source: Stallings and Kaskowitz, *Follow Through Classroom Observation Evaluation.*

SUMMARY OF ELEMENTS IN DIRECT INSTRUCTION

Table 11 presents a summary of positive elements in direct instruction and the suggested corresponding negative correlates. The variables are suggestive rather than definitive, but despite that disclaimer, they represent a convergence across similar studies conducted in primary reading and mathematics for children low in socioeconomic status and in verbal ability.

Summary

In this chapter, an attempt has been made to extend the previous reviews of relationships between classroom teaching variables and student achievement by presenting the latest results for six instructional variables and a general model of direct instruction. If one limits the generalization to primary level, low socioeconomic status classrooms in reading and mathematics—and if one gives strong weight to the Follow Through study by Stallings and Kaskowitz—several generalizations emerge:

1. Time spent on reading and mathematics instruction and time spent using reading and mathematics materials were positively related to achievement. Time spent on other activities or on students' personal concerns was negatively related.

2. Time spent by students working alone was usually negatively related to achievement, perhaps because student attention was lower in those settings. Small groups and groups of eight or more students were most functional.

3. A drill pattern consisting of questions that the students could answer, followed by feedback and subsequent questions, was most functional. But clear results were not obtained for various types of questions or types of teacher responses.

4. A pattern of direct instruction, consisting of small steps at the student's level and a great deal of work mediated by either the teacher or workbooks, all of which is directed by the teacher, appeared most functional.

5. The use of a "planned variation" program for classroom research appears to be particularly promising. But planned variation, as practiced in Follow Through, amounts to much more than installing four or five different methods and then collecting observa-

TABLE 11

A SUMMARY OF ELEMENTS IN DIRECT INSTRUCTION

Elements	Suggested Positive Correlates	Suggested Negative Correlates
Time and Activities	Time structured by the teacher	Time spent on arts, crafts, dramatic play, active play, stories
	Time spent on number and reading activities using textbooks and academic workbooks, or in verbal interactions on reading and mathematics	Gamelike activities Number of interest centers Large number of different, concurrent activities
	Time spent in seatwork with academic workbooks through which the pupils proceeded at their own pace	Hours of unstructured time Frequent socialization
Work Groupings	Students worked in groups supervised by the teacher	Free work groups Children working independently without supervision of teacher
Teacher Directions and Questions	Teacher directs activities without giving pupils choice of activities or reasons for the selection of activities	Teacher joins or participates in pupil's activities Teacher organizes learning around pupil's own problem
	Learning is organized around questions posed by the teacher	Teacher approaches subject matter in an indirect, informal way
	Teacher asks narrow question	Teacher encourages pupil to express himself freely
	Teacher asks direct questions that have only a single answer	Teacher permits pupil to suggest additional or alternative answers

TABLE 11 (continued)

A SUMMARY OF ELEMENTS IN DIRECT INSTRUCTION

Elements	Suggested Positive Correlates	Suggested Negative Correlates
	Adult commands, requests, or direct questions that had an academic focus	Pupil initiates activities
		Pupil has freedom to select activities
		Teacher commands and requests, nonacademic
		Teacher open-ended questions, nonacademic
Student Responses	Students give a high percentage of correct answers both in verbal interaction and in workbooks	Child open-ended questions and nonacademic commands
	Students are encouraged to attempt to answer questions (rather than saying "I don't know")	Adult nonacademic commands or requests, or open-ended questions
		Child nonacademic responses
		Child general comments to adults or among children
Adult Feedback	Teacher immediately reinforces pupil as to right or wrong	Adult feedback on nonacademic activities (e.g., play, music)
	Adult feedback had an academic focus	
	Teacher asks new question after correct answer	
	Teacher gives answer after incorrect answer	

SOURCES: Stallings and Kaskowitz, *Follow Through Classroom Observation Evaluation;* Soar, *Follow Through Classroom Process Measurement and Pupil Growth;* Jere E. Brophy and C. M. Evertson, *Process-Product Correlations in the Texas Teacher Effectiveness Study: Final Report* (Austin, Tex.: The University of Texas, 1974).

tions and outcomes. The Follow Through and Planned Variation programs are supervised by national sponsors, and many of these sponsors have had to work a number of years before their sites achieved adequate implementation of the intended teaching methods. Further, the instruments used by Soar, and particularly the one developed by Stallings, represent a number of years of development and refinement. The Harris study that began in 1964, the Soar study that began in 1970, and the Stallings and Kaskowitz study that began in 1972 all represent progressive development of the approach of combining both curriculum implementation and observational research. May the approach be fruitful and multiply.

6. Finally, an implication of some questions raised earlier should be made clear. Many of the variables found related to achievement may indeed have causal connections with achievement. Other variables similarly related to achievement may have merely incidental, or noncausal, relationships with achievement—relationships that arise merely because, in the Follow Through models or other programs studied, the causal and nonfunctional variables are tied together, or confounded, with one another. The task of determining which kind of variable has which kind of relationship (causal or noncausal) calls for analytic experiments in which the several variables are manipulated independently of one another. Such analytic experiments, with full or partial factorial designs, can unravel the ways of teaching and identify those that make a difference in student achievement. Until such experiments are performed, we shall not know whether, for example, working with large groups is itself desirable or merely correlates positively with achievement because it has been tied to an intensive, structured pattern of teaching that itself makes the desirable difference.

CHAPTER XI

Teachers' Decision Making

RICHARD J. SHAVELSON[1]

Decision making is pervasive in teaching. Descriptive studies have even suggested that "the list of instructional decisions made by classroom teachers is infinite."[2] Regardless of the actual number, decisions—sometimes conscious but more often not—are involved in almost every aspect of a teacher's professional life, especially in planning, implementing, and evaluating instruction.[3] Most, if not all teaching, then, is based on decisions made by the teacher after complex cognitive processing of available information.[4]

This characterization is idealized and probably attributes more rationality to teachers' behavior than is warranted. As Farr and Brown pointed out, ". . . most instructional decisions are made by forfeit; that is, by not recognizing that a decision can be made or by not being aware of possible alternatives. The usual forfeit 'decision' involves continuation of a practice whether or not it is the most appropriate procedure for the situation."[5] After observing

---

1. I am grateful to Nancy Dempsey, Richard Whitfield, and John Sutcliffe for their comments and criticisms of this chapter. I am especially indebted to Philip H. Winne, whose comments and criticisms were invaluable in developing my thinking about teachers' decision making. In all cases, I assume responsibility for errors of commission and omission.

2. Roger Farr and Virginia L. Brown, "Evaluation and Decision Making," *Reading Teacher* 24 (January 1971): 341.

3. John R. Dettre, *Decision Making in the Secondary School Classroom: Toward Preparing the Diagnostic Teacher* (Scranton, Pa.: Intext Educational Publishers, 1970); Madeline Hunter, "The Teaching Process," in *The Teacher's Handbook*, ed. Dwight W. Allen and E. Seifman (Glenview, Ill.: Scott, Foresman and Co., 1971).

4. Richard J. Shavelson, "What Is *the* Basic Teaching Skill?" *Journal of Teacher Education* 24 (Summer 1973): 144.

5. Farr and Brown, "Evaluation and Decision Making," p. 341.

science teachers, Strasser concluded that teachers decide when students are on the right track, when they are on the wrong track, and when the search for the solution to a problem has ended. But they let curriculum guides decide about theories and they let textbook authors and producers of educational materials decide about experimenting and data.[6] In developing a model of teaching from a decision-making perspective, however, our focus is on what could be rather than what is.[7]

Teaching as Decision Making

The contrast between teaching as decision making and traditional views of teaching can be illustrated by a scenario taken from research on technical skills of teaching in which interns (trainees) received training in technical skills (for example, questioning, reinforcing, probing) in a microteaching laboratory.[8] After training, the interns were videotaped in their classrooms.

One videotape showed an intern beginning a discussion with a question. (A question was chosen instead of another teaching act.) Several students responded by raising their hands. The intern called on one student. (The intern chose this student instead of others.) The student answered. The intern was dissatisfied with the answer. (A decision about the quality of the answer was made.) The intern asked the student a second question. (Given the student's response, the intern chose to question again.) The student did not respond. The student was asked a third question. (Again, a question was chosen.) Apparently distraught, he mumbled something. Eventually the intern relented and redirected his questions to other students. (The intern made a choice to redirect.)[9]

6. Ben B. Strasser, "A Conceptual Model of Instruction," *Journal of Teacher Education* 18 (Spring 1967): 63-74.

7. Lawrence M. Stolurow, "Model the Master Teacher or Master the Teaching Model," in *Learning and the Educational Process*, ed. John D. Krumboltz (Chicago: Rand McNally, 1965), pp. 223-47.

8. Frederick J. McDonald and Dwight W. Allen, *Training Effects of Feedback and Modeling Procedures on Teaching Performance*, Technical Report No. 3 (Stanford, Cal.: Stanford Center for Research and Development in Teaching, Stanford University, 1967); Robert L. Trinchero, "Three Technical Skills of Teaching: Their Stability and Effect on Pupil Attitudes and Achievement" (Ph.D. diss., Stanford University, 1975).

9. Shavelson, "What Is *the* Basic Teaching Skill?" p. 144.

In research on technical skills, the intern's "effectiveness" would probably be judged by the total number of "probes" or questions asked. But if we measured what the student learned, we might find that it did not correspond closely to what the intern intended. "The critical factor was the intern's decision or decisions to continue questioning the student instead of using some other basic skill such as 'explaining' or 'refocusing.' " [10] In considering teaching as decision making, then, one focuses on *when* a particular act is used and *which* act among other alternative acts is used, rather than on how often it is used.

FEATURES OF DECISIONS

In general, five features of decisions can be used to describe decision making in teaching, as shown in figure 1. One feature of a decision involves the choice of a teaching act from *alternative acts*. Alternatives might be individual teaching acts, sequences of teaching acts or microteaching methods, and macroteaching methods. In the scenario, the intern chose probing questions from a repertoire of teaching acts that might have included positive verbal reinforcement, factual questions, and silence.

A second feature, *states of nature*, refers to environmental conditions, which are not directly under the teacher's control but which influence the effectiveness of a particular course of action. These influences arise in or out of the classroom. Each possible state of nature occurs with some probability that is estimated subjectively by the teacher. The most important states of nature are the student's cognitive, affective, and social states. In the scenario, the intern might have thought it more probable that the student had completed and understood his homework (one possible state of nature) than that he had not understood the homework or had not done it (other possible states).

The third and fourth features are the *outcome* and *utility for the teacher* of a particular course of action under a particular state of nature. These two features are combined in figure 1 for reasons that will become apparent in the following discussion. The outcome feature means that at least one outcome can be identified for each

10. Ibid.

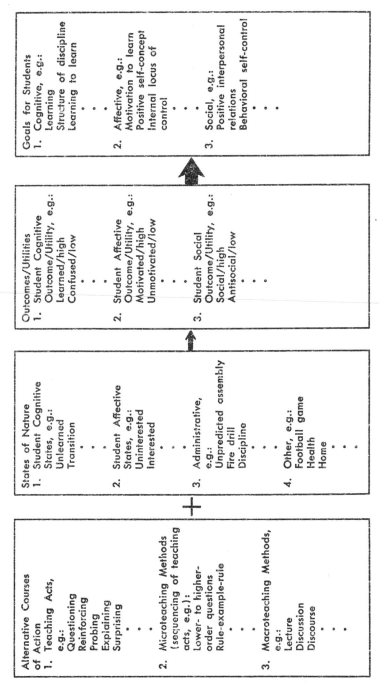

Fig. 1. Schematic representation of the elements in a decision

combination of a course of action with a state of nature. In the scenario, for example, the student may have learned to do his homework, to avoid raising his hand to answer a question, and to dislike the teacher. Quantitative measures such as achievement test scores might be used to represent an outcome. The magnitude of these scores, however, may not correspond to the teacher's subjective evaluation of the outcome. Furthermore, more than one outcome may be predicted, and some combination of their numerical values may not correspond to the teacher's subjective evaluation. Thus, by introducing the fourth feature, utility, a measure of outcome can be transformed to correspond to the teacher's subjective interpretation. In the scenario, probing questions were probably valued highly by the teacher to help his student "discover."

A fifth feature is the *goal* or set of goals the decision is intended to help attain. These goals may cover the domain of educational goals. Throughout this chapter, we deal with teacher decisions intended to optimize student outcomes (see figure 1). In the scenario, the intern's goal was perhaps to have his student "discover" something.

MODELS OF DECISION MAKING

The intern's decisions can be formally characterized as decision making under uncertainty,[11] and can be examined with concepts from statistical models of decision theory. But before doing so, a caveat is in order. Statistical models apply to situations in which sufficient time is available to carry out the five steps implied by the elements in decision making. In some teaching situations, formal models may be directly applicable. For example, in planning instruction, sufficient time and information are usually available to include all five steps. Or, in computer-assisted instruction, these formal models may have important applications.[12] But most situations in teaching do not readily correspond to statistical models. This chapter treats statistical models of decision theory as a heuristic for examining teachers' decision making.

11. R. Duncan Luce and Howard Raiffa, *Games and Decisions* (New York: John Wiley & Sons, 1967); David W. Miller and Martin K. Starr, *The Structure of Human Decisions* (Englewood Cliffs, N.J.: Prentice-Hall, 1967).

12. Richard C. Atkinson and J. A. Paulson, "An Approach to the Psychology of Instruction," *Psychological Bulletin* 78 (July 1972): 49-61.

In decision making under uncertainty, we assume that the intern has several teaching skills from which to choose the next teaching act. These alternatives might include questioning, reinforcing, explaining, refocusing, and so on. Each alternative is represented symbolically as A_1, A_2 . . ., A_i . . ., A_k in table 1. Suppose further that

TABLE 1

TEACHER'S DECISION MATRIX

Student Learning States / Alternative Teaching Acts	S_U[a] $\Pr(S_U)$[b]	S_M $\Pr(S_M)$	S_L $\Pr(S_L)$
A_1	u_{1U}	u_{1M}	u_{1L}
A_2	u_{2U}	u_{2M}	u_{2L}
A_3	u_{3U}	u_{3M}	u_{3L}
.	.	.	.
.	.	.	.
.	.	.	.
A_i	u_{iU}	u_{iM}	u_{iL}
.	.	.	.
A_k	u_{kU}	u_{kM}	u_{kL}

SOURCE: Adapted from Richard J. Shavelson, "What Is *the* Basic Teaching Skill?" *Journal of Teacher Education* 24 (Summer 1973): p. 145.

[a]S refers to a particular learning state of the student, that is, "unlearned" (U), "may have learned" (M), or "learned" (L).

[b]$\Pr(S)$ refers to the probability that a particular student is in that learning state. The probability is estimated subjectively by the teacher.

the intern's preference for a given teaching act depends on uncertain events such as the student's present state of learning. For ease of discussion, only learning states of nature are considered, but such other states as classroom interruptions or the student's attitude would also qualify. (See figure 1.) The student's possible states of learning might be "unlearned," "may be learned," or "learned." These states are symbolized as S_U, S_M, and S_L.[13] For each possible state of learning, the intern estimates the probability that the student is in that learning state. The probability is determined subjectively from information about the class as a whole and the student in particular. The subjective probabilities are symbolized in table 1 as $\Pr(S_U)$, $\Pr(S_M)$, and $\Pr(S_L)$, respectively. The intern's decision

13. The selection of three learning states is somewhat arbitrary, but it has a firm basis in mathematical learning theory, particularly in Markov models of learning. In table 1, S_U and S_L represent "guessing" and "completely learned" states of nature, respectively, while S_M represents a transition stage in learning.

problem, then, can be represented by a decision matrix (table 1) with rows as alternative teaching acts and columns as student learning states. For every cell in the matrix, there is an outcome. The intern then rank orders the cells according to some preferred outcome.[14] These preferred outcomes are represented as u_{ij} where u refers to utility, i refers to the ith alternative teaching act (a row of the decision matrix), and j refers to the jth state of nature (a column of the decision matrix).

At this point, the decision situation has been defined formally. The problem for the intern is to choose the teaching act (row) that is optimal in some sense. One strategy is the following. The value of each alternative teaching act can be represented as the sum:

$$[u_{iU} \times Pr(S_U)] + [u_{iM} \times Pr(S_M)] + [u_{iL} \times Pr(S_L)]$$

According to decision theory, the intern should choose the teaching act with the largest row sum. (For an example, see table 2.)

To describe the sequence of questions asked by the intern, each decision can be represented as a node on a decision tree. One possible representation of a decision tree is given in figure 2. The nodes on the tree are decision points; "the dotted lines represent options perceived by the teacher or an observer which were not selected, and the continuous line depicts what may be termed the teacher/ lesson vector. [On] either side of each node in the time dimension are (i) recognition or perception of a choice/decision situation . . . resulting from some stimulus or group of stimuli, . . . and (ii) action . . . arising from choice and/or decision." [15]

Several possible explanations might account for the intern's sequence of questioning and probing: the intern erred in estimating the student's learning state, the intern did not consider alternative questions or teaching acts, the intern misjudged the probable consequences of his teaching acts, the intern did not consider relevant information about the student's learning state before proceeding, or some combination of these.

Another scenario demonstrating a sequence of instructional decisions may help in understanding this kind of analysis of teachers' decision making.

14. Luce and Raiffa, *Games and Decisions*.

15. Richard C. Whitfield, "Teachers' Choices and Decisions inside the Classroom," *Australian Science Teachers Journal* 20 (November 1974): 83–90.

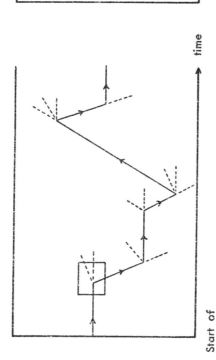

1. Stimulus or group of stimuli

2. Recognition or perception of a decision/choice situation

3. Choice or decision (see table 1)

4. Action taken in teaching

One Point in Time

time

Start of lesson

FIG. 2. Decision tree representing the sequence of a teacher's decisions.

NOTE: The box at the right shows the components of the box at the first node in the decision tree.

SOURCE: Adapted from Richard C. Whitfield, "Teachers' Choices and Decisions inside the Classroom," *Australian Science Teachers Journal* 20 (November 1974): p. 88.

When the teacher attempts to raise the level of thought very early in the discussion, this typically results in the children's returning to a lower level and in their inability to sustain discussion at the higher levels of thought. [The teacher inappropriately assigns a high utility to outcomes involving lifting questions and/or a high probability to a "learned" state of the student.] On the other hand, a strategy representing an effective pacing of shifting the thought onto higher levels seems to follow a characteristic course. [At each choice point assignment of utilities to outcomes of certain teaching acts and probabilities to states of nature should be as follows.] The level of seeking information is sustained for a considerable time during the first portion of the discussion. [Assign high utility to outcomes of such teaching acts as factual questions and explaining and high probability to the "unlearned" state.] Grouping is requested only after a large amount of information has been accumulated. [Now assign a high utility to outcomes with a higher-order question and a high probability to the learned state of nature.] The result is that in a fairly brief period, children transcend from grouping to labeling and then to providing reasons for labeling and to inferences.[16]

This sequence of decisions can also be characterized as a Test-Operate-Test-Exit sequence, or a TOTE unit.[17] (See figures 4 and 5.) The arrows in the figures represent the transfer of control from one component of the TOTE unit to the next. Shavelson applied the concept of a TOTE unit to Taba and Elzey's scenario as follows (see figure 5):[18]

The teacher begins by testing (T) whether the student has sufficient information available to group instances of a concept; for example, information available versus information needed. If the result is incongruity, that is, the information available is less than the information needed, the teacher moves to the *operate* (O) component. Here the *u* values assigned to his decision matrix [may] remain the same; he readjusts the subjective probabilities with respect to the student's learning state; he determines the optimal basic skill [teaching act], and then exercises that skill. At least four operations are carried out at the [operate] (O) component. A better representation of this component is a hierarchy of TOTE units.[19] The hierarchy, however, introduces complex-

16. Hilda Taba and F. F. Elzey, "Teaching Strategies and Thought Processes," *Teachers College Record* 65 (March 1964): 524-34.

17. George A. Miller, Eugene Galanter, and Karl H. Pribram, *Plans and the Structure of Behavior* (New York: Holt, Rinehart & Winston, 1960).

18. Shavelson, "What Is the Basic Teaching Skill?", pp. 146-47.

19. Miller, Galanter, and Pribram, *Plans and the Structure of Behavior*.

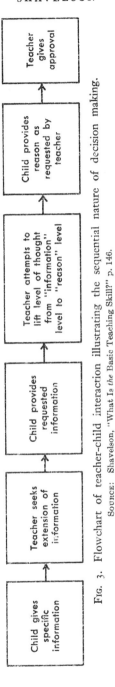

FIG. 3. Flowchart of teacher-child interaction illustrating the sequential nature of decision making.

SOURCE: Shavelson, "What Is the Basic Teaching Skill?" p. 146.

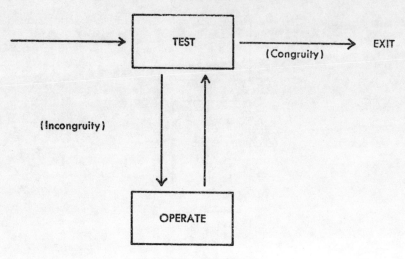

Fig. 4. The TOTE unit.
SOURCE: Shavelson, "What Is *the* Basic Teaching Skill?" p. 146.

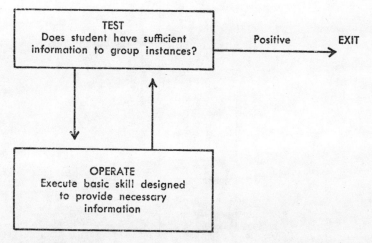

FIG. 5. Description of a sequence of decisions using the TOTE unit.
SOURCE: Shavelson, "What Is *the* Basic Teaching Skill?" p. 146.

ities beyond what is useful for the present discussion. Again, the teacher tests (T) whether the student has sufficient information. If the test result is congruity, that is, the information available equals or exceeds the information needed, the teacher *exits* (E) the phase, and moves to the next. The progress from phase to phase can be characterized as the teacher's plan (cf. the decision tree or Taba and Elzey's plan in the scenario above), with plan defined as "*any hierarchical process in the organism*

*that can control the order in which a sequence of operations is to be
performed. . . ."* [20]

TEACHING METHODS FROM THE DECISION-MAKING PERSPECTIVE

The two scenarios described in terms of the features of a decision illustrate what is meant by teaching as decision making in this chapter.[21] It is now possible to link an analysis of teaching as decision making to teaching methods.

Teaching methods may be defined as ". . . patterns of teacher behavior that are recurrent, applicable to various subject matters, characteristic of more than one teacher, and relevant to learning." [22] In the first scenario, the sequence of the intern's questions and probes, analyzed as a sequence of decisions, might be considered a pattern of teaching acts. This pattern seems applicable to various subject matters and may be relevant to learning. Bellack et al. suggest that the pattern might be recurrent and characteristic of more than one teacher.[23] The decision analysis of the first scenario and its link to teaching methods is not an isolated example. In a review of studies on interactive teaching, Shavelson found sequences of teaching acts described as recurrent patterns of teachers' behavior that could be analyzed as sequences of decisions.[24] It seems reasonable, then, to label a teaching method as a sequence of teaching acts that arise from a series of decisions a teacher has made.

The second scenario illustrates the sequential nature of decisions over an extended period of teaching. A portion of the teaching

20. Ibid., p. 16.

21. For other meanings that vary in similarity to this one see Alan J. Bishop and Richard C. Whitfield, *Situations in Teaching* (Maidenhead, U.K.: McGraw Hill, 1972); Arthur P. Coladarci, "The Teacher as Hypothesis-maker," *California Journal for Instructional Improvement* 2 (March 1959): 3-6; Frederick J. McDonald, *Educational Psychology* (Belmont, Cal.: Wadsworth, 1965); C. Kyle Packer and Toni Packer, "Cybernetics, Information Theory, and the Educative Process," *Teachers College Record* 61 (December 1959): 134-42; Shavelson, "What Is *the* Basic Teaching Skill?"; Ben B. Strasser, "Who Decides?" *Science Teacher* 34 (September 1967): 27-28.

22. N. L. Gage, "Teaching Methods," in *Encyclopedia of Educational Research*, 4th ed., ed. Robert L. Ebel (New York: Macmillan, 1969).

23. Arno A. Bellack et al., *The Language of the Classroom* (New York: Teachers College Press, 1966).

24. Shavelson, "What Is *the* Basic Teaching Skill?"

behavior might be characterized by an algorithm or computer sub-routine.[25] Once the decision is made to sustain "the level of information seeking," Taba and Elzey assume that the teacher is capable of initiating and sustaining a subroutine or habitual pattern of teaching acts. These subroutines may be considered teaching methods (microteaching methods in figure 1). In this case, then, the alternatives from which the teacher chooses are subroutines. Patterns of subroutines, such as classroom discourse, might also be considered teaching methods (macroteaching methods in figure 1).

What may be most important for research on teaching is not whether a particular teaching method should be used but *when* it should be used. Method A may produce the desired outcome in situations characterized by a particular state of nature. Under other states of nature, it may be deleterious. When states of nature are ignored, conditions under which a teaching method is effective are not differentiated from conditions under which it is not. One explanation, then, for the widely shared conclusion that teacher variables make little difference in student outcomes[26] is that teacher effects are neutralized when we simply measure use of a skill rather than *appropriate use*. The decision analysis emphasizes the latter perspective.

Furthermore, from the decision perspective, definitions of teach-

25. Lev N. Landa, "The Construction of Algorithmic and Heuristic Models of Thinking Activity and Some Problems in Programmed Learning," in *Aspects of Educational Technology*, ed. W. R. Dunn and C. Holroyd (London: Methuen & Co., 1969).

26. Robert Dubin and Thomas C. Taveggia, *The Teaching-learning Paradox: A Comparative Analysis of College Teaching Methods*, Monograph No. 18 (Eugene, Ore.: Center for the Advanced Study of Educational Administration, University of Oregon, 1968); Gage, "Teaching Methods"; Robert W. Heath and Mark A. Nielsen, "The Research Basis for Performance-based Teacher Education," *Review of Educational Research* 44 (Fall 1974): 463-84; Wilbert J. McKeachie, "Instructional Psychology," in *Annual Review of Psychology*, vol. 25, ed. Mark R. Rosenzweig and Lyman W. Porter (Palo Alto, Cal.: Annual Reviews, Inc., 1974), pp. 161-93; John D. McNeil and W. James Popham, "The Assessment of Teacher Competence," in *Second Handbook of Research on Teaching*, ed. Robert M. W. Travers (Chicago: Rand McNally, 1973), pp. 218-44; Barak Rosenshine and Norma Furst, "Research on Teacher Performance Criteria," in *Research in Teacher Education: A Symposium*, ed. B. Othanel Smith (Englewood Cliffs, N.J.: Prentice-Hall, 1971), pp. 37-72; Wilbur Schramm, "Learning from Instructional Television," *Review of Educational Research* 32 (April 1962): 156-67; Richard E. Snow, "Representative and Quasi-representative Designs for Research on Teaching," *Review of Educational Research* 44 (Summer 1974): 265-91.

ing methods are usually too general to describe adequately particular patterns of teaching behavior. This problem led Wallen and Travers to state that ". . . one man's 'lecture' may be another man's discussion."[27] No wonder research on teaching shows that variability within a teaching method often equals variability between teaching methods. To say the least, "the fact that teachers may manifest many separate and incompatible patterns of behavior makes research in this field particularly difficult."[28]

With this as background, three topics are explored in the remainder of this chapter. The first section focuses on teachers' abilities to perform the five tasks in making decisions and examines research relating to each. The second section describes a decision analysis of the preactive, interactive, and evaluative phases of teaching. The third section explores implications of the decision perspective for teacher training.

Before considering the decision analysis of teaching in detail, two caveats should be mentioned. The first is that a normative model of teaching—one that prescribes a standard of teaching—is being proposed. While reference will often be made to correspondence between the ideal decision model and actual school practice, the normative model will always be preferred to a purely descriptive model. One reason for this choice has been given by Stolurow: "The idea of modeling the master (teacher) has not worked. . . . Since there are probably fewer ways to teach effectively than to teach ineffectively, it is more likely that ineffective teaching behaviors would be identified in observational studies of teaching behavior."[29] Perhaps this tack will lead to a very much needed prescriptive model of teaching.

The second caveat is that, with few exceptions,[30] other descrip-

27. Norman E. Wallen and Robert M. W. Travers, "Analysis and Investigation of Teaching Methods," in *Handbook of Research on Teaching*, ed. N. L. Gage (Chicago: Rand McNally, 1963), p. 481.

28. Ibid., p. 463.

29. Stolurow, "Model the Master Teacher or Master the Teaching Model," p. 225.

30. Gavriel Salomon, "A Suggested Procedure for Training Teachers for Subjective Response Uncertainty Based on a Laboratory Application," *Journal of Teacher Education* 21 (Summer 1970): 244-50; Richard C. Whitfield and John Sutcliffe, personal communication, 1975.

tions of teaching from the perspective of decision making have not led to systematic, empirical study.[31] Most of the work on teachers' decisions has been limited to armchair theory. Although this chapter draws on the available empirical literature, the analysis should be viewed primarily as a heuristic for future research.

Abilities in Decision Making

The decision model assumes that a teacher chooses one teaching act or method from a set of alternatives in attempting to reach a goal or set of goals. The effectiveness or outcome of the chosen teaching method is influenced by states of nature that may arise. The teacher's problem is to select a teaching method that is most likely to be effective for the various states of nature that may exist.

From this formulation, several questions arise. To what extent can teachers identify alternative teaching acts? Can they estimate accurately the probability that each state of nature characterizes the learner? Can they estimate the probable outcomes of a particular teaching act under a particular state of nature? As will be shown, estimating the most probable outcomes poses the greatest problem for models of teacher decision making—a finding not uncommon in education.

ALTERNATIVE TEACHING ACTS

In a decision situation, the teacher has more than one teaching act or method from which to choose. Perhaps more important, the list of alternatives should be long enough to insure that a possibly effective option is not overlooked. Most research on decision models

31. Bishop and Whitfield, *Situations in Teaching*; Coladarci, "The Teacher as Hypothesis-maker"; McDonald, *Educational Psychology*; Alan J. Bishop, "Simulating Pedagogical Decision Making," *Visual Education* (November 1970): 41-43; idem, "Theory Application and Decision Making in Teacher Training," *Cambridge Journal of Education* 2 (Lent 1972): 50-61; F. Douglas Bowles, "Decision Making in Instruction," *Journal of Teacher Education* 24 (Spring 1973): 38-40; Farr and Brown, "Evaluation and Decision Making"; John R. Hill and William R. Martin, "Training for Educational Decision Making," *Journal of Teacher Education* 22 (Winter 1971): 443-47; Hunter, *The Teaching Process*; Greta Morine, "Planning Skills: Paradox and Parodies," *Journal of Teacher Education* 24 (Summer 1973): 135-43; Sa'omon, "A Suggested Procedure for Training Teachers"; Strasser, "Who Decides?"; Whitfield, "Teachers' Choices and Decisions."

has supplied the subject with a limited list of choices.[32] Seldom has the subject been free to invent his own options. This seems to be an important deficiency when translating the findings of such research to teaching. Teachers, as professionals, are free to generate their own teaching strategies. This lack of correspondence is a significant point to bear in mind in future discussions.

According to Salomon, some teachers ". . . behave as though the information they have obtained is sufficient, as though the alternative solutions they have generated account for all reasonable possibilities, and as though the chosen solution warrants high certitude."[33] In contrast, other teachers ". . . perceive quite adequately the number of choice alternatives embodied in the problem; consequently they study it very closely, generate many response alternatives, take a long time to decide on the most appropriate solution and reserve their decision. . . ."[34] Karlins and Lamm suggest that the latter teachers search for additional information to improve their estimates of which choice is likely to be most beneficial.[35] Thus, teachers are capable of considering alternative choices of teaching

32. Amnon Rapoport and Thomas S. Wallsten, "Individual Decision Behavior," in *Annual Review of Psychology*, vol. 23, ed. Paul H. Mussen and Mark R. Rosenzweig (Palo Alto, Cal.: Annual Reviews, Inc., 1972), pp. 131-76.

33. Salomon, "A Suggested Procedure for Training Teachers," 244. See also idem, "Interaction of Communication Medium and Two Procedures of Training for Subjective Response Uncertainty of Teachers" (Ph.D. diss., Stanford University, 1968); Nathan C. Claunch, "Cognitive and Motivational Characteristics Associated with Concrete and Abstract Levels of Conceptual Complexity" (Ph.D. diss., Princeton University, 1964); Joan E. Sieber, "Problem Solving Behavior of Teachers as a Function of Conceptual Structure," *Journal of Research in Science Teaching* 2, no. 1 (1964): 64-68; idem, "Lessons in Uncertainty," *Elementary School Journal* 69 (March 1969): 304-12; idem, *Individual Differences in Decision Making*, Research Memorandum No. 23 (Stanford, Cal.: Stanford Center for Research and Development in Teaching, Stanford University, 1968).

34. Salomon, "A Suggested Procedure for Training Teachers," p. 244; Joan E. Sieber and John T. Lanzetta, "Conflict and Conceptual Structure as Determinants of Decision Making Behavior," *Journal of Personality* 32 (December 1964): 622-41; idem, "Some Determinants of Individual Differences in Predecision Information-Processing Behavior," *Journal of Personality and Social Psychology* 4 (November 1966): 561-71.

35. Marvin Karlins and Helmut Lamm, "Information Search as a Function of Conceptual Structure in a Complex Problem-Solving Task," *Journal of Personality and Social Psychology* 5 (April 1967): 456-59.

methods, but they probably differ considerably in their ability to do so. Salomon and Sieber and Lanzetta showed that teacher trainees and college students can be trained to increase the number of alternative actions they consider in reaching a decision.[36] Unfortunately we have few criteria for judging whether a longer list of alternatives is more likely to contain better choices for teaching. Nor do there exist guidelines that teachers trained to generate (or recognize) alternatives can use to judge the probable effectiveness of these alternatives. Both issues warrant considerable attention in future research.

STATES OF NATURE

As noted earlier, states of nature are conditions that influence the effects of teaching but cannot be controlled directly by the teacher. In decision theory, the decision maker reviews available information on the possible states of nature and then estimates the probability that they will occur. Since information about the learner's states of nature is likely to be incomplete and inaccurate, the teacher must use available information to make an estimate of the probability that each possible state of nature will occur. Obviously, such estimates are subjective.

The critical question, then, is "How good are teachers at estimating the probability that a particular state of nature will occur?" Since no research has been done on this question, we consider first the ability of people—specifically, college sophomores enrolled in psychology classes—to estimate states of nature from limited information. A review by Peterson and Beach found that subjects' estimates of statistical parameters from sample data were extremely accurate.[37] The "goodness" of these estimates, however, varied systematically with such factors as sample size (the larger the sample, the better the estimate) and the population standard deviation (the smaller the standard deviation, the more accurate the estimate). In short, people operated somewhat like models underlying inferential

36. Salomon, "Interaction of Communication Medium and Two Procedures of Training"; Sieber and Lanzetta, "Some Determinants of Individual Differences."

37. Cameron R. Peterson and Lee Roy Beach, "Man as an Intuitive Statistician," *Psychological Bulletin* 68 (July 1967): 29-46.

statistics. But subjects tended to be considerably more conservative than the available information warranted. In other words, subjects' intuitive judgments were too conservative—they overestimated the lower boundaries and underestimated the upper boundaries of probability—because they failed to use all the information available in the environment.

An important series of studies further described the accuracy of individuals acting as intuitive statisticians.[38] They reported that ". . . people rely on a limited number of heuristic principles which reduce the complex tasks of assessing probabilities and predicting values to simpler judgmental operations. In general, these heuristics are quite useful, but sometimes they lead to severe and systematic errors."[39] Three heuristic principles have been identified: representativeness, availability, and adjustment and anchoring. According to the heuristic of representativeness, the estimate of the probability that A belongs to B depends on the degree to which A resembles B. For example, when a description of a student matches the stereotype of a slow learner, even if the description is unreliable, incomplete, or outdated, people often predict with high certainty that the student is a slow learner. In the context of teaching, Kahneman and Tversky gave students several paragraphs to read, each describing a student teacher during a practice lesson. One group of students was asked to judge the quality of the lesson. Another group was asked to predict the hypothetical teachers' performance five years in the future. Although the students were aware of limitations in making long-range predictions of teacher effectiveness from one observation, the judgments of both groups did not differ.

The second heuristic, availability, refers to the ". . . ease with which instances or occurrences can be brought to mind. For example, one may assess the risk of heart attack among middle-aged

38. Daniel Kahneman and Amos Tversky, "Subjective Probability: A Judgment of Representativeness," *Cognitive Psychology* 3 (July 1972): 430-54; idem, "On the Psychology of Prediction," *Psychological Review* 80 (July 1973): 237-51; Amos Tversky and Daniel Kahneman, "Belief in the Law of Small Numbers," *Psychological Bulletin* 76 (August 1971): 105-10; idem, "Availability: A Heuristic for Judging Frequency and Probability," *Cognitive Psychology* 5 (September 1973): 207-32; idem, "Judgment under Uncertainty: Heuristics and Biases," *Science* 185 (1974): 1124-31.

39. Tversky and Kahneman, "Judgment under Uncertainty," p. 1124.

people by recalling such occurrences among one's acquaintances." [40] Thus Chapman and Chapman presented naive subjects with information about hypothetical mental patients—information that included a clinical diagnosis and a drawing of a person made by the patient.[41] The subjects then estimated the co-occurrence of each diagnosis with various features in the drawing. Even when the correlation between a diagnosis and a feature of the drawing was actually negative, the judges overestimated the co-occurrence of stereotypically linked diagnoses and features such as suspiciousness and peculiar eyes.[42]

Finally, the heuristic of adjustment and anchoring describes how people ". . . make estimates by starting from an initial value that is adjusted to yield the final answer. The initial value . . . may be suggested by the formulation of the problem, or it may be the result of a partial computation. In either, adjustments are typically insufficient." [43] Subjects were asked to estimate percentages of African countries in the United Nations. Subjects were given an initial starting percentage, determined at random by the experimenter, and asked to indicate whether the actual percentage was above or below the starting value. Then they were asked to estimate the actual percentage. Groups of students beginning at either 10 percent or 65 percent estimated the actual percentage of African nations to be 25 and 45 respectively.

In summary, people are moderately good at estimating outcomes when given limited information about a simple situation. Apparently, they use a limited number of heuristics—for example, representativeness, availability, adjustment and anchoring—to reduce information overload in estimating states of nature. While these heuristics help people deal with complex environments, they also lead to predictable biases. These biases generate errors in estimating probabilities of various states of nature.

40. Ibid., p. 1127.

41. Loren J. Chapman and Jean P. Chapman, "Genesis of Popular but Erroneous Psychodiagnostic Observations," *Journal of Abnormal Psychology* 72 (June 1967): 193-204.

42. Tversky and Kahneman, "Judgment under Uncertainty," p. 1128.

43. Ibid.

Nothing is known about teachers' ability to estimate the probability of various states of nature relevant to classroom teaching. Furthermore, it is hazardous to generalize the results of prior research to teachers operating in classroom situations. The information available to teachers is not nearly as reliable as that given to subjects in these experiments. Also, the complexity of the teaching situation is much greater than that of the experimental setting. Finally, the information available to teachers varies in unknown ways from that which experimenters have chosen for research investigations.

At present, the best guess probably is that teachers' estimates of states of nature are moderately inaccurate and susceptible to predictable errors in judgment. The degree of inaccuracy and the magnitude of the bias introduced by errorful heuristics in estimating states of nature are matters that warrant considerable attention in future research.

ESTIMATES OF OUTCOMES FOR DECISION ALTERNATIVES

For each combination of a particular teaching act or method with a particular state of nature, an outcome can be predicted. Each outcome has some degree of *utility* to the teacher. Utility represents a numerical estimate of the value of, or preference for, a particular outcome. It must be defined in subjective terms, specific to the individual decision maker. And ". . . even for those objectives which seem to have a natural measure (profit in dollars, for example) it does not follow that the obvious measure is a measure of utility to the decision maker." [44]

The measurement of utilities is controversial. [45] In obtaining estimates of utilities, several restrictive assumptions are made. [46] For example, preferences for various alternatives should be transitive: if A is preferred to B and B to C, A should be preferred to C. Some of the assumptions find correspondence in human behavior and

44. Miller and Starr, *The Structure of Human Decisions*, p. 72.

45. Rapoport and Wallsten, "Individual Decision Behavior."

46. For a review of assumptions and problems, see Gordon M. Becker and Charles G. McClintock, "Value: Behavioral Decision Theory," in *Annual Review of Psychology*, vol. 18, ed. Paul R. Farnsworth, Olga McNemar, and Quinn McNemar (Palo Alto, Calif.: Annual Reviews, Inc., 1967), pp. 239-86.

some do not.[47] And, in cases such as the dominance or "sure-thing" outcome, the assumptions can be considered unreasonable with reference to human behavior.[48]

For present purposes, the value of estimating utilities in decision making results from their usefulness in showing that teachers should consider the consequences of each alternative teaching act under each possible state of nature. Problems of measurement aside, this means that teachers' objectives should be stated in precise, observable terms so that the utility of possible outcomes can be judged against a tangible standard for comparison.

Decisions Intended to Optimize Student Outcomes

In this section, analyses are made of teachers' decisions in pre-active, interactive, and evaluative phases of teaching. Throughout we assume that teachers' decisions are intended to optimize student outcomes. Of course, the particular type of outcome may change from time to time, and teachers may differ on the kinds of outcomes they seek. This may be a naive assumption. Whitfield pointed out that teachers often make decisions intended to minimize their personal stress. In some cases, ". . . stress may result from an awareness of the teacher's inability to optimize students' outcomes, and one way of looking at this is to say that a teacher will seek to maximize the overlap between his aims and the student's behavior by shifting to a greater or lesser extent both of these."[49] In other cases, choosing teaching acts that minimize personal stress may not optimize student outcomes.

DECISIONS DURING INSTRUCTIONAL PLANNING

Decisions made while planning instruction may be the most important ones teachers make. Unlike decisions during interactive teaching, decisions made in planning can be pondered—they have the advantage of time.

Since the teacher is an instructional designer in this phase of

47. Ibid.; Donald M. Johnson, *Systematic Introduction to the Psychology of Thinking* (New York: Harper and Row, 1972); Rapoport and Wallsten, "Individual Decision Behavior."

48. Becker and McClintock, "Value: Behavioral Decision Theory."

49. Richard C. Whitfield, personal communication, 1975.

teaching, recommendations for the design of instruction taken from models of learning and instruction should help identify decision options available in teaching. Such recommendations generally include four common elements.[50] First, features of students' learning that are to result from instruction, that is, outcomes, are stated explicitly as observable student behavior. Second, the student's present capabilities or entry behaviors are identified. Third, an instructional sequence is planned that most likely will move the student from his present capabilities toward the instructional outcomes. The sequence of instructional events is derived from whatever model of learning and motivation the teacher has adopted. Fourth, the outcomes of instruction are evaluated. This information forms the basis for decisions made in designing the next cycle of instruction.

While recommendations for designing instruction have not been cast into a decision model in previous research, this can be done as follows. Explicitly specifying outcomes of instruction is equivalent to specifying goals in decision analysis. Identifying the student's present capabilities or entry behavior in instructional design parallels determining states of nature and their corresponding probabilities of occurrence. This step uses information about the student obtained from published tests, from classroom tests and assignments, from the teacher, from experience, and so on. Specifying alternative instructional sequences and their component events that may achieve the instructional objectives in instructional design corresponds to the alternative courses of action in decision analysis. The alternative courses of action are identified from models of learning and memory, models of motivation and personality, and from the teacher's experience in teaching. Estimates of outcomes using different instructional sequences under various states of nature are based on knowledge from research, on the teacher's prior experience in similar situations, and on the teacher's value judgments. Finally, evaluating the correspondence between intended and actual instructional outcomes is equivalent in both schemes.

50. Richard C. Anderson and Gerald W. Faust, *Educational Psychology* (New York: Dodd, Mead and Co., 1973); Robert M. Gagné and Leslie L. Briggs, *Essentials of Learning for Instruction* (Hinsdale, Ill.: Dryden Press, 1974); Robert Glaser and Lauren B. Resnick, "Instructional Psychology," in *Annual Review of Psychology*, vol. 23, ed. Mussen and Rosenzweig, pp. 207-76.

Admittedly, this is a rather superficial treatment of the correspondence between decision analysis and instructional design. Many intricacies of instructional design and decision analysis have been ignored. One of the few examples of applying a decision model to instructional planning is the work of Atkinson and Paulson.[51] Atkinson used a decision model in designing computer-assisted instruction (CAI) in vocabulary. The objective of the CAI program was to teach a student the correct response to each word in a vocabulary list in a fixed number of days. On each day, a sublist of items from the total vocabulary list was presented, each item appearing only once. The instructional sequence consisted of presenting each item, soliciting the student's response, and, if the student's response was wrong, presenting the correct response for the student to study. Once the subset of items was determined for a given day, the items were presented in a random order. After the predetermined number of days, instruction was terminated, and students received a posttest covering the total vocabulary list.

The decision problem was that of choosing between alternative strategies for selecting sublists from the total list to maximize students' performance on the posttest. Five elements comprised this decision problem: (a) identifying the states of nature—learning states of the student; (b) specifying alternative courses of action— alternative ways of choosing each day's subset of vocabulary words; (c) estimating the new state of nature that results from a particular action, for example, the probability that a student will move from an unlearned to a learned state; (d) costing each action—the cost assumed to be equal over alternatives in this instance; and (e) the return or utility of pairing an instructional action with a state of nature—the distance between the actual and intended outcome of a particular course of action under a particular state of nature.[52]

A model of the learning of vocabulary items is needed to solve the decision problem. Atkinson identified three such models: the incremental model, the all-or-none model, and the random trial increments model. For present purposes, only the first two models will be discussed. Under the incremental model, the probability

51. Atkinson and Paulson, "An Approach to the Psychology of Instruction."
52. Ibid.

that a student will err on a given vocabulary item depends solely on the number of times that item has been presented. The more presentations, the greater the probability that the student will have learned the word. The following procedure for selecting a sublist from the total list of vocabulary words is optimal: "On a given day, form the sublist of M items by selecting those items that have received the fewest presentations up to that point. If more than M items satisfy this criterion, then select items at random from the set satisfying the criterion."[53]

Under the all-or-none model, the student is assumed to be in one of two states with respect to an item—learned all or unlearned. If the student is in a learned state, his response will always be correct. If he is in an unlearned state, he always responds incorrectly, unless he guesses correctly. When an unlearned item is presented, the student can move into the learned state with a certain probability. Thus, learning of the whole list appears to be gradual, but learning a particular item occurs on some particular trial. Once an item has been learned, it is assumed it cannot be forgotten. Thus, there is no reason to present it again.

Under the all-or-none model,

The optimal strategy [for selecting a subset of M items] requires that for each student a bank of counters be set up, one for each word in the list. To start, M different items are presented each day until each item has been presented once and a zero has been entered in its counter. On all subsequent days, the strategy requires that we conform to the following two rules:

1. Whenever an item is presented, increase its counter by one if the subject's response is correct, but reset it to zero if the response is incorrect.
2. Present the M items whose counters are lowest among all items. If more than M items are eligible, then select randomly as many items as are needed to complete the sublist of size M from those having the same highest counter reading, having selected all items with lower counter values.[54]

The instructional design and decisions about alternative courses of action have now been specified. The problem is to choose be-

53. Ibid., p. 54.
54. Ibid.

tween the two strategies for constructing sublists of items for presentation on a particular day. Data collected by Atkinson and Crothers suggest that the all-or-none model represents a better strategy than the incremental model.[55] (The random trial increments model was shown to be the best strategy under the conditions described above. The optimal strategy depends, however, upon the constraints placed on the instructional design.)[56]

In summary, teachers' instructional planning can be characterized as a problem in instructional design that can be described as a decision problem. In the simplest case, the decision problem involves (a) specifying the outcomes of instruction, (b) specifying instructional design alternatives, (c) specifying students' entry behavior, (d) estimating the outcome of each combination of an instructional alternative and a state of nature, (e) choosing the optimal course of action, and (f) evaluating instruction by observing student behavior.

DECISIONS DURING INTERACTIVE TEACHING

Decisions made while the teacher is interacting with students may be planned, extemporaneous, or a mixture of both. Most interactive decisions are probably modifications of decisions made in planning for instruction. But the modifications in the earlier decisions are made on the spur of the moment. This means that factors bearing on decisions made during interactive teaching probably are not defined as completely or accurately as those on which preactive decisions are based, since less than an optimal number of alternative strategies are considered. Even less perfect estimates of student learning states are available. And there is little time to consider the range of possible outcomes of different teaching methods under various states of nature. Under these conditions, a poor decision may result. An error made during interactive teaching, however, is probably not costly if it is perceived and if an immediate attempt is made to remedy the error. The temporal demands on interactive

55. Richard C. Atkinson and Edward J. Crothers, "A Comparison of Paired-Associate Learning Models Having Different Acquisition and Retention Axioms," *Journal of Mathematical Psychology* 1 (July 1964): 285-315.

56. Atkinson and Paulson, "An Approach to the Psychology of Instruction," p. 55, footnote 2.

teaching decisions, then, do not create an impossible situation. Furthermore, an adaptive teaching strategy based on a sequence of TOTE units is likely to be beneficial to student outcomes, especially as the teacher acquires skills in assessing states of nature and matching teaching methods to these conditions.

A decision analysis of interactive teaching takes the following form. As before, *goals* in decision analysis correspond to the teacher's instructional objectives. At a given point in interactive teaching, the goal might be as specific as eliciting a particular response from a student or as general as instilling a positive attitude toward the content of a lesson.

The *states of nature* of particular concern during interactive teaching are the knowledge and motivation of students relative to that which is needed to begin or continue learning at a particular point in the lesson. Which one or more of these states—knowledge and motivation—is most important in making the decision will depend upon the teacher's objectives and the relative influence of these states on achievement of the objectives. For example, the beginning of a lesson may stress motivational objectives to get the students interested, and corresponding states of students' motivation would be of concern. Later in the lesson, when cognitive or performance skills are the objectives, cognitive or psychomotor states of nature may be given priority.

Alternative courses of action refer to the teacher's repertoire of teaching acts or methods. The *utility* of a particular teaching act or method represents the teacher's best judgment about the result of using a particular teaching method when students are in a particular state of learning. The judgment is based on the teacher's prior experience in similar situations, on the teacher's philosophy of teaching, and on the teacher's formal knowledge of learning and motivation.

Finally, the outcome of the decision, or the consequence of acting on the decision, is student performance. This performance is compared with the objective the teacher intended to achieve in order to evaluate the decision and to reestimate the student's state of learning. The teacher is involved in continuous decision making that can be generally characterized as a sequence of TOTE units.

The application of decision analysis to interactive teaching is illustrated by Stanley Nicholson's study of sequences of teaching acts.[57] In examining protocols of sequences of higher- and lower-order questions, Nicholson attempted to identify a transition from one type of question to the other. He found consistent patterns of lower- and higher-order questions at the beginning of a lesson. Most teachers began a lesson with lower-order questions and then shifted to higher-order questions.[58] The exact point at which this transition was made varied from teacher to teacher. Consistent patterns of questioning were not found in the middle or at the end of the lesson.

From the decision perspective, Nicholson's study can be characterized as follows. The goals of instruction were cognitive; perhaps they could be characterized as synthesis or evaluation.[59] Nicholson examined teachers' choices from only two alternative courses of action: asking lower-order questions or asking higher-order questions. Since consistent patterns of questions were found only at the beginning of a lesson, it seems reasonable to assume that teachers judged students to be in an unlearned state when they used this pattern of questioning. A subjective estimate of the probability that this was the pupils' learning state might be .95. Thus, the probability of the learned state was .05. The decision situation involving the two alternative teaching acts and the probabilities for students' learning states is shown in table 2. The four cells in the table are ranked according to their expected outcomes in relation to the teacher's objectives. If the student is in the unlearned state, a lower-order question is the better question because it aids the teacher in identifying exactly what the student does not know. A higher-order question covering a wider range of material gives the teacher little information about specifically what the student needs to learn. Thus, the utility or value of a lower-order question ranks higher than the utility of a higher-order question when the student is in an unlearned state. This is shown in table 2 as a rank of two utility units for a lower-order question versus a rank of one utility

57. Stanley Nicholson, personal communication.

58. Taba and Elzey, "Teaching Strategies and Thought Processes."

59. Benjamin S. Bloom et al, *Taxonomy of Educational Objectives, Handbook I: The Cognitive Domain* (New York: David McKay Co., 1956).

TABLE 2

HYPOTHETICAL DECISION MATRIX FOR NICHOLSON'S DATA
ON SEQUENCES OF TEACHERS' QUESTIONING AT THE
BEGINNING OF TEACHER-STUDENT INTERACTIONS

Alternative Basic Skills	UTILITY[a]		Sum of Products of Ranks and Probabilities
	Unlearned (Probability = .95)	Learned (Probability = .05)	
Lower-order question	2	1	1.95
Higher-order question	1	2	1.05

SOURCE: Adapted from Richard J. Shavelson, "What Is the Basic Teaching Skill?" *Journal of Teacher Education* 24 (Summer 1973): p. 148.

[a]Utility of each of the four outcomes entered in each of the four cells as ranks.

unit for a higher-order question. In contrast, this logic is reversed if the student is in a learned state. For the latter condition, a rank of two utility units is assigned to the higher-order question, while a rank of one utility unit is given to the lower-order question. The expected utility of the lower-order question is given by:

$$(u_{iU} P_U) + (u_{iL} P_L)$$

where u is the ranking, P is the subjective probability of the student's learning state, U is the unlearned state, and L the learned state. The expected utility (row sum) of the lower-order question is greater than the expected utility of the higher-order question. The teacher, then, should choose the lower-order question.

As students begin to answer more and more lower-order questions, the teacher readjusts the subjective estimates of the students' learning state. A transition is made when the expected utility of a higher-order question exceeds that of a lower-order question. The variability in transition points from one teacher to another found by Nicholson might be due to different ability levels of students taught by different teachers, to differences in teachers' abilities to estimate student learning states, or to some combination of the two.

This illustration is merely heuristic. The decision model was built to fit the results of Nicholson's study. Accordingly, this does not imply that the model described what teachers actually did. But it could be used this way.

A limitation of Nicholson's study is that he focused only on questions. Clearly, other teaching acts or methods were available to the teacher and could have been observed. Although examining only questions was partly justifiable, since the teachers had just been trained in asking questions, the decision approach suggests that question asking should vary from lower-order to higher-order in accordance with many other factors, some of which involve other teaching acts and methods.[60] Patterns of questioning may be difficult to find if other alternative acts and their effects on students' states of learning are not considered.

Another shortcoming of studies on interactive teaching is that they do not take into consideration the effect of student states of learning on teachers' decisions about how to teach. The pattern of a teacher's higher- and lower-order questions when teaching students of low ability will probably differ from the pattern when teaching bright students.[61] Nicholson's study is noteworthy in its attempt to take student learning into account by determining whether a teacher's higher- or lower-order question elicited an appropriate response from a student.

In summary, "previous research on basic teaching skills examined alternative teaching acts (for example, explaining, questioning, reinforcing) without examining *how teachers choose* between one or another act at a given point in time." [62] The search for basic teaching skills and teaching methods that lead to specified pupil outcomes probably will not prove fruitful until facets of the teaching environment—states of nature (student learning states, administrative policies, physical arrangement of the classroom) and characteristics of the teacher (values, aptitudes, availability of alternative teaching acts and methods)—are systematically examined. The decision analysis model suggests that these facets should be considered in determining the relation between interactive teaching and student outcomes.

EVALUATION IN THE DECISION ANALYSIS OF TEACHING

Evaluation involves collecting and using information about the correspondence between the actual outcome of a teaching method

60. Taba and Elzey, "Teaching Strategies and Thought Processes."

61. Carol A. Moore, "Styles of Teacher Behavior under Simulated Teaching Conditions" (Ph.D. diss., Stanford University, 1973).

62. Shavelson, "What Is the Basic Teaching Skill?" 144.

and the intended outcome (the teacher's objective or goal) for judging the worth of prior decisions. This information is then extrapolated in making current and future decisions.

While there is a large body of literature on evaluation that need not be reviewed here,[63] a critical concern in the decision analysis of teaching, often not addressed in the evaluation literature, is the use of evaluative information in decision making. Teachers have been characterized a priori as rational decision makers who intuitively use evaluative information for estimating probable student states of nature and the utility of using alternative teaching methods in the presence of these various states of nature. But, is there evidence that teachers can operate in this manner? And is there evidence that teachers' subjective probability estimates correspond to objective probabilities in the data gathered?

Earlier, several papers were cited that supported the proposition that humans are fairly good intuitive statisticians. On the basis of these findings our best guess was that a model of teaching as rational decision making is not unrealistic, with the caveat that teachers, like other persons, are subject to several predictable biases.

It is one thing to judge the learning states of someone else's students. But what about teachers' estimates of the learning states of their own students? In this case, teachers are personally involved. Some evidence available to the teachers may conflict with perceptions of their teaching ability. In this case, they might ignore the information, discount it, or distort it to maintain a consistent self-image.[64] This possibility may lead teachers to minimize stress rather than to optimize student outcomes in their teaching. Teachers may not be rational decision makers when removed from the laboratory situation and placed in a classroom with the responsibility of teaching thirty children.

63. Lee J. Cronbach, "Course Improvement through Evaluation," *Teachers College Record* 64 (May 1963): 672-83; Michael Scriven, "The Methodology of Evaluation," in Ralph W. Tyler, Robert M. Gagné, and Michael Scriven, *Perspectives of Curriculum Evaluation*, American Educational Research Association Monograph Series on Curriculum Evaluation (Chicago: Rand McNally, 1967), pp. 39-83; Daniel I. Stufflebeam, *Educational Evaluation and Decision Making* (Bloomington, Ind.: Phi Delta Kappa, Inc., 1971).

64. O. J. Harvey, Harold H. Kelley, and Martin M. Shapiro, "Reactions to Unfavorable Evaluations of the Self Made by Other Persons," *Journal of Personality* 25 (June 1957): 393-411.

Several studies bear on this point.[65] Johnson et al. found that teachers gave themselves credit when a fictitious student improved but blamed the fictitious student when his performance remained low.[66] Beckman replicated and extended the Johnson study and found that teachers could accurately rank order fictitious students' skills and performance from achievement data provided them.[67] The teachers attributed increases in student performance to themselves, while they attributed decreases in performance to the environment. A group of uninvolved observers, however, were much less likely to attribute improvement in student performance to the teacher and were much more likely to attribute a decrease in performance to the teacher and the student's motivation! While the teacher may be a moderately good, intuitive statistician, his interpretations of the information about the effects of teaching are by no means the only legitimate ones possible. Teachers' interpretations have important consequences for subsequent decisions that might differ from decisions made by others given the same information.

One possible conclusion from this argument is that, in a situation low in personal involvement, teachers (like college sophomores) can estimate probabilities in their environment somewhat accurately. However, in situations where their evaluation of events affects not only their decisions but their view of themselves as well, teachers' estimates of probabilities or their interpretations of them may show biases. In this case, teachers need to be trained, if possible, to use evaluative information in a more objective manner to reach decisions that will optimize student outcomes.

The Decision Perspective and Teacher Training

The decision analysis of teaching assumes that teachers have a

65. C. Ames and R. Ames, "Teachers' Attributions of Responsibility for Student Success and Failure Following Informational Feedback: A Field Verification" (Paper presented at the annual meeting of the American Educational Research Association, New Orleans, 1973); Linda Beckman, "Effects of Students' Performance on Teachers' and Observers' Attributions of Causality," *Journal of Educational Psychology* 61 (February 1970): 76-82; Thomas J. Johnson, Rhoda Feigenbaum, and Marcia Weiby, "Some Determinants and Consequences of the Teacher's Perception of Causation," *Journal of Educational Psychology* 55 (October 1964): 237-46.

66. Johnson, Feigenbaum, and Weiby, "Some Determinants and Consequences of the Teacher's Perception of Causation."

67. Beckman, "Effects of Students' Performance."

set of goals to achieve and a set of alternative methods for achieving them. In choosing a particular teaching method, various states of nature must be taken into consideration. These states of nature influence the outcome or success of any particular teaching method. The previous review of research on these elements of a decision suggests that teachers need to be trained in pedagogical decision making. Working from a decision-making perspective, Bishop found it "surprising, to say the least, that we appear to give so little prior training in pedagogical decision making to our students before allowing them to experiment with thirty to forty children's minds during teaching practice. It is almost like allowing a learner bus driver to take his first drive in rush hour, with no instructor and a full load." [68]

To help remedy this problem, recommendations for training teachers have been drawn from the decision analysis of teaching. Generally, the proposal outlined below is to train teachers in the individual components of decision making and then to integrate these components into smooth teaching performance. The following discussion is not comprehensive. Rather, selected components of a decision-oriented training program are described. These components apply equally to inservice and pre-service training.

TRAINING IN INDIVIDUAL COMPONENTS OF DECISION MAKING

Goals. To train teachers in setting goals, several training components are needed. One component would deal with the subject matter that is taught. Another component would emphasize knowledge of students' learning abilities, particularly those of students at the developmental level where the teacher is likely to teach. A third would focus on developing useful behavioral objectives. Yet another would deal with the teacher's philosophy of education. And finally, another component would foster the teacher's "adjustment to personal problems," for lack of a better term. Since the first three components are part of most training programs as courses in subject matter, curriculum, and educational psychology, no discussion of them seems necessary. This is not to say that these components do not need improvement. But since the last two com-

68. Bishop, "Simulating Pedagogical Decision Making," p. 41.

ponents—philosophy and personal adjustment—appear in few training programs, especially in the context of teacher decision making, they deserve attention.

Inconsistencies in goal setting may arise from inconsistencies in teachers' beliefs about the nature of children, beliefs about themselves and their roles as teachers, and beliefs about the aims of education and how to achieve them. For example, beginning teachers sometimes find a conflict between the goals of friendship with their students and instructional goals, such as providing objective feedback on students' cognitive performance. Often these inconsistencies are not readily apparent and so they are not dealt with systematically in training programs.[69] Or, they are just ignored.

Not only do inconsistencies or conflicts arise within a teacher's values and beliefs; they also arise between a teacher's goals and the goals of parents, administrators, politicians, and so on. For example, a story in the *Los Angeles Times* for January 24, 1975 heralded the increase in mathematics scores for the city's schools from 1973 to 1974 as measured by published tests. An assistant superintendent attributed the increase to a change in mathematics textbooks from "new math" to traditional computational mathematics. Whether the result was due to the textbooks, to the teachers teaching mathematics the way they learned it, or to some other factor cannot be determined from the design used in the study. But since the published test measured mostly computational skills and much less the student's understanding of mathematical structure, this result should come as no surprise. Clearly this finding was what was wanted by the parents, politicians, and therefore, by the administrators. The goal of computational skill, however, might conflict with the goal of understanding mathematical structures.

Inconsistencies in goals, whatever their source, can lead to poor decision making because they can give rise to conflicts in selecting teaching methods. To avoid conflict, less than optimal teaching methods are selected to achieve conflicting goals. This problem surfaces in the formal requirements of decision theory. One such requirement is consistency. Under a given state of nature, if teaching method A is preferred to method B, and method B is preferred to

69. Alan J. Bishop and Laura B. Levy, "Analysis of Teaching Behaviors," *Education for Teaching* 76 (Summer, 1968): 61-65.

method C, consistency implies that method A should be preferred to method C. But if teachers have not resolved inconsistencies in their goals, method A may or may not be preferred to method C.

One possible solution to these kinds of problems is to have teachers systematically examine their beliefs and philosophy of education to identify these types of inconsistencies and to resolve them. Decision analysis does not dictate a particular educational philosophy. Any philosophy is acceptable as long as it is internally consistent within the limits of human nature. Bishop and Levy concur: ". . . the choice of approach [philosophy] is purely a value judgment. Perhaps the values of some sections of society, such as employers, [teachers], and pupils, are not given enough consideration." [70]

The relation between a teacher's personal adjustment and the setting of goals is relatively straightforward. To make decisions that can optimize student outcomes, the teacher should state goals in terms of student outcomes. If the teacher is working under a high level of "stress," he or she may set goals to reduce that stress. Sometimes this may lead to optimization of the revised student outcomes.[71] Sometimes reduction of teacher stress becomes the goal instead of student outcomes. In training teachers, especially preservice teachers, experience is probably valuable. But without attention to the teacher's personal adjustment, experience alone may lead to less than optimal decisions when guided by the need or desire to reduce stress.

Alternative teaching strategies. The teacher is assumed to have available alternative teaching acts or methods. Thus, teachers need to be trained to use a variety of teaching acts and methods. They also need to be trained to generate relevant, alternative teaching methods when confronted with a decision situation.[72]

Teachers can be trained to use various teaching acts, such as questioning and reinforcing. For example, modeling and micro-

70. Ibid., p. 65.

71. John Sutcliffe and Richard C. Whitfield, "An Investigation of Classroom Decision Making by Teachers: An Applied Psychological Study of Teaching" (Proposal presented to the Social Science Research Council, 1974).

72. Bishop, "Theory Application and Decision Making in Teacher Training."

teaching techniques have been successfully employed in training technical skills of teaching.[73] Whether teachers can be trained to combine teaching acts into teaching methods is less certain.[74] There is some evidence that teachers can be trained to use macroteaching methods, such as lecture, discussion, and discourse.[75] In fact, such training often comprises the entire teaching skill component of many teacher training programs. From the perspective of decision analysis, however, it should be only one part of such programs.[76]

The second part of this aspect of training deals with the generation of relevant, alternative teaching acts or methods. Little research has been done on training teachers to generate these alternatives. Extrapolating from work by Salomon[77] and Sieber,[78] we can hypothesize that even simple instructions increase the number of relevant, alternative teaching strategies considered.

States of nature. The term "states of nature" has been defined earlier as environmental conditions over which teachers have little or no control but which influence the effectiveness of a particular teaching method. In this chapter, states of nature were described primarily as alternative learning states of students. Teachers have only indirect control over these states of nature by manipulating important factors in the instructional environment; learning is clearly an *intraindividual* phenomenon. In addition to learning states, affective factors, situational features such as class size, class-

73. David C. Berliner, *Microteaching and the Technical Skills Approach to Teacher Training*, Technical Report No. 8 (Stanford, Calif.: Stanford Center for Research and Development in Teaching, Stanford University, 1969); Walter R. Borg, "The Minicourse as a Vehicle for Changing Teacher Behavior: A Three-year Follow-up," *Journal of Educational Psychology* 63 (December 1972): 572-79; Trinchero, "Three Technical Skills of Teaching."

74. Christopher Clark, Richard E. Snow, and Richard J. Shavelson, "Three Experiments on Learning to Teach" (Paper presented at the annual meeting of the American Psychological Association, Chicago, 1975).

75. Bruce Joyce, "Conceptions of Man and Their Implications for Teacher Education," in *Teacher Education*, ed. Kevin Ryan, Seventy-fourth Yearbook of the National Society for the Study of Education, Part II (Chicago: University of Chicago Press, 1975), pp. 111-45.

76. Shavelson, "What Is *the* Basic Teaching Skill?"

77. Salomon, "Interaction of Communication Medium and Two Procedures of Training."

78. Sieber, "Lessons in Uncertainty."

room layout, and so on, will influence the complete configuration of the state of nature, and hence determine the effectiveness of any particular teaching method.

The teacher's task, then, is to identify the factors comprising the states of nature influencing his or her teaching and to estimate subjectively their probability of occurrence. Clearly, this requires training. For the planning stage of teaching, teachers need to be trained to identify alternative states of nature that may affect their instruction and to estimate the probability of those states. During interactive teaching, teachers need to be able to identify the prevailing set of states of nature and their corresponding probabilities.

Research suggests that people can estimate states of nature reasonably well when reliable information is available and they are not personally involved. But the heuristics used in doing so lead to predictable errors in these estimates. Furthermore, research on attribution theory suggests that teachers may have additional difficulty in making accurate estimates of states of nature because of their high commitment to their own teaching. This means that teachers will have to be trained to estimate states of nature in their own classrooms. The author knows of no research on this topic.

Research on training teachers to identify alternative states of nature likely to prevail in their classrooms is also unavailable.[79] It may be that simple instructions accompanied by a list of important states of nature in the classroom would suffice, but this is an unconfirmed hypothesis.

Outcomes and utilities. In formal decision theory, using a particular strategy (teaching act or method) when a particular state of nature is present produces an outcome that has some utility for the decision maker. While some outcomes can be measured objectively for precisely stated teaching goals, these measurements may not correspond to the decision maker's subjective feelings about the outcome. For example, increments in average scores on an achievement test may correspond to one teacher's subjective preference for outcomes while, for another teacher, large gains from low mean scores might be preferred to small gains from already high achievement scores.

79. But see Sutcliffe and Whitfield, "An Investigation of Classroom Decision Making."

In considering the utility component of decision analysis in training teachers, we can identify two types of training. The first type would train teachers to obtain information about the outcomes of various teaching acts or methods. This also would entail collecting information on which states of nature characterized the teaching situation. The second type would train teachers to be consistent in evaluating the utilities of various outcomes; that is, if they prefer method A to B and B to C, they should prefer method A to C. Typically, courses in educational psychology or measurement and evaluation are expected to fulfill the first type of training. Teachers are often assumed to meet the consistency criterion.

Knowledge about outcomes of various teaching acts or methods is extremely limited.[80] When states of nature are considered, few if any studies contribute to knowledge about the effects of teaching acts or methods under specific conditions. This state of knowledge gives rise to a major criticism of many teacher training programs, namely, that teachers deal with the practical while teacher trainers often focus primarily on theory.[81]

In order to train teachers in decision-making skills, this gap must be closed. At present, the best resolution seems to be one that provides teachers with training in skills for evaluating the effectiveness of their own teaching in different situations on the basis of available theory and knowledge.

While teacher training programs must use knowledge, only further research on teacher effectiveness can provide adequately for the knowledge portion of this prescription. The element pertaining to research by the teacher in improving classroom teaching seldom receives sufficient emphasis in teacher training. Thus, it has been proposed that teaching be viewed as hypothesis generating and testing.[82] Where outcomes of teaching acts or methods are not

80. For reviews, see Michael J. Dunkin and Bruce J. Biddle, *The Study of Teaching* (New York: Holt, Rinehart and Winston, 1974); Gage, *Handbook of Research on Teaching*; Barak Rosenshine and Norma Furst, "The Use of Direct Observation to Study Teaching," in *Second Handbook of Research on Teaching*, ed. Robert M. W. Travers (Chicago: Rand McNally, 1973), pp. 122-83.

81. Gene V Glass, "The Wisdom of Scientific Inquiry on Education," *Journal of Research in Science Teaching* 9, no. 1 (1972): 3-18.

82. Coladarci, "The Teacher as Hypothesis-maker."

known for a particular situation, the teacher must obtain this information. To be worthwhile, the method for obtaining relevant information must conform to the conditions typical of teaching. Opinions or case studies are not sufficient. What is needed in addition to supplement these methods are quasi-experiments implemented by the teacher.[83] Time series designs when teachers have only one class and nonequivalent control group designs when teachers have more than one class seem particularly well suited to the purpose. Teachers should become fluent in these methods so that the information gathered is useful. Training along these lines should become an integral component of teacher training.

INTEGRATION OF DECISION-MAKING COMPONENTS

A number of elements of decision making have been identified as important ingredients of a teacher training program. While most training programs foster distinct skills, they often fail to train teachers to *integrate* these skills into smooth teaching performance. This type of training might best be accomplished by simulation. Specifically, it is proposed that integration of the elements of decision making can be improved by simulating pedagogical decision making.

The applicability of simulation for training teachers in decision making is evident in Bishop's analogy between teacher training and aviator training:

The training of pilots is extremely rigorous and usually involves the following stages . . .:

1. Much classwork, background reading and learning about, for example, aerodynamics, meteorology and aviation generally. [This stage can be compared with the coursework required in most teacher training programs.]
2. Sessions in various training devices (e.g., the Link Trainer) to learn and practice the basic skills. [This stage parallels skill training, such as microteaching, in many teacher training programs.]
3. Sessions in a flight simulator, an artificial representation for learning the co-ordination of skills and practicing decisions (for example, accident avoidance). [This stage is seldom available in teacher training programs.]

83. James R. Okey and Jerome L. Ciesla, "Designs for the Evaluation of Teacher Training Materials," *AV Communication Review* 21 (Fall 1973): 299-310.

4. Sessions in dual control aircraft, a real situation but with a control mechanism to allow learner responsibility to be increased while still maintaining safety. [This stage corresponds to supervised or practice classroom teaching.]

5. Solo flight, a real situation with the pilot now fully responsible for his own decisions and actions. [This stage can be compared with unsupervised classroom teaching.] [84]

Stage 3, simulation, could prove valuable in training teachers to integrate the component decision skills into smooth teaching performance. The simulation, according to Bishop, would include planning and interactive decision making in several teaching conditions, such as tutoring, using media, and so on.[85] The situations would proceed from easy to complex, and the trainee would be given decreasing amounts of time in which to reach a decision.[86]

For one activity in the planning phase, Bishop proposed that trainees write a branching programmed text. In effect, this simulation would allow the teacher to build a pedagogical decision tree. "It is often said that even if the pupils don't learn much from a program, the writer learns a lot by writing it. . . . The use of programmed instruction has the additional advantage that the branching decisions can be validated by actual experimental use of the programs."[87]

For interactive teacher decision making, Bishop and Whitfield classified decisions into three general areas, each with subclasses: learning (cognition and attitude), relationships (pupil-pupil, pupil-teacher, teacher-adult), and environment (apparatus and aids, organization and administration). Training in each of these areas might proceed by posing a series of problems like: "In introducing 'matrices' to a group of sharp eleven-year-olds, you remark casually that one reason the topic is taught in school now is because it has so many applications. A rather spotty-faced boy with glasses, sitting in the front row, asks: 'Can you show us one, Sir?'" Or, "You are in the middle of a lesson that is going well, the class is involved and

84. Bishop, "Simulating Pedagogical Decision Making," p. 41.

85. Ibid.

86. Bishop and Whitfield, *Situations in Teaching*.

87. Bishop, "Simulating Pedagogical Decision Making," p. 41.

discussion is at a high level. Suddenly, a ladder is plonked against the window sill, a window cleaner appears and begins to clean the large picture window behind you."[88]

In building the simulation, various media can be useful. Audio-visual taped lessons can be stopped and the trainee can indicate his choice for the next teaching act. Videotapes can be used in the same way or with branches so that the next segment of tape depends on the trainee's decision. This procedure could provide practice in sequential decision making.[89] Or simulations of teaching can be arranged so that trainees could teach hypothetical students.[90] For example, Moore gave the teacher a large number of pedagogical moves from which to choose in teaching the pressure-temperature-volume gas laws to a hypothetical student. The "student" followed rules that governed his responses and learning, contingent on teacher moves. The teacher taught the "student" until the latter had learned the ideal gas law. The teacher's decisions at each step were recorded and examined. The analysis of such teaching could provide feedback for training effective decision making.

One further point deserves mention. From the decision perspective, *there is not a single correct decision.* This means that three teachers who are equally proficient decision makers might teach quite differently with equally positive results. Differences between their teaching would arise from differences in their values and beliefs that, in turn, would be reflected in their goals, the alternative teaching methods considered, and their evaluation of the utility of certain outcomes in reaching those goals. If the criterion of effectiveness were cognitive, the data would rank order these teachers in one way. If an affective criterion of effectiveness were imposed, their rank order might be quite different.

Summary and Implications for Research

In this chapter, teaching has been described as a process by which teachers consciously make rational decisions with the inten-

88. Bishop and Whitfield, *Situations in Teaching*, pp. 19-20.

89. Bishop, "Simulating Pedagogical Decision Making."

90. J. L. Flake, "The Use of Interactive Computer Simulations for Sensitizing Mathematics Methods Students to Questioning Behaviors" (Ph.D. diss., University of Illinois, 1973); Moore, "Styles of Teacher Behavior."

tion of optimizing student outcomes. While teachers' decision making does not always match this description, the model seems to apply to many goal-oriented teaching situations. It also has value in making teachers aware of decisions that they might otherwise make without awareness. In both cases, the model identifies key elements in teaching that can be incorporated into teacher training and research.

In conceiving of teaching as decision making, we assume that teachers have a number of strategies (for example, teaching acts, teaching methods) available to help their students attain a goal or set of goals. In choosing a particular strategy, teachers attempt to achieve a desired outcome by matching events—both within the student (for example, attention, learning, motivation) and within the classroom (for example, distractions, facilities)—with a particular teaching strategy. Since these events, called states of nature, are not certain but occur with some probability, the teacher must subjectively estimate the probability of a particular state. Information about alternative teaching strategies, states of nature and their probabilities, and outcomes resulting from pairing a single strategy with a particular state of nature is used to make pedagogical decisions.

This model seems best to fit the kinds of decisions made in *planning* instruction; teachers' decisions parallel those made by instructional designers. There is sufficient time to consider alternative instructional strategies, student entry behavior (states of nature), classroom facilities and context (other states of nature), and the probable outcomes of instructional strategies under each of the possible states of nature.

In contrast, during *interactive* teaching, teachers cannot be as aware of their decisions or deliberate about them. Nevertheless, the decision model is important as a heuristic in this case. It suggests that teachers "test" (for example, ask a question) to determine student states of nature at the beginning of a lesson. Using this information, the teacher "operates" to move the student from an initial state of nature toward the desired state or instructional goal. Periodically during the lesson, teachers "test" their students to determine the effectiveness of the immediately preceding teaching acts. On the basis of this information, a teaching strategy may be terminated because a goal has been reached, it may be continued because it seems to be effective, or the strategy may be changed because students' learning states have not changed.

With few exceptions, this and other conceptions of teaching as decision making have not led directly to empirical research. We know, for example, that humans are moderately good intuitive statisticians who use a limited number of heuristics in judging states of nature. Yet we also know that these heuristics lead to predictable errors. What we do not know is whether teachers use similar heuristics while teaching and how the errors associated with these heuristics affect teachers' decisions and student outcomes. Further, although teachers' differ in their ability to generate alternative courses of action for teaching, we have not demonstrated that they can be helped to improve this ability. Finally, the model assumes that teachers can estimate the probable outcomes of different teaching acts or methods in a number of states of nature. But there is a paucity of information about teachers' ability to estimate these outcomes accurately. In short, the decision model of teaching suggests a number of areas for research on how teachers do and should teach.

The teaching profession and particularly preservice and inservice training programs cannot wait, however, until such research has been completed. One possible approach to this problem would be to use, as well as is currently possible, alternative methods for training teachers in the several components of decision making, such as generating alternative strategies and estimating student learning states. Research and evaluation then could determine the most effective methods and components for the teachers involved in the training.

A major part of such action research should involve training teachers to integrate the component skills into a smooth and skilled teaching performance. Such training might use simulation methods and audiotape, videotape, or computer support systems. Another approach would be to train teachers (a) to consider their teaching as hypothesis generating and testing and (b) to use quasi-experimental designs to test their hypotheses, that is, to identify which teaching strategies worked for them under different classroom conditions. A third possibility is some combination of the first two.

Training with any of these strategies should be accompanied by research on basic questions about teaching and by evaluation of the utility of the training. Attempts to reach generalizable findings from either basic research or action research may meet with only limited success.[91] But there also is reason for optimism. The major contribution of the decision model is to focus attention on providing teachers with a means for determining teaching acts or methods that are effective for them under certain teaching situations. While the findings may vary from teacher to teacher, the cumulative effect would be to improve their teaching.

91. Lee J. Cronbach, "Beyond the Two Disciplines of Scientific Psychology", *American Psychologist* 30 (February 1975): 116-27; Glass, "The Wisdom of Scientific Inquiry on Education."

Index

Abelard, Pierre, 256

Absence (student), correlations of student achievement with (table), 343

Academic ability, relation of, to effectiveness in simulation games, 244-45

Achievement: factors correlating positively and negatively with (table), 367; overview of recent studies of, 339-42

Adult feedback, variable of, in major studies of achievement, 361-64

Adult questioning, correlations of student achievement with, in grades one and three (table), 356

Affective objectives, realization of, through simulation/games, 231, 239-41

Allen, Layman E., 220, 226

All-machine simulations, limitations in the use of, 221

All-man simulations, nature and use of, 221-22

Allport, Gordon W., 2

Alternative teaching acts, choice of, by teacher, 386-88

Alternative teaching strategies, teacher need for, 405-6

Andersen, Martin P., 168

Anderson, Alan R., 218

Anderson, C. Raymond, 243

Anderson, John R., 26

Anderson, Lee F., 236

Anderson, Richard C., 194; quoted, 195

Aristotle, 78, 97

Artificial intelligence (AI): application of, 80-82; goal of research on, 80-83; Sophisticated Instructional Environment (SOPHIE) in relation to, 82-83

Assimilation and retention, length of lecture in relation to, 267-68

Atherton, Charles R., 287

Atkinson, Richard C., 26, 67, 78, 79, 80, 87, 394, 396; quoted (with Paulson), 395

Attention: process of, in learning, 26; seven methods of teaching in terms of, 290

Attitude change: differences in, linked to sex, 245; effective conditions for, 36; effectiveness of discussion method in, 200-3; influence of teacher on, 246

Attitudes: change of, as goal of issue-oriented discussion, 172; effectiveness of discussion method for effecting change in, 200-3; learning of, 35-36; see also Attitude change

Attneave, Fred, 14

Ausubel, David P., 32, 39, 117

Authoring language, work on, 72-73

Back, Kurt W., 183

Baker, Eugene H., 238, 240

Bales, Robert F., 192, 193

Bandura, Albert, 36, 41, 42

Bany, Mary A., 187

Barnes, D. S., 285

Bartlett, Frederic C., 267

BASIC language, development of, at Dartmouth College, 66

Baskin, Samuel, 279

Bass, Bernard M., 201

Bass, R. K., 68

Beach, Lee Roy, 388

Beach, Leslie R., 291

Beckman, Linda, 402

Beez, W. Victor, 352

Behaviorism: learning theory derived from, 37-38; Skinner's representation of, 38

Behavior theory, role of, implied by use of games, 227; see also Learning theory, Learning

Beliefs, fostering control of, through simulation/games, 232-33, 241-44

Bellack, Arno A., quoted, 383

Bennett, Edith B., 201

Berliner, David C., 172, 174, 177, 298, 336; quoted (with Gage), 173

Bernheim, Ernst, 256

Berry, Paul C., 204

Biddle, Bruce J., 336, 337, 356, 361

Biggs, J. B., 202
Billington, Marjorie J., 123
Bishop, Alan J., quoted, 403, 409-10, 410; quoted (with Whitfield), 410-11
Bitzer, Donald, 66, 71
Bjork, Robert A., 23
Block, Clifford H., 204
Bloom, Benjamin S., 172, 198, 200, 279, 290
Boocock, Sarane S., 225
Borton, Terry, 332
Bower, Gordon H., 26
Brenner, Marlin, 204
Briggs, Leslie J., 62, 306
Brophy, Jere E., 335, 337, 338, 341, 347, 348, 355, 356, 357, 360, 361, 362, 363, 366; review of study by (with Evertson), 338-66
Brown, Albert E., 177
Brown, Virginia L., quoted (with Farr), 372
Brown, William E., 352
Bruner, Jerome S., 3, 34, 40, 42, 307, 310
Buggey, L. J., 199
Burke, Ronald J., 209

CAI, author's definition of, 47; see also Computer-assisted instruction
Caillois, Roger, 219
Calfee, Robert, 359
Cameron, A., 272
Campbell, John, 208
Campeau, C., 306
Cantor, Joanne, 300
Cantrell, E. G., 300
Capabilities (learned), varieties of, 31
Carbonell, Jaime R., 82
Carlson, Roger L., 283
Carpenter, Edmund, 309
Carroll, John B., 105
Carter, J. L., 144
Carter, Ronald M., 352
Cartwright, Dorwin, 179; quoted (with Zander), 181
Chanbarisov, Sh. Kh., 260
Chang, Sunnyich Shin, 350
Chapman, Loren J. and Jean P., 390
Chen, Milton, 330
Cherryholmes, Cleo H., 238, 240
Cheydleur, Frederick D., 176
Chickering, Arthur W., 280

Children's interests, capture of, by television and film, 332
Child responses: relationship of, to mean class achievement in grades one and three (table), 360; variable of, in studies of achievement, 170
Chomsky, Noam, 14
Chu, Godwin C., 16, 305, 330
Churchill, Ruth, 274
Classroom discussion, interactive communication in, 170
Classroom instruction, chap. 10
Classroom structure and processes, simulation/games with reference to, 229-32
Classroom teaching: integration of television and film teaching with, 329-34; recent reviews of research on, 335-37
Class size: lecture method in relation to, 273-74; teaching methods in relation to, 6-7; see also Group size
Cloward, R. D., 145
Coding, examples of process of, in learning, 26
Cognitive content, teaching of, by television and film, 203-7
Cognitive learning, discussion of, 12
Cognitive objectives: contribution of simulation/games to, 230-31; realization of, through simulation/games, 237-38
Cognitive skills, tutoring in relation to the development of, 135-36
Cognitive strategies, nature and role of, 34-35
Cognitive style, differences in, linked to sex, 245
Cognitive theories, Ausubel and Bruner on, 39-40
Cohen, David, 208
Coke, Esther U., 108
Coleman, James S., 223, 226, 230, 239
Collins, Barry E., 184, 189, 206
Communication: alteration of pattern of, by simulation/games, 230-35; attributes of pattern of, in discussion method, 186-90; enhancement of, as goal of simulation/games, 229-30
Competence: development of, 241-44; elements of, 232; gains in, from use of simulation/games, 232-34
Computer-assisted instruction (CAI), chap. 3; boom and decline of, 69-70;

definition of, as a process, 44-48; delivery system definition of, 46-49; economic and intellectual potential of, 33-34; four pioneers in development of, 65-69; opposing views of hardware and instructional-materials specialists on, 50-51; possible future of, 87-90

Computer-assisted simulations, characteristics of, 225

Content: different kinds of representation of, 101-4; effect of sequence of, on learning, 104; four ways of characterization of, 98-101; nature of, conveyed by television and films, 303-15

Content analysis: approach of, to solving teacher's problems, 140; variety of procedures of, for analyzing instructional outcomes, 61

Content covered, variable of, in major studies of achievement, 348-53

Contiguity theory, discussion of, 10-11

Cost effectiveness, comparison of, with respect to tutoring and classroom teaching, 162-64

Coursewriter language, development of, by International Business Machines (IBM), 68-69

Craik, Fergus I. M., 110, 111, 116, 123

Creativity, encouragement of, by simulation/games, 231-32

Crothers, Edward J., 396

Cukier, Lillian, 117

Curriculum, integration of simulation/games into, 251

Cybernetic theory: application of, in U.S., 83-87; Pask's procedures based on, 83-87

Davis, James H., 205; quoted, 184-85

Davitz, Joel, 204

Dearing, Bruce, 280

De Cecco, John P., 273, 274

Decision alternatives, estimates of outcomes for, 391-92

Decision analysis of teaching, evaluation in, 400-2

Decision making: flowchart of teacher-child interaction illustrating sequential nature of, 381; integration of components of, 409-11

Decision matrix (teacher's), tabular presentation of, 377

Decision tree, sequences of a teacher's decisions represented by (figure), 379

Decisions: description of a sequence of, using TOTE unit (figures), 382; features of, 374-76; making of, during planning, 392-94; schematic representation of elements in, 375

De Kock, Paul, 240

Design science, learning and instruction as, 77-78

De Vries, David L., 235, 237

Dewey, John, 1, 218

Direct instruction: construction of model of, based on major studies of achievement, 364; elements in, 364-70; summary of elements in (table), 369

Discussion group dynamics: communication patterns in relation to, 186-90; group cohesion in relation to, 181-86; group composition in relation to, 178-81; group size as variable in studies of, 174-78; leadership in relation to, 190-96

Discussion group vs. lecture situation, 277

Discussion method, chap. 6; attributes of, 168-74; effectiveness of, 196-209; group processes in, 174-96; individual differences in relation to, 209-13

Discussion skills: development of, as objectives of discussion method, 173; improvement of, by classroom discussion, 207-9

Dittes, J. E., 183

Doty, B. A., 18

Dowaliby, Fred J., 18, 211, 212

Druker, Peter, 177

Dubin, Robert, 15, 196, 281, 305, 352; quoted (with Taveggia), 197, 198

Duell, Orpha K., 124

Duhring, Eugen, 256

Dunkin, Michael J., 336, 337, 356, 361

Dunnette, Marvin D., 208

Ebbinghaus, Hermann, 149, 266

Edmondson, J. B., 176

Educational games, factors in increased use of, 219; see also Simulation/games

Educational Testing Service, evaluation of CAI projects by, 70

Edwards, Keith, J., 235, 237, 244

Eisner, Sigmund, 272
"Electric Company," 325, 330; evaluation of, 305
Elementary school teaching, effectiveness of discussion method in, 198-200
Ellson, Douglas G., 153, 157 161
Ely, D. P., 62
Elzey, F. F., 380, 384
Englemann, Siegfried, quoted, 146
Enjoyment (student), influence of teacher on, in simulation/games, 246
Entertainment programs: content variables of, influencing learning, 319-20; uses of, 319-20
Entwisle, Doris R., 237
Environment, simulation/games in relation to control of, 241-42
Estes, William K., 11, 25
Evertson, C. M., 338, 341, 347, 348, 355, 356, 357, 360, 361, 362, 363, 366; review of major study by (with Brophy), 338-66
Exline, Ralph V., 184
Eyestone, Merle L., 276

Failure (academic): affective factors related to, 146-51; emotional theory of, 145-46; learning factors related to, 146-51; structural factors related to, 143-44
Farr, Roger, quoted (with Brown), 372
Farran, Dale C., 250, 251
Feedback: discussion method in relation to, 173-74; relation of, to reinforcement in learning, 173-74; use of videotape for, 333-34
Feedback (adult), relation of, to mean class achievement in grades one and three (table), 362
Fennessey, Gail M., 240
Fichte, Johann Gottlieb, 256
Film vs. lecture without film, 288
Finch, Curtis R., 242
Fisher, Frank L., 202
Fitts, Paul M., 36
Flanders, Ned A., 335, 337
Flesch, Rudolph: Reading Ease Formula by, 106; evaluation of formula devised by, 107-8
Fletcher, Jerry L., 244, 250
Fletcher, John, 284
Follow Through programs, 338, 339, 340, 341, 346, 353, 354, 359, 366, 370,

371; setting of, for major studies of achievement, 338 ff.
Fox, David, 204
Frase, Lawrence T., 118
Freyberg, P. S., 268
Funk, Wilmer H., 208
Furst, Norma, 133, 134, 136, 137, 145, 337; quoted (with Rosenshine), 135

Gage, N. L., 172, 174, 177, 298, 336, 337; quoted (with Berliner), 173
Gagné, Robert M., 12, 42, 61, 62, 119, 146, 147, 165, 234, 247
Gallagher, James B., 284, 336
Gall, Meredith D., 198, 199, 202, 359
Gallup poll, report of, on volunteers for reading programs, 131
Geis, George L., 45
Generalization, importance of, to design and conduct of instruction, 27; see also Transfer of training
George, John E., 153
Gerard, Harold B., 185
Gerlach, V. S., 62
Gibb, Cecil A., quoted, 190, 195
Gibb, Jack R., 190
Gibson, Eleanor J., 34
Gilbert, Thomas F., quoted, 57
Glass, Gene V, 169
Globig, Linda, 299
Good, Thomas L., 335, 337, 347
Goodman, Frederick L., 232
Gray, H. W., 300
Greeno, James G., 23
Gross, Edward, 179
Group cohesiveness: approaches to measurement of, 182; effect of, in discussion, 181-86; effect of, on interpersonal processes, 182-86
Group composition, effects of, on discussion, 178-81
Group interaction, unequal sharing of learning by students through, 211-13
Group size: effects of, on discussion, 178; methods of teaching in relation to, 6; see also Class size
Gruber, H. E., 278
Guetzkow, Harold, 184
Guskin, Samuel, 352
Gutenberg, Johann, 6
Guthrie, Edwin R., 11
Guthrie, John T., 241

Hale, Edward, 258
Hall, Katherine P., 209
Haravey, Francois, 201
Harburg, Ernest, 180
Hare, Alexander Paul, quoted, 175
Harnischfeger, Annegrete, 342
Harris, Arthur J., 342, 345, 371
Harrison, Grant Von, 153, 154, 155
Hartley, James, 272
Hartmann, Karl Robert von, 256
Haskell, Roger W., 296
Hassinger, Jack, 134
Hedley, R. A., 305
Heider, Fritz, 178
Heinkel, Otto A., 241
Heyns, Roger W., 184
Hicks, Robert A., 351
Hilgard, Ernest R., 16, 77
Hill, William Fawcett, 171, 208
Himmel, Clark E., 288
Hoffman, L. Richard, 180-209
Holloway, Philip J., 275, 285
Homans, George C., quoted, 183
Hoover, Kathryn, 359
Hopkins, Kenneth D., 169
Horn, Robert E., 218
Horst, D., 134
Hudson, Liam, 295
Hull, Clark L., 37, 150
Hymes, Jonah P., 64

Implicit curriculum, discussion of,
with respect to television and film
teaching, 312-14
Independent study vs. lecture, 278-81
Individual attention, giving of, to
learners, 136-27
Individual differences, discussion of,
with respect to verbal participation,
209-11; see also Sex differences
Individualization of instruction, proposal of, for solving classroom problems, 140-41
Information-processing skills, teaching
of, by television and films, 309
Institute for Mathematical Studies in
the Social Sciences (Stanford), early
and continuing contributions of, to
CAI, 67-68
Instruction: decision-theoretic analysis of, 79-80; design science and technology of, 77-79; phases of, 27-30
Instructional development: approaches

to, 57-63; phases in systematic approach to (figure), 56
Instructional effectiveness, attributes
related to (table), 97
Instructional materials, development of
principles in design and development of, 62-63; see also Written instructional material, Programmed instruction
Instructional methods and media:
problem of classification of, 63-65;
selection of, 63-65
Instructional objectives, proposal of,
for different types of discussion,
171-74
Instructional outcomes, content analysis procedures in relation to, 61-62
Instructional programs, three approaches to one process in design
of, 56-57
Instructional variables, reviews of (by
Stallings and Kaskowitz, Brophy and
Evertson, and Soar), 338-39
Instructional writings, kinds of, 92; see
also Written instructional material
Intellectual skills, learning of, 32-34
Interactive communication, classroom
discussion in relation to, 170; see also
Communication
Interactive teaching, decisions made
during process of, 396-400
Interpersonal processes, effects of
group characteristics on, 175-83
Interpersonal strategies, improvement
of by simulation games, 234
Item program, flowchart of, for
Rosenbaum's Peer-Mediated Instruc-
tion, 158
Ivashchenco, F. I., 260

Jamieson, G. H., 283
Jamison, Dean, quoted (with Suppes
and Wells), 16
John, Paula, 274
Johnson, Lois V., 187
Johnson, Lyndon B., 69
Johnson, Samuel, quoted, 257
Johnson, Thomas J., 402
Jones, Harold E., 266, 267, 301
Joyce, Bruce, 172, 337
Joyce, C. R. B., 277, 278, 295
Julian, James W., 230
Jungk, Robert, 231, 232

Kahneman, Daniel, quoted (with Tversky), 389-90
Kaplan, Robert, 101, 117
Karlins, Marva, 387
Kaskowitz, David H., 338, 339, 340, 341, 343, 345, 346, 347, 348, 351, 353, 355, 356, 359, 360, 361, 362, 363, 366, 368, 371; review of major study by (with Stallings), 338-71
Keach, Everett T., Jr., 239
Keeling, B., 275
Kelley, Harold H., 183; quoted (with Thibaut), 206
Kent, Thomas H., 286
Kidder, Steven J., 227, 243
King, Estelle M., 289
Kintsch, Walter, 126
Klare, George R., 106
Knott, Tom, 284
Koenig, Kathryn E., 292
Koether, Mary E., 99, 101
Kreitzberg, Valerie S., 118
Kumar, V. K., 25

Lamm, Helmut, 387
Landau, Erika, 241
Lanzetta, John T., 388
Leaderless group discussion, nature and purpose of, 192-93
Leadership: group as source of, 190; opposing styles of, 194-95; teacher's role of, in discussion, 191-92
Learning: cognitive theories in, 39-40; contiguity theory in, 10-11; criteria of, from use of simulations, 228-29; effect of content variables from television and film on, 317-21; effect of sequence of content on, 104; effects of, 42-43; forms, structure, and sentence length of written materials in relation to, 105; influence of content variables in entertainment programs on, 317; influence of teacher on, in simulation/games, 246; operant conditioning theory in relation to, 8-10; outcomes of, 30-37; phases of, 27-30; production techniques (television and film) in relation to, 321-22; significance of individual attention in, 136-37; teaching about modes of, by television and film, 314-15
Learning-hierarchy theory (Gagné), discussion of, 147
Learning models: framework of learning processes provided by, 22; func-

tion of, 43; prototype of, employed by contemporary information-processing theories of learning and memory (figure), 24
Learning outcomes, see Outcomes of learning
Learning processes, list of, 25-27
Learning theory: learning outcomes in relation to, 41-42; Skinner's behavioristic type of, 37-39
Leavitt, Howard J., 188
Lecture: effectiveness of, 266-91; experiment on improvement of, 259-66; improvement of, 259-66, 296; student reaction to, 261, 291-96; student recall from, 266; subject differences in preference for method of the, 295-96; vs. discovery method, 290; vs. discussion, 286-87; vs. independent study, 286-87; vs. tutorial vs. seminar, 292-93
Lecture-discussion: vs. group counseling, 287-88; vs. lecture-independent study, 292
Lecture-discussion group vs. large lecture class, 274-75
Lecture method, chap. 9; scores expressing preference for, in comparison with tutorial and seminar methods (table), 293
Lecture period, cycle of effectiveness in, 262-64
Lecturer: effect of personality of, 265-66; five attributes of, favored by students, 298-99
Lecture script, use of, 280-81
Lecture sequence: improvement of details of, 264; reactions to, 261-64
Lecture system: attack on, 254-59; defense of, 255-59
Lecturing: components of, for effectiveness, 268; disputed economies of, 284; origin and purpose of, 252-61; substitute for, 284-86
Lee, Robert S., 241, 242
Lenz, E. O., 275
Levy, L. B., 405
Lewin, Kurt, 200, 201, 279
Lewis, R. E., 285
Linear programmed instruction vs. discussion, 296
Lippitt, Ronald, 194
Listening, factors in ability of, 268

Livingston, Samuel L., 240; quoted, 235-36
Lloyd, D. H., 261, 262, 301
Lockhart, Robert S., 116
Lockheed, Marlaine, 209
Lorge, Irving, 204, 206
Lundberg, Donald L. V., 134

Maar, John N., 272
McClendon, Paul I., 268
Maccoby, Nathan, 330, 331
McCrea, Marion W., 282
McCullough, Celeste, 278
McDonald, James B., 263
McDougall, I. R., 300
McFarlane, Paul T., 243
McGinnies, Elliott, 180, 212
McKeachie, Wilbert J., 191, 192, 195, 198, 292; quoted, 211
McLeish, John, 16; quoted, 271
McLuhan, Marshall, 309, 310
MacManaway, Lancelot A., 280, 284
McNicol, G. P., 300
McWilliams, Perry, 290, 293
Maier, Norman R. F., 180, 191, 192, 193, 205, 210; quoted, 207
Manatt, Richard P., 284
Man-machine simulations, nature of, 221
Markle, Susan, 55, 62; quoted, 44
Marquis, Donald G., 184
Mathemagenic activities: control of, 116-19; inductive control of, 119-23; nature of, 114-16; relation of, to nominal text, 123-25
Mathemagenic processing, control of (figure), 112
Mathemagenic topographies, basis for inference of (figure), 115
May, M. A., 306
Mead, George Herbert, 217
Memory and learning, prototype of models employed by information-processing theories of (figure), 24
Menges, Robert J., 295
Merrill, M. David, 61, 62, 64, 74
Methods of study, student characteristics in relation to, 281
Methods of teaching: definition of, 5; descriptive concepts of a number of, 12-15; factors in choice of, 18; group size in relation to, 6-7; historical survey of, 1-3; implication of a hypothetical equivalence of, 15;

lecture method compared to a range of, 272-91; recent trends in, 3-5; teacher choice of, 19-20; teacher objectives in relation to choice of, 298
Michael, Donald N., 330, 331
Miller, David W., quoted (with Starr), 391
Miller, J. G., 328
Miller, K. M., 202
Miller, Neal E., 37, 38
Milton, Ohmer, 272
Minsky, Marvin, 82
Mishler, Elliott G., 175
Mitnich, Leonard L., 180, 212
Moore, Carol A., 411
Moore, Omar K., 218, 241
Mowrer, O. H., 150
"Mr. Rogers' Neighborhood," 308, 316
Motivation: learning in relation to, 25-26; provision of, by simulation/games, 230
Motor skills, place and learning of 36-37
Mueller, A. D., 176
Mulder, F. J., 176
Murray, H. T., Jr., 285
Musella, Donald, 298

Nachman, Marvin, 275
National Science Foundation, funding of PLATO and TICCIT by, 70
National Society for the Study of Education: contributions to teaching by, 1; relation of education to psychology as treated by current yearbook of, 5; schism between general and educational psychology reflected by yearbooks of, 2; Theories of Learning by, 3
Nekrasova, K. A., 259
Nichols, Ralph G., 268
Nicholson, Stanley, 398, 399, 400
Noble, Clyde E., 102
Nominal and effective stimuli, distinction between, in analysis of learning from written material, 96-97
Nominal stimulus, text as (table), 97
Nondirective teaching, students' reaction to, 276-77
Nonsimulation games: learning from, 225-26; nature and purpose of, 219
Note taking: effect of, on comprehension of lecture, 268; Eisner and

Kidder on, 272; results of an experiment on (table), 281
Novak, K., 285
Nuthall, Graham, 210, 337

O'Bryan, Kenneth, 312
Observational and listening processes, use of, in discussion method, 170
Observation learning: discussion of, 11-12; television and film teaching in relation to, 315-17
O'Leary, Arlene, 241, 242
Oliver, Donald W., 172
Olson, David R., 307, 310, 312
Operant conditioning: assumptions underlying concept of, applied to lecture situation, 9-10; terms used to describe elements of, 7-8; theory of, 8-10; transfer of training in relation to, 8-9
Opochinsky, Seymour, 275
O'Reilly, Patrick A., 241
Organization of content, effect of, on learning, 104
Outcomes of learning: decisions intended for optimization of, for student, 392-402; importance of learner's processing activities to, 109; limitations on discussion of, in terms of school subjects, 30; relation of learning theories to, 41-42

Panada, Karen, 352
Papert, Seymour, 80, 81
Parisi, D., 261
Pascal, Charles E., 282, 294
Pask, Gordon, 61, 74, 83, 84, 85, 86, 87
Paulsen, Friedrich, 254, 259; quoted, 256
Paulson, J. A., 394; quoted (with Atkinson), 395
Pavlov, Ivan, 11, 149, 153
Pearn, M. A., 290
Peckham, Percy D., 169
Pellegrini, Robert J., 351
Pennington, D. F., Jr., 201
Perceptivity of students, factors influential in, in lecture situation, 264
Performance, effect of size of discussion group on, 176-78
Performance learning, difficulty of assessment, in simulation/game situation, 247
Perry, Franklyn A., 230
Personality (student), relation of, to

preference for teaching method, 294-95
Peterson, Cameron, 388
Peterson, Penelope L., 212
Petri, Charles R., Jr., 300
Piaget, Jean, 3, 217
Pidgeon, Douglas A., 349
Pierfy, David A., 239
Pikas, Anatol, 282, 283
Planned Variation programs, 338, 339, 340, 341, 348, 353, 359, 366, 370; setting of, for major studies of achievement, 338 ff.
PLATO, see Programmed Logic for Automated Teaching Operations
Play, socializing function of, 217-19
Popham, W. James, 278
Porter, Robert M., 210
Posner, Michael J., 36
Postlethwait, S. N., 285
Postman, Leo, 109, 118
Potter, David, 168
Premack, D., 150
Problem solving: effectiveness of group discussion in, 203-7; group discussion in relation to, 172-73
Program instruction on procedures in decoding exercises (table), 155
Programmed instruction (PI), chap. 3; definition of, as a process, 44-48; introduction and development of, 54-56; possible future of, 87-90
Programmed instruction vs. lecture, 283, 288
Programmed Logic for Automated Teaching Operations (PLATO): Coursewriter and TUTOR, the language of, 76; development of, at University of Illinois, 66-67; differences of, from TICCIT, 76-78; discussion of, 70-72
Programming: selection, designing, and evaluation of, 322-26
Prototypical learning model, features of, 22-23

Questions: direct effects of, in mathemagenic activities, 122-23; variable of, in studies of achievement, 355-60
Quiller-Couch, Sir Arthur Thomas, 257

Raths, James P., 350
Raven, Bertram H., 184

Readability: evaluation of measures and indices of, 107; relation of measures of, to document characteristics, 100-9; variables in formulas of, 106-7

Receptivity (student), formula suggesting causal relation of, to other variables, 264

Reflective thinking: application of basic rules of, in lecture sessions, 259-60; lecture vs. discussion method, with respect to, 279

Rehearsal, function of, in learning, 26

Reinforcement: demonstration of effect of, 331-32; derivation of, from simulated system, 229; see also Operant conditioning

Rennie, D. L., 319

Respondent learning, theory of, 11

Response generation, function of, in learning, 27

Restle, Frank, 205

Retention: decrement in, of a lecture (figure), 263; experiments in, 269-72; traditional teaching in relation to, 282-83

Retrieval, function of, in learning, 27

Riley, J. W., 299

Robbins, Lionel Charles, 258

Rogers, George W., 268

Rohde, Kermit, 272

Rohwer, William D., Jr., 34

Role playing: fostering skills of, by use of videotape, 333; reliance of simulation/games on, 224

Ronshausen, Nina L., 162

Rosenbaum, Peter S., 153, 156, 161, 163; quoted, 157, 159

Rosenshine, Barak, 133, 134, 136, 137, 145, 336, 337, 343, 345, 350, 351, 356, 361; quoted (with Furst), 135

Ross, Edward A., quoted, 166

Rothkopf, Ernst Z., 98, 99, 101, 108, 109, 114, 119, 122, 123

Ruja, Harry, 276

Rusch, Reuben, 298

Russell, Bertrand, 131, 138; quoted, 130

Ryan, T. Antoinette, 279

Salomon, Gavriel, 307, 310, 312; quoted, 387, 388, 406

Savage, T. V., 199

Schaffarzick, Jon, 348, 349, 352; quoted (with Walker), 17

Schellenberg, J. A., 176

Schild, E. O., 224, 225, 243

Schleiermacher, Friedrich Ernst Daniel, 256

Schlesinger, I. M., 105

Schmuck, Richard A. and Patricia A., 170; quoted, 182, 184, 185

Schoen, James R., 290

Schpoont, Seymour H., 117

Schramm, Wilbur, 16, 305, 307, 317, 318, 321, 330

Schumer, Harry, 18, 211, 212

Seashore, Stanley, 185

Self-concept, effect of simulation/games on, 233

Self-instruction (programmed material) vs. lecture courses (text), 283

Self-motivating environments, creativity-inducing potential of, 241

Seminar method, scores expressing preference for, in comparison with lecture and tutorial methods (table), 293

"Sesame Street," 304, 316, 324, 325, 327, 328, 329; effects of repetition demonstrated by, 318; evaluation of, by Educational Testing Service, 305; field study of, on Israeli children, 310-11; segments in, 308

Sex differences, attitude change linked to, 245

Shank, Roger C., 104

Shavelson, Richard J., 381; quoted, 380, 400

Shaver, James P., 172

Shaw, M. E., 189

Shutes, Robert E., 350

Sidgwick, Henry, 257

Sieber, Joan E., 388, 406

Siegel, Edward M., 287

Silver, A. B., 135

Simmel, Georg, 217

Simmons, Francine G., 117

Simon, Herbert, 78

Simulated environments, hypothesis concerning use of, 233

Simulation games: author's definition of, 223-24; discussion of, as instructional model, 226-27; nature of student's response to, 226-27; teaching with, chap. 7; type of behavior theory implied by use of, 227-28; types of, 219-24; see also Simulation/games

Simulation/games: author's definition of, 223-24; correlates of effectiveness of, 244-48; criticism of research designs for study of, 247-48; effectiveness of, 234-44; goals of use of, 229-34; learning from, 225-29; management of, by teacher, 250-51; relation of, to other teaching techniques, 224-29; research issues with respect to, 247; role of teacher with respect to, 249; see also Simulation games

Simulations, three categories of, 221

Skill types, Gagné's taxonomy of, 147-48

Skinner, B. F., 2, 3, 8, 11, 38, 39, 150, 281; quoted, 10

Small-group teaching, superiority of, masked by equalization phenomenon, 275

Smith, Martin E., 99, 101

Smith, M. Brewster, 232

Smith, M. C., 290

Smithers, Alan, 299

Snook, Ivan, 337

Soar, Robert S., 338, 339, 340, 345, 353, 355, 356, 357, 359, 364, 366, 371; review of study by, 338-71

Social content, television and film teaching of, 307-9

Socialization, relation of play to, 217-19

Social learning theory, Bandura as leading proponent of, 41

Solem, Allen R., 191, 192, 193

Sommer, Robert, 187

Spilerman, Seymour, 230

Spivey, Bruce E., 286

Stallings, James A., 338, 339, 340, 341, 343, 345, 346, 347, 348, 351, 353, 355, 356, 357, 359, 360, 361, 362, 363, 366, 368, 371; review of study by (with Kaskowitz), 330-71

Stanford, Gene and Barbara Dodds. 72; quoted, 166

Starr, Martin K., quoted (with D. W. Miller), 391

States of nature: author's definition of, 388; estimate of, 388-89; teacher's task in relation to, 407-8

Steinzor, Bernard, 187

Stephan, Frederick F., 175

Stockton, J. J., 285

Stodgill, Ralph, 185

Stolurow, Lawrence M., 67; quoted, 385

Stones, Edgar, 283

Stovall, Thomas F., 198

Strasser, Ben B., 373

Strategy analysis procedures, basic categories of, 62-63

Structured teaching, structuring behaviors in (table), 365

Stuck, Dean L., 284

Student achievement: correlations of, with time on reading activities (table), 346; correlations of, with teacher and student absence (table), 343; difficulties in evaluation of, 16-17; relationship of, to time spent on instruction (table), 346; teaching methods in relation to, 15-19; see also Achievement

Students: attitudes of, toward different methods, 281-83; types of, with respect to attitudes toward teaching methods, 294

Subject matter mastery, effectiveness of discussion method on, 196-200

Subject matter mastery discussions, instructional objectives of, 171-74

Successive approximation, approach of, to development of written instructional methods, 126-27

Success opportunities, provision of, through simulation/games, 233

Suppes, Patrick, 67; quoted (with Jamison and Wells), 16

Synetics, scores of three groups on test on (table), 271

Swanson, Ernest A., Jr., 282

Taba, Hilda, 380, 384

Tallmadge, G. K., 134

Taylor, Donald W., 204, 206

Teacher absence, correlations of student achievement with (table), 343

Teacher-child interaction, flowchart of, illustrating sequential nature of decision making, 381

Teachers: description of procedures and methods of, 21-22; essential task of, 42; facilitating television and film teaching by, 329-37; factors determining choice of method by, 214-15; five recommendations regarding use of discussion method by, 214-15; learning and attitude change affected by, 246-47; management role of, in use of simulated games, 250-51; primary purpose of, 21-22; reduction of load by, by delegation, 141-42; roles of, in use of simulated games, 249; solutions for selected problems of, 139-42; task of, in selection of simulated games, 249; task of, in tutoring, 118-19

Teachers' decision making, chap. 11

Teacher training, recommendation for, from decision analysis of teaching, 403-9

Teaching, utility of, by television and film, 326-29

Teaching act, limited knowledge about, 408-9

Teaching and tutoring, theory of, 142-51

Teaching as decision making, research implications of concept of, 412-14

Teaching methods: learning basis of, chap. 2; psychology of, chap. 1; see Methods of teaching

Teaching models, discussion of, 337-38

Teaching techniques, relation of simulation/games to types of, 224-25

Technical strategies, development of, for coping with environment, 233-34

Test-Operate-Test-Exit (TOTE), application of sequences of, 380-83

Text: activities required by student in learning from, 110; flow model for translation of, into internal representation, 112; model for learning from, 111-14

Thelen, Herbert A., 176

Thelen, Mark H., 319

Thibaut, John W., quoted (with Kelley), 206

Thistlethwaite, Donald L., 279

Thomas, E. J., 262, 301

Thompson, W. N., 300

Thorndike, Edward L., 1, 149, 150

TICCIT, see Time-shared Interactive Computer-Controlled Information Television

Tieman, P. W., 62

Tillerson, Charles W., 293

Time, variable of, in major studies of achievement, 342-48

Time-shared Interactive Computer-Controlled Information Television (TICCIT): basic concepts provided by Pask for, 74-75; differences of, from PLATO, 76-78; discussion of, 70; nature and description of, 72-74

Time spent, activities, and materials, correlations between, and achievement in mathematics and reading in grades one and three (table), 344

Tistaert, G., 276

Tolman, E. C., 2

TOTE unit, graphical presentation of, 382

Touhey, John C., 299

Traditional classroom situation vs. open atmosphere, 290-91

Training simulations, nature of, 226

Transfer of training: importance of, to instruction, 27; traditional teaching in relation to, 282-83; see also Generalization

Travers, Robert M. W., quoted (with Wallen), 385

Trenaman, Joseph M., 267, 269, 270

Truscot, Bruce (E. Alison Peers), 257

Tulving, Endel, 110, 111, 123

Turner, Richard E., 337

Tutees: affective factor as cause of academic failure of, 146-51; effects of tutoring on, 133; factors responsible for academic failure of, 143-44; learning factors in relation to academic failure of, 146-51; number of, in projects (table), 132

Tutorial method, scores expressing preference for, in comparison with lecture and seminar methods (table), 293

Tutoring, chap. 5; cost effectiveness of, 162-64; effectiveness of, 133-38; present status of, 131-33; programmed systems of, 151-62; psychological aspects of, 138-51

Tutoring programs: effects of, on tutees, 133; evaluation of, 133-34; examples of four forms of, 153; grade level and subject classification of, 132; identification of examples of, 152-62; advantages of, qualified, 164-65

Tutors: changing tasks of, 138-39; effects of tutoring on, 137-38; number of, in projects (table), 132

Tutor-student system, grade equivalent study of (table), 154

Tversky, Amos, quoted (with Kahneman), 389-90

Tyler, J. F., 199, 200

Universal education, task of tutor (teacher) changed by coming of, 138-39

Vaastad, Kay, 208

Validated instruction, three-step process in production of, 46

Van Atta, E. L., 278

Verbal information, instruction for learning item of, 31-32

Via, Murray, 134

Vinsonhaler, John F., 67

Walker, Decker F., 348, 349, 352; quoted (with Schaffarzick), 17

Wallen, Norman E., quoted (with Travers), 385

Ward, John N., 277

Watson, John B., 11, 150

Weatherall, M., 277, 278

Webb, Neill J., 278

Weil, Marsha, 172, 337

Weitman, M., 278

Wells, Jane, 145

Wells, Stuart, 16; quoted (with Jamison and Suppes), 16

Welser, J. R., 285

Whitfield, Richard C., quoted, 392; quoted (with Bishop), 410-11

Whitmyre, John W., 208

Wickens, Thomas D., 26

Wiley, David E., 342

Wispe, Lauren G., 276

Wood, Norman D., 62, 63

Work groups: correlations between program means and achievement in grades one and three (table), 354; size and character of, as variables in studies of achievement, 353-55

Wright, M. Erik, 183

Written instruction, psychology of, chap. 4

Written instructional material: approaches to development of, 126-27; evaluation of, in terms of four characteristics, 98-101; learning in relation to nominal stimulus characteristics of, 125; measuring outcomes of use of, 94-96; properties of, 92-93; two kinds of determinants of learning from, 128-29; use of selected procedures for development of, 128-29

Written material (text): attributes of, related to instructional effectiveness in learning (table), 97; method for development of, 123-29; research on learning from, 125

Zander, Alvin, quoted (with Cartwright), 181

Zillman, Dolf, 300

Zipf, G. K., principle of law by, 106

Zukerman, David, 218

INFORMATION CONCERNING
THE NATIONAL SOCIETY FOR THE STUDY OF EDUCATION

1. *Purpose.* The purpose of the National Society is to promote the investigation and discussion of educational questions. To this end it holds an annual meeting and publishes a series of yearbooks and a series of paperbacks on Contemporary Educational Issues.

2. *Membership.* Any person interested in the purpose of the Society and in receiving its publications may become a member by sending in name, title, address, and a check covering dues and the entrance fee (see items 4 and 5). Graduate students may become members, upon recommendation of a faculty member, at a reduced rate for the first year of membership. Dues for all subsequent years are the same as for other members.

Membership is not transferable. It is limited to individuals and may not be held by libraries, schools, or other institutions, either directly or indirectly.

3. *Period of Membership.* Membership is for the calendar year and terminates automatically on December 31, unless dues for the ensuing year are paid as indicated in item 6. Applicants for membership may not date their entrance back of the current calendar year.

4. *Categories of Membership.* The following categories of membership have been established:

Regular. Annual dues are $10.00. The member receives a clothbound copy of each part of the yearbook.

Comprehensive. Annual dues are $20.00. The member receives a clothbound copy of the yearbook and all volumes in the current year's series on Contemporary Educational Issues.

Life Membership. Persons sixty years of age or above may become life members on payment of a fee based on the average life expectancy of their age group. Regular life members may take out a Comprehensive membership for any year by payment of an additional fee of 10.00. For information apply to the Secretary-Treasurer.

Graduate Students. First year dues for the Regular and Comprehensive membership are $8.00 and $18.00 respectively, plus the $1.00 entrance fee in either case.

5. *Privileges of Membership.* Members receive the publications of the Society as described above. All members are entitled to vote, to participate in meetings of the Society, and (under certain conditions) to hold office.

6. *Entrance Fee.* New members are required to pay an entrance fee of one dollar, in addition to the dues, for the first year of membership.

7. *Payment of Dues.* Statements of dues are rendered in October for the following calendar year. Any member so notified whose dues remain unpaid on January 1 thereby loses membership and can be reinstated only by paying the dues plus a reinstatement fee of fifty cents ($.50).

School warrants and vouchers from institutions must be accompanied by definite information concerning the name and address of the person for whom the membership fee is being paid. Statements of dues are rendered on our own form only. The Secretary's office cannot undertake to fill out special invoice forms of any kind or to a affix a notary's affidavit to statements or receipts.

Cancelled checks serve as receipts. Members desiring an additional receipt must enclose a stamped and addressed envelope therefor.

8. *Distribution of Yearbooks to Members.* The yearbooks, normally ready prior to the February meeting of the Society, will be mailed from the office of the distributor only to members whose dues for that year have been paid.

9. *Commercial Sales.* The distribution of all yearbooks prior to the

427

current year, and also of those of the current year not regularly mailed to members in exchange for their dues, is in the hands of the distributor, not of the Secretary. Orders may be placed with the University of Chicago Press, Chicago, Illinois 60637, which distributes the yearbooks of the Society. Orders for paperbacks in the series on Contemporary Educational Issues should be placed with the designated publisher of that series. The list of the Society's publications is printed in each yearbook.

10. *Yearbooks.* The yearbooks are issued about one month before the February meeting. Published in two volumes, each of which contains 300 to 400 pages, the yearbooks are planned to be of immediate practical value as well as representative of sound scholarship and scientific investigation.

11. *Series on Contemporary Educational Issues.* This series, in paperback format, is designed to supplement the yearbooks by timely publications on topics of current interest. There will usually be three of these volumes each year.

12. *Meetings.* The annual meeting, at which the yearbooks are presented and critiqued, is held as a rule in February at the same time and place as the meeting of the American Association of School Administrators. Members will be notified of other meetings.

Applications for membership will be handled promptly at any time. New members will receive the yearbook scheduled for publication during the calendar year in which application for Regular Membership is made. New members who elect to take out the Comprehensive membership will receive both the yearbook and the paperbacks scheduled for publication during the year in which application is made.

KENNETH J. REHAGE, Secretary-Treasurer

5835 Kimbark Avenue
Chicago, Illinois 60637